LANDLORD AND TENANT LAW

LANDLORD AND TENANT LAW

BARBARA MITCHELL
BA(Hons)
Barrister-at-Law of Gray's Inn
Senior Lecturer in Landlord and Tenant Law,
Kingston Polytechnic

BSP PROFESSIONAL BOOKS
OXFORD LONDON EDINBURGH
BOSTON PALO ALTO MELBOURNE

First published 1987

British Library
Cataloguing in Publication Data
Mitchell, Barbara
Landlord and tenant law.
1. Landlord and tenant—England
I. Title
344.2064'34 KD899

ISBN 0-632-01861-5

BSP Professional Books
Editorial offices:
Osney Mead, Oxford OX2 0EL
(*Orders:* Tel. 0865 240201)
8 John Street, London WC1N 2ES
23 Ainslie Place, Edinburgh EH3 6AJ
52 Beacon Street, Boston
Massachusetts 02108, USA
667 Lytton Avenue, Palo Alto
California 94301, USA
107 Barry Street, Carlton
Victoria 3053, Australia

Set by Scribe Design,
Gillingham, Kent
Printed and bound in
Great Britain by
Mackays of Chatham, Kent

Contents

To Gregory

Preface

At first sight landlord and tenant law is extremely off-putting. It appears to be a labyrinth of technicality, complexity and difficult concepts. This is especially true for the uninitiated.

This book unravels as much complexity as possible without oversimplification. The author's aim is to lay bare the essential elements of the subject so as to provide a comprehensible and yet detailed account for the benefit of surveyors, estate managers, students and general practitioners.

The subject is given a modern treatment. Key concepts are set out in a practical and helpful manner. Before venturing into the intricacies of any subject, the text provides a clear overview of each new topic. Specific landlord and tenant problems which frequently arise are considered in detail from a practitioner's point of view. The underlying legal principles are examined in some depth.

Part One introduces the statutory schemes applicable to business, residential and agricultural tenancies at an early stage in the text. This is a unique feature and provides a clear summary of the statutory framework which modern landlord and tenant law operates within. The detailed provisions are set out later.

The book includes the main statutes required for examination purposes, the 1985 Law Society/RICS Model Forms of Rent Review Clauses, diagrams to illustrate the application of key areas of law, and a comprehensive bibliography.

Warm thanks are due to all who supported this work, particularly to my family, friends and Mary Jackson. I thank my former students for giving me short shrift when I trespassed too far into 'lawyers' law' in reply to specific questions. The greatest debt of all is owed to Barry Denyer-Green who taught me the value of education without obfuscation. The good-humoured patience of Julia Burden, Commissioning Editor of Collins Professional and Technical Books, is gratefully acknowledged. I am grateful to Sheila Young and Maureen Smith for typing the table of cases and index at a late stage.

Barbara Mitchell
14 February 1987

Chapter 1

Starting Out

WHAT IS A LANDLORD AND TENANT RELATIONSHIP?

The relationship of landlord and tenant can be created in a number of diverse ways, from a simple oral agreement between the parties to a lengthy formal lease drawn up by lawyers. The simple act of handing over a key to a room coupled with the acceptance of rent lies at one end of the spectrum whilst the letting of commercial premises by way of a carefully drawn lease containing the most up-to-date rent review clauses lies at the other. The following examples illustrate three typical situations where the relationship of landlord and tenant has been created by the parties.

EXAMPLES

Informal oral agreement

Thomas requires accommodation in London whilst he is studying for the RICS finals and hears that Lyndon lets out rooms at £30 per week. He visits Lyndon and is shown a room which he likes. Lyndon tells him that he wants to avoid any possible trouble with the Rent Acts so nothing is put in writing. Thomas moves into the room and pays Lyndon £30 cash each Friday, thereby creating an oral weekly tenancy. Note that this agreement does not necessarily succeed in avoiding the Rent Acts. The relationship is illustrated by the following diagram:

Lyndon
(landlord)
|
Thomas
(tenant)

Formal lease

London Properties PLC is developing a large site on the Isle of Dogs with a view to leasing out office units to financial institutions. The company proposes to take the following steps before granting any leases:

(a) seek valuation advice from an independent expert in order to determine the most efficient way to maximise profits.

(b) take legal advice in order to determine the extent to which the law will regulate the proposed leases.
(c) advertise the leasehold premises.
(d) negotiate the grant of a lease with prospective tenants. The landlord's lawyers will draw up the legal documentation which will be sent to the tenant or to his legal advisers for approval.
(e) the prospective tenants will normally be asked to sign an 'agreement for a lease'. Note that it is not usual for parties to sign a 'lease' straight away since each side will require time to complete all the formalities, e.g. to take up references, to carry out a survey, or to arrange finance. At the same time it would be unsatisfactory from the landlord's point of view if no formal agreement was entered into at this stage. It is, therefore, customary for a tenant to sign an 'agreement for a lease' which states that the tenant has agreed to take up a lease. The agreement for a lease may be made conditional, e.g. on a satisfactory surveyor's report.
(f) payment of a deposit where appropriate.
(g) take up references for prospective tenants (especially financial references) where appropriate. The landlord may also require a third party to guarantee any indebtedness on the part of the tenant. A guarantee is often required in the case of a limited liability company in order to provide the landlord with a form of security should the company be wound up in an insolvent liquidation. The landlord could then call on the guarantee e.g. for unpaid rent and monies which the landlord will have to spend on repairs which the tenant ought to have carried out.
(h) the leases will normally be granted for a fixed number of years. The parties to a formal lease are more usually described as 'lessor' and 'lessee' rather than 'landlord' and 'tenant'.
(i) the lease will be signed once its terms have been approved by the tenant. If the lease takes the form of a deed it will also be under seal, which means that a seal will be fixed to the document. A seal used to be made of wax but is nowadays more likely to be in the form of a red self-adhesive star.

London Properties PLC
(lessor)
|
X.Y.Z
(lessees)

Lease purchase by third party

Accounts PLC is a property investment company which buys up leases of residential property from landlords with sitting tenants i.e. tenants who cannot be evicted because their tenancies are protected by the Rent

Acts and who are unlikely to give up possession of the leasehold property voluntarily.

The company has just bought Rackman Mansions, a 1930s block of flats, from Leonard for half its vacant possession market valuation since it is occupied by sitting tenants, all of whom have tenancies which are protected by the Rent Acts. Accounts PLC is confident that it can induce half of the tenants to leave by offering them a money settlement. The remainder, or rump, will be unlikely to vacate the premises before their own deaths. But Rackman Mansions will ultimately be fully vacated. Accounts PLC will thereupon refurbish the flats and sell them with vacant possession at a full market rent.

Meanwhile, Accounts PLC becomes the landlord by purchase. Leonard (the original landlord) has transferred his interest to Accounts PLC upon sale. This is referred to as an 'assignment' because the landlord has assigned, i.e. transferred, his entire interest in the property to a third party. Accounts PLC enters into a relationship of landlord and tenant with the tenants of Rackman Mansions.

Leonard (original landlord) ———— Accounts PLC (landlord)
(assignor) (assignee)
|
Sitting tenants

WHAT IS LANDLORD AND TENANT LAW?

The law of landlord and tenant is the body of law which regulates the relationship of landlord and tenant. The starting point of any landlord and tenant problem is an assessment of the facts together with a consideration of the lease or tenancy agreement, which may be written or oral. The law will determine the true nature of the facts and decide the proper construction to be placed on any terms or clauses which are doubted or disputed.

Landlord and tenant law was originally developed by the common law through the courts and presently comprises the accretion of centuries of case law. In addition, specific areas of landlord and tenant law are regulated by statute law, most notably the residential sector. This in turn has led to a further development of case law designed to interpret the statutory provisions.

Landlord and tenant law has been described as a hybrid subject since it draws on both contractual doctrines and property law principles. This is because landlord and tenant relationships originate in a contract which transfers an interest in land (a leasehold interest) from one party to the other. However, it is more than a hybrid subject since it has developed rules and principles unique to itself. Thus it is a separate strain of law in its own right.

The codification of landlord and tenant law is long overdue in order to remove archaic rules, to streamline and simplify terminology, and to set out a comprehensive code of the parties' respective obligations. The Landlord and Tenant Act 1985, Housing Act 1985, Housing Associations Act 1985, and Agricultural Holdings Act 1986 provide a consolidation of previous legislation relating to landlord and tenant law and housing law. However, more needs to be done since landlord and tenant law is presently over-complicated and far from easy to master. Landlord and tenant law impinges on most people's lives, perhaps more than any other area of law, and ought accordingly to be set out in a clear modern code.

Chapter 2

First Principles

ESSENTIAL CHARACTERISTICS OF A LEASE

In order for a lease to arise there must be an agreement whereby the landlord grants the tenant exclusive possession of leasehold premises for a period of time whilst retaining a reversionary interest in the property. Two points require clarification.

Exclusive possession

The chief characteristic of a lease is the grant of exclusive possession of leasehold premises to the tenant. This means that a tenant has the sole right to possession of the premises, and that he is entitled to exclude others from the premises. If a landlord wishes to enter the premises he must specifically reserve the right to do so, e.g. by reserving the right to enter the premises for the purpose of inspecting its state of repair. It is often stated that exclusive possession exists when an occupier of land has the right to exclude all others from the premises, including his landlord.

Licence

No tenancy can arise if a person has permission to occupy land belonging to another but does not have exclusive possession of the premises. In this situation the occupier simply has permission to occupy the premises, which takes the legal form of a 'licence'. The right to exclusive possession is crucial to the question of whether an occupier has a tenancy or a licence. Licences are discussed fully in Chapter 6.

Meaning of exclusive possession

The meaning of exclusive possession was analysed in *Heslop* v. *Burn* (1974) by Lord Justice Stamp who stated that:

> 'The expression "exclusive possession" in relation to the occupier of a property may be used in more than one sense. It may, as I see it, be used to mean that, as a factual matter, the occupant, alone or together with his family, occupies the premises and does not share

> them with any other person. Such a situation is not inconsistent with the occupation being enjoyed under a mere licence. Or the expression may be used to mean that the occupant has the right to exclude the owner from the premises... where the expression is used in the latter sense... it is clearly more difficult to reconcile it with the existence of a mere licence to occupy. But rights do not arise *in vacuo* and before concluding that an occupant was intended to be in a position to exclude the owner from the premises, one must ask...the question: did the parties intend that the occupant should have such a right?

This analysis may be refined further by distinguishing the lesser right of 'exclusive occupation' from a right to 'exclusive possession'. Lord Justice Stamp's first example of the occupier who resides in premises alone or together with his family can fall into either category. An occupier who has a right of 'exclusive occupation' has the right to occupy the premises exclusively and will not be forced to share the premises with anyone else. If the occupier also has the right to exclude his landlord from the premises he will have the greater right of exclusive possession.

Establishing exclusive possession

The Court of Appeal stated that exclusive possession is a question of fact in each case, and has to be decided by reviewing the evidence: *Brooker Settled Estates Ltd* v. *Ayers* (1987).

The terms of the lease or tenancy agreement may establish conclusively that an occupier has been granted exclusive possession of premises. But it will sometimes be necessary for the courts to decide whether an agreement has conferred a right to exclusive possession. This is generally for the purpose of deciding the broader question of whether a tenancy or a licence has been created: see Chapter 6.

Exclusive possession can be established by a consideration of the degree of control which the landlord and his agents exercise over the leasehold premises. The greater the degree of control which is exercised by the landlord the less likely it is that the occupier has exclusive possession. Lord Templeman considered this issue in the House of Lords decision of *Street* v. *Mountford* (1985), where he observed that:

> 'In the case of residential accommodation there is no difficulty in deciding whether the grant confers exclusive possession. An occupier of residential accommodation at a rent is either a lodger or a tenant. The occupier is a lodger if the landlord provides attendance or services which require the landlord or his servants to exercise unrestricted access to and use of the premises. A lodger is entitled to live in the premises but cannot call the place his own. If, on the other hand, residential accommodation is granted for a term at a rent with exclusive possession, the landlord providing neither

attendance nor services, the grant is a tenancy. Any express reservation to the landlord of limited rights to enter and view the state of the premises and to repair and maintain the premises only serves to emphasise the fact that the grantee is entitled to exclusive possession and is a tenant.'

Reversionary interest

A landlord must retain a proprietary interest in the premises so that the property returns to him (or to his successors) when the lease ends. The proprietary interest which the landlord retains is known as a 'reversionary interest' since the property will revert back to the landlord in the future. Meanwhile the tenant will have possession of the premises.

Immediate and future possession

A legal distinction is drawn between immediate and future rights to possession. If a tenant has a present right to possession it is described as an 'immediate' right; for example, where the tenant is presently in possession of leasehold premises under a fixed term lease. A landlord will have a future right to possession based on his reversionary interest during the currency of a lease. But once the lease is at an end, he too will have an immediate right to possession.

Definition of possession

Possession has a wide definition in law. The legal definition of possession is not confined to physical possession but includes the right to the receipt of rents and profits: s.205(1)(xix) Law of Property Act 1925. Therefore, if a tenant chooses to rent out the leasehold premises to another he will nonetheless be in possession even though he is not in physical possession of the premises whilst it is rented out to another.

For example, Leslie owns the freehold of Wells Farm and grants Timothy a thirty-year lease. Timothy will enjoy exclusive possession of the leasehold premises for thirty years. During this time, Timothy will have a right of 'immediate possession' regardless of whether he occupies the premises himself or rents them out to another since he is the person presently entitled to possession of the premises. Meanwhile Leslie has no right to immediate possession since his legal right to possession is a future right and not an immediate right. But possession will revert back to Leslie at the end of Timothy's lease:

Leslie (landlord) (reversionary interest)

30 years

Timothy (tenant) (right of immediate possession)

Note that if Leslie were to transfer his entire proprietary interest in Wells Farm to Timothy he would, in fact, convey the freehold instead of creating a thirty-year lease. A landlord must retain a reversionary interest in the property in order to create a lease.

Sub-tenancies

The same principles apply to sub-tenancies. Tenants are entitled to sub-let either the entire leasehold premises or part of them provided that there is no express prohibition against sub-letting.

If a tenant creates a sub-tenancy he must retain a reversionary interest in the premises. This means that he must ensure that the premises revert back to him before his own tenancy expires, if only for a day. Otherwise the tenant would not create a sub-tenancy but would in fact be assigning (transferring) his entire proprietary interest in the sub-let premises to the sub-tenant. In the example above, if Timothy grants a sub-tenancy to Sam for twenty-five years he must retain at least one day's interest in the premises in order to create a reversionary interest. The last date on which he could grant a sub-lease for a twenty-five-year term would be at a point which represented five years less one day in the life of the head-tenancy. The parties' respective interests are set out in the following diagram:

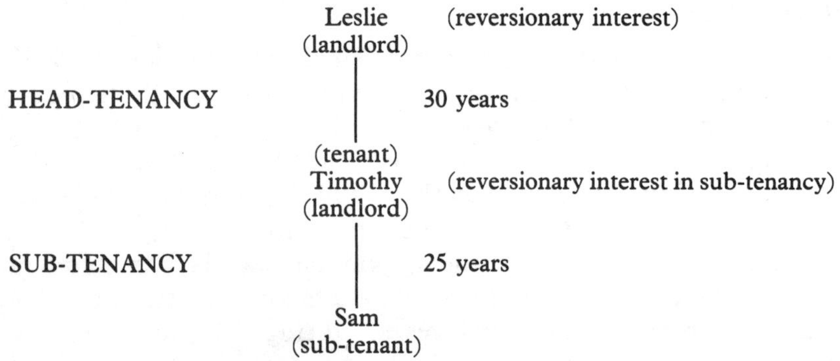

LEASEHOLD ESTATES AND INTERESTS

English land law

English land law draws a distinction between legal estates and equitable interests in land so that only one type of legal leasehold estate and one type of legal freehold estate exist in law. No other legal interests can be created. All other interests in land are classified as equitable interests: s.1(8) Law of Property Act 1925. The sole leasehold estate, the 'term of years absolute', provides the basis for all leasehold conveyancing just as the sole freehold estate, the 'fee simple absolute in possession', provides the basis for all freehold conveyancing (all other interest in land being equitable interests). The rationale for this system of landholding is to ensure that property holding and conveyancing are kept as simple as possible. Consequently, English land law divides leasehold interests into two categories, the term of years absolute and equitable interests:

Classification of leasehold property interests

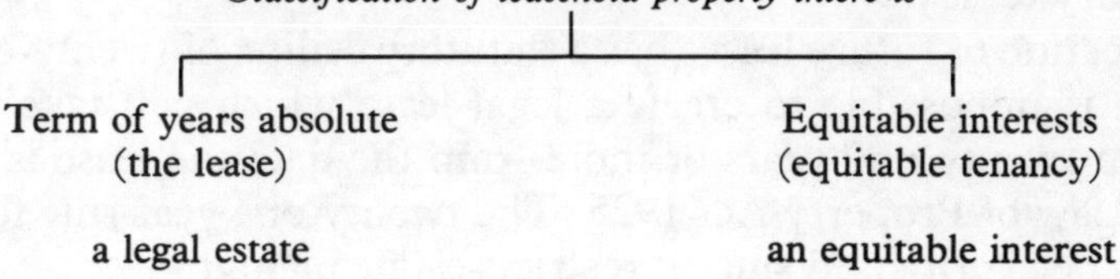

Term of years absolute

The term of years absolute is the only legal leasehold estate and is statutorily defined by s.205(1)(xxvii) Law of Property Act 1925. The key characteristics of the statutory definition are as follows.

In possession or in reversion

A term of years is capable of taking effect either in possession or in reversion.

In possession: A lease in possession gives a tenant immediate possession of the premises but does not necessarily give him physical possession since the legal definition of possession includes the receipt of rents and profits. For example, Lynch leases out a block of twenty flats to twenty tenants for ninety-nine years, and leases the reversion to a management company for the same period.

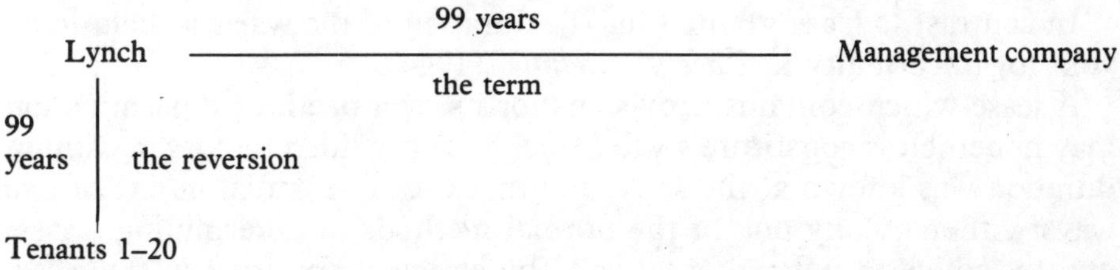

Here Lynch retains the ultimate reversion since the premises will revert back to him when the lease expires. He meanwhile relieves himself of the responsibility of maintaining and managing the block for the duration of the ninety-nine years. This achieves the effect of creating concurrent leases of the reversion and term, both giving a right to immediate possession. The management company will not take up physical possession of the premises under their lease of the reversion but are entitled to receive the rent and service charges due under the existing leases and thereby step into the landlord's shoes.

*In reversion:*A lease in reversion is a lease which is to take effect from a date in the future rather than immediately. For example, Long grants Time a twenty-one year lease which is to commence on the 1st January 2000. Leases which commence at a future date are often referred to as reversionary leases.

The creation of future leases has a statutory ceiling of twenty-one years so that it is impossible to create a legal lease which will take effect in possession twenty-one years or more from the date the lease is created: s.149(3) Law of Property Act 1925. The twenty-one year rule for future leases has been criticised since it restricts estate planning.

Certain or liable to determination

A valid lease can only arise if either the term of years 'is certain or liable to determination'. In other words, a lease's duration must be certain at the outset although a lease may be determined within that period.

The correct construction of the rule that ' a term of years must be certain' can be expressed in the form of two alternatives. Either the maximum duration of the lease and its commencement date should be fixed when the lease commences. For example, L grants T a ninety-nine year lease commencing on the 1st April 1990. Alternatively, the maximum duration and commencement date should be capable of being ascertained by reference to a collateral matter. For example, L agrees to grant T a lease on the 25th December 1985 provided that T gives up possession by Christmas Day 1990. The maximum duration of the lease is certain here, even though T may give up possession at an earlier date: *Joseph* v. *Joseph* (1966) per Lord Denning MR.

In contrast, a lease granted for the duration of the war was held to be void for uncertainty in *Lace* v. *Chantler* (1944).

A lease which contains provisions for its own death or determination may nonetheless constitute a valid legal lease provided that its maximum duration was known at the start, and that it can be ended in one of two ways: either by any one of the normal methods of determining leases, e.g. by notice to quit; alternatively, by an event specified in the lease: *Re. Midland Railway Company's* agreement, *Charles Clay & Sons Ltd* v. *British Railway Board* (1971).

Terms for less than a year

A phase 'term of years absolute' is an inaccurate label for two reasons. First of all, the definition of a legal lease includes terms for periods of less than a year. A term of years may be created for any certain length of time. A term for one week is just as valid a legal lease as a term for nine hundred and ninety-nine years. Secondly, the word 'absolute' adds little and can be ignored for all practical purposes.

Payment of rent is not essential

Although it is usual for leases to be granted for a rent, the payment of rent is not a legal requirement for a lease. Neither the general law nor the legal definition of a lease stipulates that rent is a necessary criterion for the creation of a legal lease.

However, special rules relate to leases which do not exceed three years in duration: see p. 21. The general rule is that a deed is required in order to create a legal lease for a term which exceeds three years: s.52 Law of Property Act 1925, but it is possible for leases for less than three years to be created orally without the formality of a deed: s.54(2) Law of Property Act 1925. In order for the requirement of a deed to be waived the lease for less than three years must be at a market rent. In other words, oral leases for less than three years must be at a market rent in order to create a legal leasehold estate. An equitable tenancy will be created if there is no market rent or no rent at all in respect of a lease for less than three years which has been created orally.

Leases for lives and marriage

The definition of a term of years specifically excludes any term of years which purports to create a lease for a life or lives. However, a lease for a life or lives is not invalid. A lease granted for a term which is measured by a person's life is automatically converted into a ninety-year lease which will end upon the death of the person to whom it refers: s.149(6) Law of Property Act 1925. For example, Larry grants his retired gardener Tommy a lease 'for the remainder of Tommy's life'. Tommy's lease will operate as though it were a ninety-year lease. But it will end when Tommy dies.

Identical rules apply to leases which are expressed to be determinable upon the tenant's marriage: s.149(6) Law of Property Act 1925.

Equitable interests

In English land law all proprietary interests in land apart from the two legal estates (legal freehold and legal leasehold estates) are categorised as equitable interests. In the context of landlord and tenant law, this means that tenancies which fail to qualify as a legal leasehold estate must necessarily be classified as an equitable interest. The most important equitable interest in the context of landlord and tenant law is an 'agreement for a lease' which is introduced at page 12 and discussed fully at pp. 21–3.

THE CONTRACT

Types of contract

Landlord and tenant contracts can be categorised in a number of different ways. There is no limit to the diversity of contracts which can be created at law. At the same time, two types of contract merit special consideration.

The lease

A lease is the contract which creates the leasehold interest. The term 'lease' refers to either the legal document which creates the leasehold interest or to the leasehold interest itself. In addition, the word 'lease' can be used as a generic term in which case it includes tenancy agreements. In practice, however, the label 'tenancy agreement' is normally used to describe an informal letting agreement of relatively short duration, e.g. a weekly tenancy or a bed-sitting room. A lease usually indicates a more formal contract, e.g. a ninety-nine year lease created by deed. But there is no hard and fast rule.

Agreement for a lease

An agreement for a lease is a contract to create a lease at a future date, and generally precedes the grant of a lease. Landlords often ask prospective tenants to sign an agreement to take up a lease in order to enter into a formal contract at an early stage during negotiations for a lease.

The expression 'agreement for a lease' can also be used in a different context. This is because a lease which is invalid may nonetheless amount to an agreement for a lease; see p. 21.

These two types of contract can give rise to the following factual situations:

Pre-contractual		*Contracts*
negotiations	→	lease
negotiations	→	agreement for a lease → lease
negotiations	→	invalid lease (may amount to an agreement for a lease)

Original parties

Every landlord and tenant relationship originates in a contract, that is, a legally enforceable agreement for consideration. The original parties to the contract can enforce the terms of the contract, and have the right to bring legal proceedings against the other party if he should fail to perform any of his contractual obligations whereupon the primary remedy will be damages for breach of contract. There is a legal relationship between the original parties, namely privity of contract.

Privity of contract

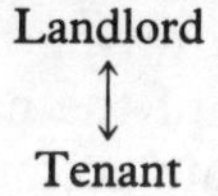

Third parties

Although all landlord and tenant relationships originate in a contract, one or both parties may, with the passage of time, have become strangers (third parties) to the original contract. Interests in leasehold property are transferred in two ways: either *inter vivos* upon a sale or transfer of the interests, or alternatively, by succession upon the death of one of the parties.

The following diagram illustrates the transfer of the last fifty years of a ninety-nine year lease in its forty-ninth year by:

(a) voluntary transfer of the reversion by sale from L to A: and
(b) involuntary transfer of the term from T to B, upon T's death.

Transfer of reversion by sale

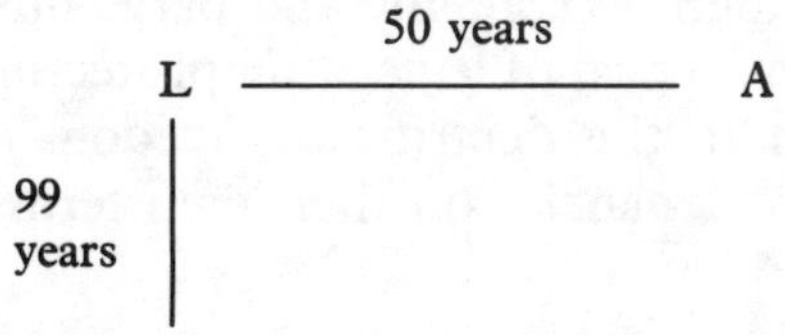

Transfer of term by succession

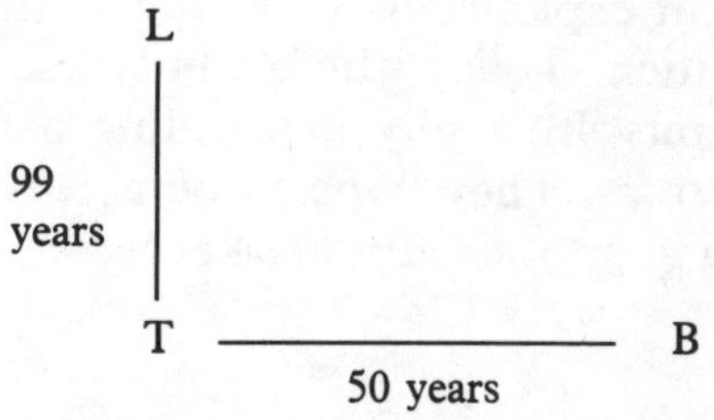

Both A and B are third parties to the original contract between L and T.

Freedom of contract

One of the traditionally held tenets of English contract law is that parties are free to enter into a contract on their own terms under the 'doctrine of freedom of contract'. The doctrine reached its highest point in the nineteenth century where it was firmly accepted by the courts. In *Printing and Numberical Co.* v. *Sampson* (1875), Lord Jessel MR said that:

> 'If there is one thing which more than another public policy requires, it is that men of full and competent understanding shall have the utmost liberty of contracting, and that their contracts when entered into freely and voluntarily shall be held sacred and shall be enforced by courts of justice. Therefore you have this paramount public policy to consider in that you are not lightly to interfere with this freedom of contract.'

This doctrine was influential in the development of landlord and tenant law. Today some areas of modern landlord and tenant law are largely regulated by statute.

The doctrine declined largely owing to changes in the economic and social structure of society. One of the main weaknesses of the doctrine was that it failed to take adequate account of the rights of third parties who might want to adjust the contract. Moreover, consumers demanded greater security when entering into contracts with those who were in a stronger bargaining position.

Inroads have been made into the doctrine of freedom of contract in areas of landlord and tenant law where the courts or the legislature have formed the view that it would be unjust or inequitable for certain terms in certain contracts to be enforced (see *The Rise and Fall of Freedom of Contract* by Atiyah, Clarence Press, 1979). For example, courts of equity were prepared to prevent tenants from being evicted for non-payment of rent, despite a term in the lease entitling landlords to repossession of the leasehold property on failure to pay rent, provided that the tenant could show that he could pay the outstanding rent, albeit late.

It is fair to say that the courts and legislature have intervened to inhibit the enforcement of contract terms in response to fears that landlords might exploit tenants owing to their superior economic and bargaining position. Today, those who argue for the repeal of legislation protecting tenants are really demanding a return to the doctrine of freedom of contract. They hope to be able to grant tenancies on their own terms, taking into account market forces.

Construing contracts

It is crucial to commence any analysis of a landlord and tenant problem with a detailed study of the original contract together with the facts presented. Most landlords and tenants shade and colour a contract with their own hand so that what appears at first sight to be a typical standard form of contract may, in fact, contain novel terms which may be significant. Oral contracts present special evidential problems of their own since it will often be difficult to ascertain the precise terms of these contracts.

Enforcing contract terms

Whether or not one can enforce the terms agreed will depend upon the general law. Prima facie, the parties are free to contract upon their own terms, and can expect the majority of those terms to be enforced: see chapter 8. At the same time, the doctrine of freedom of contract has been eroded in many areas of landlord and tenant law, most notably in the residential sector. This means that some contract terms are rendered unenforceable by statute.

LEGAL CONSEQUENCES

The phrase 'landlord and tenant relationship' conveys not simply the information that a particular relationship exists between the parties, but also the fact that certain legal consequences will automatically flow from that relationship. Two of these legal consequences merit consideration here.

Rent

Landlords are entitled to exercise an ancient right to seize the tenant's property if any rent due remains unpaid. Goods can be seized up to the value of the unpaid rent under the ancient remedy of distress.

The payment of rent is not an essential requirement of a lease so that rent-free leases can be created. However, if a tenant does recompense his landlord for the exclusive possession of leasehold premises then that recompense constitutes rent. It may take the form of monetary consideration or the provision of goods or services.

Obligations

The general law implies a minimal number of obligations which landlords and tenants must perform, referred to collectively as 'implied covenants'. The obligations balance the parties' respective interests in the leasehold property. They ensure that a tenant is permitted to occupy the leasehold property without being disturbed by his landlord. In return, the tenant must pay any rent agreed and look after the property, taking care that it does not fall into disrepair through neglecting to do odd jobs, such as replacing washers on taps.

The creation of a landlord and tenant relationship clearly has legal consequences which far exceed the bounds of contract law. Obligations and duties are imposed upon the parties which may exceed the terms agreed by the parties.

Chapter 3

Creating the Relationship

FORMALITIES

No special method of creating a landlord and tenant relationship is prescribed by law. English land law does, however, require landlords and tenants to observe the following legal formalities with certain exceptions (see p.21):

(1) writing or part performance in order to enforce the contract;
(2) a deed in order to create a legal estate (some oral leases for three years or less are exempt from this requirement).

Failure to satisfy these formalities will create great difficulties should a landlord or tenant wish to commence legal proceedings in respect of the leasehold property and may well prevent the enforcement of legal claims.

Enforceability of contracts

General

All contracts for the sale or disposal of leasehold interests must be sufficiently evidenced in order to be enforced by a court. They must either be evidenced in writing or performed in part: s.40 Law of Property Act 1925.

This rule originates in s.1 Statute of Frauds 1677 which first introduced the requirement of writing for leases. The rule was designed to prevent interests in leasehold property being sold or transferred in a fraudulent manner and is now set out in s.40(1) Law of Property Act 1925. Written evidence provides the clearest evidence of a contract.

It was not long before courts of equity disposed of the requirement of writing in cases where the plaintiff had partly performed an oral contract, applying the equitable maxim that 'statutes should not be made an instrument of fraud': *Lester* v. *Foxcroft* (1701). It would have been inequitable to refuse to enforce a contract which had been partly performed, simply on the grounds that the contract was not evidenced in writing.

Section 40(1) of the Law of Property Act 1925 provides that a plaintiff is unable to bring legal proceedings in relation to a contract for the sale or disposal of land or any interest in land (excluding leasehold interests) unless:

(a) either the agreement or a note of the agreement is in writing, and
(b) it is signed by the defendant or his agent.

Evidenced in writing

The operation of s.40(1) depends upon the existence of a concluded contract between the parties for the sale or transfer, in this context, of leasehold property. A 'subject to contract' agreement will not usually create a concluded contract: see *Law* v. *Jones* (1973), and *Tiverton Estates Ltd* v. *Wearwell Ltd* (1974). The parties and property must be identified, and the consideration and duration of the lease known. Failure to satisfy s.40(1) renders the contract unenforceable by action in the court but does not make the contract void. Consequently, any consideration transferred under the contract by the defaulting party cannot be recovered. Thus, if a tenant pays a deposit under an agreement to take up a tenancy, and later changes his mind and refuses to take up the tenancy, the landlord is entitled to retain the deposit. Losses may be recovered in full if this is made a condition of a sale or transfer of a leasehold interest: see 'Damages on the resale of land' by M. Wilkinson, *New Law Journal*, March 16th 1984.

There is no legal requirement for the contract itself to be in writing and an oral contract may suffice. There are two possible alternatives: either the full contract is in writing or there is a written memorandum or note which provides evidence of the contract. In the latter case, no statutory form is prescribed and parties have often unwittingly entered into enforceable contracts inadvertently. Receipts for deposits, correspondence between the parties, letters written by one party to his solicitor, and even a letter repudiating an agreement, have all been held to amount to a written note or memorandum of a contract.

Essential terms

If the contract is evidenced by a note or memorandum it should contain all the essential terms of the contract, that is:

(a) *Parties' identification*. Either the names of all the parties or a reasonable description must appear so that there can be no dispute as to their identity: *Warner* v. *Wellington* (1856).

A reference to 'the landlord' would be inadequate by itself since the leasehold property could have a number of landlords, for example, where several different leases have been created.

(b) *Leasehold property*. The general rule requires a physical description of the premises which are to be leased but expressions such as 'Bill's flat' would be adequate if Bill only had a proprietary interest in one flat.
(c) *Price*. The contract price must be agreed and ascertainable. In other words, the consideration (rent and/or premium) or method by which the consideration is to be calculated must be stated. For example, the rent on a farm may either be fixed at £*x* per annum, or calculated as a specified percentage of the tenant's annual net profits.
(d) *Period*. The period of the tenancy or lease must be known so that both the commencement date of the lease and its duration ought to be specified: *Harvey* v. *Pratt* (1965). If L purports to grant T a ten-year lease, without specifying the proposed commencement date, no valid agreement will exist since the courts are not prepared to imply a commencement date, e.g. within a reasonable time, in order to cure this invalidity.
(e) *Special provisions*. Additionally, the memorandum or note should set out any other special provisions agreed between the parties which are essential to a particular contract. If one of the parties wishes to incorporate any other term which is essential to conclude the contract, that term must be unconditionally accepted by the other party.

One further difficulty can be caused when the parties wish to rely on more than one document, e.g. a series of correspondence, to evidence the contract. The issue here is whether or not the documents can be joined together. The right approach is to start by looking at the document which the defendant has signed in order to ascertain whether it refers to the other document or can be connected to it by inference. It has been held that a cheque signed by the defendant could not be joined to a receipt setting out the essential terms of the contract since a cheque is simply an order for payment and cannot indicate the nature of the transaction between the parties: *Timmins* v. *Moreland Street Property Co. Ltd* (1958).

Signature

There is a great deal of latitude as regards the form of signature. The minimum requirement would be the inclusion of the name or initials of the defendant or his agent which may be printed or handwritten. The handwritten phrase 'I Tim Tenant have agreed' would amount to a sufficient signature since it shows that Tim Tenant recognises the existence of a contract. Finally, note that the memorandum must be signed by the person against whom proceedings are to be brought i.e. the defendant, or by an agent who is authorised to sign it on his principal's behalf.

Doctrine of part performance

Section 40(2) of the Law of Property Act 1925 specifically retains the equitable doctrine of part performance. Consequently, oral evidence of a contract may be given in a legal action where the contract has been partly performed notwithstanding s.40(1). If a defendant were to attempt to take advantage of the absence of a signed written contract or memorandum after having stood by and allowed the plaintiff to partly perform the contract, oral evidence could be introduced in proceedings for specific performance of the contract: *Wakeham* v. *Mackenzie* (1968).

For example, Louise enters into an oral contract to let premises to Thomas provided that Thomas repairs the premises first. Thomas performs this part of the agreement whereupon Louise refuses to grant him the tenancy promised. Thomas would be able to bring proceedings for specific performance of the contract despite the absence of written evidence bearing Louise's signature. Incidentally the fact of a tenant going into actual occupation of leasehold premises provides the best evidence of part performance: see *Kingswood Estate Co. Ltd* v. *Anderson* (1962).

Note that:

(a) The operation of s.40(2), like s.40(1), depends upon the existence of a concluded contract where the essential terms have been agreed; see (a)–(e) in the text above. The doctrine of part performance will not make good a contract which is void for uncertainty, nor turn a 'subject to contract' agreement into an enforceable contract.

(b) The act of part performance which is relied upon must be referable to some contract between the parties. The acts of part performance are considered in the light of the surrounding circumstances and should point to the existence of some contract between the parties. They should either reveal the nature of the contract, for example where L lets T into possession of premises, or be consistent with the oral contract alleged by the plaintiff.

The drawing up of a deed of transfer together with the payment of money by a purchaser were held to amount to sufficient acts of part performance by the House of Lords in *Steadman* v. *Steadman* (1974) in the light of unusual surrounding circumstances. The outcome of this case prompted academics to argue that the doctrine of part performance has rendered s.40(1) unnecessary since most sales and transfers of land or interests in land are accompanied by draft deeds of transfer together with the payment of a deposit. The traditional position was that money payment could not amount to a sufficient act of part performance.

(c) The contract must be specifically enforceable. In other words, the plaintiff must be entitled to the remedy of specific performance which is a matter entirely for the court's discretion.

Specific performance

Specific performance is a court order which directs a party to do something in order to perform his contractual obligations. For example, a tenant moves into possession under a twenty-one-year lease whereupon the landlord refuses to draw up a deed vesting the legal estate in the tenant. It would be open to the tenant to ask for specific performance of the contract to grant a twenty-one-year lease; a court could direct the landlord to execute a deed in order to create a legal term of twenty-one years.

The remedy of specific performance is an equitable remedy which is available in cases where a valid binding contract exists. An order of specific performance will not be granted if it would be futile in the circumstances, e.g. if the term has already expired. The remedy of specific performance is only available where damages would *not* be an adequate remedy. So, for example, specific performance may be granted to enforce a covenant to repair but not a covenant to pay rent.

A court exercises its own discretion when considering applications for specific performance, and can refuse to grant an order for specific performance. Examples of grounds on which the court will refuse to make an order are delay, misconduct on the part of the plaintiff, the possibility that the order will cause hardship, or the fact that the enforcement of the order would require supervision by the court.

DEED REQUIRED

General rule

The general rule, stated by s.52 Law of Property Act 1925, is that all estates and interests in land must be created or transferred by deed in order to convey or create legal estate. A deed is a document which is signed, sealed and delivered. This requirement is easily satisfied since mass-produced red adhesive paper discs are simply attached to the bottom of the appropriate document. It has been held that a document containing the letters 'LS' printed inside a circle satisfied this requirement, since they are an abbreviation for *locus sigilli* (the place of a seal): *First National Securities Ltd* v. *Jones* (1978).

Leases for three years or less may be created orally

One notable exception to the general rule is the creation of leases which take effect in possession for a term not exceeding three years granted at a market or rack rent: s.54(2) Law of Property Act 1925. Leases can be created orally provided that they satisfy these three requirements. In other words, it should:

(a) give immediate possession; and
(b) be for three years or less; and
(c) be at a market rent.

Periodic tenancies are deemed to be tenancies for not more than three years even though they may continue for a longer period. For example, Linda granted Tracy a monthly tenancy in 1980 which is still continuing. Providing that Tracy took up immediate possession and paid a market rent, a legal lease has been created even though no deed was executed. Note that the tenancy can be enforced, regardless of whether it was created orally or by writing, since s.40 is satisfied in either event, given that the contract has been partly performed by Tracy's moving into possession.

This exception does not, however, extend to the transfer of existing leases, which must always be by deed. For example, Len grants Tron a ten-year lease and assigns the last two years to Anne. Tron and Anne will only receive legal leases if deeds are executed in both cases.

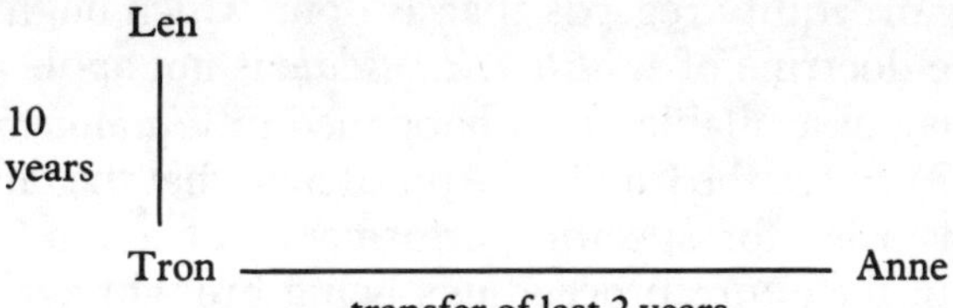

Invalid leases

Agreement for a lease

Leases which are invalid because they have failed to satisfy the requirement of a deed are not void in law. Instead an invalid lease is construed as an 'agreement for a lease'. Any such agreement for a lease is necessarily an equitable interest and is usually referred to as an equitable tenancy.

Doctrine of Walsh v. Lonsdale

The legal distinction between a lease and an agreement for a lease is that a lease creates a tenancy whereas an agreement for a lease binds the parties to granting and accepting a lease. If the agreement for a lease falls into the category of being specifically enforceable the parties to the agreement will to all intents and purposes be in almost the same position as if a lease had been granted in the first place. This is known as the 'doctrine of *Walsh* v. *Lonsdale*'.

In *Walsh* v. *Lonsdale* (1882), the landlord entered a written agreement in which he contracted to grant the tenant a seven-year lease of a mill. One of the terms of the contract was that the landlord could demand payment of rent in advance. Subsequently, the tenant entered into possession, and paid the rent quarterly (not in advance). There was no lease because the seven-year term was not granted by a deed. The landlord asked the tenant for payment of rent in advance. In subsequent legal proceedings the tenant argued that the landlord was not entitled to rely on this term since no lease had been drawn up. It was conceded that the tenant had a right to specific performance of the agreement for a lease. In those circumstances, the Court of Appeal stated that the case was to proceed as if specific performance had been granted. Sir George Jessel MR said that:

> 'A tenant holding under an agreement for a lease of which specific performance would be decreed, stands in the same position as to liability as if the lease had been granted.'

In applying the doctrine of *Walsh* v. *Lonsdale*, the courts observe the equitable maxim 'equity regards that as done which ought to have been done'. But the doctrine of *Walsh* v. *Lonsdale* is not applicable if specific performance is not available. This happened in *Warmington and Another* v. *Miller* (1973) where the Court of Appeal held that the landlord was not entitled to an order for specific performance of a sub-lease since this would result in forfeiture proceedings being brought against the tenant who had sub-let the premises in breach of a covenant prohibiting sub-letting.

The doctrine of *Walsh* v. *Lonsdale* applies even if the parties are not in a direct contractual relationship. The Court of Appeal held *per incuriam* (not as a binding precedent) in *Industrial Properties* v. *Associated Electrical Industries Limited* (1977) that the doctrine need not be limited to cases where there was only one agreement and to cases where there was a direct contractual relationship between the parties. In that case the freeholder agreed to sell the freehold to the landlord. The premises were never conveyed to the landlord even though the purchase price had been paid; this was a deliberate attempt to avoid stamp duty. The landlord agreed to grant a twenty-one-year lease to the tenant who occupied the premises for seven years and then ended the 'lease' properly, leaving the premises in a bad state of repair. The landlord brought proceedings for dilapidations. The Court of Appeal found no obstacle in treating both contracts as specifically enforceable, and applied the doctrine of *Walsh* v. *Lonsdale* to the agreement for a lease.

In conclusion, the doctrine of *Walsh* v. *Lonsdale* operates so as to create equitable rights to cases where a lease is imperfectly drawn up. If the agreement for a lease is specifically enforceable it is as good as a lease, save that it may be necessary to have recourse to the courts to establish this fact for the purpose of enforcing the terms of the lease.

REGISTRATION

Conveyancing systems

There are currently two different systems of conveyancing in operation in England and Wales. The old system of unregistered conveyancing is gradually being replaced by a new system of registered conveyancing. The main distinction between the two conveyancing systems is that land itself is not registrable in the unregistered system, but a number of miscellaneous categories of specified third party interests and charges over land are registrable in a Land Charges Register, e.g. easements and mortgages. Under the new registered system title to land itself is registrable.

Unregistered conveyancing

A number of land charges are registrable in the unregistered system under the consolidating provisions of the Land Charges Act 1972. The main registrable land charge which concerns leasehold conveyancing is the 'estate contract'. An 'estate contract' is a contract to convey or create a leasehold estate. Leases, agreements for leases, and options to purchase and to renew are all estate contracts which should be registered in the Land Charges Register as a Class C(iv) land charge: s.2(4) Land Charges Act 1972.

If the tenant fails to register an estate contract, it will be void against a 'purchaser for value' of the legal estate: s.4(6) Land Charges Act 1972. For example, if L agrees to grant T a short lease and then sells his legal freehold estate to a purchaser before the lease has been granted, the purchaser may take the property free of the lease if T has failed to register the agreement for a lease as an estate contract. But it will not be void against the landlord. Thus if a landlord sells land to a purchaser who takes free of the tenant's lease because the tenant has failed to register it as an estate contract, the tenant can enforce a claim in damages for breach of contract against the landlord: see *Wright* v. *Dean* (1948).

Registered conveyancing

General

The object of the new system of registration of title to land is the simplification of conveyancing. Under the new system of registered conveyancing title to all freehold property, and to leasehold property with more than twenty-one years to run, is registrable under the provisions of the Land Registration Acts 1925 and 1986. The new system presently covers eighty per cent of the country. It is compulsory to register title to land upon sale in areas which have been designated as areas of compulory registration.

Registration of leases

One of the objectives of the Land Registration Act 1986 was the widening of the class of leases which are compulsorily registrable. Prior to the enactment of the 1986 Act, leases granted out of unregistered land in areas of compulsory registration were compulsorily registrable only if granted for a term of forty years or more, or assigned with an unexpired term of forty years or more. Voluntary registration could be applied for in the case of the grant or assignment of leases for between twenty-one and forty years.

Compulsory registration

The 1986 Act introduced a single registration period for leases of 'more than twenty-one years'. This means that the period of reference for which the registration of leases becomes mandatory is twenty-one years for the great majority of leases. The general rule is that leases granted for more than twenty-one years or assigned with more than twenty-one years to run must be registered: s.123(1) Land Registration Act 1925 as amended by s.2(1) Land Registration Act 1986.

Inalienable leases

There are no mandatory provisions which require the registration of inalienable leases. An inalienable lease is a lease which cannot be transferred because the lease itself contains an absolute prohibition against assignment. Prior to the enactment of the 1986 Act, the registration of a lease which contained an absolute prohibition on assignment was prohibited by s.8 Land Registration Act 1925. But it is now possible for landlords to enter a restriction in respect of leases granted or assigned before the commencement of the 1986 Act. However, any restriction entered in respect of leases which pre-date the

Act's commencement date will not operate retrospectively so as to alter the effect of any dealing in the property prior to the commencement of the 1986 Act: s.3(2) Land Registration Act 1986.

Consequences of failure to register

In an area where registration is compulsory the grant or assignment of a lease for more than twenty-one years must be registered within two months. The consequence of failure to register within the prescribed two-month time-limit is that the grant or assignment becomes void for the purpose of transferring a legal leasehold estate: s.123(1) Land Registration Act 1925. The legal estate will notionally pass back to the grantor or assignor who will hold the leasehold estate on trust for the grantee or assignee. The onus is then placed on the grantee or assignee to ask for a new deed of transfer to be drawn up so that the legal leasehold estate can be conveyed anew, and time will run afresh. For example, Late grants Two a ninety-year lease by deed in an area of compulsory registration. The following illustrations demonstrate the two alternative technical legal positions of the parties, according to whether the leasehold title has been registered or not:

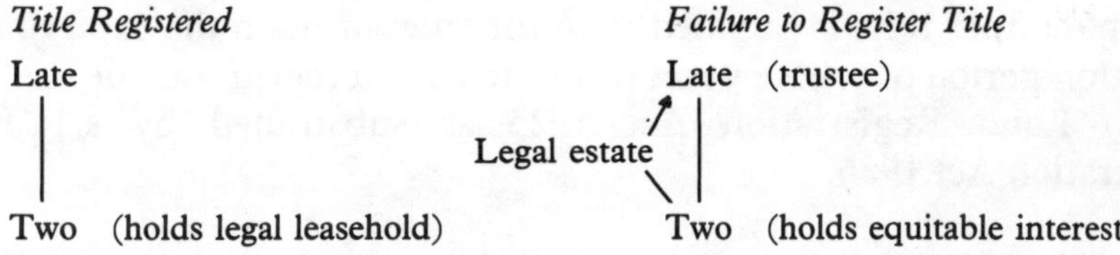

In practice, the two-month time limit can be extended so that the issues raised in this illustration are of greater academic than practical significance.

Classes of title

Tenants may apply for one of the three classes of title to be registered as described in the following text. It is possible for inferior classes of title to be upgraded and converted into a superior title. The proprietor has to submit a formal application to the Registrar for title to be converted: s.77 Land Registration Act 1925 as substituted by s.1 Land Registration Act 1986.

Absolute title: This is the best title which can be registered, and can only be applied for if both the freehold and any intermediate leasehold title can be approved by the Land Registrar: s.8(1)(b)(i) Land Registration Act 1925. Note that the Registrar will enter a 'qualified title' where an absolute title is required if it appears either that the title can only be established for a limited period or that title is subject to certain reservations: s.7 Land Registration Act 1925. The Registrar may convert a possessory title to good leasehold title is he is satisfied about title to the land: s.77(3) Land Registration Act 1925 as substituted by s.1 Land Registration Act 1986.

Good leasehold title: If title is registered as good leasehold title this means that only the leasehold title has been approved by the Land Registry. In this case no guarantee is given by the Registrar to show that the lease was validly granted in the first place: s.8(1)(b)(ii) Land Registration Act 1925.

Good leasehold titles can be converted to absolute titles if the Registrar is satisfied as to the freehold title and as to any intermediate leasehold title: s.77(1) Land Registration Act 1925 as substituted by s.1 Land Registration Act 1986.

Possessory title: It is rare for a lease to be registered with possessory title, and only occurs in cases where there is evidence of possession, but no evidence of title to the leasehold interest: s.8(1)(b)(iii), (iv) Land Registration Act 1925.

The Registrar may upgrade a possessory leasehold title to good leasehold either if he is satisfied as to the title, or upon the expiry of the limitation period of twelve years from the date of registration of the land: s.77(2) Land Registration Act 1925 as substituted by s.1 Land Registration Act 1986.

Overriding interests

An overriding interest is an interest which is protected under the provisions of the Land Registration Acts 1925 to 1986 even though the interest does not appear on the land register. It is public policy to protect certain specified proprietary interests in land regardless of registration. The 1986 Act enlarged the category of leases which qualify as overriding interests.

All leases for more than twenty-one years created or conveyed after the commencement of the 1986 Act are overriding interests and quality for protection regardless of registration: s.70(1)(k) Land Registration Act 1925 as amended by s.4 Land Registration Act 1986. Prior to the 1986 Act a distinction was drawn between leases granted in return for a premium and gratuitous leases, whereby only the former qualified as overriding interests. This distinction has been abolished in respect of transfers of leasehold estates after the commencement date of the 1986 Act: s.4 Land Registration Act 1986.

Protection by entry

Agreements for a lease, options to purchase and options to renew should be protected by entry of a notice or caution on the register.

FURTHER READING

Registered Land 3rd ed., 1981, by D. Hayton, Modern Legal Series (this edition does not include the Land Registration Act 1986).

COSTS OF LEASES

The Costs of Leases Act 1958 provides that a party to a lease shall, unless the parties agree otherwise, be under no obligation to pay any part of the other party's solicitor's costs. In practice, the landlord's solicitor prepares the draft lease which he sends to the tenant (or his solicitor). The tenant will bear these costs only if there is an express agreement to contract out of the Costs of Leases Act.

STAMPING LEASES

Tax has to be paid in respect of many leases. This is known as 'stamping leases' since an official mark is stamped on the deed as evidence that the tax due has been paid. Leases and agreements for leases should be stamped in accordance with the provisions of the Stamp Act 1891 as amended. The stamp is assessed according to the value of the rent, premium or other consideration with reference to a scale set out in Schedule 1 to the Stamp Act 1891.

Failure to stamp a lease means that it cannot be put in evidence before a civil court, arbitrator or referee: s.14 Stamp Act 1891. It is also an offence not to stamp a lease: s.15 Stamp Act 1891. Schemes which are designed to avoid paying stamp duty are destined to fail: *Ingram* v. *Inland Revenue Commissioners* (1985). The courts will invariably apply the principles established by the House of Lords in *Ramsey (W.T.) Ltd* v. *Inland Revenue Commissioners* (1982) to counteract tax avoidance schemes which rely on paper transactions. In these cases, the courts will give effect to the substance of the transaction and not to its form on paper.

DRAFTING LEASES

It is self-evident that a well-drafted lease which sets out mutually agreed obligations and liabilities is the best insurance against future disputes. Badly drafted leases (containing ambiguous or conflicting provisions), and unduly onerous leases, both provide fertile ground for disputes and litigation, which is poor estate management practice. Similarly, oral tenancy agreements can lead to disputes over important matters, such as the demarcation point between the repairing and maintenance obligations of landlord and tenant. This results from either a failure to decide these points at the tenancy's commencement, or simply as a result of the absence of written terms to evidence the oral agreement which was reached.

The importance of negotiating fair terms should not be underestimated, given the fact that the average life of an institutional lease is twenty-five years with the possibility of a renewal or continuation at the end of the contractual term. For example, leases with unusual or unduly onerous obligations may be difficult to transfer.

It is, therefore, imperative for landlords and their advisors to ensure the use of properly drafted leases which incorporate well understood clauses. Standard form leases and legal precedents are available; the problem here is knowing how to use and apply them. Skill and specialist knowledge are prerequisites for those drafting leases since it demands a clear understanding of landlord and tenant law coupled with a knowledge of contemporary practice. For instance, will a tenant be prepared to accept responsibility for a latent defect in a newly constructed shopping development, or is it customary to make provision for a sinking fund in a high quality office development?

Finally, draftsmen also require the vision to anticipate future trends. If it is necessary to incorporate novel clauses, this is not without its own risks since the new clauses can lead to lengthy disputes and result in expensive litigation if there is no clear decided legal authority on the proper construction to be placed on the clause in issue.

FURTHER READING

Drafting Commercial Leases by Murray J. Ross, Butterworths, 1980.

RECTIFICATION AND RESCISSION

Rectification

It may be necessary to rectify a lease where a mistake has occurred in its original drafting so that it fails to represent the parties' intentions. In this case, the courts will be prepared to rectify a lease on the basis of a common mistake. In *Co-operative Insurance Society* v. *Centremoor Ltd* (1983), the Court of Appeal agreed to the rectification of a lease when a sub-lease under whch the lessee and sub-lessee were to share increases of rent paid by an occupying sub-underlessee failed to dove-tail correctly owing to a drafting error c.f. *London Regional Transport* v. *Wimpey Group Services Ltd* (1986).

If the mistake is a unilateral mistake (made by one party only) the traditional rule was that the lease could be rectified if it could be shown that the other party had been guilty of sharp practice. But in *Thomas Bates & Son Ltd* v. *Wyndham's (Lingerie) Ltd* (1981) the Court of Appeal held that it was not always necessary to show that the defendant was guilty of sharp practice. The Court of Appeal held that a lease could be rectified in cases where a unilateral mistake had been made in circumstances where the parties had a common intention to include the omitted provision in the lease, and where the plaintiff thought that the lease gave effect to that intention, and the defendant knew of the mistake and failed to bring it to his attention, thereby benefitting from it. In that case, the Court of Appeal held that a lease could be rectified so as to include an arbitration provision in a rent review clause at the request of a landlord in a case where the lease failed to give effect to the parties' common intention due to a unilateral mistake by the landlord.

Finally, if a clerical error or grammatical mistake has been made, the courts will rectify the provision on the basis that the parties intended a different construction. Nonetheless, it is clear that if eccentric language has been used, that, by itself, is not a sufficient reason for the courts to order a rewriting of the provisions in order to produce a document likely to be approved in Lincoln's Inn: per Lord Justice Lawton in *East* v. *Pantiles (Plant Hire) Ltd* (1982) where the Court of Appeal refused an application to alter a date in a lease.

Rescission

General

The courts have a discretion to rescind a lease on the ground that a mutual or unilateral mistake has been made, in cases where the plaintiff can either show that he has been misled or will suffer considerable hardship: *Goddard* v. *Jeffreys* (1881). This remedy is only applicable in cases where a fundamental mistake has been made, and where the parties can be restored to their original position.

Misrepresentation

A lease may be rescinded on the ground that it was induced by a misrepresentation where rescission is available as a remedy: Misrepresentation Act 1967.

FURTHER READING

Cheshire and Fifoot's *Law of Contract* by M.P. Furmston, 11th edition, Butterworths, 1986: see Chapters 8 and 9 on *'Mistake'* and *'Misrepresentation'* respectively.

IMPLIED TERMS

It sometimes happens that landlords omit to include important terms in the lease through negligence or inadvertence. This can result in the lease failing to set out the landlord's intentions unless this omission is remedied.

In certain circumstances the courts are prepared to imply terms in a contract which have not been expressly agreed between the parties. This arises where the parties have failed to express a term which both would consider as clearly part of the contract. The courts will not seek to perfect a contract but only to imply a term when it is necessary to give 'business efficacy' to the contract. In such a case the court will supply a further term to implement the presumed intention of the parties: *The Moorcock* (1889).

This principle was extended by the House of Lords in *Liverpool City Council* v. *Irwin* (1976), who supplied an implied term obliging the landlord to keep the common parts of a block of residential flats in reasonable repair as a matter of necessity: see p.155 for a full consideration of the facts of the case. Lord Wilberforce summarised the applicable principles as follows: firstly, the courts start off by ascertaining what the contract is by looking at the documentary material. Secondly, the courts will consider the actions of the parties and the circumstances. Thirdly, the courts will then establish what the contract is, the parties not having themselves fully stated the terms. To this extent the court will imply a term in order to complete the contract as a matter of necessity.

Finally, Lord Wilberforce's speech alone draws a distinction between introducing a 'Moorcock' term into a contract and completing an incomplete contract. He stated that the objectives are different in that the object of implying a Moorcock term is to imply a term either which both parties would unhesitatingly agree to be part of the bargain or without which the contract would not work. But in this case, the exercise required the implication of a term to complete a contract as a matter of necessity and not simply for business efficacy. In other words, Lord Wilberforce drew subtle distinctions between different ways in which the courts are prepared to imply a term.

Chapter 4

Classification of Leases and Tenancies at Common Law

English common law recognises four main types of leases and tenancies (see Fig. 1). The tenancy from year to year is normally treated as a separate fifth category but can be more conveniently classified as a type of periodic tenancy (Fig. 1). Fixed term leases and periodic tenancies are by far the most prevalent whilst tenancies at will and tenancies at sufferance are comparatively rare. A tenancy by estoppel is not, strictly speaking, a true tenancy, but may have the same consequences as an ordinary tenancy.

FIXED TERM

A fixed term lease or tenancy is a lease or tenancy which is granted for a determinate period of time commencing on date 1 and expiring automatically on date 2 by effluxion (the passage) of time. For example, L granted T a fixed term lease for ninety-nine years which commenced on the 1st January 1900 and is due to expire by effluxion of time at midnight on the 31st December 1999.

The fixed term lease is the most common type of commercial lease. It is usually created by express agreement between the parties, as in the example above. However, two statutes provide for the creation of new fixed term tenancies on the expiry of an existing lease. Business tenants may apply for a new fixed tenancy for up to fourteen years, under s.33 Landlord and Tenant Act 1954, when their lease expires. Similarly, residential tenants with long leases which come within the scope of the Leasehold Reform Act 1967 may apply for new leases of fifty years in duration.

Fixed term leases can be granted for any minimum period of time including periods of less than a year. The minimum period for a fixed term was at least two years at common law: *Bishop of Bath's* case; but s.205(1)(xxvii) Law of Property Act 1925 specifically includes leases for a period of less than a year in its definition of a term of years.

FIXED TERM (most common)	PERIODIC TENANCY	TENANCY AT WILL	TENANCY AT SUFFERANCE (comparatively rare)
(term certain/term of years)			
REMARKS			
(a) Must be for a term certain. (b) Usually created by deed. (c) Most common form of commercial lease.	(a) Continues from period to period unless and until determined. (b) Traditional method of leasing residential accommodation and agricultural holdings.	Must be evidence of a genuine common intention to create a tenancy at will.	Arises by implication of law only when a tenant continues in possession after termination of his tenancy.
TERMINATION AT COMMON LAW			
by effluxion of time on the last day of the term	By a notice to quit served by either party.	(a) by choice or intention. (b) on the death of either party.	at any time.

Periodic tenancy:

TENANCY FROM YEAR TO YEAR	OTHER PERIODIC TENANCIES
6 months notice expiring at end of a year of the tenancy.	Notice = length of tenancy and expires at end of period. N.B. Minimum length of notice in the case of residential tenancies is 4 weeks: s.5 Protection from Eviction Act 1977.

Fig. 1 Classification of leases and tenancies at common law.

Term must be certain

The term for which the lease is to run must be certain at the time the lease commences. This rule is satisfied if the lease's duration is either fixed (as in the example above) or is capable of being ascertained before the lease's term has begun to run. Thus in *Lace* v. *Chantler* (1944) a lease for the duration of the war was held to be invalid because its term was not certain. Although it would have been possible to calculate the term retrospectively it was impossible to calculate the lease's term at the time the lease would take effect since no one could say how long the war would last.

There is no reason why the term of a lease should not be measured with reference to a collateral matter, so long as the date on which the term is to end can be ascertained precisely when the lease begins to run.

If a lease contains an option to determine the lease mid-term, the term is still said to be certain despite the fact that at the time the lease takes effect it will not be known whether the lease will run its full term or whether the option to determine will be exercised. For example, Lord Denning MR stated in *Joseph* v. *Joseph* (1966) that a lease under which a tenant agrees to give up possession by a certain date is valid even though the tenant may give up possession earlier.

Consider whether the following hypothetical leases might be void for uncertainty:

(a) *a fixed term lease created on the 10th October and due to commence on the 20th November*: This lease would be void for uncertainty because the date on which it is to commence is uncertain as no year is mentioned.

(b) *a fixed term lease due to commence 'when the leasehold premises became vacant for so long as L may specify'*. There is, in principle, no reason why this lease should be void for uncertainty although this is a border-line example. A lease's commencement date can be made conditional upon some uncertain event provided that the event occurs before the lease takes effect. Although the length of the term is not yet known, it can be ascertained before it begins to run if it specifies a term when the premises fall vacant.

Renewal

A lease for a fixed term will expire automatically at common law by effluxion of time unless:

(a) the tenant has a statutory right to a new tenancy, e.g. in the case of business tenancies which fall within the scope of Part II Landlord and Tenant Act 1954; or

(b) the lease contains a covenant for renewal.

Many leases give tenants a right to renew the lease for a further term at or near the end of the current term. If a lease does contain a provision for renewal, the tenant has a right of election at the end of his lease. He can either vacate the premises or ask for his lease to be renewed. The lease usually stipulates that the request for renewal should be made in writing.

Statutory restrictions on renewal

A right to renew a lease is subject to two statutory limitations as follows.

*Sixty-year limit:*The option to renew will state the length of the new term which is to be granted. This term should not exceed sixty years since any covenant which attempts to operate a renewal for a term exceeding sixty years is void: s.145, Schedule XV, para 7(2) Law of Property Act 1922. This means that if effect is to be given to the option to renew, the length of the new lease or sub-lease should not exceed sixty years.

Perpetually renewable leases: If the covenant for the lease's renewal has the effect of creating a situation where every new lease thereby created also contains a covenant for renewal, the legal effect of this may be to create a covenant for 'perpetual' renewal. In other words, the lease contains the mechanism for the lease's perpetual renewal since each new lease is automatically renewable at the end of each term. This would occur where the tenant was granted a fresh lease on exactly the same terms as the original lease, including the same covenant for renewal. In *Hare* v. *Burges* (1857) a lease which contained a covenant for renewal containing the words 'including this clause' was said to create a right to perpetual renewal.

Leases which contain covenants for perpetual renewal are converted into terms of two thousand years by the Law of Property Act 1922, Schedule XV, para 2(1) and s.202 Law of Property Act 1925. This also applies to sub-leases, in which case the term of the sub-lease is one day less than the lease's term.

PERIODIC TENANCIES

A periodic tenancy is a tenancy which continues from one period to the next unless and until one of the parties ends it by proper notice to quit, e.g. L grants T a monthly tenancy which will continue from one month until the next until L or T serves a notice to quit on the other party. The general rule is that the notice to quit should expire at the end of the current period and be equal in length to it. In this example, the notice to quit should be given one month before it is to take effect. The grant of a periodic tenancy is the traditional method of letting residential accommodation and agricultural holdings.

Creation

A periodic tenancy may be created by express agreement, arise by implication or be created by statute.

By express agreement

The parties may enter into an express agreement to create a periodic tenancy, e.g. L agrees to grant T a monthly tenancy.

Implied by law

Periodic tenancies often arise informally when a landlord grants a tenant the exclusive possession of leasehold premises in return for a rent which is paid on a periodic basis, and where no fixed term is mentioned. In this instance, a periodic tenancy will arise by implication rather than as the result of an express agreement. A periodic tenancy will arise by implication when the following conditions are satisfied:

(a) a tenant has exclusive possession of premises with the consent of the landlord. This can occur either when a tenant takes up possession of premises or when a tenant remains in possession of premises (holds over) on the expiry of a prior tenancy; and
(b) rent is paid and accepted; and
(c) the rent is measured with reference to a period, e.g. L asks T to pay him £*x* a week.

Created by statute

Periodic tenancies may be created under the provisions of the following statutory schemes.

Agricultural holdings: Agricultural holdings for periods shorter than annual periodic tenancies are automatically converted into annual periodic tenancies by statute. Section 2 Agricultural Holdings Act 1986 provides that a letting of land used as agricultural land shall take effect as if it were an agreement to let land as a tenancy from year to year. This provision includes all periodic tenancies which are less than yearly periodic tenancies, and fixed term tenancies for periods of one year or less. It has the effect of enlarging short lettings of agricultural land into tenancies from year to year.

The main object of enlarging short agricultural tenancies is to prevent what would otherwise be a widespread evasion of the security of tenure provisions which protect tenants of agricultural holdings. Landlords could otherwise use the device of granting a series of short tenancies to avoid the security of tenure provisions.

Secure tenancies: A secure tenancy is a tenancy of public sector residential accommodation. Section 86 Housing Act 1985 provides that a periodic tenancy will arise automatically on the expiry of a fixed term secure tenancy, unless a further secure tenancy is granted. The new periodic tenancy will not be a secure tenancy but a periodic tenancy. The type of periodic tenancy, i.e. weekly, monthly, or yearly, will be determined by reference to the period for which rent was payable under the secure tenancy. For example, Lamebet Council granted Ted a five-year secure tenancy at a rent payable on a weekly basis. A weekly periodic tenancy will automatically arise at the end of the five-year term unless Lamebet Council grants Ted a further secure tenancy.

Type of periodic tenancy

It will be important to determine the type of periodic tenancy which has been created, not least because the type of tenancy determines the length of notice which must be given before it can be ended. The test is the period by reference to which the parties calculate the rent. In most cases this will be a relatively easy exercise, e.g. if L grants T a tenancy at a rent of £25 per week, a weekly tenancy will arise since the rent is calculated on a weekly basis. But if T pays a weekly rent of £50 it cannot necessarily be inferred that he has a weekly tenancy. He might have been granted a monthly tenancy, at a rent of £200 per month, payable weekly.

The law has traditionally distinguished yearly periodic tenancies from all other types of periodic tenancy but little turns on this today. All periodic tenancies share the same characteristics. They have a duration which is periodic in nature rather than a duration which is fixed from the outset. This means that it is a very flexible leasehold interest. They can be assigned, and notice is required to determine them. Periodic tenancies are sub-classified according to the period for which they are created, the most common types being weekly, monthly and yearly.

Once a periodic tenancy is created it runs on relentlessly until one of the parties serves a notice to quit to end it. The tenancy, however, arises out of the original contract. For example, Lion granted Tiger a weekly tenancy in 1985 which still continues today so that Tiger has been in possession of the leasehold property for x weeks. Tiger is not treated as having been granted x separate weekly tenancies. The original 1985 contract created a single weekly tenancy which is still continuing, and which will continue into the future until it is ended by the service of a valid notice to quit.

One consequence of this is that if a landlord wants to determine a periodic tenancy which is regulated by one of the statutory schemes he must:

(a) serve a valid notice to quit; and
(b) end the tenancy in accordance with the method prescribed by the statutory scheme.

Termination of periodic tenancies

A periodic tenancy can only be ended by the service of a valid notice to quit by either party (in the absence of special circumstances, e.g. forfeiture or surrender up of the lease). It is rare for this requirement to be dispensed with, although there is no reason why the parties should not include special stipulations of their own in this matter. In order to constitute a valid notice to quit, the notice should be of the correct length and served on the appropriate day, and include information prescribed by statute where required.

Length of notice

The length of the notice to quit may either be stipulated by the parties or it can be ascertained from the common law rules. The general common law rule is that the appropriate length of notice is the period which corresponds to the period of the tenancy. A weekly tenancy requires one week's notice, a monthly tenancy one month's notice, and so on. But a yearly periodic tenancy requires six months' notice and not a year.

Residential tenancies

The law provides a minimum requirement of not less than four weeks' notice in the case of premises let as a dwelling: s.5 Protection from Eviction Act 1977. This section also contains two further requirements: firstly, the notice to quit must be in writing; secondly, it must contain certain information prescribed by the Secretary of State in a statutory instrument. (See Appendix 2 for current prescribed information on notices to quit (SI 1980 No. 1624).)

Express agreement

The length of any notice to quit can be agreed expressly by the parties, provided that s.5 of the Protection from Eviction Act 1977 is satisfied.

Served on the appropriate day

A notice to quit must expire either at the end of the current period or on the first day of any period. For this reason, the appropriate day on which the notice to quit is to be served must be calculated precisely so that it expires on the right day. Otherwise, it may be necessary to wait until the next period before notice can be served. For example, Timeon's landlord wants to determine Timeon's weekly residential tenancy which began on a Monday. He should serve a notice to quit which will expire either on Sunday or Monday. The notice should be in writing and four weeks in length in order to comply with the provisions of s.5 of the Protection from Eviction Act 1977.

In practice, most medium and large sized firms dealing with tenancies have computers programmed to serve notices to quit on the appropriate dates. Alternatively, charts are available for the purpose of aiding the calculation of the correct day.

TENANCIES AT WILL

A tenancy at will is a tenancy where the tenant is in possession with the consent of the landlord. There are two factual situations in which a tenancy at will is the most appropriate form of tenancy. Firstly, where a landlord has let a tenant into possession early, pursuant to a lease which has not yet commenced. Secondly, upon the expiry of a lease when a landlord permits a tenant to 'hold over' pending the conclusion of negotiations for a new lease. But note that once rent is paid and accepted, there is an argument for saying that a periodic tenancy has been created.

Tenants at will do not have the security of fixed term or periodic tenants since their tenancies may be terminated at any time by the landlord. The Court of Appeal have said in *Heslop* v. *Burns* (1974) that the law leans against finding a tenancy at will in the context of a residential occupancy. But there is an argument for saying that if the courts lean against tenancies at will, this only applies in the residential sector. Business tenancies at will at a rent may possibly be used to evade Part II of the Landlord and Tenant Act 1954 which entitles business tenants to apply to renew their lease.

TENANCIES AT SUFFERANCE

The meaning of this form of tenancy can be deduced from the use of the word 'sufferance'. A tenancy at sufferance arises where a landlord suffers a tenant to remain in possession after his tenancy has expired. The landlord has neither given his consent to the holding over nor has he dissented from the tenant's continued occupation of the premise. Tenants in this position are technically in a vulnerable position since the tenancy at sufferance can be ended at any time without notice, rendering the tenant a trespasser. On the other hand, the tenant's status can be upgraded to a tenancy at will if the landlord consents to the tenant's occupation, or to a periodic tenancy if rent is paid and accepted, or the landlord may simply agree to renew the old tenancy.

TENANCIES BY ESTOPPEL

A tenancy by estoppel is not initially an ordinary tenancy. What happens is that a tenancy has been granted by a landlord who does not himself have power to grant a tenancy since he does not have title to the relevant legal estate. But once the landlord owns the legal estate he is estopped (prevented) from repudiating the existence of any tenancy which he has created. The landlord's subsequent acquisition of the legal estate is said to 'feed the estoppel' so that the legal estate vests in the tenant. A tenancy by estoppel once fed has exactly the same consequences as an ordinary tenancy.

Chapter 5

Tenancies Defined by Statute

INTRODUCTORY

There are a number of statutes which provide protection for residential, business, and agricultural tenants respectively. Each statutory scheme creates a different set of rights and degrees of protection for tenants. For example, if a residential tenancy falls within the scope of the Rent Act 1977, the tenant has an automatic right to remain in possession of the leasehold premises even if the tenancy has expired, and the right to register a 'fair rent' (which may be lower than the contractual rent agreed by the parties). Landlords are only entitled to regain possession of tenancies protected by the Rent Act 1977 by a court order under one of the limited statutory grounds for possession.

By contrast, business tenants are provided with entirely different statutory rights from Rent Act tenants by Part II Landlord and Tenant Act 1954. Business tenants whose tenancies fall within the scope of Part II are entitled to request a renewal of their tenancy at the end of the contractual term on normal commercial terms. The legislation provides a procedure enabling the tenant to seek the grant of a new tenancy from his landlord, and in default of agreement by way of an order of the court.

A consideration of the common law classification of tenancies would be incomplete without an early reference to the statutory definitions of tenancies. Tenancies defined by statute have to be analysed in the context of the relevant legislation, which is often complex. Accordingly, the relevant legislation and its objective will be introduced in this chapter but the details of each scheme are set out in later chapters.

BACKGROUND TO LEGISLATION

Overview

Legislation protecting tenants first developed in the private residential sector at the beginning of the twentieth century when the provision of housing first became a major political issue. At the end of the First World War there were allegations that servicemen were returning home from war to find that their families had been evicted during their

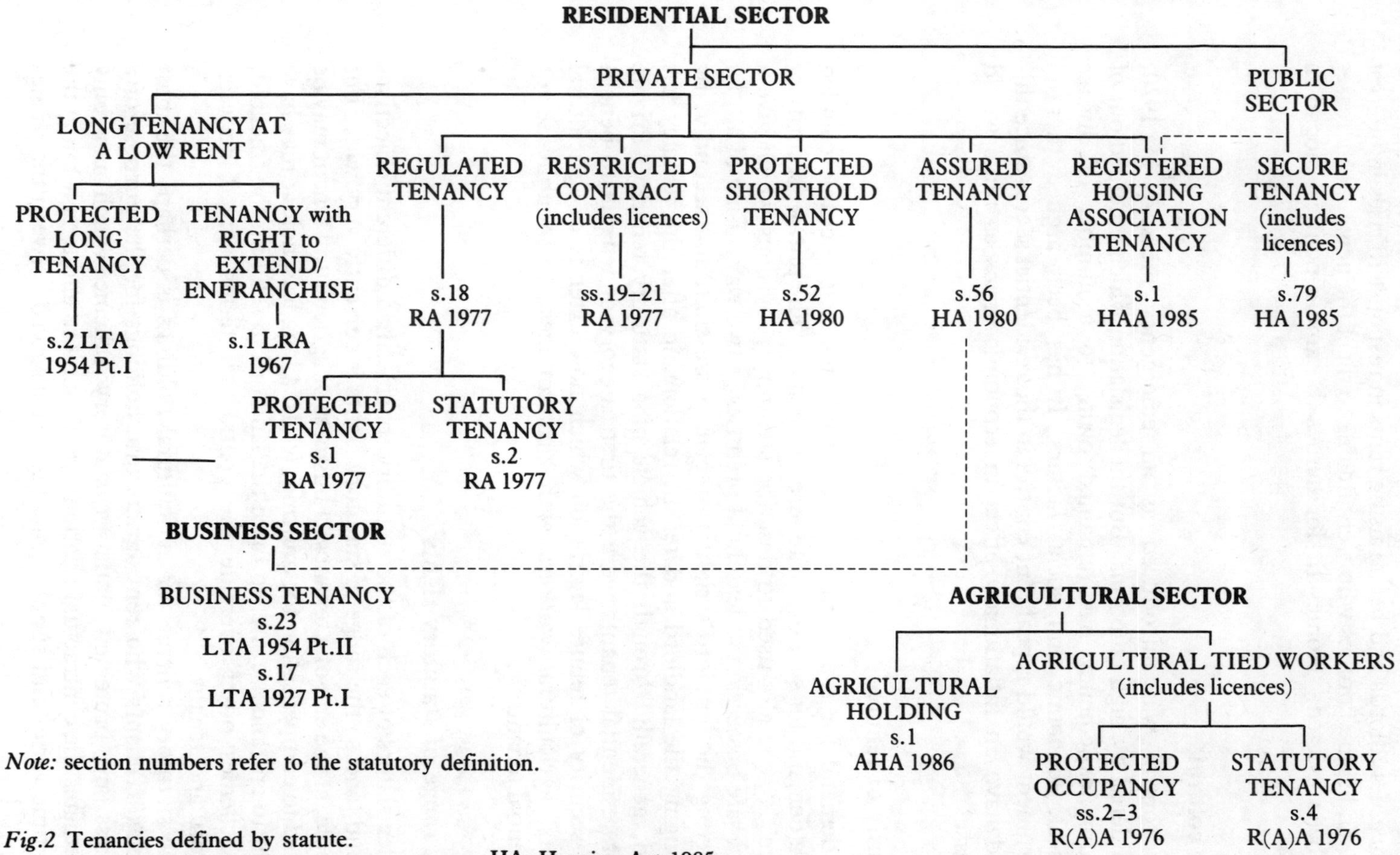

Note: section numbers refer to the statutory definition.

Fig.2 Tenancies defined by statute.

LTA–Landlord and Tenant Acts 1927 & 1954;
LRA–Leasehold Reform Act 1967;
RA–Rent Act 1977;
HA–Housing Act 1985;
HAA–Housing Associations Act 1985;
AHA–Agricultural Holdings Act 1986;
R(A)A–Rent (Agriculture) Act 1976.

absence. Landlords had been raising rents in response to rises in interest rates, and some families who were unable to meet the new rent increases had been evicted. 'Homes fit for heroes' became a political slogan in 1918.

Rent control

Rent control was introduced as an emergency measure in 1920, engendered by high emotions. But the legislation which emerged out of war-time expediency has remained owing to a number of diverse political, economic and social factors. It has been argued that no government would repeal rent control in the residential sector since this would have an inflationary effect in economic terms as rents would increase.

Security of tenure

The demand for rent control of residential tenancies became coupled with a demand for security of tenure for tenants. The phrase 'security of tenure' is generally used to describe statutory provisions which give a tenant safe possession of leasehold premises in two ways. First of all, by restricting the landlord's right to regain possession, and secondly, by prolonging the landlord and tenant relationship after the tenancy has ended, generally through the vehicle of a statutory tenancy. Private sector residential tenants were the first category of tenants to benefit from security of tenure legislation which now extends to agricultural tenants, agricultural workers with tied cottages, and public sector residential tenants.

Wide range of statutory rights

The legislators of each of the statutory schemes had different objectives in mind, and so the range of statutory rights is currently very wide. For example, at the end of a tenancy, a business or agricultural tenant may be entitled to compensation for quitting, whilst a long leaseholder may have a right to enfranchise, i.e. to force the landlord to sell him the freehold. The schemes often override the contractual terms agreed between landlord and tenant.

The statutory scheme for agricultural holdings is perhaps the most complex. Tenants who rent agricultural holdings for the purpose of a business are protected under a statutory scheme which not only perpetuates the contractual relationship of landlord and tenant but at the same time varies and supplements the terms agreed between the parties extensively.

THE CONTRACTUAL TERM

The contractual term is the duration of the tenancy as agreed under the original contract, e.g. a fixed term ten-year tenancy has a contractual term of ten years. It should be noted that some of the statutory schemes apply from the time the tenancy commences whilst other schemes only take effect at the end of the contractual term. This can be illustrated by comparing private sector residential tenancies with business tenancies. The majority of tenancies in the former sector will be protected by statute from the tenancy's inception. Business tenancies, on the other hand, are only regulated by statute towards the end of the contractual term.

STATUTORY SCHEMES ARE MUTUALLY EXCLUSIVE

Generally speaking, the statutory schemes are mutually exclusive so that a tenancy is only regulated by one scheme, although the scheme itself may be set out in one or more statutes. There are two exceptions to this: firstly, registered housing associations are quasi-public in nature; secondly, an assured tenancy is a hybrid residential/business tenancy.

It is not always easy to decide which scheme applies in cases where the tenancy satisfies the formal requirements of more than one scheme. This occurs most often in cases where there is mixed user. For example:

(a) Trader leases a shop and lives on the premises, combining business and residential user.
(b) Tiller farms land, sells its produce, and lives in a cottage; all on the same leasehold premises.

A good rule of thumb to apply in order to determine which statutory scheme regulates tenancies with mixed users is the 'predominant user test'. Thus, if Trader's predominant user is business and Tiller's agricultural, the tenancies will be designated business and agricultural respectively. All the tenancies created by statute will be introduced in this chapter whilst greater detail of the more important tenancies will be found in later chapters.

THE RESIDENTIAL SECTOR

Introduction

The residential sector comprises three main sub-divisions: long tenancies at low rents, private sector, and public sector tenancies. The division of residential tenancies into private sector tenancies and public sector tenancies first appeared in the Housing Act 1980. This sub-classification draws a distinction between private and public landlords. Public sector landlords are defined as local authorities and other public bodies and associations by s.80 Housing Act 1985. Private sector landlords are private individuals, companies, trusts or charities.

PRIVATE SECTOR

Long residential tenancies

Meaning

A long tenancy is a tenancy which exceeds twenty-one years. A low rent is defined with reference to the rateable value of the premises as set out in the valuation list on a designated date known as the 'appropriate day'. The appropriate day for this calculation is the 23 March 1965 for dwellings for which a rateable value was shown in the valuation list at that time, or the date on which the value first appeared in the valuation list.

Legislation's objectives

*Introductory:*Long tenancies at low rents fall within the scope of two statutory schemes which co-exist together, namely Part I Landlord and Tenant Act 1954 ('the 1954 Act') and the Leasehold Reform Act 1967 ('the 1967 Act'). Both these statutory schemes and the Rent Acts are mutually exclusive during the currency of the tenancy: s.5(1) Rent Act 1977.

The 1954 Act: The object of the 1954 Act is to provide certain residential tenants who would otherwise be excluded from the Rent Act scheme, owing to a low rent, with security of tenure. The Rent Act 1977 specifically excludes tenancies at a low rent from qualifying for Rent Act protection: s.5 Rent Act 1977. But if a long tenancy at a low rent is ended in accordance with the provisions of Part I, the tenant is entitled to Rent Act protection: s.1 Landlord and Tenant Act 1954.

In order to qualify for protection under the 1954 Act there must be a long tenancy at a low rent which satisfies the 'qualifying condition': s.2(1) Landlord and Tenant Act 1954. To do so, a tenant must show that on the coming to an end of his tenancy, he would be entitled to Rent Act protection but for the low rent. In other words, the tenancy must in all other respects fall within the scope of a Rent Act tenancy.

The 1954 Act achieves its objective of providing security of tenure for certain long leaseholders in four ways. Firstly, the long tenancy continues automatically after the tenancy's term has expired: s.3

Landlord and Tenant Act 1954. Secondly, the tenancy can only be ended by following the correct statutory procedure: ss.4–5 Landlord and Tenant Act 1954. The tenancy is known as a 'continuation tenancy' until it is ended in accordance with the provisions of the 1954 Act: s.3 Landlord and Tenant Act 1954. Thirdly, once a landlord ends the tenancy in accordance with Part I, a statutory tenancy (within the meaning of the Rent Acts) arises which is governed by the Rent Act 1977. Fourthly, a landlord can only regain possession of the leasehold premises if he can show that one or more of the limited statutory grounds for possession apply: s.12 Landlord and Tenant Act 1954.

The 1967 Act: The 1967 Act has a totally different objective from the 1954 Act. The 1967 Act is designed to give certain residential tenants with long leases at low rents the opportunity either to extend their leases by up to fifty years or to purchase the freehold compulsorily at the end of the term of their lease. If a tenant elects to extend his lease he may later purchase the freehold provided that he does so before the extended lease expires. The compulsory purchase of the freehold is known as 'enfranchisement'.

The 1967 Act only applies to certain categories of leasehold premises in order to avoid practical difficulties which would arise if tenants who occupy one floor in a building were granted the freehold of it.

A tenant with a long tenancy at a low rent has a right to purchase the freehold or an extended lease on fair terms provided that he has occupied the premises as his residence for the last three years of the lease or for periods amounting to three years in the last ten years, and the property falls within the prescribed appropriate rateable value limits: s.1 Leasehold Reform Act 1967.

Qualifying tenancies

In order for a tenancy to qualify for the protection afforded by the 1954 Act or the rights granted under the 1967 Act, the tenancy must be a long tenancy at a low rent. It is very often the case that long residential leases are in fact granted at a low rent where a premium (lump sum) is payable e.g. a ninety-nine year lease of a two-bedroomed house granted for a premium of £50,000 and a ground rent of £50 per annum.

Regulated tenancies

The Rent Act

A regulated tenancy is a tenancy which is protected by the Rent Act 1977 ('the Rent Act'): s.18 Rent Act 1977. The Rent Act 1977 is a consolidation Act which draws together legislation dating back to the Increase of Rent and Mortgage Interest (War Restrictions) Act 1915.

Types of tenancies

There are two types of Rent Act tenancies, namely protected and statutory tenancies. A tenancy which falls within the scope of the Rent Act is known as a Rent Act 'protected tenancy' for the duration of its contractual term. Once the tenancy is terminated at common law it is continued automatically by statute, and is referred to as a 'statutory tenancy'. The expression 'regulated tenancy' includes both terms: s.18 Rent Act 1977. The position can be represented diagrammatically as follows:

PROTECTED TENANCY ————→ STATUTORY TENANCY
(contractual term) (indefinite duration)
Rent Act regulated tenancy

Objectives

The aim of the Rent Act is twofold, namely to provide security of tenure to private sector residential tenants, and to set rent controls for regulated tenants. Controlled tenancies were converted to regulated tenancies as from 28th November 1980 by s.64(1) Housing Act 1980.

Security of tenure

The Rent Act provides regulated tenants with security of tenure in two ways. First of all, the original tenancy is continued automatically by statute after it has been determined at common law. A statutory tenancy cannot be transferred by the tenant and continues so long as the tenant resides in the leasehold premises. Accordingly, it may continue indefinitely until the tenant dies. In the eventuality of the death of a statutory tenant, members of the tenant's family who lived with him are entitled to 'inherit' the statutory tenancy. For example, the tenant's spouse could succeed to the tenancy. If a statutory tenancy is transferred in this manner it is described as a 'statutory tenancy by succession'. It is possible for the statutory tenancy to be transferred twice e.g. if a tenant dies his widow could be the first successor to the statutory tenancy, and then their child could inherit the statutory tenancy by a second succession.

Secondly, a landlord can only regain possession if he obtains a court order for possession. This is difficult to obtain because a landlord may only regain possession if he can show that one of a limited number of grounds for possession applies. In many cases, even if one of the grounds for possession can be shown to apply the court has a discretion in the matter and may decide that it is unreasonable to grant an order for possession when taking into account the whole circumstances of the case.

Fair rents

Rent Act tenants have a statutory right to apply to a Rent Officer for a 'fair rent' to be registered: ss.62–75 Rent Act 1977. A registered fair rent may be set at a level which is below the market rent, and may well be less than the rent the tenant has contracted to pay.

Restricted contract

Meaning

A restricted contract is a contract to occupy a dwelling where one of the following three circumstances applies: the rent includes payment for the use of furniture or services; there is a resident landlord; or the tenant shares some accommodation with his landlord: ss.19–21 Rent Act 1977.

Protection

A person with a restricted contract has very limited protection under the Rent Act, which takes two forms. First of all, the occupier is entitled to apply to the courts for the effect of a possession order to be postponed for up to six months in the case of contracts made prior to the 28th November 1980, and for up to three months for contracts made after that date: ss.103–6 Rent Act 1977. This gives the occupier a very limited form of security.

Secondly, the occupier is entitled to refer the contract to a Rent Tribunal in order for a 'reasonable rent' to be registered. The procedure and effect are similar to the registration of a fair rent. But it has to be said that if an occupier with a periodic tenancy registers a reasonable rent which is lower than the contractual rent, a landlord may well determine the tenancy by serving a notice to quit and obtain a court order for possession. In this situation the tenant will not be able to reap the benefit of a lower rent for very long since he can only ask the court to postpone a possession order for three months.

Protected shorthold tenancy

Protection

The protected shorthold tenancy was introduced by the Housing Act 1980 in response to concern about the shortage of letting accommodation. It was devised as a short tenancy with no security of tenure beyond the contractual term. The fair rent provisions of the Rent Acts applied originally but have now been removed for all shorthold tenancies outside London by the Protected Shorthold Tenancies (Rent Registration)

Order 1981 (SI 1981 No.1578). It is now a moderately popular form of letting outside London.

Definition

A protected shorthold tenancy is a protected tenancy which is granted for a term certain of not less than one year and not more than five years which satisfies the following conditions: it cannot be ended before the term expires except by forfeiture; the landlord gives the tenant a valid notice stating that the tenancy is a protected shorthold tenancy before it begins; and a certificate of fair rent has been issued or applied for if the leasehold premises are situated in London.

Assured tenancy

Introduction

Assured tenancies were introduced by the Housing Act 1980 in order to stimulate the construction of new residential letting accommodation. The main aim of the statutory provisions is to encourage approved bodies to construct new buildings for residential letting by eliminating the application of the Rent Acts to the lettings. Instead, the tenancy will be treated as if it were a business tenancy, and Part II Landlord and Tenant Act 1954 will apply subject to modifications: s.58 Housing Act 1980. The tenancy has a hybrid character since it is residential in nature but is treated as though it were a business tenancy.

The Housing and Planning Act 1986 extends the assured tenancy scheme to cases where works have been carried out up to a prescribed value when the premises were either unoccupied or not used for residential occupation: s.12 Housing and Planning Act 1986. The prescribed amount is: (a) for a dwelling house in Greater London £7000; and (b) elsewhere in England and Wales £5000: see The Assured Tenancies (Prescribed Amount) Order 1987 SI 1987 No.122.

Definition

A tenancy is an assured tenancy and not a housing association or protected tenancy if it is a tenancy under which a dwelling house is let as a separate dwelling and:

(a) the conditions in s.56A (new buildings) or 56B (existing buildings to which work has been carried out) are satisfied;
(b) the landlord belongs to a body approved by the Secretary of State for the purpose of creating assured tenancies;
(c) the tenancy would, when created, have been a protected tenancy or housing association but for s.56.

See s.56 Housing Act 1980 as amended by s.12 Housing and Planning Act 1986.

REGISTERED HOUSING ASSOCIATION TENANCY

Housing associations provide, manage and build accommodation for letting. Although they are run primarily by private trusts and companies, they rely on public funds and so can be described as quasi public in nature. The Housing Associations Act 1985 consolidates the law relating to the registration, auditing and financing of housing associations. Housing Corporations were first established in 1964 and have the general statutory function of promoting and assisting the development of housing associations: s.75 Housing Associations Act 1985.

Registered housing association tenants are specifically exempt from Rent Act protection by s.15 Rent Act 1977 and are, theoretically, a vulnerable group of tenants. But the rent payable is limited by statute: see p.100 in Chapter 10.

PUBLIC SECTOR

Secure tenancy

General

A secure tenancy is the only form of public sector tenancy and was first introduced by the Housing Act 1980. These provisions have been consolidated by the Housing Act 1985 which regulates secure tenancies from the 1st April 1985 (the Act's commencement date).

The Housing Act 1980 was introduced by the Conservatives with the stated object of engineering social revolution through the transfer of capital wealth from the State to the people, by stimulating council tenants to improve and purchase their council homes. In addition, the new legislation gave council tenants security of tenure comparable to private sector Rent Act tenants.

These provisions have now been consolidated into the Housing Act 1985: Parts IV and V Housing Act 1985. The Housing and Planning Act 1986 introduces further discounts and financial assistance in respect of the right to buy: ss. 1–3 Housing and Planning Act 1986.

Protection

A secure tenancy is modelled on the Rent Act tenancy, and is accordingly very similar, save that the landlord is a public body rather than a private individual or institution. Secure tenants have security of tenure analogous to that enjoyed by Rent Act tenants, as the name 'secure tenancy' implies. Thus a statutory tenancy arises upon the determination of a secure tenancy's contractual term. The main distinction between a public and private sector statutory tenancy is that only a single transfer of the statutory tenancy to relatives, after the tenant's death, is permitted in the case of a secure tenancy.

A secure tenancy can only be ended by court order if one of the limited statutory grounds for possession applies.

BUSINESS SECTOR

Meaning of business tenancies

A business tenancy is a tenancy where the whole or part of the leasehold premises are occupied by the tenant for the purpose of carrying on a business.

Legislation's objectives

The legislation regarding business tenancies has totally different objectives to that regulating residential tenancies. It is primarily directed at providing a procedure which enables a business tenant to seek the grant of a new tenancy from his landlord, and in default of agreement by way of an order of the court, when the contractual term expires. Part II Landlord and Tenant Act 1954 ('Part II') was introduced to prevent landlords from 'blackmailing' tenants to pay more than the market rent upon the renewal of a business tenancy. Tenants who failed to meet the landlord's demands upon renewal risked losing their trading premises and the consequential loss of any business goodwill which they had built up at a particular location.

The provisions of Part II enable tenants to request a renewal of their business tenancy for up to fourteen years at an open market rent, on substantially the same terms as their existing lease. A 'continuation tenancy' is created by statute during negotiations for a new business tenancy if they take place after the contractual term has ended.

Some business tenants qualify for compensation under Part II for loss of business goodwill if a request for the renewal of a business tenancy is refused. In addition, some tenants are entitled to compensation for improvements which they have carried out under the provisions of Part I of the Landlord and Tenant Act 1927. The right to compensation arises when the tenant leaves the leasehold premises at the end of his tenancy.

AGRICULTURAL SECTOR

Introduction

The agricultural sector is regulated by its own complex statutory framework, most of which is beyond the purview of this book which is primarily directed towards a consideration of urban leasehold premises. Nonetheless the agricultural sector deserves some consideration, if only to elucidate problems involving mixed user and to complete the statutory picture.

Agricultural holdings

Introduction

Agricultural holdings are holdings of agricultural land which are let for the purpose of a trade or business. The scheme of the current legislation is designed to perpetuate the contractual relationship by continuing tenancies after the contractual term has ended, and contains a number of diverse rights.

The statutory provisions relating to agricultural holdings are consolidated in the Agricultural Holdings Act 1986 ('the 1986 Act').

Meaning

An agricultural holding is a holding of agricultural land which is let for the purpose of a trade or business: s.1 Agricultural Holdings Act 1986.

Legislation's objectives

The main objective of the 1986 Act can be summarised as follows:

Arbitration: The statutory control of agricultural holdings is dependent upon an arbitration system which contains wide powers for referring disputes between landlords and tenants to the Agricultural Lands Tribunal for arbitration. The Agricultural Lands Tribunal has statutory powers to arbitrate in a wide range of matters relating to agricultural holdings. For example, either a landlord or a tenant may refer a written tenancy agreement to the Tribunal for arbitration: s.8 Agricultural Holdings Act 1986, at p.103 in Chapter 10.

Security of tenure: Until recently, tenants of agricultural holdings had security of tenure comparable to Rent Act tenants insofar as relatives of a deceased tenant were entitled to succeed to the agricultural holding, and two successions were permissible. But these provisions were abolished in respect of tenancies granted after the 12 July 1984 by s.2 Agricultural Holdings Act 1984 in order to halt the decline of the tenancy system. It has been calculated that whereas nearly ninety per cent of farm land was rented at the beginning of the century, this figure had decreased to less than forty per cent by 1984.

The current security of tenure provisions take the form of restrictions on the length and operation of notices to quit: ss.25–29 Agricultural Holdings Act 1986.

Compensation: When a tenant leaves an agricultural holding he may be entitled to compensation for disturbance if his tenancy is ended by a notice to quit, and for improvements which he has made to the leasehold premises: ss.60–9 Agricultural Holdings Act 1986.

Damages: For his part, a landlord may be able to recover damages from the tenant e.g. for deterioration of the holding: ss.71–2 Agricultural Holdings Act 1986.

Agricultural tied houses

Introduction

The Rent (Agriculture) Act 1976 ('the 1976 Act') was introduced in order to give security of tenure to agricultural workers housed in tied houses by their employers, and to their successors. In addition, provision is made to control rent levels. The Act is designed to take effect on the termination of the contract of occupancy. Hitherto, agricultural workers with tied houses were a vulnerable group of residential occupiers since they could lose both their job and their home together once their employment had been terminated.

For example, Lord employed Oddy as a farm hand for a number of years and housed him together with his family on a farm cottage on one of his farms. Lord has recently terminated Oddy's employment since he wishes to engage a younger man. He has also brought proceedings to evict the Oddy family from the cottage since he requires the accommodation for his new employee.

Since service occupiers, that is, occupiers housed by their employers for the performance of their service contract, are not strictly speaking tenants they do not normally qualify under the statutory schemes protecting residential tenants: see pp.60–1 for a discussion of the distinction between service occupiers and tenants. In the last example, Oddy would have lost both his job and his home if it were not for the protection afforded by the 1976 Act.

Form of protection

The structure of the 1976 Act is that an agricultural worker will be regarded as a protected occupier during the existence of the contract of employment and collateral contract relating to the provision of accommodation. A statutory tenancy arises automatically when the contracts are terminated.

An agricultural worker's occupancy is classified as a protected occupancy under the provisions of s.2(1) if the worker has a relevant agricultural licence or tenancy, and the worker, the premises, and the employer qualify.

Security of tenure

The Act's security of tenure provisions only come into effect upon the termination of the contractual term whereupon the protected occupancy is automatically converted into a statutory tenancy provided that the dwelling-house is occupied as a residence under the provisions of ss.2(4),(4)(1) of the Act. The grounds for regaining possession are limited, and are broadly speaking similar to the grounds for regaining possession of a Rent Act tenancy.

Rent control

The effect of the Act's rent control provisions means that the maximum rent that can be demanded in respect of a statutory tenancy is a multiplier of 1.5 times the rateable value. The parties may either agree a rent limit of not more than 1.5 times the rateable value or apply for the registration of a rent pursuant to the fair rent provisions in Part IV Rent Act 1977 under the provisions of ss.11 and 13 of the Act: see also p.103 in Chapter 10.

CONTRACTING OUT

The vast majority of the statutory schemes do not permit the parties to enter into a contract or agreement to exclude the statutory provisions, which is known as 'contracting out'. If the landlord has asked the tenant to sign an agreement which contains a contracting out provision he may well find that he cannot enforce it, unless of course the tenant accepts the term. The fact that a statute is silent on this question does not mean that contracting out is permitted: the contrary is the case. In other words, the parties can only contract out of statutory provisions if there is express power to do so within the statutory scheme.

The rule against contracting out was settled in *Barton* v. *Fincham* (1931) where the tenant had agreed to serve a notice to quit in return for payment. The landlord's application for possession was refused even though the tenant had served a notice to quit and received payment. In *Brown* v. *Draper* (1944) Lord Greene MR stated that:

> 'A tenant remaining in possession cannot lawfully contract not to avail himself of the protection which the Acts give him, if and when

> the landlord takes proceedings against him to recover possession. If he wishes to place himself outside the protection of the Acts without putting the landlord to the necessity of taking proceedings, his proper course of action is to deliver up possession. Unless and until he does so, he is under the shelter of the Act, whether or not he so desires. No contract, and, a fortiori, no mere statement of his wishes or intentions, can deprive him of the statutory protection'.

Landlords can only avoid the consequences of protective legislation by arranging their affairs so that the transaction falls outside the scope of the relevant Act. Tenants cannot, for example, be deprived of protection by the operation of the doctrine of estoppel or any other legal principle.

The position under the statutory schemes relating to the residential sector compares unfavourably with the position regarding business tenancies. The parties to a business tenancy are entitled to contract out of the provisions of Part II Landlord and Tenant Act 1954 with the consent of the court: s.38(4) Landlord and Tenant Act 1954. However, it has been held by the Court of Appeal in *Allnatt London Properties Ltd* v. *Newton* (1984) that an agreement which had the effect of precluding a tenant from requesting a new tenancy was void and unenforceable. The parties had not obtained the court's consent to contract out of the provisions of Part II.

Chapter 6

Leases and Licences

INTRODUCTION

Leases belong to the law of property whilst licences to occupy land arise out of contracts or agreements which fall short of creating interests in land. A licence is permission to allow someone to use or occupy another's property. A lease creates a term of years whereas a licence is a personal agreement between the licensor and licensee which is not generally enforceable against third parties to the contract. Suppose that Louis grants Oscar the right to occupy No.1, High Street, in return for a weekly payment of £50. Louis later transfers his reversionary interest to Ace. Differing legal consequences will arise, according to whether the agreement is construed as a lease or a licence in law.

Louis (landlord/licensor) ———————— Ace (assignee)

|

Oscar (tenant/occupier)

If the agreement is construed as a lease, it will create a term of years, and the relationship will be governed by property law principles. Thus Oscar will be able to enjoy his interest in land until it is determined in the appropriate manner. He will be able to enforce his tenancy rights against third parties to the contract, including Ace. He will be able to transfer (assign) his tenancy, provided that there is no prohibition against assignment in the tenancy agreement. Finally, the tenancy may be protected by one of the statutory schemes if the tenancy qualifies for protection thereunder.

On the other hand, if Oscar's occupation of No.1 amounts to a licence, a strict application of traditional rules relating to contractual licences will render his position far less secure. First of all, the doctrine of privity of contract will be applicable, which means that Oscar will not be able to enforce his licence against third parties to the contract, including Ace. So that, if Ace chooses to terminate the licence by revoking it, Oscar will have to give up possession of No.1 upon reasonable notice. Oscar's only remedy in these circumstances would be to sue Louis for damages for breach of their agreement; he cannot resist eviction through court proceedings. Secondly, Oscar has very limited right of assignment so that he will be unable to transfer his licence of No.1 to another.

LICENCES

Licences are primarily used by landlords who hope to avoid the Rent Acts.

Varieties

There is no formal limit to the possible scope and variety of licences to occupy land since they are the product of agreements and contracts between individuals which are diverse in nature and extent. They range from agreements which permit entry onto the licensor's land for a limited time and a specific purpose (for example, to attend lectures or to watch a sport, play or film), to agreements which grant the licensee the right to occupy land for lengthy periods of time (for example, a student's use and occupation of the parental home for an indefinite duration).

The law adopts a threefold classification of licences, as follows.

Bare or gratuitous licences

A bare licence is not supported by valuable consideration, and is simply a permission to enter onto another's land without becoming a trespasser in the process: *Thomas* v. *Sorrel* (1673), for example, where permission is granted to enter land for the purpose of a survey. It is an agreement rather than a contract, due to the absence of consideration. It may be revoked at any time upon reasonable notice; damages may be awarded if a bare licensee is evicted without reasonable notice: *Aldin* v. *Latimer Clark, Muirhead & Co.* (1894).

Licences coupled with an interest

Licences coupled with the grant of an interest comprise two elements: a licence to enter onto land, and the grant of an interest in property. The interest may take many forms, e.g. the right to cut and remove timber or growing crops; hunting, shooting or fishing rights; rights to remove chattels such as hay. (See *London Borough of Hounslow* v. *Twickenham Garden Developments Ltd* (1970) for the meaning of 'interest'.) Since the licence is coupled with a proprietary interest, the licence assumes the characteristics of a property right. Accordingly, licences coupled with interests are irrevocable, assignable and enforceable against third parties.

Contractual licences

Contractual licences are by far the most important type of licence in matters relating to landlord and tenant law. This is because it is not always easy to distinguish tenancies from contractual licences. Furthermore, some landlords have tried to avoid the consequences of legislation designed to protect tenants by purporting to create a contractual licence rather than a tenancy, since many of the statutory schemes specifically exclude licences.

A contractual licence is a licence to occupy land which is supported by valuable consideration. Traditionally, contractual licences were governed by contract law principles, although the subject-matter of the contract is the occupation of land. This means that contractual licences could not adopt the mantle of a proprietary interest in land. The main distinctions between a contractual interest and an interest in property are enforceability against third parties, revocation and assignability.

(a) Enforceability

The general rule is that contractual licences cannot be enforced against third parties to the contract. If either the licensor or the licensee assigns his interests, the licence will not bind his successors in title. Thus in the last example, the assignment by Louis to Ace results in Ace becoming a third party to the contract between Louis and Oscar. Neither Oscar nor Ace have the right to enforce the terms of the original contract against each other. Thus any obligation that Oscar might have entered into, e.g. to repair the premises, cannot be enforced by Ace. Conversely, Ace can revoke Oscar's contract. Indeed, if Oscar could enforce his licence against Ace and other successors in title, it would amount to an interest in land. This is because it is only in property law that interests can be enforced as against third parties to a contract.

The traditional view that a contractual licence can never bind third parties has been partially eroded in a series of cases involving special arrangements between the parties, where the licensor's successor in title had full notice of the occupational rights of the licensee. The modern position is that in certain special circumstances, contractual licences may assume the status of an equitable interest in land (as opposed to contractual rights).

The Court of Appeal first held that a contractual licence was binding on successors in title who had notice of the contract, in a case involving family arrangements for a house: *Errington* v. *Errington and Woods* (1952); the successor in title was the licensee's mother-in-law. The Court of Appeal refused the mother-in-law's application for possession of the house, and held that the daughter-in-law could remain in the house provided that she complied with the terms of the licence agreement. Thus the contractual licence created an equitable interest in land binding on third parties who had notice. It would clearly be inequitable to enforce a contractual licence against a successor in title who had no notice of the licence. In *Errington*, Lord Justice Denning said that:

> 'Neither the licensor nor anyone who claims through him can disregard the contract except a purchaser for value without notice'.

(b) Revocability
The traditional common law rule was that contractual licences were revocable at will. For instance, imagine that Oddy pays to watch a rugby match on Oust's ground and is subsequently turned off the premises at half-time for no good reason. Even though Oddy has not broken the conditions of the contract, he is treated as though he were a trespasser. Oddy's traditional remedy lay in damages, since Oddy had no claim or property interest in the land; he simply occupied the owner's land under a contract. This point was illustrated graphically by Latham CJ in *Cowell* v. *Rosehill Racecourse Co.* (1937) who said that:

> '50,000 people who pay to see a football match do not obtain 50,000 interests in the football ground'.

The House of Lords finally repudiated the rule that contractual licences could be revoked at will without notice in *Winter Gardens Theatre (London) Ltd* v. *Millennium Productions Ltd* (1947). Viscount Simon said that a licensee has a right to remain on the licensor's land, and that where a licence is revoked, the licensee must be given a reasonable time to leave.

A contractual licence can only be revoked in accordance with its terms, and it is possible for irrevocable licences to be created. An irrevocable licence is a licence which cannot be revoked prematurely. For example, a member of a family or an employee might be granted a licence to occupy premises 'for life' or 'for so long as he requires the premises'. In neither case can the licence be revoked by either the licensor or those who acquire the premises by purchase, with notice of the terms of the licence; to this extent the licence is irrevocable. The terms of the licence will specify its duration, otherwise the courts are prepared to imply a term as to the duration of the licence: see *Hardwick* v. *Johnson and Another* (1978).

(c) Assignability
The general rule is that a licence creates purely personal rights under the contract which are not assignable. However, the benefit of a contract may be assigned, so that in the first example, Louis may assign the benefit of the licence with Oscar to Ace, entitling Ace to receive any consideration payable under the contract. There are two alternative methods of assigning the benefit of a contract: either in equity or in law under the provisions of s.136 Law of Property Act 1925, provided that

there is no prohibition against assignment. The benefit may only be assigned in equity if this does not increase the burden on the other party: *Tolhurst* v. *Associated Cements Manufacturers* (1900). This is a question of fact. An assignment under the provisions of s.136 is the preferred method of assignment.

For an assignment to operate as a valid assignment under s.136 it must be an unconditional assignment and in writing under the assignor's own hand: *Wilson* v. *Vallani* (1880). Moreover, written notice of the assignment must be given by the assignor to the party affected. In the example above, Louis should give Oscar notice of the assignment to Ace. The assignment will operate from the date of the notice.

Finally, many contractual licences contain provisions which prohibit the assignment of rights arising under the contract, rendering any purported assignment invalid: *United Dominium Trust (Commercial) Ltd* v. *Parkway Motors Ltd* (1955).

Terms of contractual licences

Since many contractual licences are assuming the status of equitable interests in land, it is important to consider whether the law implies any special terms into the contract equivalent in nature to the covenants implied by law to landlord and tenant relationships. The courts have always been prepared to imply terms so as to give 'business efficacy' to a contract in cases where the parties have omitted to include a term which, unless remedied, may negative their intention: *The Moorcock* (1889). What is not yet settled are the terms which should be implied in a contract for the use and occupation of premises. Where a property owner grants a licence to another allowing the use and occupation of his property, and the licence is silent on the liability for repairs, there is not necessarily any implied term on the part of the owner to keep the premises in repair. His only obligation is to use reasonable care: *Morris, Thomas* v. *Petticoat Lane Rentals* (1986).

The future

The law relating to contractual licences is now sufficiently developed to give occupiers extensive proprietary rights. Landlords should be cautious when attempting to create a licence as a means of avoiding legislation protecting tenants, because there is a slight risk of creating an irrevocable contractual licence which is binding on successors in title. For example, in *D.H.N. Food Distributors Ltd* v. *Tower Hamlets London Borough Council* (1976) it was held that a company occupied premises under an irrevocable licence which entitled them to full compensation for disturbance when the local council acquired the property pursuant to a compulsory purchase order.

Special cases

Employees

Special principles apply in cases where residential accommodation is provided by an employer to an employee. The most typical illustrations are domestic staff who live in, e.g. caretakers, housekeepers, nannies, cooks, wardens and security officers. The provision of a 'home with the job' will generally give rise to a licence, sometimes referred to as a service occupancy. The use of the terms 'service tenant' and 'service occupier' are ambiguous; tenant and licensee are preferred descriptions: see Halsbury's *Laws of England*, volume 27, paragraph 14.

An employee in occupation of premises belonging to his employer may be either a licensee or a tenant, depending on the facts of the case. The test for distinguishing between licensees and tenants for this purpose is whether the occupation of the accommodation is either necessary for the performance of the employee's services or a requirement of the contract of employment: *Glasgow Corporation* v. *Johnstone* (1965). If the occupation is either necessary or required for the performance of these services, then a licence and not a tenancy will have been created. The rationale for this rule is that an employer will wish to ensure that he can regain possession of the accommodation upon the termination of his employee's service contract, in order to be able to replace him effectively in situations where the employee is required to live in the accommodation for the performance of his duties.

Consider the following cases:

(a) Olive has been a warden of Redbrick University's female Hall of Residence for the past five years. She occupies a ground-floor flat in the Hall, which has its own separate entrance. The Vice-Chancellor has recently discovered that Olive has been keeping her pet toy spaniel dog in her flat, contrary to Hall regulations, and has terminated her contract of employment as a warden. Olive seeks legal advice as to whether she can stay on in the flat, as she would qualify for Rent Act protection if she could establish the existence of a tenancy.

(b) Lindos employs Thomson as a clerk in his travel agency. When Thomson was evicted from his last home, Lindos allowed him to occupy the flat above the travel agency's shop which was empty at that time. Lindos deducts the rent from Thomson's wages. Thomson has now found a better job in the area but wishes to continue to rent the flat as his home. It is within the rateable value limits of the Rent Acts.

In both these cases, the decision of whether a licence or tenancy has arisen is crucial to the occupiers, since it may mean the difference between eviction and full Rent Act protection. Olive will find it difficult to substantiate a claim for a tenancy, if it can be shown that it is either necessary for her to live in the Hall for the performance of her duties or it is a requirement of her contract of employment. Lindos' position is quite different on these facts. Prima facie, the provision of the flat appears unrelated to his job as a clerk. Moreover, the fact that Lindos deducts his rent from his wage at source will not in itself be enough to raise the presumption of a licence. A quantified rent was deducted from wages in *Montague* v. *Browning* (1954) but it was nonetheless held that the employee had a Rent Act protected tenancy.

An employee who is provided with a 'home with job' by his employer traditionally enjoyed very little protection. The only security of tenure provided by statute is enjoyed by agricultural tied workers: see p.53. However, a recent Court of Appeal decision has established that occupiers provided with accommodation by their employers who have exclusive possession for a term at a rent can assert a tenancy. In *Royal Philanthropic Society* v. *County* (1985) the occupier was employed as a house parent in one of the landlord's schools and was granted occupation of a school house with the job. The occupier refused to give up possession of the school house when his employment terminated, and the landlord brought proceedings to recover possession. The Court of Appeal had no difficulty in holding that a tenancy had been created since exclusive possession had been granted in return for a rent.

Lodgers

Lodgers have also been treated as a special category of licensee. The word 'lodger' is used in cases where the landlord lives in the same house as the occupier. A lodger is really no more than a paying guest. The lodger may have his own separate rooms or self-contained apartment or may share part of his accommodation with his landlord. These types of sharing arrangements are particularly common in urban areas where houses are split up into separate units and occupied by a number of lodgers, in addition to the landlord.

The distinction between lodgers and tenants was considered by Lord Goddard CJ in *Helman* v. *Horsham and Worthing Committee* (1948), who said that:

> '...the fact that the landlord is living on the premises does seem to me to raise the presumption...that he intends to retain control of the whole of the premises...,that, I think, prima facie at least negatives the fact that the person who is occupying rooms in the other part of the house than that in which the landlord lives is a tenant in the true sense and not a lodger'.

The issue of whether a licence or tenancy has been created is decided by the nature of the landlord's occupation. If a landlord retains a high degree of control and access, this will be sufficient to preclude the occupier from having exclusive possession of the lodgings, and thereby create a licence: per Mr Justice Blackburn in *Allan* v. *Liverpool Overseers* (1874). However, the occupation of the lodgings may be described as 'exclusive occupation' in the sense that the occupier has the sole right to occupy the lodgings, which may still give rise to a licence. On the other hand, if a landlord exercises no control whatsoever over the premises, the occupier will have exclusive possession of the accommodation and is a tenant: *Fenn* v. *Grafton* (1836).

Landlords wishing to avoid the statutory protection afforded to tenants have attempted to draft lodging agreements, particularly in the light of the House of Lords decision in *Street* v. *Mountford* (1985) which highlighted lodging agreements as a possible route for creating licences (see pp.63–5 for a consideration of the House of Lords decision).

The first of these agreements to come before the Court of Appeal after *Street* v. *Mountford* was the case of *Crancour Ltd* v. *Da Silvaesa* (1986) where the court considered the proper construction of two lodging agreements. In both cases the landlord was seeking possession from the occupiers upon the expiry of the agreements. The Court of Appeal adopted the approach of considering which terms of the agreement were obviously shams and then considered the remainder of the agreement in order to decide whether exclusive possession had been conferred on the occupiers. In other words, the existence of terms which were considered shams, e.g. a clause restricting the hours of occupation, did not render the entire agreement a sham.

DISTINGUISHING LEASES FROM LICENCES

Introduction

The traditional approach to distinguishing leases from licences was to ask whether the occupier had been granted exclusive possession of the premises which he was occupying. If he had, a lease was created; if not, a mere licence. This test for distinguishing leases from licences was never wholly satisfactory because there could be many instances where a person was let into exclusive occupation of premises where there was no intention to create a landlord and tenant relationship e.g. where a person was let into exclusive possession under a contract to purchase the freehold. This occurred in *Howard* v. *Shaw* (1841) where Lord Abinger CB stated that:

> 'While the defendant occupied under a valid contract for the sale of property to him, he could not be considered as a tenant'.

Accordingly, there was a strong movement away from a single test of exclusive possession to a two-stage test. Firstly, a consideration of whether exclusive possession has been granted; no lease can be created without exclusive possession. Secondly, if exclusive possession has been granted, a consideration of whether it was the intention of the parties to create a lease. The first case which demonstrated that exclusive possession could no longer be regarded as the sole test was *Booker* v. *Palmer* (1942), where an owner gave some evacuees permission to stay in a cottage rent-free for the duration of the war. Lord Greene MR said that:

> 'There is one golden rule which is of very general application, namely, that the law does not impute intention to enter into legal relationships where the circumstances and the conduct of the parties negative any intention of the kind'.

Street v. *Mountford*

The House of Lords decision in *Street* v. *Mountford* (1985) signals a return to the traditional test for distinguishing leases from licences, which is the primary test of whether exclusive possession has been granted. In this case the landlord had granted the occupier the right to occupy a furnished flatlet on the top floor of a building divided into flatlets, at a licence fee of £37 per week, in March 1983. This was subject to a written licence agreement drawn up by the landlord's agent. The issue which the House of Lords had to determine was whether a licence or tenancy had been created. The Court of Appeal had held that Mrs Mountford was a licensee, and was accordingly not entitled to the protection of the Rent Acts. But this decision was overturned by the House of Lords who held that a tenancy had been created.

Exclusive possession

Lord Templeman stated that the true test was whether, on the true construction of the agreement, the occupier had been granted exclusive possession of the accommodation for a fixed or periodic term at a stated rent. If these requirements have been satisfied, a tenancy arises unless there are some special circumstances which negative the presumption of a tenancy. Lord Templeman said that:

> 'If the agreement satisfied all the requirements of a tenancy, then the agreement produced a tenancy and the parties cannot alter the effect of the agreement by insisting that they only created a licence. The manufacture of a five-pronged implement for manual digging results in a fork even if the manufacturer, unfamiliar with the

English language, insists that he intended a spade and has made a spade'.

Exclusive possession is now the primary criterion for establishing a tenancy. The House of Lords was not required to analyse exclusive possession in *Street* v. *Mountford* since the landlord's counsel had conceded that the agreement granted exclusive possession. Instead Lord Templeman illustrated the meaning of exclusive possession by comparing a tenant with a lodger, and said that:

> 'In the case of residential accommodation there is no difficulty in deciding whether the grant confers exclusive possession. An occupier of residential accommodation at a rent is either a lodger or a tenant. The occupier is a lodger if the landlord provides attendance or services which require the landlord or his servants to exercise unrestricted access to and use of the premises. A lodger is entitled to live in the premises but cannot call the place his own. If, on the other hand, residential accommodation is granted for a term at a rent with exclusive possession, the landlord providing neither attendance nor services, the grant is a tenancy. Any express reservation to the landlord of limited rights to enter and view the state of the premises and to repair and maintain the premises only serves to emphasise the fact that the grantee is entitled to exclusive possession and is a tenant'.

Intention of the parties

The intention of the parties may be a relevant consideration when deciding whether exclusive possession has been granted, depending on the facts of the case. The circumstances might be such that it is apparent that the parties did not intend to create a tenancy. In *Heslop* v. *Burns* (1974) a family had been housed by another as an act of generosity and it was held that the parties had not intended to create a tenancy. The following passage from the judgment of Lord Justice Scarman in *Heslop* v. *Burns* was approved by Lord Templeman in *Street* v. *Mountford*:

> 'In all the cases where an occupier has been held to be a licensee there has been something in the circumstances, such as a family arrangement, an act of friendship or generosity, or such like, to negative any intention to create a tenancy'.

In all other circumstances it will be difficult to show a contrary intention if the hallmarks of a tenancy exist. In *Bretherton* v. *Paton* (1986) the Court of Appeal, applying the principles in *Street* v. *Mountford*, held that although the parties had contemplated a possible sale of the property to the occupier at the time she went into occupation, the only intention which was relevant was that demonstrated by the facts of the transaction, namely, the grant of exclusive possession at a rent for a periodic term.

Construction of agreements

It will often be necessary to construe a written agreement in order to decide whether a licence or tenancy has been created. The written agreement may be described as a licence or lodging agreement. The case of *Addiscombe Garden Estates Ltd and Another* v. *Crabbe and Others* (1957) sets out the relevant principles and establishes firstly that the label of the document is not paramount, and secondly that the true substance of the document will be given effect to. In that case, Lord Justice Jenkins said that:

> 'The principles applicable in resolving a question of this sort are, I apprehend, these. It does not necessarily follow that a document described as a licence is, merely on that account, to be regarded as amounting only to a licence in law. The whole of the document must be looked at; and if, after it has been examined, the right conclusion appears to be that, whatever label may have attached to it, it in fact conferred and imposed on the grantee in substance the rights and obligations of a tenant, and on the grantor in substance the rights and obligations of a landlord, then it must be given the appropriate effect...'.

(See also 'Distinguishing between Tenancies and Licences, *New Law Journal* parts I and II, 11th & 16th October 1980, for an analysis of this 'balance sheet' approach.)

The future

The main impact of the House of Lords decision in *Street* v. *Mountford* is that landlords will find it increasingly difficult to avoid the consequences of protective legislation by creating artificial contractual licences. Techniques which were successfully employed in recent years, ranging from the crude labelling of a tenancy as a 'licence agreement' to the complex 'non-exclusive occupation' licence agreements which succeeded in avoiding the status of a tenancy in *Somma* v. *Hazlehurst* (1978) have been specifically disapproved. The ramifications have already started to be felt.

The House of Lords decision can be interpreted at a number of different levels. It can be seen as an exercise in outlawing anti-avoidance devices: see Lord Justice Denning in *Faccini* v. *Bryson* (1952). Alternatively, it can be construed as a decision which deprives landlords of the right to freedom of contract. The occupier had signed a statement agreeing that no Rent Act tenancy could be created by her occupation of the flatlet. On this point, Lord Templeman stated that the parties only had freedom of contract to agree lawful terms. There is no lawful method of excluding the Rent Acts once a tenancy is established, unless one of the statutory exceptions applies. Compare the business sector where the parties have the power to 'contract out' of the provisions of Part II Landlord and Tenant Act 1954, provided that the courts concur: s.38(4)(a) Landlord and Tenant Act 1954.

Business licences

The decision in *Street* v. *Mountford* (1985) applies equally to business tenancies. Although the licence was never important in the business sector it did have its uses. For example, a property owner might wish to let out premises under a licence agreement pending redevelopment whilst he is arranging finance, and applying for planning permission. If a business occupancy meets the principles of *Street* v. *Mountford*, namely exclusive possession for a term at a rent, the arrangement constitutes a tenancy and not a licence: *London & Associated Investment Trust PLC* v. *Calow* (1986).

The leading case on business licences to date is *Shell-Mex and BP Ltd* v. *Manchester Garages Ltd* (1971) where the occupiers of a petrol filling station claimed a Part II business tenancy, even though the agreement described the relationship as a 'licence'. The Court of Appeal rejected their claim and upheld the agreement as a licence. They relied on the fact that there was no proviso for re-entry; the high degree of control which the owners exercised; and the fact that the occupiers could only sell the owner's petrol, which amounted to a personal tie between the parties. Lord Templeman considered *Shell-Mex* in the context of the decisive test of exclusive possession, and distinguished it from *Street* v. *Mountford* on the following ground:

> 'In my opinion the agreement was only 'personal in its nature' and created a 'personal privilege' if the agreement did not confer the right to exclusive possession of the filling station. No other test for distinguishing between a contractual tenancy and a contractual licence appears to be understandable or workable'.

Contractual licences

Lord Templeman endorses the traditional view that the main hallmark of a contractual licence is that it creates personal privileges. The House of Lords recognises two main circumstances in which a contractual licence and not a tenancy will arise. Firstly, circumstances where the parties' conduct negatives the intention to create legal relations. This can only be deduced from the circumstances at the time of the letting, and not the wording of a document. For example, in *Cobb* v. *Lane* (1952), the Court of Appeal held that there was no intention to enter into a legal relationship when an owner allowed her brother to live in a house rent-free. (See 'Licences and tenancies–the generosity factor' by J.W. Harris, volume 32, *Modern Law Review*, pp.92–6, for a review of the early case-law.) Secondly, where special circumstances prevent exclusive possession from creating a tenancy. For example, the special categories of licensees (lodgers and employees who live in the accommodation for the performance of a job); and where a vendor allows a purchaser into early possession.

Note that it has been argued that the status of a contractual licence seems to have disappeared, as a result of the decision in *Street* v. *Mountford*: see *Lease or Licence–the Law after Street* v. *Mountford* by Kim Lewison, Longman Professional (1985), at p.21.

FURTHER READING

The following cases are worthy of consideration; short extracts may be found in *Rent Acts–Selected Case Law Guide*, published by Institute of Rent Officers Educational Trust.

Attendance provided:	*Appah* v. *Parncliffe Investments Ltd* (1964)
	Marchant v. *Charters* (1976)
Employees:	*Faccini* v. *Bryson* (1952)
Hotel rooms:	*Luganda* v. *Service Hotels Ltd* (1969)
Family arrangements:	*Cobb and Another* v. *Lane* (1952)
	Hardwick v. *Johnson* (1977)
Personal privilege:	*Barnes and Another* v. *Barratt and Another* (1970)
	Marcroft Wagons Ltd v. *Smith* (1951)

Kim Lewison's *Lease or Licence, the Law after* Street v. Mountford, Longman Professional Opinion (1985), provides a practical analysis; the Appendix sets out five precedent licence agreements.

Chapter 7

Introduction to Obligations

INTRODUCTORY

The purpose of this chapter is to provide an overview of the legal obligations which regulate a landlord and tenant relationship during the currency of the contractual term. The main categories of obligations will be defined, but the substantive law relating to individual obligations will be set out in Chapters 8 to 15. This approach will facilitate a consideration of the relevant law in its entirety in respect of specific matters, e.g. repairing obligations, rent etc., and avoid overlaps between the different categories of obligations.

GENERAL

Both landlords and tenants assume a number of obligations during the currency of a term in order to give effect to the lease or tenancy agreement. For example, a tenant will undertake an obligation to pay a fixed rent on agreed dates, and the parties may reach agreement on their respective maintenance and repairing obligations.

There is no statutory code setting out the parties' obligations in a comprehensive manner. The parties' obligations under a lease or tenancy are a matter which is largely governed by contract. The common law only intervened in order to provide for minimal obligations to be implied into all landlord and tenant relationships in order to give efficacy to the arrangement. In addition, legislation was introduced to impose obligations on landlords of residential accommodation to ensure that the premises were fit for habitation at the time of letting and that landlords carried out repairs both to the structure and to installations supplying essential services in leases of less than seven years: see ss.8 and 11 Landlord and Tenant Act 1985 below.

The Law Commission produced a *Report on Obligations of Landlords and Tenants* which was part of a wider brief to codify landlord and tenant law in response to the following basic problem:

> 'The basic law of landlord and tenant, even apart from legislation controlling rents and securing tenure, is unduly complicated,

anachronistic in many respects and difficult to ascertain. It is to be found in a very large number of statutes and cases, is largely self-contained and in the Commission's view is suitable for ultimate codification.' (*Law Commission No.1* (1965), p.10).

This is apposite in the context of landlord and tenant obligations. Hence the Law Commission recommended a statutory code of obligations which would be implied into all tenancies, and produced a comprehensive draft bill giving effect to their proposals. But no serious effort has been made on the part of Government to implement their detailed recommendations, and it is to be regretted that only a small proportion of their recommendations have been adopted; these can now be found in the Landlord and Tenant Act 1985.

CATEGORIES OF OBLIGATIONS

Obligations fall into two broad categories: obligations which are expressly agreed, and obligations implied by the general law:

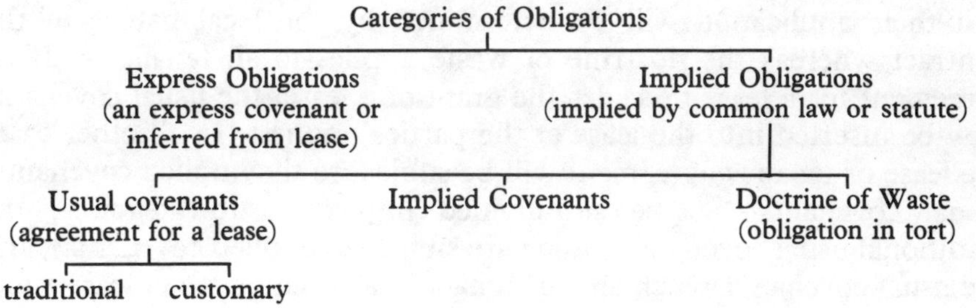

Express obligations

Express obligations are obligations which arise as the result of an express agreement between the parties, and are usually set out expressly in a lease or tenancy agreement or inferred from its wording. They are referred to by the generic term 'express covenants', and there is no limit to the leasehold obligations which may be agreed between the parties.

Only an obligation which is set out expressly in a lease may, strictly speaking, be defined as a 'covenant', i.e. a contractual promise which is contained in a deed under seal. However, the word 'covenant' is not restricted to obligations in leases under seal today, and it is customary to refer to most obligations which arise out of a landlord and tenant relationship as covenants. Problems and disputes relating to the parties' respective obligations during the contractual term are generally resolved with reference to the lease's express covenants, taking into account any binding implied obligations. The normal principles of construction apply which means, briefly, that obligations should be evidenced in writing, although oral collateral agreements may be enforced: see *City and Westminster Properties* v. *Mudd* (1958).

The most important express covenants, in practical terms, are: covenants to pay and review the rent, rates, service charges and premiums; covenants restricting user; covenants restricting assignment and sub-letting; covenants to repair; covenants prohibiting alterations and improvements; and a number of miscellaneous covenants, e.g. to clean, decorate, and insure the premises.

Implied obligations

An implied obligation is an obligation which is implied by law, as compared with an obligation which arises out of an express agreement. The legal source of an implied obligation may be either a case-law precedent or a statutory provision. Obligations implied by law can be sub-divided into three categories: usual covenants, implied covenants, and the negative obligations arising out of the doctrine of waste.

Usual and implied covenants are two mutually exclusive categories, and their application will be determined by the legal nature of the contract whereas the doctrine of waste applies to all tenancies. If an agreement for a lease precedes the grant of a lease, the usual covenants may be inserted into the lease at the parties' request. In all other cases the lease or tenancy agreement will be subject to the implied covenants. Usual covenants can be sub-divided into two sub-categories: the traditional usual covenants (which are similar to implied covenants), and the usual covenants which are customary in a specific type of lease e.g. a lease of offices.

There are two main distinctions between usual covenants and implied covenants. First of all, traditional usual covenants impose more extensive rights and liabilities than implied covenants e.g. a proviso for re-entry for non-payment of rent is a usual but not an implied covenant. Secondly, the list of customary usual covenants is not fixed at common law and is capable of being extended by the judiciary according to the circumstances of an individual case.

Usual covenants

Strict technical meaning

It is an implied term in every agreement for a lease that the lease will contain the usual and proper covenants. If the parties have failed to specify the express covenants which are to be inserted in the lease, then either party may request the usual covenants to be inserted: *Propert* v. *Parker* (1832). In other words, a lease drawn up pursuant to an agreement to grant a lease which fails to include the usual covenants may be rectified so as to include the usual covenants. *Hampshire* v. *Wickens* (1878) lists the usual covenants which will apply in all cases as follows.

Landlord's usual covenant

A landlord is liable under a qualified covenant for quiet enjoyment (it only applies to actions by the landlord and his agent): see pp.72–7.

Tenant's usual covenants

(a) a covenant to pay rent;
(b) a covenant to pay the tenant's rates and taxes;
(c) a condition entitling the landlord the remedy of re-entry for non-payment of rent;

These three obligations are considered in Chapter 10 on Rent.

(d) a covenant to keep and deliver up the premises in repair;
(e) a covenant to permit the landlord to enter and view the state of repair.

These two obligations are considered in Chapter 14 on Repairs.

Technically, the above list comprises the traditional usual covenants which are implied into agreements for a lease.

Customary covenants

In addition, criteria have been established for deciding which covenants are 'usual', in the less technical sense of customary. For example, an agreement for a lease may state that the lease is to contain the 'usual covenants' rather than set out a number of express covenants. In this case, the agreement for a lease requires additional covenants to be inserted into the lease; these will be tailored according to the special facts and circumstances of the agreement. In *Chester* v. *Buckingham Travel* (1981), Mr Justice Foster held that the test for determining what were or were not usual covenants (in addition to the 'usual covenants' in the technical sense as set out in *Hampshire* v. *Wickens* (1878) above) was the same for both an agreement for a lease and an agreement to assign an existing lease. The full list of usual covenants is not fixed, and largely depends on the type of premises and conveyancing practice. In the event of a dispute, the judge will decide what covenants ought to be included by considering the facts and by looking at:

(a) the nature of the premises and its situation;
(b) the purpose of the letting;
(c) the length of the term;
(d) the evidence of local conveyancers, and the leading books of precedent.

Implied covenants

The general law implies a fixed number of covenants into leases and tenancy agreements for the dual purpose of enabling the tenant to enjoy the benefit of the leasehold premises without interruption, whilst protecting the landlord's reversion. Thus harassment of a tenant by a landlord was made unlawful, and tenants became responsible for carrying out minor repairs. The main implied covenants are:

Tenant's implied covenants

(a) an obligation to pay rent;
(b) an obligation to pay tenant's rates and taxes;

These two obligations are considered in Chapter 10 on Rent.

(c) an obligation to use the premises in a tenant-like manner;
(d) an obligation permitting a landlord the right to view the state of repair of the premises, in cases where the landlord has a repairing liability.

These two obligations are considered in Chapter 14 on Repairing Obligations.

(e) there is an implied covenant, in respect of agricultural tenancies only, to manage and cultivate the lands in accordance with the custom of the country and good husbandry.

Landlord's implied covenants

Covenant for quiet enjoyment: A covenant for quiet enjoyment is not a covenant in the acoustic sense of the word 'quiet', but imposes an obligation on the landlord to ensure that the tenant will have peaceful possession of the premises.

Scope: It would obviously be impracticable for landlords to 'police' the premises to ensure that the tenant's occupation is not being disturbed. Accordingly, the law has always drawn a distinction between acts performed by the landlord and his agents, on the one hand, and torts committed by a third party. A landlord is liable for the former but cannot be liable for the behaviour of a third party. If a third party does commit an act of nuisance, the tenant's remedy is against the wrongdoer and not against the landlord.

For example, in *Richards* v. *Lothian* (1913) it was held that a landlord of a building let out as offices is not liable under the covenant for quiet enjoyment for damage caused by an escape of water from a lavatory on the premises, caused by the malicious act of an unknown person.

This case illustrates the proposition that scope of a landlord's covenant for quiet enjoyment only extends to his own acts and to those for whom he is responsible and that he cannot be held responsible for the acts of a stranger.

A limited covenant: An implied covenant for quiet enjoyment is not an absolute covenant. It is restricted to the landlord and persons for whom he is responsible. It does not protect the tenant from someone claiming a greater title to the property than the landlord's title, and does not protect the tenant against someone with paramount title (as once thought prior to *Jones* v. *Lavington* (1903)). Thus if a landlord turns out to have a bad title due to some defect in it, the tenant will not be able to bring proceedings against the person with superior title to the landlord. The covenant cannot amount to a guarantee of title: *Celsteel Ltd and Others* v. *Alton House Holdings Ltd and Another* (No. 2) (1986).

What will amount to a breach of a covenant for quiet enjoyment?: The former rule was that a tenant had to show that there was substantial interference with his ordinary enjoyment of the premises. This is a question of fact. The classic illustration of this principle is the case of *Lavender* v. *Betts* (1942).

In order to get rid of the tenant, the landlord had removed the doors and windows of the premises, and was found to be in breach of the covenant of quiet enjoyment, because his acts constituted substantial interference with the enjoyment of the demised premises.

Not only did a tenant have to show some substantial interference with ordinary enjoyment, but also some physical interference to constitute a breach of covenant of quiet enjoyment under the former law. This can be illustrated by the case of *Brown* v. *Flower* (1911) where a landlord erected an external staircase which passed the tenant's bedroom window, and, as a result, destroyed the tenant's privacy. It was held that the tenant's action for damages failed since the tenant had not suffered physical interference with his enjoyment of the property, simply loss of privacy. Mr Justice Parker dismissed the action because it appeared to him:

> 'to constitute a breach of such a covenant there must be some physical interference with the enjoyment of the demised premises, and that a mere interference with the comfort of persons using the leasehold premises by the creation of a personal annoyance such as might arise from noise, invasion of privacy, or otherwise is not enough.'

There was no physical intrusion into the leasehold premises although a physical structure outside inconvenienced the tenants.

Brown v. *Flower* can be compared with the later case of *Owen* v. *Gadd* (1956) where the tenant of a shop had his shop window temporarily obscured when the landlord erected scaffolding. There was also evidence that the scaffolding seriously interfered with the ordinary access of the public to the shop and shop window. The Court of Appeal held that the erection of scaffolding poles in close proximity to the shop window constituted a breach of covenant. The Court of Appeal assumed that Mr Justice Parker's statement in *Brown* v. *Flower* was correct and held that erection of scaffolding was 'certainly physical'. The facts in these two cases show just how narrow the margin is between an interference which is a breach of covenant and one which is not a breach of covenant.

A new point arose on similar facts in *Queensway Marketing Ltd* v. *Associated Restaurants Ltd* (1984) where sub-tenants complained about scaffolding erected by the head landlord. It was held that since 'landlord' had been defined in the lease to include the head landlord, liability arose under the covenant for quiet enjoyment.

Modern view: There is now a tendency to move away from the view that there must be physical interference before one can establish a breach of covenant for quiet enjoyment. There is now modern authority to the effect that the covenant is not confined to direct physical interference but may be broken by conduct of the landlord or his agent which interferes with the tenant's freedom of action in exercising his rights as tenant. The breakthrough came with the Court of Appeal decision in *Kenny* v. *Preen* (1962) where the landlord made threats to the tenant by letter and by shouting. It was held that there had been a breach of covenant for quiet enjoyment, although there was no physical interference. Lord Justice Pearson was prepared to find in the tenant's favour on the basis that the landlord's conduct:

> 'Seriously interfered with the tenant's proper freedom of action in exercising her right of possession, and had deprived her of the full benefit of it... and would in itself constitute a breach of covenant, even if there were no direct physical interference with the tenant's possession and enjoyment'.

This was followed by *McCall* v. *Abelesz* (1976) where Lord Denning MR said that the covenant for quiet enjoyment was not confined to direct physical interference by the landlord.

> 'It extends to any conduct of the landlord or his agents which interferes with the tenant's freedom of action in exercising his rights as a tenant'.

See 'The Sound of Peace: Quiet Enjoyment', an article by H. Wilkinson, *New Law Journal* (21/12/84).

Unlawful eviction and harassment: Tenants of residential premises are now protected by s.1 of the Protection from Eviction Act 1977 which makes the unlawful eviction of a residential occupier and the harassment of an occupier an offence. Section 1(3) provides that if any person with intent to cause the residential occupier of the premises to either give up occupation or to refrain from exercising his rights in respect of the property, and does acts calculated to interfere with the peace or comfort of the residential occupier or persistently withdraws or withholds services reasonably required for the occupation of premises, he shall be guilty of an offence. The penalties are a fine or imprisonment, or both.

The statutory offence applies to 'any person' and is not limited to the landlord. 'Tenant' is also construed widely to include 'members of household' which is wider than a tenant's family at common law.

The tenant must satisfy the court that there was a positive intention to cause the giving up of occupation or restriction on rights. There must be some calculated act, not simply inactivity. For example, a failure by a landlord to pay a gas or electricity bill resulting in the disconnection of supplies to the tenant, is not sufficient to establish the statutory offence. In this case, the tenant's remedy is for breach of covenant for quiet enjoyment.

It is necessary to prove that there was a specific intent to harass a person who was known or believed by the defendant to be a residential occupier: *R* v. *Phekoo* (1981). A landlord who persuades a tenant to leave the premises for a limited period to enable essential work to be done and thereafter to return could not be said to have formed the requisite intention to cause the tenant to give up occupation: *Schon* v. *Camden London Borough* (1986).

Remedies for breach of covenant for quiet enjoyment: The appropriate remedy is the award of damages on the breach of contract. Damages will be measured by the loss resulting from the breach. In addition, it has been settled since *Jarvis* v. *Swan Tours Ltd* (1973) that the court can grant damages for mental upset and distress. The wrongful conduct of the landlord may also amount to a tort in which case aggravated or exemplary damages may be awarded in an appropriate case. Exemplary damages of £1,000 were awarded to the plaintiff in the case of *Drane* v. *Evangelou and Others* (1978).

The facts were all too common. The tenant rented a furnished flat at £25 per week and lived there with his girlfriend from August 1975. A year later he applied to the rent officer for a revision of rent. On 8 October 1975 the rent officer fixed the rent at £16 per week. Meanwhile the landlord had attempted to evict the tenant unsuccessfully. On the 14 October, the landlord's agents invaded the premises. On his return, the tenant found a Greek Cypriot barring the entrance, and all his belongings had been put outside. The door was bolted on the inside and four or five people were inside the premises. Some of the tenant's belongings were damaged. The tenant and his girlfriend slept on a friend's floor and asked the county court to restore their possession of the furnished flat.

The county court judge described the landlord's behaviour as 'monstrous behaviour' and granted the injunction restoring possession. But the landlord would not give up possession and defied the injunction. The landlord was committed for contempt of court. Eventually the tenant moved back in on 1 January 1976 to find everything dirty and damaged. He began an action for damages, and was subsequently awarded £1,000 exemplary damages. The Court of Appeal upheld the County Court's award and Lord Justice Lawton said that:

> 'If there ever was a case where a landlord like this landlord should be taught a lesson, it is this case.'

Exemplary damages were also awarded in *Guppys (Bridport) Ltd* v. *Brookling* (1984) where the landlord had disconnected services during conservation work, forcing the tenants out of their premises.

Injunction: It is quite clear from the decision in *Drane* v. *Evangelou* that the courts will not only grant injunctions to restrain eviction, but will also grant an injunction to restore a tenant to possession in appropriate circumstances. Lord Denning MR was prepared to grant an injunction in the unusual case of *Smith and Others* v. *Nottingham County Council* (1981). Students had complained of noise and the consequential disturbance to their studies owing to building work being carried out during their examination period, near to their residence. Although the students were only licensees, Lord Denning MR was prepared to imply a term that the landlord council should do nothing by making noise or other disturbance to prevent the students getting on with their studies in their rooms in reasonable quietude. This implied term produced a similar result to the remedy of an injunction for a breach of covenant for quiet enjoyment.

Criminal compensation: Where the conduct complained of amounts not only to a breach of covenant for quiet enjoyment, but also amounts to harassment within the terms of s.1(3) of the Protection from Eviction Act 1977, an order for criminal compensation may be made. In this case, one does not of course need to establish breach of covenant for quiet enjoyment, or the tort of trespass, one simply pleads compensation for the criminal offence of harassment.

Criminal compensation can also be awarded for unlawful harassment under s.1 Protection from Eviction Act 1977 in addition to any civil liabilities arising under the covenant for quiet enjoyment.

This means that the same facts may give rise to a number of alternative actions. Either a civil action for breach of covenant for quiet enjoyment, with damages in contract, and/or a civil action for the tort of trespass for damages in tort with a possibility of obtaining exemplary damages not available for the breach of contract.

Obligations not to derogate from his grant:

> 'The maxim...embodies the principle that a lessor may not by his voluntary acts prejudice any rights which he has created–having given a thing with one hand, he is not to take away the means of enjoying it with the other.'

per Lord Justice Bowen in *Birmingham, Dudley and District Banking Co.* v. *Ross* (1888).

The obligation not to derogate from grant only applies where the landlord retains adjacent land. The underlying principle is that a landlord may not do any act which is inconsistent with the purpose for which the demised premises are let. In essence, this can be summed up by saying that the landlord must not seek to take away with one hand what he has given with the other. Therefore to constitute derogation from grant there must be some act which renders the land substantially less fit for the purposes for which it was let: *Aldin* v. *Latimer Clarke, Muirhead and Co.* (1894).

This principle has a limited application and only applies to two cases. First where the landlord has granted easements over retained land he cannot derogate from these. Second, where the landlord uses retained land so as to render demised land unfit for the purpose for which it is demised. For example, in *Aldin* v. *Latimer Clarke, Muirhead and Co.* (1894) a landlord demised premises to a timber merchant for the purpose of storing timber. It was held that a landlord will be prevented from building on adjoining land so as to interrupt flow of air to sheds used for drying timber. Tenants do not often rely on this obligation. It is useful where there is no other cause of action, i.e. where covenant for quiet enjoyment has not been broken and where the landlord has not acted unlawfully–as in *Aldin's* case where the landlord's building programme did not amount to a breach of covenant, neither did it amount to a tort. The true distinction between breach of covenant for quiet enjoyment and non-derogation from grant seems to be that the duty not to derogate is concerned with the retained part, which makes the premises less fit for the purpose for which they were let; the covenant for quiet enjoyment is concerned with the enjoyment of the premises and actual interruption or disturbance on them. For a tenant to benefit from this obligation the landlord must appreciate the particular sensitivity of the tenant at the time of letting: *Robinson* v. *Kilvert* (1889).

Implied condition of fitness for human habitation: see s.8 Landlord and Tenant Act 1985;
Implied repairing obligation in leases for less than seven years: see s.11 Landlord and Tenant Act 1985.

These two obligations are considered in Chapter 14 on Repairs.

Doctrine of waste

The doctrine of waste imposes a limited repairing obligation in tort on tenants, and is discussed fully in Chapter 14. The common law doctrine of waste can be found in several branches of property law since it was designed to ensure that a temporary occupier of land, e.g. a 'tenant for life' under a trust settlement, returned the land to the reversioner in the same or similar condition as at the start of the occupancy. The doctrine of waste provided an important remedy for reversioners who wanted a temporary occupier to ensure that the property was maintained. It is relied on today primarily by landlords who cannot rely on an express repairing obligation, although the doctrine applies universally to all fixed term leases and to the majority of periodic tenancies.

Conflicts

It is possible for a conflict to arise between express and implied obligations where an express covenant in a lease purports to override an implied obligation. For example, a short lease might purport to exclude the landlord's statutory s.11 obligation to carry out structural repairs to a house: see s.11 Landlord and Tenant Act 1985. The following rules apply in the case of a conflict:

(a) The general rule is that parties may, by express agreement, exclude any 'implied covenants' which are implied by case-law;
(b) Covenants implied by statute will generally override any express agreement. But the statutory provisions may provide the parties with the possibility of 'contracting out' of the statutory obligation, in

which case any prescribed statutory procedure for excluding the implied statutory covenant should be observed;

(c) The doctrine of waste is part of the law of tort, and cannot be excluded by an express covenant since it does not constitute an implied covenant: *Kinlyside* v. *Thornton* (1776).

Thus in the hypothetical example above, the landlord can only contract out of his s. 11 statutory repairing obligations if he follows the strict contracting out provisions prescribed by s. 12 Landlord and Tenant Act 1985, and the doctrine of waste will apply.

Chapter 8

Overview of Remedies for Breach of Covenant

INTRODUCTORY

Specialist legal advice should be sought if proceedings are contemplated for breach of covenant. The most appropriate remedy or remedies can only be identified by persons qualified to construe specific covenants with accuracy after taking into account any limitations imposed by the statutory schemes. In addition, commercial and tactical decisions will often have to be taken and these require a detailed understanding of procedural matters.

MAIN REMEDIES FOR BREACH OF COVENANT

The vast majority of advisory work for landlords and tenants involves a consideration of the remedies available if one party has defaulted in performing some part of the agreement e.g. the landlord has failed to carry out repairs or the tenant has fallen behind with payment of rent. The substantive law relating to remedies is introduced in this chapter but considered in later chapters in the context of specific landlord and tenant problems.

Action for damages

The most common remedy for the non-performance of a covenant is an action for damages for breach of covenant. Damages are generally assessed according to normal contractual principles in order to place the plaintiff in the position that he would have been in but for the breach of covenant. The most common situations in which damages are sought are for breach of either a landlord's or tenant's repairing covenant or where the tenant has assigned the lease in breach of a covenant against assignment.

Forfeiture

A lease which contains a forfeiture clause for a tenant's breach of covenant entitles the landlord to eject the tenant and regain possession of the leasehold premises. For example, the landlord may wish to forfeit the lease if the tenant has failed to comply with his repairing obligations or transferred the lease to another in breach of a covenant against assignment. If the lease is forfeited, then at common law any sub-tenancies end automatically: *Great Western Rly Co.* v. *Smith* (1876). However, where a statutory scheme applies both the tenant and any sub-tenant may have security of tenure preventing the landlord from regaining possession.

A lease can only be forfeited with the court's consent and the landlord must comply with the statutory procedure for forfeiting a lease unless possession is given up voluntarily. Courts tend to 'lean against forfeiture', and have wide discretionary powers to grant both tenants and sub-tenants relief from forfeiture. For instance, forfeiture of the lease is likely to be refused if the tenant has remedied the defects before the hearing and paid any compensation due. A landlord may 'waive' his right to forfeit a lease if his conduct demonstrates that he is continuing the relationship of landlord and tenant after he knows of the breach of covenant, for example by accepting rent with knowledge of the breach.

(Chapter 20 contains a full discussion of forfeiture.)

Action for double rent or double value

Landlords are entitled to recover double the rent or double the rent's value if the tenant 'holds over' (remains in possession) after the tenancy has ended. But in practice this remedy is seldom used since many tenants have statutory rights once their tenancies end.

Specific performance

Occasionally a landlord or tenant may be entitled to ask the court to grant the discretionary remedy of specific performance in order to compel the other party to fulfil an obligation under the lease.

A covenant to employ a resident porter in leases of a luxury flat in a block has been held to be specifically enforceable: *Posner and Others* v. *Scott-Lewis and Others* (1986).

Specific performance is only granted where damages would not be an adequate remedy. For example, the circumstances would have to be unusual for a landlord to be able to obtain specific performance of a repairing covenant against a tenant at the end of the term, because damages would usually be adequate. By contrast, a tenant will more usually be able to obtain an order for specific performance of his landlord's repairing obligations because damages would not properly compensate a tenant for having to live in premises which are in bad repair. (See p.20 for a general consideration of specific performance.)

Injunction

The grant of an injunction is also a discretionary remedy. As with specific performance an injunction will only be granted where damages would not be an adequate remedy. A landlord might obtain an injunction in order to prevent a tenant from making an unlawful assignment. In such a case damages are not an adequate remedy because it is difficult to quantify the amount of damages. A tenant might obtain an injunction to prevent a landlord from unlawfully evicting him. Once again damages could not compensate for the inconvenience that could be caused. In general it is difficult to obtain injunctions in the whole field of landlord and tenant law because most breaches of covenant can be compensated for by an award of damages.

Declaratory relief

If the parties wish to have a particular matter determined by the court they can apply to the court for a declaration on a specific point. For example, a declaration that the landlord has unreasonably withheld his consent to an assignment, to improvements, or to a change in user.

Recovery of costs

Many leases and some statutory provisions provide that the landlord is entitled to recover his legal and other costs in a number of situations. For example, in recovering rent, or for costs incurred when giving consent to an assignment or sub-letting, or to an alteration or improvement. In some circumstances, costs can also be recovered in carrying out repairs for which the other party is liable: see p.161.

APPOINTMENT OF RECEIVER

It is possible for tenants to appoint a reciver to manage property and collect rents where the landlord has defaulted in his obligations: see p.165.

Chapter 9

Enforcing Leasehold Obligations

BASIC PRINCIPLES

Introductory

The rules relating to the enforcement of obligations as between landlord and tenant are somewhat curious. This is because long chains of landlords and tenants can develop, particularly in the case of a long fixed term lease, owing to the fact that both the original parties may have assigned their respective interests in the reversion and term to successors. This is distinct from a chain created by the grant of sub-tenancies.

The question here is whether the terms of the original lease or tenancy agreement can be enforced against assignees who are in contractual terms third parties to the lease. The application of the contractual principle of privity of contract means that only the original parties to a contract are bound by its terms: see p. 13. Accordingly, the terms agreed by the original parties to the contract will be enforceable as between those parties. Generally speaking, third parties are not bound by the terms of a contract. However, special rules apply to the enforcement of leasehold obligations against assignees providing an exception to the doctrine of privity of contract.

Position at common law

Landlord and tenant law devised its own special rules and principles at common law to enable the terms of a lease to be enforced not only as between the original parties, but also against assignees. These rules are now enshrined in the statutory provisions of ss.141–2 Law of Property Act 1925.

Only obligations which affect the leasehold property itself are enforceable against assignees. Personal covenants are unenforceable against assignees, whether they are successors in title to the term or the reversion. The appropriate legal shorthand for this rule, as devised by the common law, is to say that, covenants which 'touch and concern the land' are enforceable against assignees: *Spencer's case* (1583). This became known as *the first resolution in Spencer's case*. Contractual obligations which were purely personal in nature and which did not touch and concern the leasehold property were only held to be binding on the contracting parties (known as *the second resolution in Spencer's case*).

The former common law rules were incorporated into ss.141 and 142 of the Law of Property Act 1925. Today, the question of whether leasehold obligations are enforceable against successors is a matter of applying these statutory provisions to the facts of the case: per Lord Justices Upjohn and Diplock in *Re King, Robinson and Gray* (1963).

HYPOTHETICAL PROBLEM

The following hypothetical problem provides a simple illustration of the difficulties which arise upon assignment. Lamaco PLC, an oil company, granted Teetotal Limited a twenty-one year lease of a petrol filling station in Margate. Teetotal Limited's lease contains: a covenant to pay rent quarterly in advance; a full repairing covenant; and a covenant stipulating that Teetotal Limited should purchase all its petrol supplies from Lamaco PLC. Teetotal Limited was unable to pay last year's rent owing to financial difficulties and has recently assigned the remaining ten year term to A1 Garages Limited. The reversion was subsequently sold to Anglican Petroleum. A1 Garages Limited has refused to pay the first quarter's rent because it claims that the premises are out of repair, and has refused to accept supplies of petrol from Anglican Petroleum since it has its own independent supplier. You are asked to advise Anglican Petroleum who wish to: (a) recover the year's unpaid rent from Teetotal Limited; (b) recover the quarter's rent from A1 Garages Limited; (c) enforce the repairing covenant; and (d) enforce the covenant to supply Anglican Petrol to A1 Garages Limited. It is hoped that the reader will be able to draw his own conclusions as to the correct answer to this problem from the discussion in the ensuing pages.

The following diagram provides an illustration of the relationship between the parties.

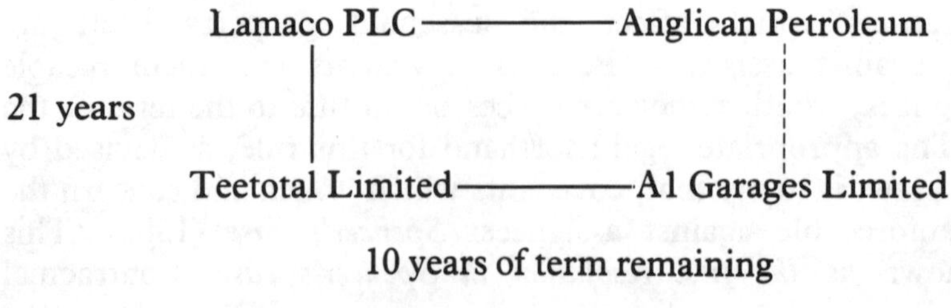

LANDLORDS AND THEIR SUCCESSORS

Privity of estate

At common law, covenants which touch and concern the land could only be enforced where there was 'privity of estate'. These covenants only bound assignees if and so long as they held the estate with which the covenant ran; the covenants could not bound sub-tenants or squatters.

Application of sections 141 and 142

The enforcement of leasehold obligations against successors in title is regulated by the provisions of ss. 141 and 142 Law of Property Act 1925.

Benefit and burden

The rights and liabilities of landlords and their successors fall into two legal categories for the purpose of ss.141 and 142, namely benefits and burdens. The benefit of a covenant entitles a person to sue on the covenant in order to enforce it, i.e. to benefit from its terms. The burden creates an obligation or liability so that a person can be sued by another who wishes to enforce a covenant, i.e. one party is burdened with the provisions of a covenant.

Covenant must refer to leasehold premises

S.141 and 142 only apply to covenants which refer to the leasehold property, that is to covenants which 'have reference to the subject-matter of the lease'.

In order to determine which covenants fall within the scope of these provisions it is necessary to have recourse to the considerable body of case-law which developed prior to the enactment of ss.141 and 142. This is because the sections are a statutory restatement of the two resolutions in *Spencer's case*. Covenants which have 'reference to the subject matter of the lease' are the statutory equivalent of the former common law covenants which 'touch and concern the land'. Thus in order to determine whether a covenant has reference to the subject-matter of the lease it is necessary to determine whether it has been considered judicially before. If it has, the relevant case-law relating to covenants which touch and concern land can be applied, otherwise the point will be decided by arguing by analogy with reference to decided case-law.

Examples of covenants which have been held to touch and concern the land are:

(a) tenant's covenants
To pay rent: *Parker* v. *Webb* (1693)
To pay rates and taxes: *South of England Dairies Limited* v. *Baker* (1906)
To repair: *Dean and Chapter of Windsor* v. *Hyde* (1601)

Restriction on use to residential use only: *Wilkinson* v. *Rogers* (1864)
Prohibition on assignment without consent: *Goldstein* v. *Sanders* (1915)
Covenant by a tenant of a public house to buy liquor from the lessor: *Fleetwood* v. *Hull* (1889)
Prohibition on selling petrol on the premises other than that supplied by the landlord: *Cleveland Petroleum Co Ltd* v. *Dartstone Ltd* (1969)

(b) landlord's covenants
For quiet enjoyment: *Campbell* v. *Lewis* (1820)
To renew: *Richardson* v. *Sydenham* (1703)

Examples of covenants which do not touch and concern the land are:

(a) tenant's covenants
To pay a premium for the grant of a lease: *Hill* v. *Booth* (1930)
To pay rates in respect of other land: *Gower* v. *Postmaster-General* (1887)

(b) landlord's covenants
Providing the tenant with an option to purchase: *Woodall* v. *Clifton* (1905)
To keep in repair other houses in the district: *Dewar* v. *Goodman* (1909)
To pay for items which are not fixtures at the end of the term: *Gorton* v. *Gregory* (1862)

Rent and benefit–section 141

Landlords and their assignees have a statutory right to benefit from covenants which refer to the leasehold premises. Section 141(1) provides that rent reserved by a lease and the benefit of covenants which refer to the subject matter of the lease and which impose an obligation on the tenant, together with conditions of re-entry are specifically annexed to the reversionary estate. In other words, these obligations will continue for the lease's duration notwithstanding the fact that an assignment has taken place.

Who is entitled to the benefit?

In some situations the original landlord and the assignee of the reversion may both attempt to claim the same benefit where the reversion has been assigned after a breach of covenant by the tenant. This would obviously work injustice. For example, a tenant fails to pay a quarter's rent and the landlord assigns the reversion soon afterwards. It would obviously be unfair to the tenant if both the landlord and the assignee were entitled to claim the unpaid quarter's rent.

The rule here is that the rent or benefit of the covenant can be recovered, received or enforced by the person who is from time to time entitled to the lease's income: s.141(2) Law of Property Act 1925. A successor is entitled to sue for and recover arrears of rent which pre-date the assignment under this rule because he has acquired all the benefits of the tenant's covenants. The Court of Appeal held in *Arlesford Trading Co Ltd* v. *Servansingh* (1971) that a landlord's successor could recover arrears of rent from the original tenant which were due before the assignment: see also *London County (A and D) Ltd* v. *Wilfred Sportsman Ltd* (1971). Thus in the last example, the assignee could claim the unpaid quarter's rent since the assignee is the person who is currently entitled to the lease's income, the landlord having lost his right of action.

This problem also arises in the hypothetical problem above since Anglican Petroleum wishes to sue for breaches of covenant which arise both before and after the assignment, and will be entitled to do so. Lamaco PLC will be unable to enforce the covenants for non-payment of rent against A1 Garages Ltd after the assignment of the reversion to Anglican Petroleum since only the assignee can sue the tenant for breaches of covenant under the provisions of s.141.

The burden—section 142

If the landlord has assumed obligations under the lease, e.g. repairing obligations, these obligations will be enforceable by the person who currently holds the term provided that they refer to the leasehold premises. Section 142 provides that the obligations of covenants entered into by landlords which have reference to the subject-matter of the lease are annexed to the reversionary estate, and may be enforced by the tenant in whom the term is from time to time vested.

A tenant can sue after assignment. It has recently been held that a tenant who had suffered a loss as a result of a breach of a landlord's repairing covenant, committed while he was tenant, could sue the landlord for the loss after he had assigned the lease: *City and Metropolitan Properties Ltd* v. *Greycroft Ltd* (1987). Mr John Mowbray QC said that 'the landlord's liability to the tenant for the existing breaches survived the assignment of the lease in the same way as the tenant's liability to the landlord.'

Scope of sections 141 and 142

Sections 141 and 142 apply to leases, sub-leases, and other tenancies: see s.154 Law of Property Act 1925. In addition, it appears that these sections may also apply to the terms of oral leases for less than three years which are exempt from the requirement to be in writing by s.54(2), although this matter has not yet been tested in the courts: see Hill and Redman's *Law of Landlord and Tenant*, 17th ed., at pp. 569, 573.

EQUITABLE TENANCIES

In some circumstances the courts are prepared to grant an order for specific performance of an 'agreement for a lease'. If the courts grant an order for specific performance and a lease is drawn up, ss.141 and 142 apply in the normal way. Indeed one of the main objects of obtaining an order for specific performance is to enable one party to enforce the terms of the agreement against an assignee.

Collateral agreements

A provision in an agreement to a lease which is not subsequently incorporated into the lease does not cease to have effect because it may amount to a collateral agreement which can be enforced in contract. This occurred in *International Press Centre* v. *Norwich Union* (1986) where a covenant in an agreement to a lease to erect a building in good and workmanlike manner was held to survive the grant of a lease which did not refer to it (but only to repair).

Assignment of equitable tenancy

Not specifically enforceable

If the remedy of specific performance would not be available, e.g. because there has been delay or bad conduct on the part of the party who wishes to apply for specific performance the position of the parties is governed by contractual principles. The benefit of a contract may be assigned under the provisions of s. 136 Law of Property Act 1925, but the burden of a contract cannot be assigned: *Purchase* v. *Lichfield Brewery Co* (1915). The application of these principles is considered in the following examples:

(a) assignment of an equitable tenancy by a tenant

If the tenant assigns an equitable tenancy, the assignee will be able to enforce the benefit of the covenants in the tenancy e.g. an assignee can sue the landlord for breach of covenant for quiet enjoyment if he is wrongfully evicted or for breach of a landlord's repairing covenant. But the landlord cannot sue the assignee since the burden of a tenant's covenant is not assignable: *Marquis of Camden* v. *Batterbury* (1860); and article by R.J. Smith, vol. 37 *Cambridge Law Journal*, at p.98 (1978). For example, the landlord will not be entitled to enforce a covenant by the tenant to repair the interior against an assignee.

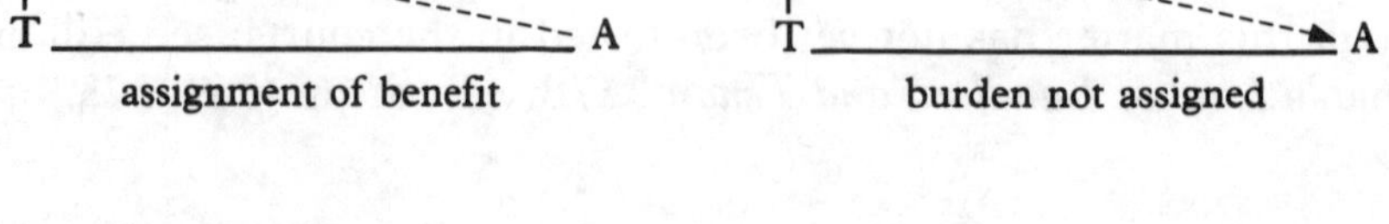

(b) assignment of an equitable tenancy by the landlord

If the landlord assigns the reversion, the benefit of the equitable tenancy will be assigned under the provisions of s. 136 Law of Property Act 1925, but not the burden. The assignee is entitled to the benefit of the covenants in the tenancy, but cannot be sued for breach of covenant by the tenant.

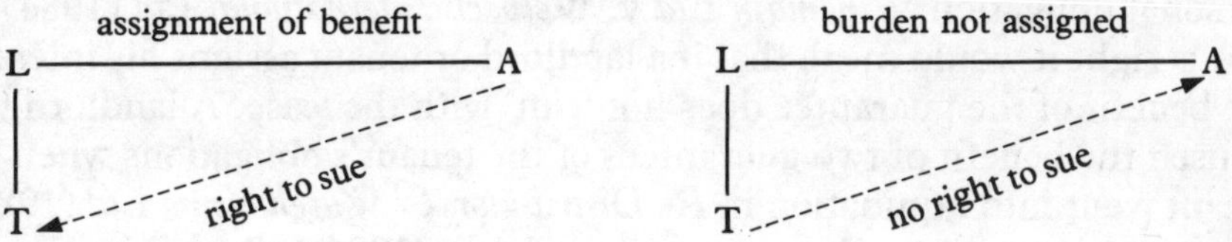

Hypothetical problem if an equitable tenancy

In the hypothetical problem on page 84, suppose that the twenty-one year term granted by Lamaco PLC to Teetotal Limited was not granted by deed and created an agreement for a lease. Anglican Petroleum would be advised to seek specific performance of the agreement in order to enforce its terms against A1 Garages Limited. If this remedy was refused, the position would be as follows. The benefit of the contract between Teetotal Limited and A1 Garages Limited would have been assigned so that A1 Garages Limited could sue Lamaco PLC for breach of its repairing obligation. Lamaco PLC would not be able to recover the unpaid rent from A1 Garages Limited since the burden would not be assigned. The benefit of the contract between Lamaco PLC and Anglican Petroleum has been assigned so that Anglican Petroleum would be entitled to sue A1 Garages Limited for unpaid rent and in respect of the covenant to supply petrol. A1 Garages Limited cannot enforce the repairing covenant against Anglican Petroleum since the burden has not been assigned.

Entitlement to specific performance

The rules as to who is entitled to apply for an order for specific performance are complicated if there has been an assignment of an equitable tenancy. The equitable tenancy is treated in law as a contract and not a lease and is subject to normal contractual principles. Thus an assignee will only be entitled to an order for specific performance (thereby enabling him to enforce the terms of the contract against a third party assignee) if he is entitled to the benefit of the contract.

SURETIES

Many modern commercial leases contain a surety covenant whereby the obligations of one party are guaranteed by a third party to the lease. For example a surety may covenant with the landlord and his successors in title that the surety would pay the rent in the event of the tenants failing to do so, guaranteeing the payment of rent. It was thought until recently that a surety covenant does not 'touch and concern' the land and is a personal obligation: *Pinemain Ltd* v. *Welbeck International Ltd* (1984). If that is right it would mean that if a landlord or tenant assigns his interest, the benefit of the guarantee does not 'run' with the lease. A landlord was refused the benefit of two guarantees of the tenant's obligations when the tenant went into liquidation in *Re Distributors & Warehousing Ltd* (1986). See also *Kumar* v. *Dunning and Another* (1986). But this line of authorities was doubted in *Coastplace Ltd* v. *Hartley* (1987) where Mr Justice French held that the benefit of a surety covenant passed on the assignment of a reversion without express mention, relying on *Griffith* v. *Pelton* (1958) not cited in the earlier cases.

FURTHER READING

Hill and Redman's *Law of Landlord and Tenant*, 17th ed., 1982, volume 1, chapter 7.

RESTRICTIVE COVENANTS

A restrictive covenant is a covenant which is negative in nature if not in form e.g. a covenant restricting user. A restrictive covenant which affects freehold land will only bind a tenant if he has notice of it: *Tulk* v. *Moxon* (1848). Post-1925 restrictive covenants are registrable as a class D(ii) land charge if the land is unregistered land, or as a minor interest if the land is registered: see s.2(5) Land Charges Act 1972 and s.3 Land Registration Act 1925. The registration system is defective in one significant way. An intending tenant may have no means of discovering the names of the covenantor unless he has access to the title deeds or register or is given this information. This means he cannot carry out a search to discover the existence of any registered restrictive covenant. Yet he will be bound by a covenant which he has no means of discovering. A tenant may be entitled to compensation: see s.25 Law of Property Act 1925. In the case of pre-1925 restrictive covenants which are not registrable, the tenant is not bound by covenants of which he has no notice. Restrictive covenants which touch and concern the land are binding if the benefit has been passed on with the land by annexation, by assignment or under a scheme of development.

FURTHER READING

The Law of Real Property by R. Megarry and H. Wade, 5th ed., 1984, pp.770–98.

Chapter 10
Rent

INTRODUCTION

Tenants commonly assume a number of separate and distinct obligations by way of payments to a landlord in return for the use and occupation of leasehold premises. The majority of tenants agree to pay either a premium (lump sum) or rent at the commencement of a tenancy. Additionally, many tenants agree to pay a separate sum in respect of service charges so that a landlord can be reimbursed for costs which he has incurred in providing services to a tenant. For example, Theodore owns a small residential block of twenty flats which is managed by Milk Limited. The flats have recently been let on new fixed term leases of ninety-nine years, at a premium of £50,000 and a ground rent of £50 (doubling every thirty three years). In addition, there is a service charge which covers management fees, cleaning and gardening expenses, lighting, decorating and cleaning of the common parts. In this example, the premium and rent are fixed at the outset whilst the service charge will be assessed quarterly.

RENT

Legal concept

Rent is compensation for the exclusive use and occupation of leasehold premises, and is reserved formally in a lease by the 'reddendum' which simply reserves the payment of rent. It used to be considered to be an acknowledgement of the obligations of service at common law, and was accordingly described as 'rent service'. This no longer represents the modern position although this label has been retained:

> 'The medieval concept of rent as a service rendered by the tenant to the landlord has been displaced by the modern concept of a payment which a tenant is bound by his contract to pay to the landlord for the use of his land. The medieval concept has, however left as its only surviving relic the ancient remedy of distress.'
> (Per Lord Diplock in *United Scientific Holdings Ltd* v. *Burnley Borough Council* (1977).)

The remedy of distress permits a landlord to recover any outstanding unpaid rent by seizing property belonging to the tenant, from the leasehold premises, up to the value of the unpaid rent. Note that this remedy is not available if there are arrears of any monies other than rent.

The 'rent must be certain' but need not be monetary in nature, and may consist of the provision of goods or services: see *Montague* v. *Browning* (1954). However, the rule as to certainty was never applied strictly, and it is satisfied if the rent is either certain or capable of being ascertained when payment is required: *Parker* v. *Harris* (1692). Coke said that: '*Id certum est quod certum reddi post*' (rent is certain when it is ascertained). This means that variable rents are permissible so that the rent can vary according to the profits generated by a business or agricultural tenancy. Furthermore, rents can be increased if the lease contains a rent review provision: see Chapter 13 and Clarke and Adams *Rent Reviews and Variable Rents*, Oyez 1981.

Reservation

No particular method of reserving rent is prescribed by law so that any expression which shows that the parties intended rent to be payable will be sufficient: *London and Westminster Loan Co.* v. *London & North Western Railway* (1893). A formal lease will contain a reddendum which will specify that the tenant will yield or pay a rent. But the law implies a covenant to pay rent in the case of periodic and fixed term tenancies, in the absence of a formal lease or written agreement: *Drake* v. *Munday* (1631).

Payment

General

The date of payment will normally either be agreed between the parties or set out in a lease's reddendum. The tenant is free to pay his rent at any time on the agreed date and it is not in arrears until after midnight: *Dibble* v. *Bowater* (1853). If a landlord requires rent to be paid in advance, this should be specifically provided for by the lease (this is customary). Payment may be made either to the landlord or to his authorised agent: *Hitchings* v. *Thompson* (1850). It is often paid by post rather than in person, and this will be at the tenant's own risk; registered or recorded delivery is a wise precaution.

Assignment of reversion

The position is more complicated if there has been an assignment. If the reversion has been assigned by the landlord, the assignee is entitled to the rent under the provisions of s.141(1) Law of Property Act 1925. However, the rent may be validly paid by the tenant to the assignor, until notice of the assignment is received from the assignee: s.151(1) Law of Property Act 1925.

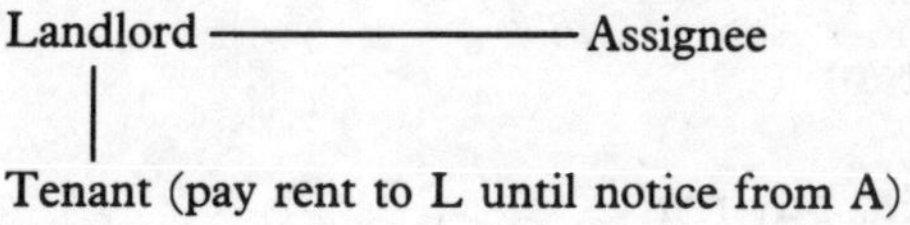

Assignment of term

A tenant's obligation to pay rent is attached to the leasehold property. The general rule is that rent is payable by the person entitled to the lease or tenancy: s.141(2) Law of Property Act 1925. Thus, if a tenant assigns his term to an assignee, the assignee is bound to pay the rent from the date of the assignment. The landlord can sue the assignee for the non-payment of rent which has accrued from the date of the assignment; but he cannot recover unpaid rent from the assignee which accrued prior to the assignment.

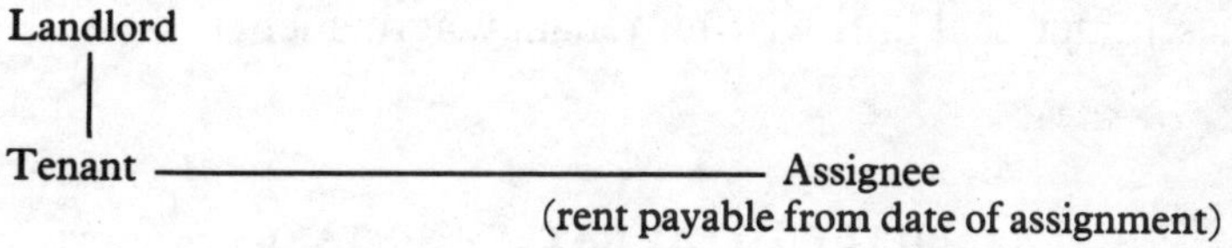

Original parties

The original tenant will remain liable to the original landlord for any unpaid rent for the duration of the lease, as a result of the contractual relationship between the two. The original tenant's liability will only end upon an assignment of the reversion, when the contractual relationship between the original parties will be severed, as from the date of the assignment.

However, the landlord cannot recover rent twice, i.e. from both the original tenant and an assignee of the term.

Implied indemnity

A covenant to pay the rent and indemnify the original tenant is implied into all leases made since 31st December 1925: s.77 and Schedule 2 Parts IX and X. The effect of these provisions is that a landlord should sue the assignee for any unpaid rent which accrued after the assignment in the first instance, but can bring a claim against the original tenant.

The tenant would thereupon be entitled to an indemnity from the assignee. The indemnity would be valueless in practical terms where the assignee is a bankrupt.

Liability to pay rent

Implied covenant to pay rent

The common law implies a covenant to pay rent where a rent was reserved by the contract of tenancy; the emphasis here is on the word 'pay'. Landlords can bring proceedings for non-payment of rent on the strength of this implied covenant. A tenant's liability is less extensive under an implied covenant to pay rent than under an express covenant in two respects. Firstly, the tenant's liability does not arise before entry; secondly, the tenant's liability ceases once the lease is assigned.

Express covenant to pay rent

It is customary for an express covenant to pay rent to be inserted into both leases under seal and written tenancy agreements.

LIABILITY TO PAY RATES AND TAXES

Implied covenant

There is an implied covenant imposing liability on the tenant to pay the tenant's rates and taxes. The tenant is, therefore, liable to pay all the rates and taxes relating to the leasehold premises as the occupier of the land, except for those for which the landlord is made solely liable by statute.

Express agreement

There is no reason why the parties should not enter into an express agreement whereby the landlord covenants to pay the rates, and this is frequently done in the case of periodic tenancies. Moreover, in certain circumstances the landlord alone will be liable to pay specified rates and taxes and will be prevented from shifting this liability by statute, in which case the tenant can deduct any amount which he has paid from his rent.

RENT BOOKS

Provision

Landlords have a statutory duty to supply rent books or similar documents, e.g. rent cards, to both tenants and contractual licensees who occupy premises or a residence, and pay their rent weekly: s.4 Landlord and Tenant Act 1985. The scope of s.4 is cut down by s.4(2) which excludes occupiers whose rent includes a payment in respect of board. The previous statutory provisions have been criticised since they are easy to avoid and are ineffectual as a result of lack of effective sanctions for non-compliance: see Michael Haley, *New Law Journal*, 6th January 1984 at page 4. It is to be regretted that the new Act fails to deal with the problem of avoidance of these provisions, and merely repeats the provisions of earlier legislation.

Prescribed information

General

All rent books supplied by landlords in pursuance of s.4 must contain the following information prescribed by s.5 Landlord and Tenant Act 1985:

(a) the name and address of landlord;
(b) regulated tenancies: additional information prescribed by statute;
(c) restricted contracts: particulars of rent, terms and conditions of the contract, notice of prescribed matters.

Companies

Companies must give tenants written details of the names and addresses of the company secretary and all company directors if this is requested by the tenant in writing: s.6 Landlord and Tenant Act 1985.

Offences

Failure to comply with these provisions renders landlords liable to a summary fine at a modest level: s.7 Landlord and Tenant Act 1985.

STATUTORY RENT LIMITS

General

The vast majority of residential tenancies and occupancies are subject to statutory provisions which have the object of limiting the amount of rent payable, notwithstanding the contractual rent which has been agreed between landlord and tenant. The statutory provisions have not been consolidated so that all the major residential tenancies created by statute have their own statutory framework for rent control and regulation. In the following pages, each scheme will be dealt with separately, moving from left to right of Fig. 2 (page 41).

Long tenancies at a low rent

A low rent is payable in order for a tenancy to qualify as a tenancy at a low rent, and there is no form of rent control during the contractual term. However, the Rent Acts apply automatically once a long tenancy is determined in accordance with the provisions of Part I Landlord and Tenant Act 1954, so that a tenant can register a fair rent at the end of a long tenancy where a statutory tenancy arises: see Chapter 26 for the substantive law on 'Long Tenancies at Low Rents'.

Regulated tenancies

The rent payable for a regulated tenancy is regulated by Part IV Rent Act 1977 which provides for the registration of fair rents: see Chapter 27 on Rent Act tenancies generally. Every local authority is responsible to the Secretary of State for drawing up a scheme to provide Rent Officers for their area under the provisions of s.63 Rent Act 1977. A Rent Officer has a duty to draw up a Rent Register, keep it up to date, and make it available for public inspection: s.66 Rent Act 1977. The register should contain the following information, as prescribed by s.66(2) Rent Act 1977 and Schedule 2 Rent Act 1977 (Forms, etc.) Regulations 1980 (SI 1980 No. 1697):

(a) the rent payable under the regulated tenancy;
(b) the following details of the tenancy:
    (i) all tenancies: names and addresses of landlord and tenant; rental period; allocation of repairing liabilities; details of services and furniture provided by the landlord or a superior landlord; any other terms of the tenancy which are relevant to the determination of a fair rent;
    (ii) fixed term tenancies: length of term and commencement date;
    (iii) statutory tenancies arising under Part I Landlord and Tenant Act 1954: particulars of the initial repairs;
(c) the dwelling-house's specifications.

Fair rents

The registration of fair rents was originally introduced as a temporary war-time expediency but has become a central part of the statutory control of residential sector tenancies: see *The Politics Of Legislation – The Rent Act 1957* by M.J.Barnett, Weidenfeld and Nicolson, 1969, for an incisive commentary on the political process of introducing rent control.

The determination of what constitutes a fair rent is set out in s.70(1) Rent Act 1977 which directs:

(a) a consideration of the age, character, locality and state of repair of the premises, in addition to the quantity, quality and condition of any furniture provided. Comparables, that is, rents of comparable premises, are an important factor in determining a fair rent. The Court of Appeal said that the best evidence of comparables is a recent finding of a Rent Officer or rent assessment committee in *London Rent Assessment Committee* v. *St George's Court Ltd* (1984). A rent assessment committee determined a fair rent for certain flats and failed to treat its own findings on other flats in the same block as a comparable.
(b) that both tenants' improvements, and defects or disrepair which result from a tenant's failure to comply with his obligations, are disregarded. The assessment is, therefore, based on objective criteria, and the personal circumstances of the parties are specifically excluded from consideration.
(c) that a discount is given if the premises are in an area where letting accommodation is scarce since s.70(2) contains the statutory assumption that the number of persons seeking accommodation 'is not substantially greater than' the number of premises available for letting. The House of Lords considered the correct interpretation of the scarcity provision in *Weston Heritable Investment Co. Ltd.* v. *Husband* (1983) where a forty per cent deduction for scarcity was upheld. Lord Keith of Kinkel said that the statutory provision was intended to:

> 'secure that when market rents have been pushed up by a shortage of houses to let, tenants do not have to bear the burden of the increase over what would otherwise be fair which is attributable to that shortage'.

This provision has been criticised for creating wholly artificial notional market conditions, especially in urban areas. Fair rents are determined on the hypothetical basis that the local letting market is almost in a state of equilibrium. If the reality is that there is a scarcity of accommodation, the market rent levels will be brought down in order to eliminate the amount of rent attributable to scarcity. The right to charge a premium upon assignment can be taken into account when assessing a fair rent: see *Crown Estate Commissioners* v. *Connor* (1986) which has been codified as s.70(1)(c) Rent Act 1977 by s.17 Housing and Planning Act 1986 with retrospective effect.

Registration

Either or both parties may apply to the Rent Officer for the registration of a fair rent. Once a fair rent has been registered, s.67(3) Rent Act 1977 provides that it cannot be altered for two years (previously three years), unless there has been a change in:

(a) the condition of the premises, e.g. improvements have been made;
(b) the terms of the tenancy;
(c) the quantity, quality or condition of any furniture; or
(d) any other circumstances which were considered at the time the rent was registered as to make the registered rent no longer a fair rent.

A tenant who applied for the re-registration of an existing rent in the mistaken belief that the landlord could increase it without reference to a rent officer after three years was allowed to have the re-registered higher rent quashed when the mistake was discovered: *R* v. *Chief Rent Officer for Kensington and Chelsea London Borough Council* (1986).

The application has to be made on a prescribed form, the applicant must propose a specific rent, and landlords should state details of any expenditure which they incur in providing services if the application is made by a landlord who provides services: s.67(2) Rent Act 1977. If only one party applies for the registration of a fair rent, the other is informed and given a minimum period of seven days to make written representations against the proposed registration. The Rent Officer may, however, register a fair rent at this stage, if he believes that the rent is fair. But note that either party can request a consultation in order to consider what rent ought to be registered, and may be represented by agents: see s.67 and Schedule 11 Rent Act 1977 for the procedure on an application to a Rent Officer. Note that landlords often ask Rent Officers to decide the preliminary issue of whether a tenancy or licence has been created in an effort to avoid the consequences of the Rent Acts.

The parties are entitled to object to the Rent Officer's decision. Objections must be made in writing within twenty-eight days of receipt of the notice giving the Rent Officer's decision, whereupon the matter will be referred to a Rent Assessment Committee: Schedule 11 para 6. It is noteworthy that the county courts do not have jurisdiction to fix or alter a registered rent: see *Tingey* v. *Sutton* (1984).

Effect of registration

Once a fair rent is registered, any amount paid in excess is recoverable by the tenant for up to two years later, and may be deducted by the tenant from the rent he pays to the landlord: s.57(2) Rent Act 1977.

Certificate of fair rent

Prospective landlords may apply to the Rent Officer for a certificate of fair rent in order to find out in advance what the fair rent might be: s.69 Rent Act 1977. This provision applies to those who are considering letting residential property for the first time, or those who intend to construct or improve property: see Chapter 27 for the substantive law relating to Rent Act tenancies. In the public sector landlords may apply for a fair rent certificate with a view to disposing of an interest in a dwelling-house: s.69A Rent Act 1977 added by s.7 Housing and Planning Act 1986.

Restricted contracts

The procedure for registering a 'reasonable rent' in respect of a restricted contract is similar to the procedure for registering a fair rent: see Part V Rent Act 1977 and Rent Assessment Committees (England and Wales) (Rent Tribunal) Regulations 1980 (SI 1980 No 1700). But note the following differences:

(a) Rent Assessment Committees have jurisdiction as from the 28th November 1980 (formerly rent tribunals): s.72(3) Housing Act 1980;
(b) No special forms are required;
(c) The circumstances of an individual landlord, e.g. any outstanding mortgage repayments, may be considered in assessing a reasonable rent: see *R* v. *Paddington and St Marylebone Rent Tribunal, ex parte Haines* (1961).
(d) It seems that the calculation of a reasonable rent involves a far more subjective test than the registration of a fair rent: see *Private Sector Tenancies* by P.Pettit, Butterworths, 1981, at pp.166-8.

The effect of registering the rent is that it is unlawful for landlords to require or receive more than the registered rent: s.81 Rent Act 1977. See Chapter 29 for the substantive law on restricted contracts.

Protected shorthold tenancy

One of the original qualifying conditions of a protected shorthold tenancy was that a certificate of fair rent had either been granted, or had been applied for not later than twenty eight days after the beginning of the term. It was soon discovered that this provision inhibited the grant of protected shortholds, and the new scheme looked as though it was destined to become a flop. But this condition was abolished for all protected shortholds outside London, from the lst December 1981, by the Protected Shorthold Tenancies (Rent Registration) Order 1981 (SI 1981 No 1578). This means that there are no prescribed rent limits for protected shortholds granted after this date outside the areas of the councils of London and of the Common Council of the City of London: see Chapter 30 for the substantive law on protected shortholds.

Assured tenancy

The primary objective of creating assured tenancies was to encourage the construction of new residential accommodation which would be available for letting. Assured tenancies are regulated by the provisions of Part II Landlord and Tenant Act 1954. No statutory rent limits exist since these are often blamed for the present shortage of accommodation available for letting (although it has to be said that it is virtually impossible to provide empirical evidence to correlate the registration of fair rents with shortage of accommodation). The absence of rent limits does not, to date, appear to be an adequate inducement since a relatively small number of bodies have applied to the Secretary of State for approval to create assured tenancies. It may well be the case that this is partly due to the fear that future governments might introduce rent limits for assured tenancies: see Chapter 30 for the substantive law on assured tenancies.

Registered housing association tenancy

Although housing associations are non-profit making by definition, the rent payable is nonetheless limited, and the statutory provisions relating to the registration and certification of a fair rent are applicable: see Part VI Rent Act 1977. This means that fair rent procedures must be observed by Housing Associations, and any excess payment of rent may be recovered by the tenant up to two years after it has been paid: s.94(1) Rent Act 1977. Note that the Housing Association Act 1985 does not attempt to consolidate these fair rent provisions by incorporating them.

Secure tenancy

Local housing authorities have the power to 'make such reasonable charges as they may determine for the tenancy or occupation of their houses', and can review rents at any time: s.24(2) Housing Act 1985. Thus in theory, local housing authorities have considerable freedom to set rent levels but, in practice, their wide powers are invariably tempered by political expediency: see Chapter 31 for the substantive law on secure tenancies.

Power to limit rents

The Secretary of State has wide powers to limit rents on dwellings through statutory instrument. For this purpose, rent has the extended meaning of sums payable under a licence. The provisions include existing dwellings and new lettings of dwellings.

FURTHER READING

Housing Law by A.Arden and M.Partington, Chapter 3, on Rent Regulation, Sweet & Maxwell, 1983.

Business tenancies

Contractual term

Market forces have always determined rent levels for business tenancies, and Parliament has never introduced any form of rent regulation for business tenancies during the contractual period of the tenancy. This is because successive governments have sought to promote businesses, and have given commercial men a free hand in negotiating their own terms, including rent.

Renewal:

Rent levels fall to be considered at two stages upon the renewal of a business tenancy:

(a) if a new tenancy is granted, a new rent will have to be set.
(b) it may be necessary to set an interim rent for any continuation tenancy which arises on the end of the term so that landlords can obtain a proper market rent on the leasehold premises for the period of negotiations for a new tenancy – particularly where the negotiations are likely to be prolonged, and the rent payable under the lease has fallen behind market levels.

New tenancy's rent

The rent payable under a new business tenancy may either be agreed between the parties, or determined by the courts applying the formula in s.34 Landlord and Tenant Act 1954. The s.34 formula is based on a hypothetical open market letting by a willing lessor, and is the rent which might reasonably be expected from the holding, having regard to the terms in the lease (except the rent), and disregarding the following:

(a) any effect that the tenant's (or his predecessor's) occupation might have on the rent;
(b) any goodwill attached to the holding by the tenant's business;
(c) any effect of a s.34 improvement. This only relates to tenant's improvements which were carried out voluntarily (rather than as the result of an obligation under the lease): s.34(2). If the improvement was not carried out in the current tenancy, it must satisfy the three following conditions:
    (i) it must have been completed in the twenty-one year period prior to the application for a new tenancy;
    (ii) that the holding affected by the improvement must have been part of a business tenancy(ies) since the improvement was completed;
    (iii) the tenant must not have quit the part of the premises affected by the improvement at the end of the tenancies.

Note that the court has power to include a rent review provision when it determines the rent payable: s.34(3) Landlord and Tenant Act 1954.

Interim rents

The landlord may apply to the court for the determination of an interim rent 'which it would be reasonable for the tenant to pay while the tenancy continues', if either a landlord has given a s.25 notice of termination or the tenant has made a s.26 request for a new tenancy under s.24A Landlord and Tenant Act 1954. Thc new rent will commence on the date on which legal proceedings were begun or the date specified in the s.25 or s.26 notice, whichever is the later.

In determining the rent, the court applies the criteria in s.34 Landlord and Tenant Act 1954 (as if it were determining the rent of a new tenancy) and also considers the current rent. Interim rents are assessed on a yearly tenancy basis: s.24(3) Landlord and Tenant Act 1954. Thus the court approved a deduction of ten per cent from the open market value when assessing the interim rent in *UDS Tailoring Ltd* v. *BL Holdings Ltd* (1982), in order to reflect a yearly tenancy basis.

The principles which are applicable to determine an interim rent are set out in *English Exporters (London) Ltd* v. *Eldonwall Ltd* (1973) where Mr Justice Megarry held that whilst the powers under s.24A are discretionary, they ought generally to be exercised in order to promote justice. He also held that the correct formula was to determine the market rent for a hypothetical yearly letting, on the same terms as the existing lease, without considering the rent for the new hypothetical letting since s.34(1) precludes this. But he added that there was nothing to preclude a consideration of the rent under the existing tenancy. Mr Justice Megarry said that the net effect of the statutory provisions is that interim rents are based on a hypothetical letting of a new yearly tenancy, which has the effect of producing an interim rent which was less than the full market rent (as calculated by the s.34 formula), if having regard to the existing rent, the court felt it reasonable to do so. This formula was approved by the Court of Appeal in *Fawke* v. *Viscount Chelsea* (1979).

Appeals

An appeal against a court's determination of rents and interim rents will only be justified if a substantial wrong or miscarriage of justice has occurred, see: Rules of Supreme Court – Order 59 r. 11(2); and the Court of Appeal judgment in *Halberstam* v. *Tandalco Corporation NV* (1984) where Lord Justice Goff said that the Court of Appeal would not put parties to the delay and expense of a new trial unless the figures arrived at were obviously wrong.

FURTHER READING

See Chapter 24 on the renewal of business tenancies.

Statutory Valuations by A.Baum (Routledge Kegan Paul, 1983, reprinted 1986 with corrections).

Agricultural sector

Agricultural holdings

Both landlords and tenants have the right to apply to an arbitrator to review the rent under the provisions of s.12 of the Agricultural Holdings Act 1986, not more than once every three years. The formula for determining the rent was changed by s.1 Agricultural Holdings Act 1984, from the 12th July 1984, in an effort to enable arbitrators to fix rents at a market level by giving statutory support for what was widely considered to be the general practice of arbitrators, and to limit the scope for legal arguments.

The new rent formula is based on a hypothetical letting by a willing landlord to a willing tenant, after taking into account the following matters: comparable rents, the tenancy's terms, the character, situation and locality of the holding, its productive capacity and its related earning capacity. The arbitrator is directed to disregard: any appreciable element of scarcity in the comparables; any element in the rent which is due to the fact that two holdings can be conveniently combined in a single occupation by the tenant; any effect that allowances or reductions (due to the charging of premiums) have on the rent; tenant's improvements; landlord's grant-aided improvements; the effect of the tenant's occupation; and the effect of dilapidations, deterioration or damage caused or permitted by the tenant.

Agricultural workers

The Rent (Agriculture) Act 1976 makes automatic provision for the rent of a statutory tenancy at the end of the protected tenancy, and not before. Rent for the statutory tenancy does not become payable until the landlord and tenant agree a rent. Where the rent is agreed, it must not exceed the statutory maximum which is at present equal to 1.5 times the rateable value of the dwelling-house at the date of the agreement: s.11 Rent (Agriculture) Act 1976. If there is no such agreement, a provisional rent is set at 1.5 times the rateable value pending an application to register a fair rent under the provisions of Part IV Rent Act 1977. The procedure for registering a fair rent and the criteria for determining it are broadly similar to registering a fair rent in respect of a regulated tenancy (see above): s.13 Rent Act 1977.

FURTHER READING

Institute of Rent Officers Educational Trust Guidance Notes to the Rent (Agricultural) Act 1976.

Chapter 11

Premiums and Service Charges

PREMIUMS

General meaning

Premiums are sums paid for the grant of a lease, and may also be paid on the renewal of a lease. They can be to the lessor's advantage since he will receive a lump sum in advance in return for the grant of a lease. On the other hand, the property market is a volatile one, and one of the parties could be penalised in the long term by agreeing a premium at too high or too low a price, if the market fluctuates more than was envisaged at the time the lease was granted.

Premiums should not be confused with rent, and are conceptually quite different. A premium is the money paid for the purchase of a lease. It is a contractual obligation which is not attached to the leasehold estate: *Hill* v. *Booth* (1930). This means that the obligation is not transferred upon assignment, and landlords cannot distrain for non-payment of a premium. It is not always easy to distinguish rent from a premium, particularly in cases where the premium is paid in instalments: see *Samuel* v. *Salmon and Gluckstein Ltd* (1945). Indeed Pettit argues that:

> 'It is not logically necessary, and there is no decision, that 'rent' and 'premium' are mutually exclusive terms. There has, in fact, been considerable discussion as to whether rent paid in advance constitutes a premium, but the point remains undecided.' (*Private Sector Tenancies*, 1981, at page 253).

Protected tenancies

Prohibitions

The general rule is that the requirement of a premium in return for the grant or assignment of a protected tenancy is illegal. This is because rent regulation would be of little value if landlords could require tenants to pay premiums in addition to rent:

> 'In the context of housing accommodation the most obvious and facile way of operating a black market where rents are controlled is

to demand a premium, i.e. a capital payment in connection with the grant etc. of a tenancy over and above the rent as held statutorily below its true market rate.'

(Per Lord Simon in *Farrell* v. *Alexander* (1976).)

Meaning

For this purpose, a premium is described in wide terms as the payment of any sum by way of a premium or a loan, in addition to the rent. Premiums include any fine or other like sum; or pecuniary consideration in addition to rent. Thus it includes any form of consideration which has a monetary value.

The majority of residential sector landlords require a deposit to cover damage to fittings and furnishings, and to insure against a tenant's non-payment of public utility bills, e.g. gas and electricity. Deposits may amount to a prohibited premium where the deposit either exceeds one-sixth of the annual rent (two months rent) or, in the case of lesser sums, the deposit is unreasonable when taking into account the potential liability in respect of which the deposit is paid: s.128(1) Rent Act 1977.

Grant of protected tenancy

An offence is committed by any person who requires a premium or loan in return for the grant, renewal or continuance of a protected tenancy, by the provisions of s.119 Rent Act 1977: see p.276 in Chapter 27 for the meaning of a protected tenancy. This is wide enough to catch both landlords and their agents: per Lord Wilberforce in *Farrell* v. *Alexander* (1976).

Assignment of protected tenancy

The general rule is that any person who requires or receives a premium or loan as a condition of the assignment of a protected tenancy is guilty of an offence by virtue of the provisions of s.120 Rent Act 1977. The provisions prohibiting the payment of a premium or making of a loan are less stringent, in that there are a greater number of categories of exceptions to the general rule: see s.120(3),(4) Rent Act 1977. For example, a premium required by an assignor in respect of any expenditure which is reasonably incurred in altering the premises or improving the fixtures, is not an illegal premium.

Penalties

Landlords and their agents face fines of up to £100 for requiring or receiving a premium for the grant or assignment of a protected tenancy, and may be required to repay the premium: s.119(3),(4), s.120(6) Rent Act 1977.

Restricted contracts

Similar provisions prohibit the requirement of the payment of a premium for the grant, renewal, continuance or assignment of rights under a restricted contract: see s.122(2), and Chapter 29 on restricted contracts.

Excessive price for furniture

It is perfectly legal for landlords to charge reasonable amounts for the purchase of furniture. But if the price required for the purchase of furniture upon the grant, renewal, continuance or assignment of a protected tenancy or rights under a restricted contract exceeds a reasonable price, the excess will be treated as an illegal premium: see s.123 Rent Act 1977.

FURTHER READING

Housing Law by A. Arden and M. Partington, Sweet and Maxwell (1983) ch.7 'Legal and Illegal Premiums'
Private Sector Tenancies by P.H. Pettit, Butterworths (1981), ch.14 'Premiums etc.'.

SERVICE CHARGES

Meaning

Modern leases usually provide for the payment of a service charge where the leasehold premises make up only one of several units in residential or business premises. These payments reflect the value of services provided by the landlord:

'In modern conveyancing, by far the most usual and most important covenanted sum (or additional rent) is that which refers to the cost or value of repairs, maintenance, and services provided to the tenant, and those sums are here referred to compendiously as "service charges", whether reserved as rent or not.'
Halsbury's *Laws of England*, 4th edition, volume 27, para. 258.)

It is generally more convenient for the landlord to provide a common service to all the tenants in a block of flats, offices, or a shopping development rather than leaving tenants with this responsibility.

Moreover, it enables landlords to maintain a high degree of control and to retain uniform standards of maintenance–which is of particular importance if high calibre tenants are to be attracted.

Residential flats

Service charges are defined for the purpose of the Landlord and Tenant Act 1985, in connection with residential lettings of flats by s.18, as:

> 'An amount payable by a tenant as part of or in addition to the rent
>
> (a) which is payable, directly or indirectly, for services, repairs, maintenance or insurance or the landlord's costs of management, and
>
> (b) the whole or part of which varies or may vary according to the relevant costs.'

'Relevant costs' are the costs or estimated costs which a landlord incurs in relation to a service charge, including overheads and management costs: s.18(2) Landlord and Tenant Act 1985.

Liability to pay

The liability to pay a service charge will arise as a result of a covenant in the lease, and not otherwise. Service charges may be made payable to a third party, e.g. a managing agent or maintenance company. A service charge is a payment which is separate from and additional to rent. But it is possible to describe a service charge expressly as 'rent' in a lease, which has one significant advantage: the widest possible range of remedies for non-payment will then be available to landlords, including distress and re-entry (see below). Landlords can only recover interest on costs incurred in providing services if the lease employs words to that effect: *Boldmark Ltd* v. *Cohen* (1985).

Service charge clauses in commercial leases

There is no agreed published model form of service charge clause, although the Joint Sub-Committee of the Law Society and RICS on model clauses in commercial leases have considered model forms for service charge clauses. However, the sub-committee have set out the following guidelines for service charges in commercial leases.

(1) The definition of the building should include everything to be serviced.
(2) Service charges should be reserved as rent.
(3) If the service charge is a specified percentage of proportion, there should be a provision for variation by the landlord's surveyor to allow for changes in the lettable areas in the building.

(4) The service charge year should be contemporaneous with the landlord's tax year: see 'Tax and the Sinking Fund', a paper published in *Chartered Surveyor Weekly*, 28th October 1982.

(5) The service charge should consist of: the reimbursement of the actual cost incurred by the landlord; a management charge; a sweeping-up provision for incidental expenses reasonably incurred; short-term reserves for periodic redecoration and other expenditure; and a landlord's option to create a replacement fund for renewal. It is recommended that money received for short-term reserves and by way of replacement funds should be kept in a separate interest-bearing account on trust.

(6) Service charge accounts should give a break-down of charges, show the apportionments, and be certified by a qualified accountant. The certificate should be given to the tenant as soon as conveniently possible after the end of the service year. A disputes procedure should be agreed.

(7) Provision should be made for a provisional service charge to be paid in advance on the same date as the payments of rent. The provisional service charge should be a fixed amount in the first year. In subsequent years it could either be based on the amount paid in the preceding year or set by a surveyor.

(8) The landlord, and not the tenant, should bear any refurbishing costs.

(9) The landlord should covenant as follows: to use all reasonable efforts to provide the services; to contribute an amount equal to the service charge in respect of any lettable parts which are not producing a service charge; to return short-term reserves and replacement funds pro rata if the building is demolished or becomes untenantable.

Residential sector

A common cause of complaint by tenants is the level of charges for services. Generally speaking, tenants will have little control over the level of charges for services, although modern leases usually provide that landlords should supply the tenant with relevant information. Special statutory provisions have been introduced in the residential sector, which are only applicable to private sector tenancies of flats, in order to give tenants the right to obtain relevant information and to enable tenants to challenge service charges.

Limitation of charges

Service charges (as defined by s.18 Landlord and Tenant Act 1985) are subject to a dual test of reasonableness by s.19 Landlord and Tenant Act

1985. Only 'reasonably incurred' amounts in respect of services or works of a 'reasonable standard' are payable: s.19(1) Landlord and Tenant Act 1985. Furthermore, only a reasonable amount is payable in cases where the service charge is payable in advance; any adjustment must be made after the costs have been incurred and not before: s.19(2) Landlord and Tenant Act 1985.

If the cost of carrying out work on a block of flats exceeds either £25 per flat or £500 (whichever is greater), at least two estimates must be obtained; one of which must be from a person wholly unconnected with the landlord. The landlord must then give the tenants at least one month's notice of the works and invite comments on the estimates, unless the works are urgently required: s.20 Landlord and Tenant Act 1985. Landlords have a statutory duty to consider any comments or observations which are received: s.20(3)(e).

Summary of relevant costs

Tenants are entitled to ask the landlord, his agent or the person who collects the rent, for a written summary of any relevant costs either on an individual basis or collectively, if there is a recognised tenants' association: s.21 Landlord and Tenant Act 1985. The landlord has a statutory duty to comply with this request within one month or not later than six months after the accounting period: s.21(4) Landlord and Tenant Act 1985. In addition, where there are more than four flats in a building, the costs must be certified as a fair summary which is sufficiently supported by documentation by a qualified accountant: s.21(6) Landlord and Tenant Act 1985.

If the landlord to whom the request is made does not have the relevant information, because the relevant costs relate partly or wholly to costs incurred on behalf of a superior landlord, he has a statutory duty to make a written request to the superior landlord for the relevant information: s.23 Landlord and Tenant Act 1985. The superior landlord must, for his part, reply to this request within a reasonable time: s.23(1)(b).

Inspection of accounts

Tenants who have obtained a summary of relevant costs may then ask to inspect the accounts, receipts, and other documents supporting the summary within six months of receiving it. The landlord is under a statutory duty to provide facilities for this inspection for a two-month period which begins not later than one month after the inspection request is made: s.22(4) Landlord and Tenant Act 1985.

Penalties

Landlords who fail to comply with the statutory duties imposed by ss.21, 22, and 23 above are liable to be fined, unless they have a reasonable excuse: s.25 Landlord and Tenant Act 1985.

Exceptions

The service charge provisions in ss.18–30 Landlord and Tenant Act 1985 do not apply to:

(a) public sector landlords of flats: s.26 Landlord and Tenant Act 1985. But note that ss.45–51 Housing Act 1985 contain restrictions on service charges payable on houses which have been disposed of by local authorities which correspond to ss.18–30 Landlord and Tenant Act 1985.
(b) tenants of Rent Act regulated tenancies who have registered a fair rent, unless the registered rent is a variable rent: s.27 Landlord and Tenant Act 1985. This category of tenant is already sufficiently protected since a rent assessment takes into account any service charge element: s.71(4). The Court of Appeal held, *per curiam*, that the control of registered rent limits gives protected tenants all the protection that they need, in *Legal and General Assurance Society Ltd* v. *Keane* (1978).

Long tenancies at a low rent

Any element of rent which is referable to the provision of services is disregarded when calculating a low rent: s.5(4) Rent Act 1977. If service charges were not disregarded, many long tenancies would no longer qualify as an exception to the Rent Acts on the basis of a 'low rent'.

Business tenants

Business tenants have no statutory protection, and must comply with their leasehold obligations to pay service charges. This can lead to disputes when tenants believe that the standard of service provided is inadequate or where the amount charged seems unreasonable. It is important for tenants to note that landlords sometimes charge for services which are provided but not specifically referred to in a lease. For example, a landlord might appoint a managing agent although the lease is silent on the matter of the agent's fees. If a tenant pays for services over and above those specified in the lease, he cannot recover any sums paid at a later date, unless he challenged this at the time of the payment: see *Concorde Graphics Ltd* v. *Andromeda Investments SA* (1982).

Interest

Landlords who wish to pass on any interest charges on monies which they have borrowed for the purpose of carrying out their leasehold obligations to provide services to tenants, must do so expressly. The courts will not imply a term: see *Frobisher (Second Investments) Ltd* v. *Kiloran Trust Co. Ltd and Another* (1980).

FURTHER READING

Halsbury's *Laws of England*, 4th edition, Butterworths, 1981, volume 27, ch.6 on 'Rent and Service Charges'.

Chapter 12

Recovery of Rent and Related Sums

Arrears of rent may be recovered by a legal action to recover rent as a debt or by the remedy of distress. Related sums, such as premiums and service charges, may be recovered by legal action but not by distress.

ACTION TO RECOVER RENT

An action for rent arrears can be brought by an ordinary action for a debt on either an express or implied covenant to pay rent for a specific sum due under the contract to pay rent. Both the county court and High Court have jurisdiction under different statutory provisions.

County court

General

The County Court has jurisdiction if the claim does not exceed £5000: s.15 County Courts Act 1984. If the claim is less than £500 a county court registrar can act as an arbitrator: s.17 Administration of Justice Act 1977.

Rent action

A new form of action known as a 'rent action' was introduced in 1971 to provide a simplified procedure for the recovery of rent in cases where the tenant is still in occupation of the premises: see the County Court Rules 1981 Part II, Order 24 rules 8–11. A rent action is begun by summons in the County Court for the district in which the leasehold premises are situated; proceedings can be served throught the post. The tenant has the option of either appearing at the hearing or paying the monies due into court.

High Court

The High Court has jurisdiction for claims of more than £5000. High Court actions are commenced by writ.

Defences

There are a number of defences available to an action for rent. The tenant may claim that the rent has been paid; that the rent is statute-barred because it is outside the limitation period; or he may dispute liability e.g. where he has assigned the tenancy. Tenants also commonly withhold payments or rent by way of set-off in cases where they have spent their own monies on repairs when the landlord has refused to carry out his repairing or maintenance liabilities. The law relating to set-off is complex, but as a rule of thumb, the two matters have to be directly connected in order to give rise to a set-off. It would be prudent for a tenant both to warn his landlord in writing first before taking this course of action, and to send him proper estimates which demonstrate that the expenditure was reasonable.

Original lessee

Landlords may recover unpaid rent from the original lessee where the lease has been assigned:

> 'The rule of law is that a lessee remains liable upon his express covenants, notwithstanding an assignment and acceptance by the landlord of rent from the assignee, and there is an implied promise on the part of each successive assignee to indemnify the lessee against breaches of the covenants of the lease in his own time.' (per Lord Esher M.R. in *Baynton* v. *Morgan* (1888).)

Landlords are not entitled to recover rent twice from an assignee and a tenant: see p.86.

Action for use and occupation

A landlord may bring an action to recover compensation for the 'use and occupation' of land: s.14 Distress for Rent Act 1737. These provisions do not apply to tenancies granted by deed. But compensation for use and occupation may be recovered if there is an agreement for a lease: *Elliott, Executor of Thompson* v. *Rogers* (1801). Compensation may be recovered if either the rent was agreed orally or the tenant went into occupation without an agreement fixing the rent: *Arden* v. *Pullen* (1842). The action is based on the tenant's occupation of the premises under a contract where there was an intention to create a landlord and tenant relationship: see *A-G* v. *De Keyser's Royal Hotel Ltd* (1920).

Limitation period

The limitation period for the recovery of rent arrears is six years, which means that only rent arrears which became due within six years of the commencement of the action can be recovered: s.19 Limitation Act 1980.

ACTION FOR RECOVERY OF RELATED SUMS

Related sums, e.g. premiums and service charges, may be recovered by an action on the contract in just the same way as rent arrears.

DISTRESS

Landlords may seize the tenant's goods up to the value of the unpaid rent without the necessity of commencing legal proceedings, under the ancient rules of distress. The goods seized are then generally sold off to meet the rent arrears. Distress is a less popular remedy than hitherto for two main reasons. Firstly, it seems draconian in modern times: see Lord Denning MR's comments in *Abingdon RDC* v. *O'Gorman* (1968). Secondly, some of the goods seized may be protected or privileged from distress. But it is nonetheless an important proprietary remedy if the tenant is insolvent.

Right to distrain

Landlords have a common law right to distrain once rent payable under a landlord and tenant relationship falls into arrears. In practice, this means that the earliest time at which distress is available is the day after the rent is due. The right only applies in respect of unpaid rent, and does not extend to related sums. But a landlord must give the tenant five days to pay off his rent arrears before selling a tenant's goods.

Distrainable goods

The general common law rule is that all personal moveable goods on the leasehold premises are subject to distress. This includes goods belonging to the spouse of the tenant whose rent is in arrears, and goods belonging to a finance company which are being purchased under a hire purchase credit arrangement entitling the tenant to possession. But special rules apply to protect goods owned by sub-tenants and lodgers who may complete a written declaration in the prescribed form stating that the tenant does not own the goods: see s.1 Law of Distress Amendment Act 1908 which affords a degree of protection to goods owned by sub-tenants and lodgers.

Privileged goods

The remedy of distress was never used to strip tenants of all their possessions, and certain categories of property were privileged against distress. Today, the following goods are the subject of absolute privilege from distress:

(a) property in the custody of a tenant who carries on a public trade or business;
(b) tenant's fixtures;
(c) goods in actual use. The law adopted the pragmatic view that a breach of the peace would arise if goods in actual use by the tenant could be distrained, for example tools being used.
(d) clothing, bedding, and the tenant's trade tools up to a value of £50: s.4 Law of Distress Amendment Act 1888; s.124 County Courts Act 1959.
(e) perishable goods; loose money; and wild animals;
(f) agricultural machinery and livestock on the premises for breeding purposes which belong to another person, in the case of agricultural holdings: s.20(1) Agricultural Holdings Act 1948.

The following property is also the subject of an absolute privilege from distress: Crown property; the property of diplomats: see Diplomatic Privileges Act 1964; and property in the custody of the law. Finally, certain goods have a conditional privilege, which means that they can only be distrained in the last resort, if there are no other goods on the premises which can be distrained to meet the entire rent arrears. These include sheep, plough animals, and the tenant's trade tools.

Procedure

A landlord can either distrain personally or employ an authorised bailiff. In the latter case, the landlord must authorise the bailiff in writing by giving him a distress warrant, and obtain a certificate from the county court judge: see the Distress for Rent Rules 1953 printed in the County Court Practice (the Green Book).

A landlord or his authorised bailiff will have to enter the demised premises in order to seize the tenant's chattels. The rule here is that he must enter the premises peacefully in a manner which falls short of breaking into them. Articles should be seized by either actually handling the article and declaring that it is to be distrained (actual seizure), or by stating that it should not be removed until the rent arrears have been paid (constructive seizure). If a landlord is subsequently sued for damages for negligence or misconduct on the part of a bailiff who exceeds his authority, he can recover any damages payable from the bailiff.

The landlord or bailiff should then draw up an inventory of the goods which have been distrained, and include particulars of the amount owed and authorised fees and charges. Notice of the distress should be given to the tenant: see s.1 Distress for Rent Act 1689 and r. 22 Distress for Rent Rules 1953.

The goods should then be impounded either on the tenant's premises or in a safe place for at least five days, after which time they can be sold if the tenant has failed to pay the rent arrears and costs of distraining: s.1 Distress for Rent Act 1689.

FORFEITURE

General

Landlords may wish to combine the recovery of rent arrears with an action for possession founded on forfeiture for breach of covenant to pay rent. Forfeiture is dealt with in detail in Chapter 20 but the special rules relating to non-payment of rent are considered here.

Procedure

Non-payment of rent

Modern leases invariably contain a proviso for re-entry if the rent remains unpaid for more than the specified number of days (usually 21 days). This proviso enables a landlord to forfeit the lease and to evict the tenant. The lease cannot be forfeited for non-payment of rent unless it contains a proviso for re-entry for non-payment. In practice, the courts are generally reluctant to forfeit a lease for non-payment of rent.

Forfeiture proceedings may be commenced without the service of the statutory 's.146 notice' which is otherwise required in forfeiture actions, provided that non-payment of rent is the only ground relied upon for forfeiture of the lease: s.146(11) Law of Property Act 1925. It is for this reason that landlords often describe service charges as rent in arrears in order to avoid the necessity of serving a 's.146 notice'.

Non-payment of related sums

It is necessary to serve a 's.146 notice' before forfeiting a lease for breach of covenant to pay all other related sums which are not described as rent. The notice specifies the arrears, asks the tenant to remedy the position (by making payment), and requires monetary compensation. Some modern leases specify that tenants should meet the legal costs of any forfeiture proceedings, including the issue of a s.146 notice. This means that landlords issue forfeiture proceedings at the tenant's expense, and use this as a weapon in recovering arrears in service charges from recalcitrant tenants who are habitually late in paying their service charges since no tenant relishes the prospect of fighting a forfeiture action.

Mesne profits

If a landlord has commenced proceedings for forfeiture he must be careful not to claim 'rent' since that would affirm the existence of the tenancy: Rules of the Supreme Court Order 18 rule 15/2. The correct approach is for the landlord to claim 'mesne profits' which will normally be equivalent to the rent due since they are assessed on an open market rent. Mesne profits are really no more than a type of damages for trespass.

Waiver

The landlord's right to forfeit will be waived if the lessor treats the lease as continuing when he knows that there has been a breach of covenant, e.g. where a landlord or his agent demands and accepts rent: per Lord Justice Buckley in *Central Estates Ltd.* v. *Woolgar* (No 2) (1972).

Relief

The courts have traditionally exercised wide powers in order to grant tenants relief from forfeiture for non-payment of rent. These powers are now contained in statutory provisions. There are special provisions relating to relief for non-payment of rent in addition to the general power to grant relief from forfeiture as contained in s.146(2) Law of Property Act 1925: see Chapter 20, pp.220–1. The High Court and county court have different powers to grant relief, which amount to the same thing in practice. The county court's forfeiture jurisdiction is limited to cases where the net annual value for rating of the land is within the county court's forfeiture jurisdiction, i.e. does not exceed £1000.

County court jurisdiction

By legal action: Section 138 of the County Courts Act 1984 provides tenants with automatic relief from forfeiture in two situations. First of all, a lease will not be forfeited on the ground of non-payment of rent if the tenant pays the rent arrears, together with the landlord's costs, into court five clear days before the action is heard (thus dispensing with the necessity for a hearing): s.138 County Courts Act 1984 as amended by s.55 Administration of Justice Act 1985. If, however, the landlord has brought forfeiture proceedings on other grounds, the court does have power to order forfeiture.

Where there is a hearing, the court must grant possession if it is satisfied that the landlord is entitled to forfeit the lease. But the tenant may still be able to obtain relief from forfeiture at this late stage provided that he pays into court the rent arrears together with the costs of the proceedings within a specified period which will not be less than four weeks from the date of the order: s.138(5) County Courts Act 1984. Failure to pay the arrears in time will ban the tenant from seeking further relief: *Di Palma* v. *Victoria Square Property Co. Ltd and Others* (1984).

By peaceable re-entry: The county court has jurisdiction to grant relief from forfeiture for non-payment of rent, if the landlord has forfeited the lease and re-entered peaceably. The tenant must apply for relief within six months of the date of re-entry.

High court jurisdiction

By legal action: The High Court has jurisdiction to grant relief against forfeiture for non-payment of rent under the provisions of s.38 Supreme Court of Judicature Act 1981 if the landlord has taken High Court proceedings for forfeiture. A mortgagee is entitled to claim relief from forfeiture during any High Court proceedings for forfeiture for non-payment of rent.

Six months rent arrears: Sections 210–212 of the Common Law Procedure Act 1852 contain special provisions where the rent due is six months in arrears. In this situation a landlord is entitled to re-enter unless there are sufficient goods on the premises to meet the arrears. However, any order for possession will be stayed for a period of six months, giving the tenant that amount of time to apply for relief: s.210 Common Law Procedure Act 1852. In any event, the tenant or his assignee is automatically entitled to relief from forfeiture if he pays off the arrears and costs before the hearing for possession: s. 212 Common Law Procedure Act 1852.

By peaceable re-entry: The High Court has equitable jurisdiction to grant relief from forfeiture for non-payment of rent where the landlord has re-entered peaceably. The tenant should make his application within six months of the date of re-entry: s.38 Supreme Court Act 1981. But this is not an inflexible rule, and a few days outside this period will not necessarily be fatal to the tenant's success: *Thatcher* v. *C. H. Pearce & Sons (Contractors) Ltd* (1968).

Interested third parties: A mortgagee or sub-tenant has the same powers to apply for relief as a tenant. It may be the case that there has been a forfeiture by peaceable entry, and that this has not been brought to the attention of an interested mortgagee or sub-tenant until after possession has been taken. Section 38 of the Supreme Court of Judicature Act 1981 only gives the High Court powers to give relief in the forfeiture proceedings themselves, and in any event, does not give the High Court any powers to grant relief to a third party in the case of a peaceable entry. This means that a mortgagee or other party must, therefore, ask the court to grant relief on the basis of its inherent equitable jurisdiction: *Ladup Ltd* v. *Williams & Glyn's Bank PLC* (1985). Of course, the mortgagee or sub-tenant can ask for relief in the normal way if he knows about the forfeiture proceedings under either s.38 (above) or s.146(4) Law of Property Act 1925, which is applicable in all forfeiture proceedings: see Chapter 20, pp.220–1. Finally, if more than six months' rent is in arrears, the interested third party has six months in which to apply for relief: s.210 Common Law Procedure Act 1852.

Tenancies regulated by statute

Many of the statutory schemes contain provisions dealing with the effect of non-payment of rent. Each of the schemes operates its own rules regarding the effect of non-payment of rent, and the two following examples serve to illustrate the breadth of treatment of the issue by the legislature.

Residential sector

All statutory tenancies in the residential sector include special provisions restricting the landlord's right to forfeit for non-payment of rent. For example, proceedings for possession of Rent Act regulated tenancies for non-payment of rent must be framed in terms of a Case 1 ground for possession: s.98, and Case 1 of Schedule 15 Rent Act 1977. Judges have a wide discretion to refuse a landlord's request for possession under these provisions. (See Chapter 20 on Termination for a detailed consideration of these restrictions.)

Renewing business tenancies

Persistent delay in paying rent due is one of the statutory grounds for opposing the renewal of a business tenancy: s.30(1)(b) Landlord and Tenant Act 1954.

Chapter 13

Rent Review

GENERAL

Objectives

The vast majority of modern commercial leases (and some residential and agricultural leases) contain rent review provisions. The object of these provisions is to provide for regular reviews of the rent payable under a lease on an 'upwards only' basis. The review periods used to be at intervals of seven years, but five years now appears to be more common whilst shorter periods of two and three years are certainly not rare. These provisions became fashionable during the seventies, as landlords attempted to maintain rent levels during a period of rampant inflation, although they do feature in many earlier leases. There are two main methods which landlords can employ in order to ensure a full market rent return on leasehold premises: either by granting short leases which are only renewable in return for an increased rent (the practice on the continent and in America); alternatively, by granting longer leases with provisions for regular rent reviews.

Achieving the objective of raising the rent mid-term to current market levels is not always an easy task, and presents two major problems.

Procedural problems

A rent review is initiated by the service of a 'trigger notice'; this is generally served by a landlord who wishes to raise the rent, although there is no reason why a tenant cannot initiate the procedure himself if he wishes to know the level of rent increase in advance. This triggers off the rent review procedure. The other party will then be required to respond to this by serving a counter-notice setting out his intentions.

The early litigation on rent review concerned the validity of trigger notices and procedural problems relating to the timing and serving of notices. Rent review provisions used to be notorious for their bad drafting. In particular, many rent review provisions failed to include any contingency provisions setting out what would happen if the rent review did not take place on time, or where one or other party failed to serve notice on time. Rent review machinery is a matter of contract.

Valuation–legal principles

Modern rent review problems concern the legal principles which should be applied in order to value the new rent level. The problem here is that the leasehold premises have to be valued on the basis of a purely hypothetical letting. In other words, the valuer must perform the mental exercise of assuming that the premises are available for letting to a willing tenant on the open market which involves a number of notional assumptions. For example, what length of term should be notionally assumed in a twenty year business lease with five year rent reviews at the last review? Should the notional term be equivalent to the original term (twenty years) or the remainder of the term (five years)? If the lease specifies the review period as the notional term, should account be taken of the possibility of a continuation of a business lease under the provisions of Part II Landlord and Tenant Act 1954? The length of the notional term will affect the valuation of the lease. Moreover, it does not necessarily follow that the longer notional term will achieve the higher rent since longer terms may involve onerous repairing obligations which will devalue the lease.

Construction

Normal contract law principles apply to the construction of rent review provisions. In addition, the Vice-Chancellor, Browne-Wilkinson, has given some guidance in construing rent review clauses in a lease in *The British Gas Corporation* v. *Universities Superannuation Scheme Ltd.* (1986). The Vice-Chancellor stated that it was proper to give effect to the underlying commercial purpose of a rent review clause and to construe the words so as to give effect to that purpose by requiring future rent reviews to be taken into account in fixing the open market rental under the hypothetical letting. Vice-Chancellor Browne-Wilkinson said that:

> 'Landlords, tenants and their valuers need to know what is the right basis of valuation without recourse to lawyers, let alone the courts. The question cannot be left to turn on the terms of each lease without the basic approach being certain'.

NO RENT REVIEW PROVISION

Many older leases will contain no provisions for rent review, in which case the general rule is that the rent can only be increased by appropriate negotiation and agreement. The landlord must provide some consideration for any agreed increase in rent; one common form of consideration is the carrying out of repairs, improvements or alterations. Any such increased rent operates as a collateral contract, i.e. a contract which is separate from the lease but connected with it. This is significant upon an assignment of the lease since the collateral contract will only be transferred upon assignment if it is expressly assigned: *Hoby* v. *Roebuck and Palmer* (1816).

It may be possible to achieve the objective of increasing the rent by terminating the lease prematurely, and granting a new lease at a higher rent with rent review provisions. This will require the tenant's consenting to the surrender of the residue of the existing lease in return for the grant of a new lease.

Landlords of the following residential sector tenancies may increase rent levels unilaterally without terminating the tenancy:

(a) Registered rents of regulated tenancies may be increased at two year intervals: s.67(3) Rent Act 1977
(b) Local housing authorities may review rents from time to time and increase rents, unless the tenancy is a secure tenancy: ss.24(2), 25 Housing Act 1985.
(c) Rents of secure tenancies may be increased pursuant to a clause in the lease or agreement creating the tenancy, or in an agreement varying it: s.102(3) Housing Act 1985. But the rent is not to be increased on account of improvements carried out by the tenant: s.101 Housing Act 1985.

RENT REVIEW PROVISIONS

Common forms

The inclusion of rent review provisions in commercial leases is a relatively recent legal phenomenon so that each rent review case will turn on its own particular rent review provisions; the standardisation of rent review provisions is desirable. A rent review clause should:

(a) define the rent review period;
(b) if a time-table is provided, state whether the time-limits are to be adhered to strictly. The legal presumption here is that 'time is not of the essence', i.e. the time limits do not have to be complied with;
(c) set out the formula for ascertaining what rent is to be payable in each review period on an upwards only basis e.g. open market rental values current at the review date;
(d) provide the machinery for assessing the new rent levels. If this is by reference to a surveyor's opinion, state whether the assessment is to be by way of an independent valuation as an expert or whether the surveyor is to act as an arbitrator in the event of a dispute;
(e) state what matters are to be disregarded in the assessment, e.g.

tenant's improvements; goodwill attached to the tenant's business; restrictions on user;

(f) state the terms of the notional letting which are to be assumed, e.g. length of term; the existence of a willing tenant; a letting with vacant possession; tenant's compliance with leasehold obligations, e.g. repairing obligation;

(g) incorporate provisions to deal with disputes, including matters relating to the payment of an interim rent in the event of a delay and final adjustments.

ARBITRATION

Rent review clauses often provide for a process for settling rent review disputes which involves referring the matter of dispute to a third party, an arbitrator, for a binding decision. Arbitration clauses are commonly invoked where the parties fail to reach agreement on the rent payable, whereupon an arbitrator will be appointed to set the new rent level.

Arbitration is a specialist area governed by the Arbitration Acts 1950 and 1979. One statutory provision which is of importance in the context of rent review is s.27 Arbitration Act 1950. If a rent review agreement provides for an arbitration clause for tenants and sets time limits on commencing arbitration proceedings, s.27 Arbitration Act 1950 empowers the High Court to extend the time limit where 'undue hardship would otherwise be caused'. Tenants who refer a rent review dispute to arbitration outside the time limits set out in the leases can invoke s.27 if the circumstances would result in undue hardship: see *Pittalis* v. *Sherefettin* (1986) for a modern interpretation of s.27 Arbitration Act 1950 by the Court of Appeal. An appeal can be made where there is real doubt whether the arbitrator was right in the conclusion he reached: *Lucas Industries* v. *Welsh Development Agency* (1986).

MODEL FORM

The Law Society and the Royal Institution of Chartered Surveyors publish model forms of rent review clauses for a wide range of commercial leases ranging from poor quality multi-tenanted buildings to single tenant lettings of large modern properties with complex arrangements for the provisions of services. The current 1985 edition supersedes the 1980 forms in their entirety. The model forms provide for the determination of rent upon rent review where the parties have failed to reach agreement. They all contain alternative provisions for (a) upwards only review and (b) upwards or downwards review. Upwards only rent review provisions ensure that the rent can only be increased upon rent review. An upwards or downward clause enables rent to be increased or decreased so that the clause accurately reflects the market conditions prevailing at rent review.

The 1985 edition contains three main variants as follows:

Variation A, which provides for the determination of rent by arbitration. Arbitration can be a lengthy drawn-out procedure where the arbitrator hears evidence from both sides before arriving at a binding decision. One flaw in the arbitration procedure is that there is no provision for the consolidation of arbitrations with the same subject matter. Thus disputes arise out of a number of rent reviews in the same premises, but being under different leases, the disputes cannot be heard together.

Variation B, which provides for the determination of rent by an independent valuer acting as an expert. The idea here is that a quick expert decision can be obtained. However, since each party has a right to make representations, the expert may be asked to act as a quasi-arbitrator and settle disputes when faced with conflicting representations.

Variation C, which provides for the determination of rent by an independent valuer acting as an expert (at the landlord's option).

LEGAL PRINCIPLES

Time limits

The vast majority of the early rent review clauses set out a time-table for the purpose of giving effect to the review, specifying a review date and mapping out a time-table for the service of notices. The landmark case is the House of Lords decision in *United Scientific Holdings Ltd* v. *Burnley Borough Council; Cheapside Land Development Co. Ltd* v. *Messels Service Co.* (1977) (two appeals were heard together). The House of Lords held in *United Scientific* that the legal presumption is that 'time is not of the essence'. This is sometimes referred to as 'the general presumption'. In other words, the time-table specified in the review clause for the completion of the various steps for determining the rent payable in respect of the period following the review date is not of the essence of the contract.

This principle can be illustrated in the context of the *United Scientific* case where rent for each review period was to be determined during the year immediately preceding the review date. Burnley Borough Council served notice to review the rent six weeks out of time. The issue was whether the rent review clause conferred an option on the landlord. If it did, then the rule that time is of the essence would apply, and the landlord would have to wait until the next review period before reviewing the rent. The House of Lords expressly overruled the earlier authority, namely *Samuel Properties (Developments)* v. *Hayek* (1972), when they held that the rent review clause could not be construed as an option. The clause simply provided machinery for setting the rent review in motion. Since there was nothing in the lease to displace the general presumption, Burnley Borough Council were entitled to review the rent outside the prescribed time limits.

The *United Scientific* decision is noteworthy not least because of its generous construction of rent review provisions. Landlords who have missed a date or made a mistake about a date will nonetheless be able to review the rent, unless one of the following exceptions to the general presumption applies. It has been argued that this decision is part of a new trend on the part of the courts to favour a wide rather than a narrow construction of clauses in leases: see 'Some Aspects of Rent Review: An Alternative Slant' an article by P.F.Smith in *Conveyancer and Property Lawyer* (1979), at page 10. This is in direct contrast to Parliament's pro-tenant legislation, and will be welcomed by landlords with badly drafted leases.

Time of the essence

The House of Lords in *United Scientific* stated that the general presumption would not apply in the three following circumstances.

Contra-indications

Time will be of the essence if the wording of the lease contains a contra-indication to the general presumption, e.g. the lease specifies that time is of the essence for the whole or part of the rent review machinery: see *C. Bradley Ltd* v. *Telefusion Ltd* (1981). In *Drebbond Ltd* v. *Horsham District Council* (1978) the lease included an arbitration provision whereby the landlord could serve an arbitration notice (if the rent could not be agreed) within three months of the date of service of the trigger notice 'but not otherwise'. Vice-Chancellor Megarry held that these words made time of the essence.

Interrelationship with an option

Time is of the essence where the rent review clause is interlocked with another clause conferring an option which has to be exercised within strict time limits. This occurred in *Al Saloom* v. *Shirley James Travel Services Ltd* (1981) where the lease contained a rent review clause which was interrelated with a tenant's break clause. A 'break clause' gives a tenant the option of breaking or determining the lease mid-term, and it is subject to the general rule regarding options, i.e. time is of the essence. The Court of Appeal held that time was of the essence for the rent review procedure because of the interrelationship between the provisions. This decision is important for tenants who may wish to break a lease mid-term when the new rent level becomes known. The decision was applied by a differently constituted Court of Appeal presided over by Sir John Donaldson in *Legal & General Assurance (Pensions Management) Ltd* v. *Cheshire County Council* (1984).

However, the presumption that time is not of the essence will not invariably be rebutted if there is a correlation between a rent review clause and a break clause. The Court of Appeal held that the presence of a break clause did not make time of the essence in *Metrolands Investments Ltd* v. *J.H. Dewhurst Ltd* (1986) because the date of one of the relevant events was substantially outside the control of the landlords.

Surrounding circumstances

Time is of the essence where the surrounding circumstances negative the general presumption. There are some circumstances in which a landlord will be prevented from exercising his right to review the rent where his conduct gives rise to an estoppel, i.e. his conduct is such that it would be inequitable for him to rely on the rent review provisions out of time. For example, Tinker runs a shoe repair shop in a run-down urban area which is currently undergoing re-development. Tinker's lease contains a rent review provision. He is worried about the new rent which he may be asked to pay, given the fact that the re-development programme is attracting new businesses into the area at higher rents than hitherto. Consider the following hypothetical problems:

(i) Tinker's landlord told Tinker that he was not going to review the rent. Tinker (relying on this) made no provision for accrued rent.
(ii) Tinker's lease contains an absolute prohibition on assignment.
(iii) There is no provision for the initiation of a rent review by Tinker.

Delay: Perhaps the clearest illustration of the last principle is delay. The Court of Appeal in the *United Scientific* case were concerned about the possibility of landlords delaying a rent review. Accordingly, they held that the time limits for rent review must be observed strictly. Otherwise it would be to the detriment to the tenant since he would not know what his rent would be in advance of the date on which it started to accrue. One consequence of this might be that a tenant would have to assign the residue of the lease at the new rent and still be unable to pay the rent which accrued in the interim. Lord Diplock replied to this argument in the House of Lords (which reversed the Court of Appeal decision) when he said that:

> 'For my part, I find this unrealistic, if only because under this particular clause the tenant can initiate the review procedure himself and unless there is some unforeseen delay on the part of the arbitrator, has it in his power to ensure that the new rent is determined before the stipulated date'.

Lord Diplock's argument has to be considered in the light of modern practice. The RICS and Law Society Joint Committee now recommend that strict time limits should be avoided as far as possible in the light of the decision in *United Scientific*; only the rent review periods being specified since the general presumption renders most time-tables impotent. This gives the landlord a relatively free hand in selecting the best date for the initiation of rent review proceedings unless a tenant has the power to initiate proceedings himself. Hardship can clearly be caused where landlords delay their rent reviews and then review the rent well after the rent review period.

It has subsequently been argued in the Court of Appeal, in *Amherst* v. *James Walker (Goldsmith & Silversmith) Ltd* (1983), that a landlord's trigger notice was invalid on the basis that the delay in serving it was unreasonable. Lord Justice Oliver reviewed the authorities and said that:

> 'In my judgment...even delay plus hardship to the tenant would not disentitle the landlord to exercise the right which he has, on the true construction of the contract, unless the combination amounted to an estoppel'.

The Court of Appeal in Amherst's case held that the four year delay in serving the trigger notice was not unreasonable. Unreasonable delay means more than 'prolonged delay' and Lord Justice Oliver said in *Amherst* that it expresses:

> 'the notion either of delay for which no acceptable reason can be advanced or delay which no reasonable man would incur acting in his own interest'.

Note that it has been argued that there is now no logical reason to prevent landlords from stacking up reviews and exercising them all at once or after the end of the lease's term; see 'Jam today and jam tomorrow' an article by S. Murdoch in vol. 267 Estates Gazette at p.525.

VALUATIONS–LEGAL PRINCIPLES

Rent review valuations cannot easily be impugned: *Hudson ('A') Pty Ltd* v. *Legal & General Life of Australia* (1986).

The valuation of a rent on a rent review requires an assessment of the rent payable under the lease, and this necessarily involves a number of assumptions, e.g. the length of the notional term to be valued. To this extent, the exercise is hypothetical in nature. Recent cases have explored the legal principles which should be applied and have set out certain parameters. The main rule is that the intention of the lease as evidenced by its wording is paramount. The exercise is purely objective and based on a hypothetical letting rather than equitable considerations of fairness as between an individual landlord and tenant:

> '...the test of what is a reasonable rent (and the same must apply to fair rent) for the premises, is something to be decided, not as between the particular landlord and tenant, who are parties to the proceedings, but in relation to a hypothetical letting of the premises.'
>
> (Per Sir David Cairns in *99 Bishopsgate Ltd* v. *The Prudential Assurance Company Ltd* (1985).)

But it is now clear that it is proper for the effect of future rent reviews to be taken into account in fixing the open market rental under the hypothetical letting: *The British Gas Corporation* v. *Universities Superannuation Scheme Ltd* (1986).

No detailed reference to valuation methods will be mentioned in this chapter since valuations is a subject which is beyond the purview of this book, save for three general observations. Firstly, in practice, valuers assess rent on the basis of comparable properties. Secondly, those advising upon a rent review should consider the express provisions of the rent review provisions carefully in order to determine the correct basis for valuation and know what matters should be taken into account or disregarded. For example, allowance will be made if a lease contains an absolute prohibition against assignment. But there will be no deduction for an obligation to reinstate at the end of the term: *Pleasurama Properties Ltd* v. *Leisure Investments (West End) Ltd* (1986). Thirdly, in the context of some leases it may be appropriate for the parties to leave it to the valuer on each review to decide, subject only to the specific directions given to him, what terms and conditions he would in the circumstances then obtaining, regard as reasonable: *Basingstoke and Deane Borough Council* v. *Host Group Ltd* (1986). Finally, *Halberstam* v. *Tandalco Corpn NV* (1985) is a useful case on preparing valuations.

The notional term

The rent review clause should specify what length of term is to be assumed notionally for rent review purposes since this will affect the valuation of the new rent, e.g. whether the term should be assumed to be the residue of the term or the rent review period. If the notional term of a business tenancy is relatively short, account must also be taken of the possibility of the term being renewed under the provisions of Part II Landlord and Tenant Act 1954. It has been held that the valuer, whilst taking account of this possibility, should not add on a further term which may be granted under Part II in *Pivot Properties Ltd* v. *The Secretary of State for the Environment* (1979).

If the rent review provisions fail to specify the notional term it may be possible for the lease to be rectified if it is clear that the parties contemplated a particular term which had inadvertently been omitted in drafting the lease. In *Boots the Chemist Ltd* v. *Street* (1983) the lease specified seven yearly rent reviews although the parties had intended to review every five years. In those circumstances the court held that rectification would be granted because of the clear evidence of the mistake, and the fact that the lease failed to represent the parties' common intention.

Notional user

The rent review provisions should state whether or not the notional letting is to be on identical terms to the current lease in respect of restrictions on user, e.g. whether the class of tenant or type of business use is to be restricted. Most leases contain restrictions on user, and these may have the effect of depressing the rent. This exercise may involve valuers in the complex questions of the proper interpretation to be placed on a lease.

The judiciary adopt the approach of attempting to give effect to the precise terms of the lease. Thus in *Plinth Property Investments Ltd* v. *Mott, May & Anderson* (1979) the Court of Appeal assumed that the provisions of the lease were to be enforced and held that the arbitrator was correct in taking into account the depressing effect of a restriction on user to offices used in connection with the lessee's business as Consulting Engineers. Accordingly, the tenant achieved a thirty-one per cent discount: compare with *Law Land Co. Ltd* v. *The Consumers Association Ltd* (1980) discussed at p.131.

A use for premises may be notionally assumed notwithstanding the physical state of the premises. In *Trusthouse Forte Albany Hotels Ltd* v. *Daejan Investments Ltd* (1980) the Strand Palace Hotel's rent review clause provided that rent was to be assessed on the basis that an area of the hotel was 'available for letting' for shopping and banking, despite the fact that a substantial conversion would be required to achieve this use. It was held that the premises could be assumed to be on offer with vacant possession for this use (but not physically suitable for this use). This meant that the premises could be valued in their existing physical state. The Court of Appeal went further in *Bovis Group Pension Fund Ltd* v. *G.C. Flooring & Furnishers Ltd* (1984), to the tenant's detriment, when they held that a clause which provided that the rent was to be valued on the assumption that 'the demised premises might reasonably be expected to be let for office purposes' was to be given effect to. The Court of

Appeal held that the parties' intentions envisaged an agreed use, and the premises must be valued on that basis, even though that meant assuming that planning permission had been given to convert the building to office use. But an assumption by a valuer that a user clause restricted the use of premises was rejected in *Sydenham (J.T.) & Co. Ltd* v. *Enichem Elastomers Ltd* (1987).

Rent assessment

Rent will be assessed according to the provisions of the lease which may be onerous from the tenant's standpoint. The high water mark of the strict construction of rent review clauses is to be found in the House of Lords decision in *Ponsford* v. *H.M.S. Aerosols Ltd* (1978) where it was held that the new rent was to be assessed with regard to the extensive improvements which the tenant had carried out. The criteria for the valuation were purely objective and the final outcome of the case took no account of what was fair and reasonable to the parties: *Ponsford's* case has been distinguished at first instance in *Lear* v. *Blizzard* (1983).

Concept of willing tenant

Since a rent review exercise has the primary object of achieving a market rent, notional assumptions such as 'open market rent' and 'willing tenant' are frequently employed to achieve this end. In *Law Land Co. Ltd* v. *The Consumers Association Ltd* (1980) the rent review clause provided that the rent was to be that which might reasonably be obtained on the 'open market' even though the user clause restricted the use to Consumer Association offices and its associated organisations. The Court of Appeal held that the user clause could be ignored for rent review purposes since the rent review clause clearly envisaged the existence of an open market and, by implication, a willing tenant. The tenant's rent was valued on the basis of open market competition with no discount for the restrictive use. Incidentally, the main distinction between *Plinth Property* (above) and *Law Land* is that it was accepted that in *Plinth Property* the restrictive user clause would limit the class of possible assignees to civil engineering consultancy businesses whereas in *Law Land* the lease provided that the use could be changed with the landlord's prior written consent.

A different problem arose in *99 Bishopsgate Ltd* v. *The Prudential Assurance Co. Ltd* (1985). In *99 Bishopsgate*, the arbitrator was asked to determine a 'fair yearly rent' on the basis of vacant possession. The rent review provisions directed the rent to be assessed on the basis of vacant possession of the entire building, which was a substantial tower block. It was held that the tenants ought to have the equivalent of a discount for a notional rent free period of sixteen months since the effect of such a large amount of prestigious accommodation flooding the market would be that high calibre tenants would normally be able to negotiate these favourable terms.

If examination of the appropriate open market shows no 'willing lessee' at any price, the formula should not be construed as requiring a willing lessee to be invented–there is no justification for incorporating a wholly unreal factor into the hypothetical exercise demanded by rent review: per Michael Wheeler QC, sitting as a deputy judge in *Dennis and Robinson Ltd* v. *Kiossos Establishment* (1986).

Matters to be disregarded

Valuers may be specifically directed to disregard certain matters for rent review purposes, such as improvements. However, the Vice-Chancellor has recently stated that no literal effect could be given to words requiring all provisions as to rent to be disregarded: *British Gas Corporation* v. *Universities Superannuation Scheme Ltd* (1986).

Improvements

Improvements are an example of a common disregard. Indeed, it would be nonsensical for landlords to include tenant's improvements in the assessment of the rent since this would eventually deter tenants from carrying out improvements of their own volition. Unimproved properties may be used as a comparable for assessing the rent; see *Estate Projects Ltd* v. *Greenwich London Borough* (1979).

Express references to the disregard of improvements will be enforced where the improvement is carried out by the tenant. But *Ponsford's* case (above) is authority for the proposition that the courts will not imply 'disregards' in the absence of an express reference to the matter which is to be disregarded.

Section 34 Landlord and Tenant Act 1954 (as amended) is usually incorporated into commercial leases. Section 34(1)(c) provides for the disregard of improvements when reviewing the rent for a new business tenancy granted under that Act. However, for this purpose the improvements must have been carried out under a tenancy. Voluntary improvements carried out by a tenant under an earlier lease cannot be disregarded: *Brett* v. *Brett Essex Golf Club Ltd* (1986). In *Euston Centre Properties Ltd* v. *H. & J. Wilson Ltd* (1982) the tenant had improved the premises prior to the grant of a lease under a licence agreement. But it was held that at the time the improvements were carried out the tenant was a licensee and not the tenant under the new lease, and that accordingly the improvements could be taken into account: compare the decision in *Hambros Bank Executor & Trustee Co. Ltd* v. *Superdrug Stores Ltd* (1985) (see p.134). Improvements carried out under a statutory obligation cannot be disregarded in a lease containing the s.34 disregard: *Forte & Co. Ltd* v. *General Accident Life Assurance Ltd* (1986).

FURTHER READING

See 'Rent Reviews–II' by C.Meaney (1982) 264 EG 225, and 'Theory and Malpractice' by R.Lyons (1983) 265 EG 451, for an introduction to the valuation of improvements at a rent review. 'Disregarding Improvements' legal note by S.Murdoch (1986) 279 EG 75.

Other disregards

In *Jefferies and Others* v. *O'Neill and Others* (1984) the clause stipulated that rent should be assessed on an open market basis to a willing lessee. The tenant argued that the premises could not be let to anyone else since access to the first floor leasehold premises could only be gained through the tenant's adjoining premises. But it was held that the rent should be assessed on the basis of an implied disregard of the fact that access was limited, applying *Law Land* (1980) (above), where Lord Justice Brighton had said that: 'Some modification has to be made to the strict wording of the rent review clause if it is to work.'

Deeming provisions

Clauses sometimes provide for rent to be 'deemed' to be an open market rent or the rent specified by the landlord, but there are pitfalls here. The danger of deeming provisions is illustrated by *Henry Smith's Charity Trustees* v. *AWADA Trading and Promotion Services Ltd* (1984) where the clause set out a strict time-table for the service of a landlord's trigger notice and tenant's counter-notice. The clause provided that the amount stated in the landlord's notice would be deemed to be the market rent if the tenant failed to serve a counter-notice in time. Upon service of a counter-notice, the landlord should apply for the appointment of a surveyor to assess the market rent. If the landlord failed to appoint a surveyor (in the event of a dispute), the rent would be deemed to be that in the tenant's counter-notice. The landlord failed to appoint a surveyor within the time limits. The Court of Appeal held that since the parties had specified what would happen if the strict time-table was not complied with, time was of the essence, and the landlords were not entitled to a review.

The decision in the *Henry Smith's* case was distinguished in *Mecca Leisure Ltd* v. *Renown Investments* (1984) where the clause provided that the tenant was deemed to have accepted the rent specified in the landlord's trigger notice if he failed to serve a counter-notice. The Court of Appeal in *Mecca* held that time was not to be of the essence for the service of the tenant's counter-notice. The apparent conflict between these two Court of Appeal authorities was examined in *Taylor Woodrow Property Co. Ltd* v. *Lonrho Textiles Ltd* (1985), on similar facts to *Mecca*, where it was held that the Court of Appeal decisions could be reconciled on the ground that the deeming provisions were two-way in the *Henry Smith's* case and one-way (applying to the tenant only) in *Mecca* and *Taylor Woodrow*. Thus time was not of the essence in the latter cases.

Post review evidence

It has been held that an arbitrator was right to take into account evidence of a comparable rent which was agreed after the rent review date in *Segama N.V.* v. *Penny Le Roy Ltd* (1984).

Interest

A landlord is not entitled to interest where a revised rent is determined after the review date unless the lease makes provision for payment of interest: *Shield Properties & Investments Ltd* v. *Anglo Overseas Transport Co. Ltd (No. 2)* (1986).

THE FUTURE

It is clear that rent review litigation has made a tremendous impact on landlord and tenant law. Landlords who favoured tight restrictions on user in order to retain a firm control of leasehold property are now reconsidering the position in the light of *Plinth Property* (1979) above. Restrictions on user must now either be reduced or rent review clauses must be drafted so as to disregard their effect on rent assessment.

Tenants, for their part, will always find artificial user clauses and the taking into acount of tenants' improvements objectionable. The strict approach to the construction of onerous clauses has offered little hope to tenants. However, the decision by Mr Justice Scott in *Hambros Bank Executor & Trustee Co. Ltd* v. *Superdrug Stores Ltd* (1985) contains evidence of the fact that some judges are prepared to abandon a strict construction in favour of equitable principles. Mr Justice Scott rejected the landlord's argument that improvements carried out by a prospective tenant do not fall to be disregarded under the lease's disregard provisions because the lease was not yet executed; the effect was a difference of £3000 per year. Mr Justice Scott said that:

> 'It is near to being, in my view, an unconscionable attempt by a landlord to take advantage of a situation which it has itself encouraged by consenting to its tenant going into possession and commencing the shopfitting works in advance of the lease'.

FURTHER READING

Casebook on Rent Review and Lease Renewal by D.Brahams and M. Pawlowski, published by Collins, 1986.

Chapter 14

Repairing and Maintenance Obligations

OVERVIEW

Liabilities to repair and maintain impose onerous obligations on the repairing party. It is not, therefore, surprising that this area provides ample material for landlord and tenant disputes. Impecunious tenants, greedy landlords, and poor relations between tenants and estate managers only fuel the fire, particularly in the residential sector where a large amount of housing stock is of sufficient antiquity as to require major repairs. If a dispute arises, there is no easy procedure for its resolution in the absence of express arbitration provisions. The law in this area is complex and in need of urgent reform and codification along the lines suggested by the Law Commission in 1975: see pp.326–7. Codification is desirable in order to streamline the many common law principles which are uneasily juxtaposed with statutory provisions designed to protect tenants from onerous obligations. But the adventurous attempt by Lord Denning MR to introduce terms into contracts in anticipation of the legislative recommendations of the Law Commission has been disapproved: see *Liverpool City Council* v. *Irwin* (1976) per Lord Wilberforce.

The question of who is obliged to repair and maintain leasehold premises is a mixed question of fact and law. The general principles and their interrelationship may be summarised as follows.

EXPRESS OBLIGATIONS

The general rule is that the parties are free to reach express agreement as to their respective obligations.

Tenant's obligations

Tenants will commonly be required to enter into a number of separate and distinct repairing and maintenance obligations which will generally include the following covenants: a covenant to keep and leave the leasehold premises in good repair; a covenant entitling the landlord or his agents to enter the premises to view the state of repair upon reasonable notice; and a covenant to repair defects within a specified time (usually two to three months after being given notice). Additional related obligations include: a covenant to paint the interior and/or exterior with good quality paint at specified intervals of time; and a covenant to clean external windows.

In the case of buildings in multiple occupation it is usual to find the following covenants: mutual covenants detailing arrangements for the repair and maintenance of the common parts; a covenant to give neighbouring tenants adequate notice of any repair work to be undertaken; and a covenant to ensure that party walls and floors are to be adequately protected.

The law will give effect to any express agreement reached provided that it does not operate as an unlawful displacement of the statutory repairing obligation imposed on landlords of short residential tenancies by s.11 Landlord and Tenant Act 1985.

Landlord's obligations

It is comparatively rare for a landlord to enter into an express repairing covenant unless either a short lease is granted or the landlord reserves part of the premises. Landlords commonly reserve part of the property if premises are to be let on a multiple occupancy basis; the reserved property will include the main exterior structure and the common parts and grounds. There is no reason why a landlord should not carry out repairs voluntarily, apart from the usual commercial considerations.

IMPLIED OBLIGATIONS

Introductory

There are a limited number of repairing obligations which are implied by law. These obligations are useful to the extent that they entitle landlords to enforce minimum repairing obligations in cases where no express agreement has been reached, and impose repairing obligations on specific categories of landlords.

By the tenant

A tenant's liability to repair and maintain the leasehold premises depends on:

(a) the express covenants set out in the lease or tenancy agreement;

(b) obligations implied in tort by the operation of the doctrine of waste;
(c) the implied covenant to use the premises in a tenant-like manner where there is no express repairing obligation: *Horsefall* v. *Mather* (1815);
(d) if the landlord has an express or implied repairing obligation, the tenant must allow him to view the premises at reasonable times upon notice.

By the landlord

Landlords' implied repairing obligations are limited to the following cases:

(a) a tripartite covenant obliging landlords to keep premises let on short residential tenancies (tenancies for less than seven years) in repair implied by s.11 Landlord and Tenant Act 1985. This onerous statutory repairing obligation can only be excluded or modified by a county court order made pursuant to s.12 Landlord and Tenant Act 1985 if it appears to the court that it is reasonable to do so, having regard to all the circumstances of the case, and the other terms and conditions of the lease; and
(b) the implied obligation to keep the common parts of a dwelling in multiple occupancy in a reasonable state of repair and usability: *Liverpool City Council* v. *Irwin* (1976). This has a restricted practical application since it can be excluded by express provisions.

EXPRESS REPAIRING OBLIGATIONS

Construction

The principles applying to landlords' and tenants' repairing covenants are identical. If the wording creates ambiguity, the normal principles of construing documents apply so that the 'good sense' of the agreement prevails: per Lord Justice Sachs in *Brew Brothers* v. *Snax* (1970).

General covenant

A covenant for general repair, e.g. 'to keep and leave in repair' imposes a two-fold obligation on the tenant. He must first of all keep the premises in repair, and secondly deliver them up in repair at the end of the lease.

Standard of repair

The covenant obliges the tenant to maintain the premises in substantial repair: *Harris* v. *Jones* (1832). It is the condition of the premises at the lease's commencement which determines the appropriate standard of repair. The tenant will satisfy his repairing obligations provided he maintains the property to the same standard of repair which the premises were in at the beginning of the lease, taking into account the age and nature of the premises: *Lurcott* v. *Wakely and Wheeler* (1911). There is no obligation on the part of the tenant to update or modernise the premises, although there is nothing to stop the tenant updating the premises voluntarily provided it does not breach any other covenants in the lease, e.g. prohibiting alterations.

There is a legal presumption that the premises were in a tenantable condition at the time the lease commenced: *Brown* v. *Trumper* (1858), but this presumption can be rebutted by evidence to the contrary.

Qualified covenant

Good, tenantable or habitable

Modern repairing covenants are invariably qualified by additional words. For example a tenant's covenant to keep the premises in 'good' or 'tenantable' or 'habitable' repair, or any combination of those or similar words. These qualifying words all amount to the same thing, namely that a tenant has an obligation to keep the premises in tenantable repair: *Proudfoot* v. *Hart* (1890). A qualified covenant can accordingly be more onerous than a general covenant because a qualified covenant assumes that the leasehold premises are in tenantable repair at the lease's commencement so that a tenant may first be required to put the premises into tenantable repair, thereby improving its condition.

Repair and renew

Likewise, it has been held in *Collins* v. *Flynn* (1963) that the addition of the word 'renew' in a repairing covenant adds nothing to the obligation that is imposed by a covenant to repair. Sir Brett Cloutman V-C considered the construction of a covenant to 'repair and renew' in *Collins* v. *Flynn* and said that:

> 'While I am most anxious to give effect to every word of the covenant...yet every repair does involve a degree of renewal...and I feel that I can give a separate meaning to the word 'renew' only by holding that it includes rebuilding the whole property demised; and I think that if this were intended, much stronger and more specific words would have to be used'.

Standard of repair

The standard of repair is construed with reference to the age, character and locality of the premises at the time the lease commenced: see *Lurcott* v. *Wakely and Wheeler* (1911) for the tenant's liability, and *Torrens* v. *Walker* (1906) for the landlord's liability. This is essentially an evidential question which is not always susceptible to precise assessment. The argument that the standard of repair ought to be lower than the standard at the lease's commencement in order to reflect the fact that the area has become run-down in the intervening period was rejected in *Anstruther-Calthorpe* v. *McOscar* (1924).

The class of tenant who would have been likely to occupy the premises at the lease's commencement is also taken into account:

> 'Good tenantable repair...is such as, having regard to the age, character and locality of the house, would make it reasonably fit for the occupation of a reasonably-minded tenant of the class who would be likely to take it. The age of the house must be taken into account, because nobody could reasonably expect that a house 200 years old should be in the same condition as a house lately built; the character of the house must be taken into account, because the same class of repair as would be necessary to a palace would be wholly unnecessary to a cottage; and the locality of the house must be taken into account, because the state of repair necessary for a house in Grosvenor Square would be wholly different from the state of repair necessary for a house in Spitalfields.'
> (per Lord Esher MR in *Proudfoot* v. *Hart* (1890).)

Tenants are not required to repair every defect assiduously, however minor. Landlords cannot insist that holes caused by nails or cracks in plasterwork should be filled under a covenant to keep in tenantable repair: *Perry* v. *Chotzner* (1893). Furthermore, many covenants specifically exempt defects caused by 'fair wear and tear' so that tenants do not have to make good dilapidations caused by natural deterioration. On the other hand, the tenant cannot rely on a fair wear and tear exception to excuse him from consequential damage which would not arise as a result of fair wear and tear: *Regis Property Co. Ltd* v. *Dudley* (1958).

Obligation to rebuild

By the landlord

The landlord is under no obligation to rebuild the premises if they are destroyed unless he has expressly covenanted to rebuild: *Bayne* v. *Walker* (1815). This rule may appear harsh since a landlord is not liable to rebuild even if he has insured against this eventuality: see p.186, Chapter 17, on application of insurance monies.

By the tenant

An obligation to rebuild is implied from an express covenant to keep in repair unless this obligation is expressly excluded by the terms of the lease: *Paradine* v. *Jane* (1647). Tenants with express repairing obligations are accordingly required to rebuild the leasehold premises if they are destroyed, e.g. by an accident, a stranger's act or as a result of a natural disaster.

War damage

The Landlord and Tenant (War Damage) Acts 1939 and 1941 relieves landlords and tenants from an obligation to repair damage caused by war.

Repair subject to supervision

Landlords of prime leasehold property often insist on a supervision and check mechanism to ensure a high quality of repair and maintenance. There are a number of ways of doing this; one of the most common is to incorporate a covenant stating that the tenant will undertake to repair and maintain to the 'satisfaction of a surveyor appointed by the landlord' or 'subject to the supervision of a surveyor or architect'. The precise formula used in specific covenants will determine the extent of the tenant's obligation. However, it has been held that a tenant's obligation is discharged if the supervisor ought to have been satisfied with the standard of the work: *Doe d. Baker* v. *Jones* (1848).

Landlord's repairing covenant

Notice of repair

A tenant must notify the landlord of the repairs which he requires the landlord to undertake owing to the strict rule that a landlord does not become liable under his repairing covenant until the tenant notifies the landlord or his agent of the lack of repair. Landlords are not presumed to have any knowledge of defects. It has been said that nothing short of proof that the landlord had actual knowledge of the defects will relieve the tenant of his obligation to show that he gave notice of repair: per Mr Justice Glyn-Jones in *Uniproducts (Manchester) Ltd* v. *Rose Furnishers Ltd* (1956). This rule applies to both express and implied repairing covenants: see p.150 below for a discussion of the rule's application to implied obligations.

Liability for dangerous defects

Landlords will be liable for injuries caused by dangerous defects which result in injury to tenants or their visitors under two statutory provisions. First of all, landlords who retain control over part of the premises, e.g. the common parts, are 'occupiers' for the purpose of s.2 Occupiers Liability Act 1957 (as amended), and owe a duty of care to the tenant and his visitors. Secondly, s.4 Defective Premises Act 1972 imposes a duty on landlords to all persons who might reasonably be expected to be affected by defects in the leasehold premises where the landlord is under a duty to repair the premises.

SCOPE OF REPAIRING OBLIGATION

Introduction

It is far from easy to determine the scope of a repairing obligation. The test for determining a repairing covenant's scope was, until recently, decided by distinguishing repair from a renewal or improvement. This test seems to have been replaced by a 'test of degree' where the question is whether the work is repair work as a matter of fact and degree. See 'Repair, Renewal and Improvement', an article by P.F.Smith in *Conveyancer and Property Lawyer* 1979 at p.429, for a critical comparison of these two approaches.

No obligation to renew or improve

Repairs

The scope of a repairing covenant is limited to repairs which can be defined for this purpose as work which results in the restoration or replacement of subsidiary parts of the premises: per Lord Justice Buckley in *Lurcott* v. *Wakely and Wheeler* (1911). In this case joists had become rotten and needed replacing, providing a good example of a case where subsidiary parts required replacing.

Renewal

A repairing covenant does not include renewal which amounts to a reconstruction of all or most of the premises. In *Lister* v. *Lane and Nesham* (1893) a cottage built on a timber platform on muddy ground sank and the walls bagged. The cottage was condemned and pulled down. The Court of Appeal held that the tenant was not liable for the damage under his covenant to repair owing to the defect in the orginal structure. Lord Esher MR said that:

> 'if a tenant takes a house which is of such a kind that by its own inherent nature it will in the course of time fall into a particular condition, the effects of that result are not within the tenant's covenant to repair. However large the words of the covenant may be, a covenant to repair a house is not a covenant to give a different thing from that which the tenant took when he entered into the covenant. He has to repair that thing which he took; he is not obliged to make a new and different thing, and, moreover, the result of the nature and condition of the house itself, and the result of time upon that state of things is not a breach of the covenant to repair'.

Improvement–inherent defects

A repairing covenant does not include putting right defects by substituting something different from the original since this would amount to an improvement. In *Sotheby* v. *Grundy* (1947), an old house required underpinning owing to an inherent defect and was condemned and pulled down. Mr Justice Lynskey held that the expenses incurred did not come within the scope of the tenant's repairing covenant owing to the inherent defect, and he said that:

> 'The premises demised here were premises with insecure foundations. What the tenant would have had to do would be to put in a new foundation which would alter the nature and extent of the property demised turning a building which, as originally constructed, would not last more than some 80 odd years into a building that would last for probably another 100 years'.

Accordingly, a repairing covenant does not contain any obligation to repair inherent defects. In *Collins* v. *Flynn* (1963), considered above, a pier carrying one end of a girder supporting a considerable part of the back main wall, and indirectly part of the side wall of the house subsided owing to inadequate foundations. This necessitated the rebuilding of the pier and walls with newly designed foundations. It was held that the work effected an important improvement of the premises. The tenant's covenant did not impose on the tenant liability to remedy what amounted to an inherent defect. To conclude otherwise would have resulted in the tenant returning the leasehold premises in a different condition from the condition in which he took them. Sir Brett Cloutman distinguished *Lurcott* v. *Wakely* on the ground that it was an example of the doctrine of the subsidiary part in the old age cases and had no application to a case of an inherent defect dating from the construction of the premises: see also *The Post Office* v. *Aquarius Properties* (1986).

Degree test

Although it is relatively easy to draw an academic distinction between repair on the one hand, and improvements and renewal on the other, distinguishing the two in practice is not always a straightforward task. A new approach was adopted in *Ravenseft Properties Ltd* v. *Davestone (Holdings) Ltd* (1979) where Mr Justice Forbes said that:

> 'The true test is, as the cases show, that it is always a question of degree whether that which the tenant is being asked to do can properly be described as repair, or whether on the contrary it would involve giving back to the landlord a wholly different thing from that which he demised. In deciding this question, the proportion which the cost of the disputed work bears to the value or cost of the whole premises, may sometimes be helpful as a guide'.

This dictum was approved by Mr Justice French in *Halliard Property Co. Ltd* v. *Nicholas Clarke Investments Ltd* (1983) where a wall forming part of a jerry-built structure at the rear of the premises had collapsed. The landlord claimed that the tenant was liable to rebuild the jerry-built structure and to reinstate it under his covenant to repair the premises. Mr Justice French held that there was no breach of the repairing covenant since the reinstatement claimed would involve handing back an edifice entirely different from the unstable and jerry-built structure of which the tenant took possession at the start of the lease.

The Court of Appeal applied this test to a landlord's repairing obligations in *Elmcroft Developments Ltd* v. *Tankersley-Sawyer* (1984).

The Court of Appeal held that the landlord was in breach of a covenant to 'maintain and keep the exterior of the building and the roof, the main walls, timbers and drains thereof in good and tenantable repair and condition'. The landlord had contended that the remedial work required to eradicate dampness in flats in a late Victorian mansion block went beyond repair. It was found that the dampness was caused by an ineffectual damp-proof course consisting of slates laid horizontally below ground which allowed moisture to be drawn up from the ground by capillary action. Lord Justice Ackner reviewed the authorities considered in *Ravenseft Properties Ltd* and reached his conclusion by applying the test of degree.

Undertaking repairs which eliminate defects

The fact that there is an inherent defect does not by itself exclude a repairing liability. The correct approach in cases involving damage resulting from inherent defects is to begin by identifying the parts of the premises which are out of repair: per Lord Justice Lawton in *Quick* v. *Taff-Ely Borough Council* (1985). Once the disrepair has been identified it is appropriate to ask whether it is reasonable to remedy a design fault when doing the repair. This problem was considered by the Court of Appeal in *Quick* v. *Taff-Ely Borough Council* (1985) in the context of a 1970s house which suffered from a design defect causing severe condensation. The Court of Appeal held that there was no evidence of damage or lack of repair although there was ample evidence of damage to decorations, bedding and clothing; the work required to eliminate the condensation would amount to an improvement.

The factual situation in *Quick* v. *Taff-Ely B.C.* can be compared with the *Ravenseft* and *Elmcroft* cases where disrepair was established. In the *Ravenseft* case, the absence of expansion joints led to physical damage, and stone cladding had become detached from the concrete structure. Mr Justice Forbes rejected the argument that no liability could arise under a repairing covenant if the disrepair was due to an inherent defect. He held that the cost of putting in expansion joints could be recovered under the repairing covenant, even though this amounted to an improvement, on the basis that this was the only way of reinstating the stone cladding. Similarly in the *Elmcroft* case, the rising damp had caused physical damage to the walls so that it was reasonable for the landlord to bear the cost of putting in a replacement damp-proof course under his repairing covenant.

Secure tenant's repairs

Secure tenants are entitled to carry out landlord's repairs and recover the costs from their landlords provided that they make a formal application under the 'Right to Repair Scheme' before undertaking any work: see s.96(1) Housing Act 1985. The Right to Repair scheme is considered at pp.169–70.

Maintenance

Landlords often covenant to maintain premises where there are several units in a building occupied by different tenants: see pp.107–8 for financial arrangements regarding service charges. Payment of a tenant's maintenance contribution is not a condition precedent to the landlord's liability: *Yorkbrook T. Investments Ltd* v. *Batten* (1986). A landlord is not, therefore, entitled to stop providing maintenance if the tenant fails to pay his contribution, unless this is made an express provision of the lease.

Right to enter

A lease generally reserves a right to re-enter to inspect and carry out repairs. If the lease omits this covenant it will be implied where the landlord has undertaken a repairing obligation: *Saner* v. *Bilton* (1878).

Tenants often wish to know the details of the work proposed. They may either be concerned about the standard and quality of the repair work or may simply wish to know whether the end result will justify the inconvenience to themselves. Tenants are not entitled to a great deal of information. In the absence of provisions to the contrary, a tenant is only entitled to sufficient notice of the landlord's intentions. This duty will be discharged if a landlord sets out the general nature and purpose of the work to be performed; the tenant is not entitled to any information or guarantees about the adequacy of the work contemplated: per Lord Justice Ormerod in *Granada Theatres Ltd* v. *Freehold Investment (Leytonstone) Ltd* (1959).

DOCTRINE OF WASTE

Meaning

The doctrine of waste imposes a limited repairing obligation in tort on tenants: see Chapter 7 for an introduction to the doctrine. Technically, 'waste' is any act which alters the leasehold premises for better or for worse to the detriment of the reversioner. Waste falls into two main categories: voluntary waste and permissive waste.

Voluntary waste

Voluntary waste is the commission of any positive action which causes the wilful or negligent alteration or destruction of the premises, e.g. the demolition of a house; cutting down timber: *Buckland* v. *Butterfield* (1820). It has recently been held that the tenant's lawful removal of fixtures without filling holes is an act of waste: *Mancetter Developments Ltd* v. *Garmanson Ltd and Givertz* (1986). There was a strong dissenting judgment from Sir George Waller who said that all the tenant did was remove his own extractor fans from a wall without damaging it, and that no act of voluntary waste could be committed by an omission to do something. In this case the damage was not *de minimis* since the holes in the cladding, lining and brickwork let wind and weather into the premises.

All tenants are liable for voluntary waste. If a tenant at will commits voluntary waste, the tenancy is automatically terminated, and the tenant at will becomes a trespasser and is liable for wilful damage to the premises: see *Panton* v. *Isham* (1701) where the premises were destroyed by the tenant's negligence in keeping a fire.

Permissive waste

Permissive waste is an omission to take action to prevent damage to the premises, e.g. allowing a house to decay; permitting foundations to rot through failing to clear drains: *Herne* v. *Bembow* (1813). All tenants, apart from weekly tenants, tenants at will and tenants at sufferance, are liable for permissive waste.

Remedies

Landlords may have recourse to two main remedies if a tenant commits waste; either an action for damages, or an injunction in the case of voluntary waste only. The quantification of damages for waste is based on the damage to the value of the reversion, and is not related to the actual cost of making good the damage to the premises: *Whitham* v. *Kershaw* (1886). One consequence of this rule is that if the tenant alters the premises intentionally, e.g. by extending an existing building, an action in damages may well fail since it will be difficult to show that the alteration has resulted in a diminution in the value of the reversion.

The courts are prepared to grant an injunction to restrain a tenant from committing acts of voluntary waste which will result in substantial damage to the leasehold premises. But the courts will not grant an injunction if this involves supervising the tenant. Accordingly, the courts will not grant an injunction in respect of permissive waste since this involves supervising a tenant to ensure that omissions are corrected.

Landlords will generally combine an action for waste with an action for breach of the obligation to use the premises in a tenant-like manner since both relate to a tenant's liability to maintain the premises, in the absence of an express repairing covenant. Note that if the tenant can show that his use of the premises was reasonable, he will have a good defence to a claim of waste: *Manchester Bonded Warehouse Co.* v. *Carr* (1880).

TENANT'S IMPLIED COVENANTS

Duty to use premises in a tenant-like manner

The only repairing obligation imposed on a tenant at common law (apart from liability for waste) is the duty to use the premises in a tenant-like manner. This duty obliges tenants to take proper and reasonable care of the premises by doing odd jobs around the house, but excludes liability for fair wear and tear. This obligation is of particular importance in providing landlords with a remedy against weekly tenants in cases where there is no express repairing obligation, since weekly tenants are not liable for permissive waste.

Scope of duty

In *Warren* v. *Keen* (1953), the landlord brought an action against a weekly tenant to recover money which he had spent on repairing the premises. In particular, the landlord alleged defects which included damp and stained plaster on the internal walls; cracked and broken external walls; window sills which lacked weather-proof joints; decayed paintwork; and a leak in the hot-water boiler. The Court of Appeal held that the defects particularised by the landlord were due to fair wear and tear for which a weekly tenant was not liable.

Lord Denning defined the obligation to use the premises in a tenant-like manner in *Warren* v. *Keen* (1953) with reference to a number of homely illustrations:

> 'The tenant must take proper care of the premises. He must, if he is going away for the winter, turn off the water and empty the boiler; he must clean the chimneys when necessary and also the windows; he must mend the electric light when it fuses; he must unstop the sink when it is blocked by his waste. In short, he must do the little jobs around the place which a reasonable tenant would do. In addition he must not, of course, damage the house wilfully or negligently... but, apart from such things, if the house falls into disrepair through fair wear and tear or lapse of time or for any reason not caused by him, the tenant is not liable to repair it'.

Right to view

Landlords have an implied right to enter the leasehold premises in order to view their state of repair in cases where the landlord is liable to carry out repairs: *Saner* v. *Bilton* (1878). Beyond this, a landlord has no implied rights of entry. In other words, the tenant has a right to the exclusive possession of the premises unless a right to enter has been specifically reserved by the landlord. This duty will be discharged if a landlord sets out the general nature and purpose of the work to be performed; the tenant is not entitled to any information or guarantees about the adequacy of the work contemplated: per Lord Justice Ormerod in *Granada Theatres Ltd* v. *Freehold Investment (Leytonstone) Ltd* (1959).

LANDLORD'S IMPLIED COVENANTS

Statutory repairing covenant

Section 11 Landlord and Tenant Act 1985 implies a tripartite covenant on landlords to keep short leasehold premises in repair, coupled with a right to view on 24 hours notice in writing. The purpose is to relieve residential tenants with short leases from onerous repairing obligations. Section 11 re-enacts s.32 Housing Act 1961.

Scope of repairing obligations

The covenant comprises three repairing obligations as follows.

Structure and exterior

The landlord must keep in repair the structure and exterior of the dwelling-house, including drains, gutters and external pipes: s.11(1)(a).

This is an onerous obligation since a landlord may be required to carry out considerable repairs to the structure, e.g. replacing slates on roofs and repairing brickwork and rendering: *Granada Theatres Ltd* v. *Freehold Investments (Leytonstone) Ltd* (1959). The Court of Appeal have held that landlords of flats which form part of a building have an obligation to repair anything which, in the ordinary use of words, would be regarded as part of the structure or exterior, in *Campden Hill Towers Ltd* v. *Gardner* (1977), even though the exterior walls may not form part of the flat which is let: see also *Douglas-Scott* v. *Scorgie* (1984).

Installations for essential services

The landlord is obliged to keep in repair and proper working order the installations in the dwelling-house for the supply of water, gas and electricity and for sanitation. This includes basins, sinks, baths and sanitary conveniences but excludes other fixtures, fittings and appliances for making use of the supply of water, gas or electricity services: s.11(1)(b).

Demarcation problems can arise. For example, a landlord would not be liable to repair a boiler used for heating the tenant's radiators which is situated outside the dwelling-house under the provisions of s.11. The Court of Appeal confirmed that this obligation is limited to installations which are situated in the dwelling-house, in *Campden Hill Towers Ltd* v. *Gardner*.

There is no obligation to improve the installations supplying essential services. In *Wycombe Health Authority* v. *Barnett* (1982) the Court of Appeal held that it could not be said that a failure to lag water-pipes meant that water-pipes were not in proper working order.

Heating installations

Landlords are required to keep installations in the dwelling house for space heating and heating water in repair and proper working order: s.11(1)(c).

Exclusions

Three matters are excluded from the scope of s.11 as follows:

Tenant-like manner repairs

The tenant is expected to carry out minor repairs in compliance with his duty to use the premises in a tenant-like manner: s.11(2)(a). An attempt was made to extend this duty to prevent damage caused by burst water-pipes in *Wycombe Health Authority* v. *Barnett* (1982). The Court of Appeal rejected the argument that a tenant has a duty to lag water-pipes, drain the water or leave the heating on before going away.

Many landlords now ask tenants to sign a 'frost damage' agreement which obliges tenants to take these simple precautions to avoid damage from burst pipes, and making them liable for any damage which occurs. This fills a lacuna in the law.

Rebuilding and reinstatement

Section 11 exempts landlords from any obligation to rebuild or reinstate if a fire, storm, flood or other inevitable accident destroys the premises: s.11(2)(b).

Repairing tenant's chattels

A landlord is not required to repair or maintain anything which the tenant is entitled to remove: s.11(2)(c).

Tenant's repairing covenants ineffective

If the lease falls within the scope of s.11, the following covenants are ineffective: repairing covenants; covenants to paint, point or render; covenants to pay money in lieu of repairs or on account of repairs: s.11(4),(5).

Standard of repair

The standard of repair is the same as for an express repairing covenant. In other words, the age, character and prospective life of the dwelling-house and the locality in which it is situated are all taken into account: see *Proudfoot* v. *Hart* (1890) above.

No obligation to renew or improve

The common law distinction between repairs, and renewal and improvements applies to the statutory covenant. The tenant in

Wainwright v. *Leeds City Council* (1984) argued that the landlord Council were under an obligation to provide a damp-proof course in a small back-to-back terraced house which had been built at the beginning of the century without a damp-proof course. The Court of Appeal had no hesitation in deciding that this did not fall within the scope of the landlord's statutory repairing obligation following *Pembery* v. *Lamdin* (1940) on identical facts, and stated that public sector landlords are under no greater an obligation than private sector landlords.

This point arose again in *Quick* v. *Taff-Ely Borough Council* (1985) where a tenant claimed that the landlord was liable to replace existing metal windows and to insulate the lintels in order to eradicate the house's severe condensation which caused dampness and mildew. The Court of Appeal held that the landlord was not in breach of his statutory obligation since the damage was the result of an inherent design defect. This is an important decision for landlords leasing modern houses which were built in conformity with existing building regulations but have subsequently proved susceptible to condensation and mildew, provided that the term of fitness for human habitation implied by s.8(3)(4) Landlord and Tenant Act 1985 is inapplicable: see the comment made by Lord Justice Lawton at the beginning of his judgment in *Quick* v. *Taff-Ely Borough Council* (1985).

Knowledge of defect

The landlord's liability to commence repair work does not arise until the landlord has information about the existence of a defect such as would put a reasonable man on enquiry as to whether repair work was necessary: per Lord Morris of Borth-Y-Gest in the House of Lords decision of *O'Brien and Another* v. *Robinson* (1973).

Tenants should, therefore, give landlords notice of any defects requiring repair. Many landlords take advantage of the fact that notice of disrepair is required in law coupled with the fact that the majority of residential tenants may grumble about defects but relatively few begin formal proceedings against landlords.

Tenants are entitled to compensation for living in unrepaired houses from the time the landlord knew of the defects in repair: *McGreal* v. *Wake* (1984).

Right to view

Section 11 also includes an implied covenant by the tenant to permit the landlord or his authorised agent to view the condition and state of repair of the premises at reasonable times of the day upon twenty-four hours written notice: s.11(6).

Application of s.11

The application of s.11 is regulated by s.13 as follows.

General rule

The general rule states that s.11 applies to leases of a dwelling-house which were granted on or after the 24th October 1961 for a term of less than seven years.

Definitions: For this purpose 'lease' includes tenancies, sub-tenancies and agreements for leases: s.36(1)(2) Landlord and Tenant Act 1985. A 'lease of a dwelling-house' means a lease under which a building or part of a building is let entirely or partly as a private residence: s.16(b) Landlord and Tenant Act 1985. The 'dwelling-house' is the part of the building which is let wholly or partly as a private dwelling: s.16(b) Landlord and Tenant Act 1985.

Licences: Section 11 does not apply to licences but is restricted to leases and tenancies.

Periodic tenancies: Periodic tenancies qualify as a lease for less than seven years.

Fixed term leases: Section 13 is drafted in order to close possible loop-holes in the calculation of the qualifying period of less than seven years by landlords seeking to avoid their statutory repairing obligations. The two following anti-avoidance provisions were designed to achieve this result:

(a) backdating disallowed. Landlords could easily avoid their s.11 repairing obligations by purporting to grant a term which is longer than the qualifying term of less than seven years by backdating the lease's commencement date. The anti-avoidance provision leaves any period falling before the date of grant out of account: s.13(2)(a). Thus the backdating of leases to create artificially long terms to avoid s.11 is specifically disallowed.
(b) break clause exercisable before the seventh year creates a qualifying lease. Landlords could avoid their repairing obligation by granting leases for seven years or more which include a 'break clause' (option to determine the lease) which can be exercised by the landlord within the qualifying period. Thus a lease for a term of seven years or more which ostensibly falls outside s.11 could be ended within the qualifying period. The anti-avoidance provision treats leases which are determinable at the landlord's option as a qualifying lease of less

than seven years: s.13(2)(b). But the option to determine must be an unfettered option for this purpose. The Court of Appeal held that an option to determine a ninety year lease with full repairing covenants on the death of the landlord was a fettered option, and could not be treated as a lease for less than seven years in *Parker* v. *O'Connor* (1974). This provision has a materially different result as compared with the backdating avoidance provision since a lease caught by the breakclause avoidance provision renders the landlord liable to comply with the s.11 repairing obligations. There is no 'wait and see' provision enabling the courts to wait and see whether the break clause is in fact exercised before determining the parties' repairing liabilities.

Option to renew

Special rules apply to the calculation of the term if the tenant has an option to renew the term. The original term is added to the renewal period for the purposes of calculating the lease's duration. Thus a lease for a term of less than seven years is not treated as a lease for less than seven years if the original term together with the renewal period amount to more than seven years: s.13(2)(c).

Exceptions to general rule

The following leases are specifically exempt from the general rule by the provisions of ss. 13(3) and 14 Landlord and Tenant Act 1985.

Business tenancies: Section 11 does not apply to business tenancies which are within Part II Landlord and Tenant Act 1954: s.13(3). This provision applies to leases with mixed residential and business user. The question of who is liable to keep the premises in repair is determined by asking whether Part II applies to the tenancy.

Leases granted to public bodies: Section 11 does not apply to leases granted to public bodies on or after the 3rd October 1980. This includes leases granted to local authorities, registered housing associations and co-operatives and educational institutions: s.14(4).

Leases granted to the Crown or Government: Section 11 does not apply to leases granted to the Crown or to a Government department: s.14(5).

Agricultural holdings: Section 11 does not apply to agricultural holdings as defined by the Agricultural Holdings Act 1948: s.14(3).

Upon renewal: Section 11 will not apply if an existing tenant or former tenant who is still in possession is granted a new lease for less than seven years provided that the original lease was for more than seven years: s.14(1).

Contracting out

The parties may exclude or modify the landlord's s.11 repairing obligations provided that the county court authorises the contractual provision to exclude or modify s.11. This is referred to as 'contracting out' because the parties have entered into a contract excluding or modifying s.11 by way of either a covenant in the lease or an agreement collateral to the lease.

The county court will only authorise contracting out if it is satisfied that both parties consent, and that it is reasonable to do so after taking into account all the circumstances and the other terms and conditions of the lease: s.12(2).

Any term or agreement which purports to contract out of the landlord's s.11 repairing obligations is void unless authorised by the county court: s.12(1)(a). Similarly any term or agreement which purports to penalise tenants who rely on s.11 is void. For example, a forfeiture provision would be void if it provided that the lease was to be forfeited if the tenant brought an action for damages against his landlord for failing to repair the premises: s.12(1)(b).

Questions

Consider whether the landlords in the following examples are obliged to repair the dwelling-house:

(1) L grants T a lease for five years with an option to renew for a further five years.

(2) L lets T into possession on 1 April 1986 for four years under a lease which provides for a term of eight years commencing on 1 April 1982.

(3) L grants T a ten year term which contains an option to determine by the landlord exercisable in the fifth year.

(4) L grants T a ten year term on the 1st September 1986 which includes a covenant stipulating that 's. 11 of the Landlord and Tenant Act 1985 shall not apply'.

(5) L grants T a five year lease which provides that the landlord is 'entitled to recover any monies spent on repairs from the tenant if the expenditure is reasonably incurred'.

(6) L granted T a six year lease of a cottage. T makes high fashion knitwear at the cottage which she sells in Covent Garden Market on Saturdays.

Fitness for human habitation

Scope of section 8

Section 8 Landlord and Tenant Act 1985 implies a term as to fitness for human habitation. It only applies to leases of houses where the rent on or after 6 July 1957 does not exceed £80 in London or £52 elsewhere: s.8 is a consolidation of s.6 Housing Act 1957. The Act contains a table together with notes detailing the appropriate rent limits for all periods, which can be found in Appendix 1 .

The implied term ousts any express obligation and consists of a condition that the house is fit for human habitation at the commencement of the tenancy. This is coupled with an undertaking that the house will be kept fit for human habitation during the tenancy: s.8(1) Landlord and Tenant Act 1985.

Agricultural workers

If an agricultural worker's contract of employment provides him with a home with his job as part of his remuneration under a licence agreement the condition and undertaking in s.8 apply.

Section 8 inapplicable

Rent limit too high: Section 8 only applies to houses let at the low rent limits referred to above.

Licences: Section 8 does not apply to licences but is restricted to tenancies. For this purpose tenancy is defined as including sub-tenancies and agreements for tenancies: s.36(1) Landlord and Tenant Act 1985.

Houses irreparable at reasonable expense

The Court of Appeal held in *Buswell* v. *Goodwin* (1971) that the statutory implied term of fitness does not apply to premises which could not be made fit at reasonable expense. In this case a closing order had been made by the local authority which gave the landlord a statutory entitlement to possession. The Court of Appeal accepted that the closing order would only have been made if the local authority were satisfied that the house was both unfit for human habitation and could not be repaired at reasonable expense. The tenant's argument that the landlord should not profit from his own wrong in neglecting his repairing obligations was rejected as having no bearing on landlords who profited from closing orders.

Sections 264–323 (Part IX) Housing Act 1985 contains the current provisions in respect of the demolition or closing of unfit premises which are beyond repair at a reasonable cost (see pp.165–8).

Test of fitness

A house is deemed to be unfit for human habitation if it is not reasonably suited for occupation owing to the presence of one or more defects in the condition of the following matters: repair; stability; freedom from damp; internal arrangement; natural lighting; ventilation; water supply; drainage and sanitary conveniences; facilities for preparation and cooking of food and for the disposal of waste water: s.10 Landlord and Tenant Act 1985.

Implied right to view

The landlord has a right to view the premises at reasonable times of the day on twenty-four hours notice in writing: s.8(2) Landlord and Tenant Act 1985.

Common law repairing obligations

The former common law rule was that landlords were not liable to repair leasehold premises in the absence of an express repairing covenant by the landlord. This rule has been partially modified by the decision in *Liverpool City Council* v. *Irwin* (1976) where the House of Lords held that Liverpool City Council were under an obligation in the nature of an implied covenant to take reasonable care to keep the means of access to flats in a multi-storey block of council flats in a state of reasonable repair and usability. Vandalism, non-cooperation by the tenants and neglect by the council had resulted in broken lifts, blocked rubbish chutes and dangerous conditions on the staircases.

This decision appears to be of limited practical effect for two reasons. Firstly, the decision is restricted to its own facts and is only applicable to cases where landlords have retained essential rights of access in buildings in multiple occupation. Secondly, the letting agreements were silent on the question of repairing liability in respect of the common parts. Although the decision applies to both public and private sector property it would be unusual to find no mention of maintenance and repairing obligations of the common parts in private sector buildings in multiple occupation. The Court of Appeal declined to imply a landlord's covenant to repair drains where the lease provided a workable scheme of repair which represented the apparently complete bargain between the parties in *Duke of Westminster and Others* v. *Guild* (1984), in the absence of any special considerations such as those which were present in *Liverpool City Council* v. *Irwin*.

USUAL COVENANTS

An agreement for a lease should specify the repairing covenants which are to be inserted in the lease. If none is specified, there is an implied term that the lease should contain the following usual repairing covenants:

(a) a covenant to keep and deliver up the premises in repair is a usual covenant: *Hampshire* v. *Wickens* (1878).
(b) a covenant to allow the landlord to enter and view the state of repair is a usual covenant.

In special circumstances additional repairing covenants may be implied: see *Chester* v. *Buckingham Travel* (1981).

Usual covenants are defined on pp.70–1 whilst the substantive law is discussed in the text above.

Chapter 15

Remedies for Disrepair

NON-REPAIRING TENANT

Introduction

Breaches of a repairing obligation may amount to either a 'single' or a 'continuing' breach of a covenant. A single breach of covenant, e.g. a breach of a covenant to put the premises into repair, will entitle a landlord to a single remedy on one occasion only. But in the case of continuing breaches of a covenant, e.g. to *keep* the premises in repair, a landlord may theoretically bring an action at any time during the term when the premises are out of repair.

Action for damages

The most common remedy sought by landlords against a non-repairing tenant is an action for damages for breach of a repairing obligation.

Measurement of damages

Damages are assessed on the basis of the common law rule that a landlord should be placed in the position which he would have been in but for the breach of repairing obligation. This is subject to the statutory ceiling on the amount which can be claimed by way of damages for breach of a repairing covenant: s.18(1) Landlord and Tenant Act 1927.

Maximum recoverable by statute

Section 18(1) Landlord and Tenant Act 1927 imposes an upper limit on the damages which can be recovered by a landlord for a breach of a tenant's express or implied repairing covenant, and provides that:

'Damages...shall in no case exceed the amount (if any) by which the value of the reversion...in the premises is diminished owing to the breach...'

For this purpose, the maximum measure of damages is the difference between the open market value of the premises in its unrepaired state and its expected value if repaired. One consequence of this statutory limitation is that landlords cannot recover the total cost of carrying out repair work from a tenant if the amount spent is more than the amount by which the saleable value of the leasehold premises is injured by the defects in repair.

It should be noted that s.18(1) does not state that the test for measuring damages is the diminution in the reversion's value. The former common law rule that damages can be assessed by calculating the actual cost of the repairs together with a sum representing rent lost while the repairs were being carried out has not been displaced altogether, but has to be read subject to s.18: *Jacquin* v. *Holland* (1960).

Repair rendered useless by demolition or alteration

No damages can be recovered for breach of a covenant to leave or put the premises in repair at the end of the lease if it can be shown that the repairs would be rendered useless because the premises are either due to be pulled down or altered at the end of the tenancy or shortly afterwards: s.18(1) Landlord and Tenant Act 1927.

The relevant time for testing the landlord's intention is at the end of the lease. This rule was interpreted strictly in *Salisbury* v. *Gilmore* (1942) when the landlord's intention to pull down the premises at the end of the lease was thwarted by the imposition of war-time restrictions on demolition. It was held that a change of intention after the lease had been terminated was irrelevant. But if the landlord's intention is only provisional and not definite at this time, damages can be recovered from the tenant if the premises are not subsequently demolished or altered: *Cunliffe* v. *Goodman* (1950).

Long residential leases

There is a statutory restriction on the landlord's right to recover damages for breach of a repairing obligation in the case of leases of small houses for seven years or more which have three or more years unexpired. Section 1(2) of the Leasehold Property (Repairs) Act 1938 provides that a landlord cannot enforce any right to damages by a legal action for damages in respect of leases falling within the scope of s.1 unless he complies with the Act's strict procedural requirements. The object of the Act is to prevent landlords harassing residential tenants mid-term for dilapidations unless essential repair work needs to be carried out mid-term.

Scope of section 1

Leases qualify for the protection afforded by s.1 Leasehold (Property Repairs) Act 1938 if the lease is for a term of seven years or more, and three or more years are unexpired at the time a s.146 notice is served on a tenant: s.1(1) Leasehold (Property Repairs) Act 1938.

Procedure

Section 146 notice: A s.146 notice which is served in respect of a lease of the qualifying length will only be valid if it contains the information that the tenant is entitled to claim the benefit of the 1938 Act by serving a 'counter-notice' in conspicuous characters: s.1(4) Leasehold (Property Repairs) Act 1938.

Tenant's counter-notice: A tenant with a lease of the qualifying length is entitled to serve a counter-notice stating that he claims the benefit of the 1938 Act. The counter-notice should be served within twenty-eight days of the service of a s.146 notice. Once a tenant has served a counter-notice on the landlord claiming the benefit of the Act, the landlord cannot bring any proceedings against the tenant without the leave of the court: s.1(3) Leasehold (Property Repairs) Act 1938.

Grounds for granting leave to proceed

Leave to bring proceedings against a tenant will only be granted by the court if the landlord proves a prima facie or arguable case that one of the five statutory grounds lettered (a)–(e) applies: s.1(5) Leasehold (Property Repairs) Act 1938.

Ground (a). This ground is based on two alternative valuations of the reversion. The landlord must either prove that the reversion's value has already been substantially diminished by the tenant's breach of his repairing obligations, or that there is likely to be a substantial diminution in its value if the breach is not remedied immediately.

Ground (b). This ground entitles a landlord to bring proceedings if he can show that the breach must be remedied immediately in order to comply with an Act of Parliament, a bye-law, a court order or a local authority requirement.

Ground (c). This ground only relates to tenants who are not in occupation of all of the premises. The court will grant leave to proceed if it can be shown that the immediate remedying of the breach is required in the interests of the occupier of the premises.

Ground (d). Landlords will be given leave to proceed on the proverbial basis that 'a stitch in time saves nine' if they can show that the breach can be remedied immediately at a relatively small expense in comparison with the much greater expense of a postponement of the necessary work.

Ground (e). The court has an overriding discretion to grant leave to proceed in cases where the landlord can show evidence of special circumstances on the basis of which it would be just and equitable to grant leave to proceed.

Prima facie case: A landlord does not have to prove a complete case at this interlocutory stage when requesting leave to bring proceedings. But he is required to put forward evidence to prove a prima facie or arguable case that a breach of covenant exists: *Sidnall* v. *Wilson* (1966). This test was explained by Vice-Chancellor Sir Robert Megarry in *Land Securities PLC* v. *Receiver for the Metropolitan Police District* (1983) where he said that:

> 'In the end, I think that all that a landlord has to do on an application for leave is to make out a prima facie case (or perhaps a bona fide or arguable case) that at least one of the paragraphs of s.1(5) is satisfied; and this includes making out such a case for there being a breach of the repairing covenant.'

Leave to proceed granted: The court may impose terms and conditions on both the landlord and tenant in granting or refusing leave to proceed: s.1(6) Leasehold (Property Repairs) Act 1938.

Forfeiture

General principles

A landlord will usually combine forfeiture proceedings with a claim for damages. A landlord would only be likely to omit a claim for damages in forfeiture proceedings if the tenant is insolvent and not worth powder and shot.

Forfeiture clause

A landlord will only be able to commence forfeiture proceedings against a tenant for breach of a repairing obligation if the lease contains a forfeiture clause which allows the landlord to re-enter in the event of a breach of a repairing obligation.

Section 146 notice

A landlord must serve a 's. 146 notice' on the tenant requiring him to remedy the breach and asking for compensation. The tenant is then given time to carry out repairs to remedy the breach, and an opportunity to compensate the landlord for any loss which he has sustained as a result of the lack of repair.

Long residential leases

Landlords who wish to commence forfeiture proceedings for disrepair against residential tenants with long leases must comply with the provisions of s.1(1) Leasehold (Property Repairs) Act 1938. Briefly the Act requires landlords to notify tenants of their rights under the Act in conspicuous characters in the s.146 notice. If the tenant chooses to claim the benefit of the Act within twenty-eight days of service, the landlord can only bring forfeiture proceedings mid-term with the leave of the court.

Once leave to proceed is granted, the forfeiture proceedings will proceed unless the tenant has carried out the repairs and paid any compensation due, or the breach of covenant has been waived. The tenant will be entitled to claim relief from forfeiture in the normal way: s.146(2) Law of Property Act 1925.

Landlord's recovery of repair costs

Many leases give the landlord power to carry out the repairs and recover the cost from the tenant if the tenant is in breach of his repairing obligations. Such a clause can only be relied on if the full requirements of the clause, that estimates and contracts shall be submitted to the tenant first, have been satisfied: *CIN Properties Ltd* v. *Barclays Bank PLC* (1986). The recovery of costs from a tenant in these circumstances is generally by way of a claim for a 'debt' due under an express covenant in the lease which permits the recovery of the costs as a debt, and not a claim for damages: see p.113 above on actions for recovery of rent. Leave to bring proceedings for a debt against the tenant would not, therefore, be necessary: per Mr Justice Vinelott in *Hamilton* v. *Martell Securities Ltd* (1984) followed by Mr Justice Nourse in *Colchester Estates (Cardiff)* v. *Carlton Industries PLC* (1984) and in later cases.

It will only be necessary to obtain leave to bring proceedings under the 1938 Act where the landlord's claim is for 'damages'. One pitfall should be avoided. If a landlord wishes to recover the cost of repairs by way of damages he should serve a s.146 notice containing the information prescribed by the 1938 Act before carrying out the repair work. This is because the 1938 Act only contemplates a situation where a state of disrepair has not been remedied at the time when the application for leave is made. A landlord who carried out urgent repair work before serving a s.146 notice was refused leave to bring proceedings in *Sedac Investments Ltd* v. *Tanner* (1982).

Specific performance

It is rare for the courts to grant an order for specific performance of a tenant's repairing obligation since this would involve supervision by the courts. The proper remedy is damages: *Hill* v. *Barclay* (1810).

NON-REPAIRING LANDLORD

Damages

Tenants are entitled to claim damages against a landlord for breach of an express or implied obligation to repair in contract. Alternatively, it may occasionally be possible to bring proceedings for negligence. A tenant successfully sued her council landlord in negligence in *Stockley* v. *Knowsley Metropolitan Borough Council* (1986). Severe weather had caused the pipes supplying cold water to the tenant's flat to freeze. They burst flooding the flat with water and causing damage. The Court of Appeal held that the landlords were in breach of their duty to act reasonably in the circumstances since they had failed to advise her to turn off the stop-cock. A tenant may sue after assignment: see p.87.

Measurement of damages

General principle

The decision of the Court of Appeal in *Calabar Properties Ltd* v. *Stitcher* (1983) sets out the principles which apply to the assessment of damages against a non-repairing landlord. Lord Justice Stephenson said that:

> 'In measuring and assessing any tenant's damages for breach of a landlord's repairing covenant the court must, I think, always start with the fundamental principle that they are "so far as is possible by means of a monetary award, to place the plaintiff in the position which he would have occupied if he had not suffered the wrong complained of, be that wrong a tort or a breach of contract" '.

In this case the tenant had bought a lease of a flat as a home. The landlords failed to carry out their repairing obligations and rainwater penetrated the flat until it became uninhabitable. Damages were assessed on the difference between the unrepaired flat and its anticipated value if the landlord had fulfilled his repairing obligations: see 'Breach of Landlord's Covenant To Repair' by H.W. Wilkinson, *New Law Journal*, 20th April 1984 at p. 379 for a solicitor's comments on *Calabar Properties*.

Knowledge of defect

Damages can be claimed from the time from which the landlord has knowledge of the defect in repair or is notified of the same. In *Hewitt* v. *Rowlands* (1924) Lord Justice Bankes said that:

> '...the measure of damages is the difference in value to the tenant of the premises, from the date of the notice to repair down to the date of the assessment of damages, between the premises in their present condition and their value, if the landlord on receipt of the tenant's notice had fulfilled the obligations of the covenant'.

Lord Justice Stephenson applied this dictum in *Calabar Properties*, and explained that this dictum is not an authority for the proposition that a tenant is entitled to damages to be assessed on the basis of diminution in value to the tenant.

Diminution in value

Calabar Properties has finally established that diminution in the value of the leasehold premises is not necessarily the correct measure of damages against a non-repairing landlord. Moreover, a tenant is not entitled to damages assessed on this basis unless the landlord knew that the premises were acquired as a speculative investment. This is alarming for tenants who hope to lease premises for the dual purpose of a home and an investment but fail to make this clear to their landlord when the lease is granted. On this point, Lord Justice Stephenson was emphatic:

> 'If she [the tenant] had bought the lease as a speculation intending to assign it, to the knowledge of the landlords, the alleged diminution in rental (or capital) value might be the true measure of her damage. But she did not; she bought it for a home, not a saleable asset, and it would be deplorable if the court were bound to leave the real world for the complicated underworld of expert evidence on comparable properties and values, on the fictitious assumption that what the flat would have fetched had anything to do with its value to her... .

Damages by way of compensation

A tenant may be entitled to compensation against a landlord where the leasehold premises were acquired for the tenant's own personal use. Tenants are entitled to claim damages for distress, loss of enjoyment and inconvenience under the rule in *Jarvis* v. *Swan Tours* (1973): see *McCall* v. *Abelesz* (1976). Thus compensation has been held to be recoverable by way of damages for the following items of expenditure which flowed from the landlord's breach of covenant:

(a) the cost of alternative accommodation if the lack of repair renders the premises uninhabitable: *Calabar Properties*;
(b) the cost of storing furniture whilst the tenant was in temporary alternative accommodation: *McGreal* v. *Wake* (1984);
(c) the cost of any repairs paid for by the tenant: *Calabar Properties*;
(d) reasonable expenditure on redecoration: *McGreal* v. *Wake* (1984)
(e) the cost of clearing debris and cleaning up after repair work has been carried out: *McGreal* v. *Wake* (1984)
(f) for the discomfort of living in deteriorating premises: *Calabar Properties*.

Specific performance

Procedure

Tenants may ask the county court for an order for specific performance unless a monetary claim outside the county court limits of £5000 is also being sought in which case the application should be made to the High Court. This is an equitable remedy, and the judge is entitled to exercise his discretion and refuse to grant the order if, for example, the tenant has not come with clean hands or has delayed in bringing proceedings.

This remedy is by way of an exception to the rule that a court will not compel performance of an obligation which requires supervision. There is no comparable remedy which is available to a landlord against a non-repairing tenant.

Residential tenants

Residential tenants have a statutory right to ask a court for the remedy of specific performance in cases where the tenant is bringing proceedings against his landlord for breach of a covenant to repair, maintain, renew, construct or replace property under the provisions of s.17 Landlord and Tenant Act 1985. This remedy is of practical importance to residential tenants who wish to compel a non-repairing landlord to fulfil his repairing obligations. But it can only be exercised if the tenant is bringing legal proceedings for breach of a repairing covenant. The remedy extends to obligations to repair or maintain common parts and is not restricted to non-repair of the leasehold premises.

APPOINTMENT OF RECEIVER

The High Court has always had a discretionary power to appoint a receiver where it appears to be just and convenient to do so: see s.37 Supreme Court Act 1981. Mr Justice Goulding exercised this power and appointed a surveyor as a receiver in *Hart* v. *Emelkirk Ltd* (1983) to manage a block of flats on long leases in Battersea until trial or further order. The landlord had neither collected rents and charges for maintenance nor carried out his repairing obligations which resulted in a serious deterioration in the condition of the properties.

The *Hart* v. *Emelkirk* procedure was used in *Clayhope Properties Ltd* v. *Evans and Another* (1986) where Lord Justice Dillon made the following observations on its benefit to tenants:

> '...the procedure provided by Mr Justice Goulding in *Hart* v. *Emelkirk Ltd* ... is, as it seems to me, a very valuable procedure for the protection of tenants who find that their landlords, particularly in blocks of flats, whether the landlords be companies or individuals, are wholly failing to perform vital repairing obligations under the terms of the relevant leases. The landlords can often not easily be traced. They collect rents, they are prepared to sell off long leases for premiums, but they allow premises to fall into serious disrepair without regard to their repairing obligations. In such circumstances, the appointment of the receiver is a valuable protection to the tenant who has a tenancy or lease of the flat.'

In subsequent proceedings the receiver failed to ensure that his assets would cover his expenses and was unable to claim the excess expenditure from the landlords: *Evans* v. *Clayhope Properties Ltd* (1986).

The county court has similar jurisdictional powers: see County Court Rules 1981 Order 32 rule 1.

REPAIR NOTICES

Introductory

Local housing authorities have wide statutory powers controlling local housing conditions. For example, local authorities have power to serve repair notices on landlords, to assist owners of defective housing, to clear areas designated as slum areas and to issue compulsory purchase orders. The main objective of the Housing Act 1985 is the consolidation of these extensive powers. To deal with these provisions is beyond the ambit of this book, save the service of repair notices which is one means by which repairs against landlords can be enforced.

Local authorities have statutory duties to serve repair notices on a 'person having control' of a house which is either unfit for human habitation or in a state of serious disrepair under the provisions of Part VI Housing Act 1985. A repair notice requires landlords to carry out specified repairs within a reasonable time. Copies of the repair notice may be served on any interested party including tenants and mortgagees: ss. 189(3), 190(3) Housing Act 1985. These powers are designed to deal with landlords who allow housing stock to fall into substantial disrepair, unless the expense fails to justify the means.

Person having control

Repair notices can be served on any person who appears to control the premises whether it is the landlord or his agent or trustee. The repair notice scheme permits the local housing authority to serve a repair notice on the 'person having control'. He is defined as the person who receives the rack rent regardless of whether he is the landlord or the landlord's agent or trustee; the rack rent is defined as 'not less than 2/3rds of the full net annual value of the premises': s.207 Housing Act 1985.

House unfit for human habitation

A local authority has a mandatory statutory obligation to serve a repair notice against the 'person having control' of a house which is 'unfit for human habitation' unless it is satisfied that the cost of repairs to make it fit for habitation is not a reasonable expense: s.189(1) Housing Act 1985.

Fit for human habitation

The criteria to establish whether a house is fit for human habitation are set out in s.604 Housing Act 1985, and are identical to those set out in s.10 Landlord and Tenant Act 1985: see page 154 above. In other words, the premises shall be deemed to be unfit if one or more of the defects set out in s.604 means that the house is not reasonably suitable for occupation in that condition. This is essentially an evidential question of fact.

Basement rooms

Special rules apply to 'underground rooms', i.e. basement rooms. Basement rooms will be closed down as unfit for human habitation if they fail to comply with the minimum statutory regulations in respect of height or ventilation: s.282 Housing Act 1985. Basement rooms will be closed on the ground that they are unfit for human habitation if they fail to comply with:

(a) the minimum height of seven feet from floor to ceiling: s.281-2 Housing Act 1985 or;
(b) the minimum regulations made by the local housing authority under s.281 Housing Act 1985 to secure the proper ventilation, lighting and protection against dampness, effluvia or exhalation in underground rooms.

Reasonable expense

It is a complete defence to a repair notice if it can be shown that the end does not justify the means. Landlords are entitled to appeal against a repair notice on this basis but must do so within twenty-one days of service: see s.189(4) Housing Act 1985 below.

The cost of the specified repair work is compared with the estimated open market value of the repaired house, in order to determine whether the house can be rendered fit for human habitation at a reasonable expense: s.206 Housing Act 1985. This test creates a number of valuation problems, e.g. should the open market value be calculated on the basis of vacant possession?:

> 'The authorities appear to agree in requiring the court to make a realistic approach to the value of dwelling-houses as a saleable asset in the hands of the landlord when considering the reasonableness of the expense required to improve them, and therefore, to have regard to the presence of tenants and their rights of continued occupation and the effect that they have on the market value.'
> (Per Lord Justice Stephenson in *F.F.F.Estates Ltd* v. *Hackney London Borough Council* (1981).)

See also *Bacon* v. *Grimsby Corporation* (1949) for the common-sense approach. In addition geographical anomalies are created since the repair work is more likely to be deemed a reasonable expense in areas with high house prices.

Contents of repair notice

The repair notice must specify the repair work, state that the work will render the house fit for human habitation, and set out a reasonable time-table for the work's completion of not less than 21 days: s.189(2) Housing Act 1985.

Slum clearance

One consequence of a house being designated unfit for human habitation is that the local housing authority must order its demolition or closure, unless the landlord or freeholder undertakes either to reconstruct the house or that the house will not be used for human habitation: s.264 Housing Act 1985. Possession of the house can be regained from Rent Act tenants if the owner undertakes that it will not be used for human habitation, notwithstanding the Rent Acts: s.264 Housing Act 1985. The homeless tenant will be rehoused by the local housing authority: s.39 Land Compensation Act 1973 and Sch 2 Para 24(4) Housing (Consequential Provisions) Act 1985. It is not hard to see why a minority of landlords have been tempted to allow a house to fall into an unfit condition, sometimes with the tenant's connivance.

House in state of disrepair (but not unfit)

The local housing authority has a discretionary power to serve a repair notice on a person having control of a house which is in a serious 'state of disrepair': s.190 Housing Act 1985. In this case, the disrepair falls short of rendering the house unfit for human habitation. Before issuing a repair notice, the local authority must be satisfied that the house requires substantial repairs in order to bring it up to a reasonable standard: s.190 (1)(a) Housing Act 1985. The appropriate standard of repair is measured with reference to the house's age, character and locality: see *Proudfoot* v. *Hart* (1890) at p.139 above.

Tenant's application

Tenants may ask the local authority to serve a repair notice on their landlord requiring him to carry out substantial repairs. Tenants are not entitled to ask for the repair of minor defects or internal decorations.

The tenant has to satisfy the local authority that the house is in a condition which interferes with the 'personal comfort' of the occupying tenant in some material way: s.190(1)(b) Housing Act 1985. There is no statutory definition or guide to the criteria which will be considered here. This gives local housing authorities a very wide discretion, and it is likely that authorities have developed different criteria in deciding when to issue a repair notice.

Reasonable expense

There is no qualification that the expense must be reasonable in the case of disrepair which does not render the house unfit, but the Court of Appeal have said that the former statutory provision applies to notices for disrepair: *Hillbank Properties Ltd* v. *Hackney London Borough Council* (1978). Although the Housing Act 1985 does not adopt the 'reasonable expense' test for houses which are not unfit for habitation, it is assumed that the previous law remains unaltered given the fact that the new Act is a consolidation Act: s.2 Housing (Consequential Provisions) Act 1985.

Contents of repair notice

The repair notice must require the person on whom it is served to carry out specified repairs within a reasonable time. A minimum period of at least 21 days must be given. The repair notice must not require any works of internal decorative repair: s.190(2) Housing Act 1985.

Appeals against repair notices

Twenty-one days to appeal

Landlords and their agents must respond immediately to any repairs notice which is served on them since they only have a period of twenty-one days from date of service in which to appeal against the repair notice. If they fail to appeal, the notice operates after twenty-one days from service, and is final and conclusive as to matters which could have been raised on appeal: s.189(4), 190(4) Housing Act 1985.

Procedure

The landlord or any aggrieved person can appeal against the notice to the county court and has a further right of appeal to the Court of Appeal: s.191 Housing Act 1985. The appeal procedure can be used as a delay tactic by landlords who want a longer time in which to complete the work.

Enforcement of repair notice

Local authorities have very wide powers to enforce the specified repairs: see ss 193-8 Housing Act 1985. For example, they have power to carry out the repair work themselves if the landlord fails to complete the works within the specified time or, in the case of an appeal against the notice, within a longer period fixed by the court: s.193 Housing Act 1985. But they must first notify the person having control of the house in writing of their intention to carry out the repairs: s.194 Housing Act 1985.

FURTHER READING

Housing Law, Part III by A.Arden and M.Partington, Sweet & Maxwell (1983).

SECURE TENANT'S RIGHT TO REPAIR SCHEME

The repair scheme

One common complaint of secure tenants was the length of time landlords took to carry out their repairing obligations. The law has recently been changed to enable secure tenants to carry out 'landlord' repairs to their dwelling-houses and to recover the cost from their landlords: s.96(1) Housing Act 1985. The scheme is set out in Statutory Instrument 1985/1493 and commenced on the 1st January 1986.

Qualifying repairs

A secure tenant has a statutory right to recover sums expended on 'qualifying repairs' provided that he complies with the scheme's procedural requirements. Qualifying repairs are repairs which the landlord is obliged by a repairing covenant to carry out, other than a repair to the structure or exterior of a flat: para 1(2) of the Schedule to SI 1985 No. 1493.

Procedure

A tenant who wishes to carry out a qualifying repair must make a repair claim by serving a notice claiming a right to repair on a prescribed Tenant's Repair Claim Form. He is required to set out a description of the work and materials, detail the repair defects, and state whether he intends to carry out the work himself or give details of the person who is to carry out the repair works.

The landlord has twenty-one days in which to refuse or accept the claim; the grounds for refusing a claim are limited.

If the landlord fails to notify the tenant of its acceptance or refusal of the repair claim within twenty-one days of service, the tenant is entitled to serve a default notice on the landlord, provided that the estimate for the repair work is less than £200. Whereupon the tenant is entitled to carry out the work and claim the cost from the landlord if the landlord still fails to deal with the claim or does not carry out the repairs within seven days.

Grounds for refusal

The landlord must accept the tenant's repair claim if none of the following statutory grounds for refusal set out in Annex 8 to the Statutory Instrument applies:

(1) The landlord's costs would be less than £20.
(2) The repair works specified are not qualifying repairs.
(3) The works and materials specified would not remedy the repair defect.
(4) The landlord's costs would be more than £200.
(5) The landlord intends to carry out the work within 28 days from service.
(6) The works specified are not reasonably necessary for the personal comfort or safety of the dwelling-house's occupiers, and the landlord intends to carry out the works within one year of service as part of a maintenance programme.
(7) Carrying out the specified work would infringe a guarantee of which the landlord has the benefit in respect of work already done and materials supplied.
(8) The tenant has failed to provide reasonable access for the landlord to inspect the site of the works specified.

Chapter 16

Assignment and Sub-letting

INTRODUCTION

Prospective tenants who are contemplating the purchase of a lease will invariably want to know what restrictions, if any, will be placed on their future ability to sell the lease. This is an important issue regardless of whether a lease is bought for the purposes of a home, business or investment since restrictions on transfer will affect its saleability.

The general rule is that tenants are entitled to transfer a lease provided that it does not contain a provision to the contrary. However, landlords commonly restrict the tenant's right to transfer the leasehold premises during the term in order to retain control over the choice of tenant.

The transfer of a lease involves parting with possession of the leasehold premises, usually by an assignment or by sub-letting. A tenant has a right to assign or sub-let unless the lease contains a provision to the contrary: *Bruerton* v. *Rainsford* (1583).

ASSIGNMENT

General

Meaning

An assignment is the transfer of the whole of a lease's term or reversion. The transferor is called the 'assignor' and the transferee (the person who takes the assignment) is called the 'assignee'. For example, Lisa grants Thelma a ninety-nine year lease of a flat. Thelma lives in the flat for five years before assigning the remaining ninety-four year term to Anna.

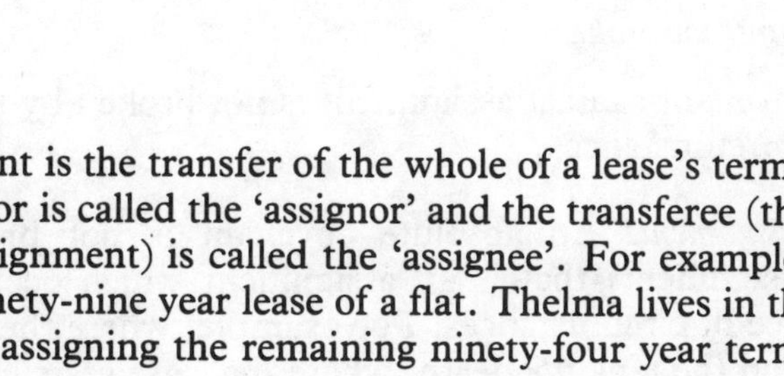

Methods of restricting assignment

There are two legal methods of prohibiting an assignment. A landlord can make it a condition of the lease that an assignment by the tenant will render the lease void: *Greenaway* v. *Adams* (1806). Alternatively, a landlord can insert a covenant into the lease which prohibits the assignment of a lease. A covenant against assignment can be in an absolute or qualified form.

Absolute covenants

An absolute covenant against assignment prohibits all voluntary legal assignments, and often takes the following form:

the tenant is 'not to assign or otherwise part with the premises or any part thereof'.

The additional words 'not to part with possession' have the effect of widening the scope of the covenant against assignment to any grant of possession to another including sub-letting: see *Lam Kee Ying Sdn Bhd* v. *Lam Shes Tong* (1974). Landlords who wish to restrict the class of persons in occupation of the premises will have to change the covenant's formula to reflect any further restrictions contemplated.

A tenant has no power to create a legal assignment if the lease is subject to an absolute prohibition on assignment. This can have harsh consequences for a tenant who may wish to transfer the lease if its obligations have become onerous e.g. owing to rent increases upon review. A tenant can assign a lease which is subject to an absolute prohibition against assignment if the landlord gives his permission for an assignment. But there is no legal compulsion on a landlord to grant his consent to an assignment, and he is entitled to rely on the covenant which prohibits assignment absolutely.

Absolute covenant not broken

An absolute covenant against assignment is not broken by the tenant in the following circumstances.

Involuntary assignment: An absolute covenant is not broken by an involuntary assignment, that is an assignment which occurs unintentionally by force of circumstances. For example, where the lease passes to an assignee on the tenant's death; where the lease vests in a trustee in bankruptcy because the tenant is insolvent; or where the lease is acquired by a local authority under a compulsory purchase order.

Sub-letting: An absolute covenant against assignment is not broken by sub-letting unless the covenant also prohibits sub-letting or parting with possession: *Russell* v. *Beecham* (1924).

Partnerships: A tenant who is a partner in a business can allow his partner to use the leasehold premises for business purposes without being in breach of an absolute covenant against assignment: *Gian Singh & Co.* v. *Nahar* (1965). But if the partnership is dissolved the lease cannot be assigned into the sole name of the non-tenant partner without causing a breach of an absolute covenant against assignment: *Varley* v. *Coppar* (1872). The question of the ownership of partnership property always presents special difficulties when partnerships are dissolved.

Lease as security: Many tenants obtain financial assistance when purchasing a lease. For example a home owner may obtain a mortgage from a bank or Building Society whereupon the lease will be charged as security for the loan. If the tenant fails to meet the loan repayments the lender will be entitled to possession. Notwithstanding this possible eventuality a covenant against assignment or parting with possession is not broken by the deposit of the lease as security: *Doe d. Pitt* v. *Hogg* (1824).

Entitlement to security of tenure: It has been held that even though a purported assignment by a housing association tenant to his daughter was unlawful because it was in breach of an absolute covenant, the daughter could remain in possession because she would have succeeded to the tenancy in any event: *Peabody Donation Fund Governors* v. *Higgins and Another* (1983).

Qualified covenants

A qualified covenant against assignment is a covenant which stipulates that the tenant cannot assign the lease unless he has first obtained the landlord's consent. It is commonly in the following form: the tenant is 'not to assign or part with possession of the premises or any part thereof without the landlord's prior written consent or licence'.

The purpose of a qualified covenant is to protect the landlord from having his premises occupied in an undesirable way or by an undesirable assignee: *Houlder Brothers & Co. Ltd* v. *Gibbs* (1925).

Landlord's consent

A qualified covenant may include the proviso that the landlord's consent to an assignment is 'not to be unreasonably withheld'. If the lease fails to include this proviso it will be implied by s.19(1)(a) Landlord and Tenant Act 1927 (see pp.176–7).

SUB-TENANCIES

A sub-lease is created when a third party is granted a leasehold interest in part only of the subject-matter of the original lease, the 'head lease'. A sub-lease may be carved out of the original estate in one of two ways. Either the entire premises may be sub-let for up to a day less than the original term; if the premises are purported to be sub-let for the entirety of the term this would amount to an assignment since the whole term would be transferred. Alternatively, part only of the premises may be sub-let. For example:

(a) Leonard grants Titian a five year lease of an artist's studio. Titian goes to Italy to study design and meanwhile sub-lets the studio to Stubb for the remainder of the term less one day. Titian has sub-let the entire premises.
(b) London Properties grants Tandy a 21 year lease of a shop with a flat above. Tandy has no use for the flat and sub-lets it to Sally for three years. This creates a physical sub-letting of part of the premises to Sally.

Absolute covenant

The precise wording of the covenant should be considered in order to determine which type of sub-letting is prohibited.

If the covenant states that the tenant is 'not to under-let', the covenant prohibits sub-letting of the entire premises (see example (a)), but does not prohibit sub-letting of part only (see example (b)).

If the covenant is 'not to under-let the premises or any part thereof', both sub-lettings in examples (a) and (b) are prohibited.

A covenant against sub-letting (or parting with possession) will be broken by a tenant if he allows another person into exclusive possession of the whole or part of the leasehold premises. But the grant of a licence will not amount to sub-letting: *Doe d. Pitt* v. *Laming* (1814). Incidentally an absolute covenant against assignment does not prohibit sub-letting: *Crusoe d. Blencowe* v. *Bugby* (1771).

Qualified covenant

A qualified covenant against sub-letting operates in a similar way to a qualified covenant against assignment in that it will stipulate that the tenant is 'not to under-let without the prior consent of the landlord'.

Relationship with head-landlord

The relationship between sub-tenant and head-landlord requires special consideration. When a tenancy is sub-let, there is no direct landlord and tenant relationship between the head-landlord and sub-tenant, and no privity of contract.

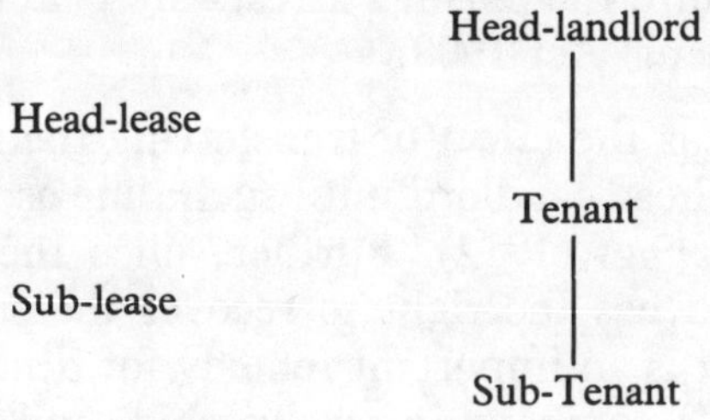

General

Although the sub-tenant is not in a direct landlord and tenant relationship with the head-landlord, he may be liable to him under the terms of the head-lease. This can work injustice in practice, because many sub-tenants have no opportunity of seeing the head lease but may nonetheless have agreed to be bound by its terms.

The sub-tenant has a duty to discover the terms of the head lease. He must also comply with any covenants of a negative character, e.g. a covenant prohibiting a change in user: *Cosser* v. *Collinge* (1832). This rule is founded on the general property law principle that restrictive covenants bind all those who have either actual notice of the restriction or who could discover the restriction if they had made the usual inquiries (constructive notice): rule in *Tulk* v. *Moxhay* (1848): see p.90.

Restrictions on sub-letting

The sub-tenant is in a vulnerable position should the head-lease contain a restriction on sub-letting. Any sub-letting would be unlawful in these circumstances and the head-landlord would be entitled to an order for possession against both the tenant and sub-tenant if the lease contains a forfeiture clause for breach of covenant: *Patoner Ltd* v. *Alexandrakis* (1984).

Enforcement of covenants against head-landlord

The sub-tenant may enforce covenants which 'touch and concern' the land against the head-landlord: ss. 78–9 Law of Property Act 1925, *Smith and Snipes Hill Farm Ltd* v. *River Douglas Catchment Board* (1949).

Recovery of rent from a sub-tenant

A head-landlord can claim rent directly from a sub-tenant if:

(a) the tenant is in arrears with rent; and

(b) the landlord serves a notice prescribed by statute on the sub-tenant stating that the rent is due, and requiring him to pay the rent to the head-landlord until the tenant's arrears are paid off: s.6 Distress for Rent (Amendment) Act 1908.

This procedure has the effect of transferring the right to receive the tenant's rent to the head-landlord until such time as the arrears are paid off: *Jarvis* v. *Hemmings* (1912). Further, once the notice for rent is served, the landlord has the right to recover the sub-tenant's rent by action or distress. It is an important remedy for head-landlords in cases where the tenant is a company in receivership, and a receiver has been appointed to collect rents due to a company tenant from sub-tenants but is not repaying the rent received to the head-landlord: note that this remedy was not relied on in *Official Custodian for Charities* v. *Parway Estates* (1985).

FURTHER READING

Corporate Receivers and Administrators by Lightman and Moss, Sweet & Maxwell, 1986, Chapter XVI.

STATUTORY INTERVENTION

Implied statutory proviso–qualified covenants

Qualified covenants against assignment, sub-letting and parting with possession are all subject to the important implied statutory proviso set out in s.19 Landlord and Tenant Act 1927. The effect of the proviso is that landlords cannot withhold their consent to an assignment unreasonably. Moreover, landlords are not entitled to ask the tenant to pay any money in return for consent to an assignment or sub-letting, apart from reasonable costs connected with the consent, unless this is expressly provided for by the lease: s.19(1) Landlord and Tenant Act 1927 and s.144 Law of Property Act 1925.

Withholding consent unreasonably

A body of case-law sets out guide-lines for the interpretation of the proviso that a landlord is not to withhold his consent unreasonably. Each case turns on its own facts. The onus of proving that consent has been unreasonably withheld is on the tenant: *Pimms Ltd* v. *Tallow Chandlers Co.* (1964).

Request for consent

A tenant must ask for his landlord's consent prior to the assignment or sub-letting: *Eastern Telegraph Co* v. *Dent* (1899). This is a strict rule. A tenant who fails to seek consent prior to assignment is liable to have his lease forfeited for breach of covenant: *Barrow* v. *Isaacs & Son* (1891). The fact that the landlord could not have withheld his consent to the assignee or sub-tenant is no defence to forfeiture proceedings.

Unreasonably

The general rule is that landlords may consider their own interests. The meaning of 'unreasonably' was judicially considered in *Viscount Tredegar* v. *Harwood* (1929) where Cozens-Hardy MR said that:

> 'It was not enough to show that other landlords might have accepted the proposed assignees; the landlords were not to be held to have withheld consent unreasonably, if in the action they took they acted as a reasonable man might have done in the circumstances'.

This is because the object of a covenant against assignment is to prevent undesirable tenants being foisted upon landlords. This is why it is often said that the landlord's reasons for refusal must have reference to an objection which is based either on the personality of the tenant or his proposed use of the premises: *Houlder Bros & Co Ltd* v. *Gibbs* (1925).

Object of assignment

The object of the assignment might have to be considered in determining whether the consent was withheld unreasonably. It has been held that a landlord's refusal to give consent to the assignment of the 'fag-end' of a lease was not unreasonable when the object of the assignment was to use the 'nuisance value' of the last few years of the term as a lever to persuade the landlord to share the profits of a redevelopment scheme: *Pimms* v. *Tallow Chandlers Co.* (1964). A landlord can reasonably refuse consent if granting consent would prejudice the landlord's rights to enforce a user covenant: *Woolworth (F.W.) PLC* v. *Charlwood Alliance Properties Ltd* (1986).

Surrender-back clause

A lease may require a tenant to offer to surrender the lease back to the landlord before any proposed assignment or sub-letting. If the tenant fails to offer to surrender the lease back in accordance with this covenant, a landlord's withholding of consent is not unreasonable: see *Adler* v. *Upper Grosvenor Street Investment* (1957) applied in *Bocardo SA* v. *S and M Hotels Ltd* (1979) where Lord Justice Megaw emphasised the importance of the doctrine of freedom of contract.

Business tenancies

If an agreement to surrender a lease back to the landlord has the effect of precluding the tenant from applying for a new business tenancy under the provisions of Part II Landlord and Tenant Act 1954, the agreement to surrender is invalidated by s.38(1) Landlord and Tenant Act 1954. This difference in the treatment of business leases arises as a result of the decision in *Allnatt London Properties Ltd* v. *Newton* (1981): see 'Restrictions on Assignment of Lease' an article by R. Sheldon and M. Friend (1982) 98 Law Quarterly Review 14.

Creation of statutory tenancy

A landlord will be justified in withholding his consent if the effect of an assignment or sub-letting would be the creation of a statutory tenancy. The Court of Appeal held in *West Layton Ltd* v. *Ford* (1979) that a landlord had not withheld his consent unreasonably to a sub-letting which would create a Rent Act protected tenancy: see also *Leeward Securities Ltd* v. *Lilyheath Properties Ltd* (1984).

Detriment to tenant

It has recently been held that it is unreasonable for a landlord to omit to consider the detriment which the tenant would suffer if consent to an assignment was refused in cases where the detriment to the tenant is greater than the benefit gained by the landlord. This balancing exercise was applied in *International Drilling Fluids Ltd* v. *Louisville Investments (Uxbridge) Ltd* (1986) where the Court of Appeal held that the damage to the landlord's reversion would be minimal as compared with the harm to the tenant; the tenant having already vacated the building but remaining liable under the lease's covenants. It is not altogether clear what the position is if the landlord takes into account the detriment to the tenant but still fails to consent to an assignment.

Leases for more than forty years

No consent is required for an assignment of a lease for more than forty years which has seven or more years to run if the lease is subject to a condition that the tenant erects, improves, adds or alters buildings: s.19(1)(b) Landlord and Tenant Act 1927. This does not apply to local authority and Government department landlords.

Payment for consent

Legal and other expenses: Landlords are entitled to require the tenant to pay any legal or other expenses incurred in connection with the consent to an assignment: s.19(1)(a) Landlord and Tenant Act 1927. The point here is that it is not open for a tenant to argue that the landlord, by requiring the tenant to pay any reasonable expenses which he has incurred, is withholding his consent unreasonably.

Sums by way of a fine: But some leases go further, and require the tenant to pay a sum of money to the landlord by way of a fine in return for his consent to an assignment in which case the landlord may lawfully require a sum of money to be paid. But if the lease is silent on this matter s.144 Law of Property Act 1925 stipulates that the lease is to be subject to the proviso that 'no sum of money or fine shall be payable for the landlord's consent'.

Discrimination

The race and sex discrimination legislation provides that landlords are not entitled to discriminate against prospective assignees on the grounds of race or sex.

Racial discrimination

It is unlawful for a landlord to discriminate against a proposed assignee on grounds of colour, race, nationality, ethnic or national origin when considering whether to withhold consent to an assignment: s.24 Race Relations Act 1976.

Small premises exemption: The only permitted statutory exception is where the landlord or a near relative lives in small residential premises and has to share accommodation with the tenant other than storage places and access areas. Small premises are premises which will accommodate either no more than three households including the assignor or six persons excluding the assignor and his family: s.22(1) Race Relations Act 1976.

Sexual discrimination

Similarly it is unlawful for landlords to discriminate against proposed tenants on the ground of his or her sex when considering the question of whether to consent to the assignment of a right of occupation. The only exception is where the landlord or a close relative of his fulfills the conditions of the 'small premises' exemption: s.31 Sex Discrimination Act 1975.

REMEDIES

Landlord's remedies

Injunction

A landlord can ask the court for an injunction to prevent a proposed assignment: *McEacharn* v. *Colton* (1902). This is a discretionary remedy.

Damages

A landlord is entitled to damages for breach of covenant against assignment. The correct measure of damages is the loss flowing from the assignment or sub-letting: *Williams* v. *Earle* (1868). There will be cases where the loss to the landlord will not be great e.g. where the assignee has a better reputation or greater financial standing than the assignor.

Forfeiture

If the lease contains a forfeiture clause for breach of covenant, the landlord is entitled to bring forfeiture proceedings against the tenant. An assignment is an irremediable breach of covenant, therefore a landlord does not have to ask the tenant to remedy it in the s.146 notice.

The acceptance of rent by a landlord who knows that an assignment or sub-letting has taken place will amount to a waiver of the breach of covenant. If rent is collected by an agent on behalf of a landlord, the agent's knowledge of an assignment or sub-letting is imputed to the landlord once a reasonable time has elapsed in which the facts can be communicated to the landlord by his agent: *Metropolitan Properties Co. Ltd* v. *Cordery and Another* (1979).

Tenant's remedies

Declaration

The tenant may apply to the court for a declaration that the landlord has unreasonably withheld his consent to an assignment or sub-letting together with his legal costs: *Young* v. *Ashley Gardens Properties Ltd* (1903). The county court has jurisdiction to grant a declaration regardless of the leasehold property's rateable value: s.53(1)(a) Landlord and Tenant Act 1954 as amended. A tenant is entitled to a declaration under this provision if he satisfies the court that the landlord's consent was unreasonably withheld: s.53(1),(2).

Specific performance

A tenant may ask for specific performance of a qualified covenant against assignment or sub-letting if the landlord is withholding his consent improperly: *White* v. *Hay* (1895). This is a discretionary remedy which may be sought as an alternative or an additional remedy to a declaration.

Damages

It seems that a tenant is not entitled to damages if a landlord has unreasonably withheld his consent to an assignment or sub-letting. But it has been pointed out that this point is not entirely settled: see Hill & Readman's *Law of Landlord and Tenant* 17th ed. (1982), volume 1 at p.560 n.(f).

Self-help

The tenant may take the risky course of proceeding with the assignment without the landlord's consent. In *Bromley Park Garden Estates Ltd* v. *Moss* (1983) a landlord provoked a tenant into assigning a flat by giving an unqualified refusal of consent based on the reason that it was not the landlord's practice to permit assignments of residential tenancies. In reality the landlords had refused consent in order to achieve the collateral purpose of furthering their investment plans. The Court of Appeal held that the landlords were not entitled to refuse their consent in order to achieve a collateral purpose. Lord Justice Slade gave the following warning to tenants contemplating proceeding with an assignment without their landlord's consent:

> 'A tenant who decides to proceed with an assignment following an unqualified refusal of consent on the part of the landlord must be entitled to take this course in the light of the facts as they exist at the date of the assignment. Even on this footing, he must still accept a degree of risk in adopting this course inasmuch as he may not be aware of all the factors which have in truth influenced the landlord in his refusal.'

This course is inadvisable if the lease contains a forfeiture clause for breach of covenant. If there is no forfeiture provision the tenant can minimise the risk to himself by ensuring that any damages payable will be minimal by selecting a reputable assignee so that the landlord cannot prove any loss flowing from the assignment.

FURTHER READING

Hill and Redman's *Law of Landlord and Tenant* 17th ed. 1982, Chapter 7.

'Assignment of leases–advising the client' D.W.Williams (1983) 266 EG 793.

Chapter 17

User, Insurance, Alterations and Improvements

RESTRICTIONS ON USER

Introductory

Landlords have historically insisted on inserting covenants in leases restricting the tenant's use of the leasehold premises. There were a number of explanations for this: the landlord may have wished to retain the character of the leasehold premises; the landlord may have traded from neighbouring premises and restricted the tenant's business activities in order to prevent the tenant setting up a competing business; or the covenant might be designed to prevent a nuisance or annoyance arising. Today restrictions are inserted for a variety of commercial reasons. For example, lettings of shop units in modern shopping arcades often contain a formula which restricts the trade of individual shop units to prevent competition between businesses within the same shopping development. The object of the restriction is to maximise rents since tenants will pay higher rents in a shopping arcade if they can be ensured a monopoly position.

The general rule is that tenants are entitled to use the leasehold premises for any lawful purpose, subject to any express or implied restrictions on user.

Illegal or immoral use

Tenants who use premises for illegal or immoral purposes are in a precarious position since the courts will not injunct a landlord who evicts a tenant in these circumstances, even if the lease did not contain a proviso for re-entry: *Litvinoff* v. *Kent* (1918). Landlords who either let premises in the knowledge that they will be used for illegal or immoral purposes or fail to take steps to end the lease when this fact comes to light will not be able to enforce the lease against the tenant, e.g. rent cannot be recovered: *Girardy* v. *Richardson* (1793).

Construing express restrictions

The interpretation of user covenants is obviously important to prospective tenants who need to know whether they can use the premises for the purpose desired: see 'Interpreting user covenants', an article by D. Williams (1986) 280 EG 21.

Common restrictions

Trade or business: Covenants which prohibit specified trades or businesses or prohibit certain uses will not be broken by a slight degree of the prohibited use on the part of the tenant. Thus a covenant prohibiting certain trading activities will not be broken by a tenant who sells a few of the prohibited class of goods together with his own class of goods: *Stuart* v. *Diplock* (1889). In *Calabar (Woolwich) Ltd* v. *Tesco Stores Ltd* (1977), it was held that a covenant restricting use to supermarket and allied purposes was not broken by the ancillary sale of freezer cabinets at a supermarket. Similarly, a covenant restricting use to business offices only is not broken by either eating there during the day or sleeping on the premises at night since those acts did not convert the use to residential use: *Macmillan & Co Ltd* v. *Rees* (1946).

Residential user: Conversely, where the use is restricted to use as a private dwelling-house only, any degree of business use amounts to a breach of covenant: *German* v. *Chapman* (1877). This covenant will not, however, preclude tenants from taking in paying guests or lodgers where the sharing amounts to the taking in of a friend who shares family life: *Segal Securities Ltd* v. *Thoseby* (1963). On the other hand, there will be a breach of covenant if the taking of lodgers is an arm's length business transaction and the lodger does not live as a member of the family: *Thorn* v. *Madden* (1925).

Nuisance or annoyance: One prerequisite of good estate management practice is to ensure that leases contain covenants against nuisance and annoyance which can be enforced against tenants whose activities disrupt others.

Nuisance has the narrow technical meaning of an inconvenience which materially interferes with the ordinary human existence in a physical sense, not merely according to elegant or dainty life: per Vice-Chancellor Knight-Bruce in *Walter* v. *Selfe* (1851). A nuisance in the colloquial sense of the word may not amount to a nuisance in law. Thus an actress tenant was held not to be in breach of a covenant 'not to permit anything which might be a nuisance or annoyance' to the landlord in a case where the nuisance complained of was shouting from outside the premises and the persistent telephonic use of an entry-phone by an over-persistent admirer: *Commercial General Administration Ltd* v. *Thomsett* (1979).

The addition of the word 'annoyance' widens the covenant considerably since it is not restricted to interruptions of a physical nature. Any act which interrupts the reasonable peace of mind of an adjoining occupier constitutes an annoyance. For example, a fried fish shop creates an annoyance but not a nuisance: per Mr Justice Avory in *Errington* v. *Birt* (1911).

Implied restrictions

Planning law

Planning legislation imposes a number of restrictions on the use of property; this subject is outside the ambit of this book. See B. Denyer-Green's *Planning and Development Law* (Estates Gazette, 1982).

Overcrowding

The overcrowding of residential accommodation is prohibited by Part X Housing Act 1985. For this purpose overcrowding is defined with reference to either a 'room standard' or a 'space standard'. The room standard is contravened when two persons of the opposite sex (who are not living together as husband and wife) must sleep in the same room: s.325 Housing Act 1985. The space standard is contravened if the number of people occupying a floor space exceeds the permitted number: see Table 1, s.326 Housing Act 1985. For both purposes children under ten years of age are left out of account. Both landlords and occupiers of overcrowded dwelling-houses are guilty of an offence, and may be fined or convicted of the offence.

Distinction between absolute and qualified prohibitions

Covenants restricting user either prohibit the use altogether (absolute prohibition) or provide that the tenant may use the premises for the user prohibited by the lease provided that the landlord's consent has been obtained first (qualified prohibition).

Absolute prohibitions

Landlords who refuse to consent to an alteration in a use which is subject to an absolute prohibition in the lease are not liable in damages, even where the refusal to consent to a change in use can be shown to be unreasonable: per Mr Justice Mervyn Davies in *Guardian Assurance Co. Ltd* v. *Gants Hill Holdings Ltd* (1983).

Qualified prohibitions

If the lease specifically states that consent to a change in use is not to be unreasonably withheld, and a landlord refuses to agree to a change of use, the tenant is entitled to ask the court for a declaration that consent was unreasonably withheld: s.53(1) Landlord and Tenant Act 1954.

Landlords are prohibited from charging a premium for giving consent to a change in use in cases where the lease contains a qualified prohibition on change of user. This is because there is an implied statutory term that no premium or fine may be charged by the landlord for giving his consent to a proposed aleration in use where the prohibition on user is qualified by the words 'without licence or consent' provided that no structural alteration of the premises is required to give effect to the changed use: s.19(3) Landlord and Tenant Act 1927.

Releasing the restriction

If the landlord has accepted rent in full knowledge of the breach of covenant restricting user over a considerable period of time, there is a strong argument for saying that he has either waived or acquiesced in the breach, or granted a licence permitting the breach: *Gibson* v. *Doeg* (1857) (twenty years acquiescence). However, if rent has been accepted by the landlord with knowledge of the breach for a relatively short period of time, the Court of Appeal has held that only the past breaches have been waived and that the tenant was not impliedly released from the covenant for the future: *City and Westminster Properties* v. *Mudd* (1958).

Discharge or modification

The Lands Tribunal has power to discharge or modify a restrictive covenant in cases of long leases of more than forty years where more than twenty-five years have expired: s.84 Law of Property Act 1925 as amended. The Lands Tribunal is directed to consider the value or advantage of the restriction to those who benefit from it. The restrictive covenant will only be discharged or modified if it is truly obsolete, impedes reasonable user of the land, or where everyone concerned has agreed to this course of action.

Effect of restriction upon rent review

Landlords and tenants face a predicament when agreeing modern user clauses since their construction often has a marked impact upon rent review. The more restricted the user, the lower the open market valuation at rent review. One way for landlords to circumvent this problem whilst retaining restrictions on user is to stipulate that the rent should be reviewed on the notional assumption that there are no restrictions on user: see pp.130–1. But in the absence of a stipulation of this sort, landlords cannot unilaterally attempt to widen the user clause ex post facto simply in order to ensure a greater increase in rent at rent review: *C & A Pensions Trustees Ltd* v. *British Vita Investments Ltd* (1984).

COVENANTS TO INSURE

It is the practice for leases of seven years or more to contain either a landlord's or tenant's covenant to insure. Leases with shorter terms may contain covenants to insure.

Landlord's covenant

The landlord will generally pay for the insurance and recover it from the tenants by way of additional 'rent' in cases where the landlord has covenanted to insure the leasehold premises. The tenant will be required to pay the full costs involved, and will generally have no part to play in the choice of insurance or insurers. Tenants may be required to meet the higher insurance premiums demanded by an insurance policy which provides for the full cost of reinstatement which contains an element of inflation-proofing: *Gleniffer Finance Corpn Ltd* v. *Bamar Wood and Products Ltd* (1978).

Tenant's covenants

Tenants may be required under the terms of the covenant to insure the leasehold premises themselves, in which case it will be at their own expense. But the landlords may have to approve or specify the insurers. Note that it is now possible to obtain relief from forfeiture for non-insurance.

Application of insurance monies

A landlord is under no obligation to apply any insurance monies he receives to rebuilding in the absence of an express term requiring him to rebuild the leasehold premises in the event of their destruction: *Leeds* v. *Cheetham* (1827). A tenant who insures the premises voluntarily is in an identical position. By contrast, a landlord who has imposed an express insuring obligation on his tenant must apply any monies recovered to rebuilding: *Mumford Hotels Ltd* v. *Wheeler* (1963).

ALTERATIONS AND IMPROVEMENTS

Leases often prohibit or restrict the tenant's right to carry out alterations. Alterations will be considered separately from improvements, although in practice both matters will generally be dealt with under the generic term 'alterations' in a lease. It is rare for a lease to include the term 'improvement' since this term is largely redundant if the term 'alteration' is used. After all, an improvement is an alteration which makes the leasehold premises better than before.

ALTERATIONS

Meaning

An alteration is a change to the construction or fabric of the leasehold premises: *Bickmore* v. *Dimmer* (1903). For example, the conversion of a house into flats: *Duke of Westminster* v. *Swinton* (1948).

Absolute covenants

The precise form and wording of a covenant which prohibits alterations will depend upon the type of premises and the length of the lease. For example, business tenants will often insist on specific modifications to an absolute covenant in order to carry on their business activity properly or to alter premises in order to lay cabling for high technology equipment into old buildings. An express covenant prohibiting alterations is often in the following form:

the tenant is

> 'not to make any alterations to the demised premises, and not to cut or maim the main walls and timbers of the premises'.

No alteration can be made in the case of an absolute covenant unless the landlord chooses to give his consent to the tenant's proposed alterations.

Qualified covenant

A qualified covenant will contain the qualification that a tenant is only entitled to alter the premises if he has first obtained the landlord's consent, and this qualification commonly takes the following form:

the tenant is

> 'not to make any alteration or additions to the demised premises without the prior written licence or consent of the landlord, such licence or consent is not to be unreasonably withheld'.

In order to comply with a qualified covenant tenants should seek and obtain the landlord's permission before carrying out the improvement. If the covenant states that consent is not to be unreasonably withheld, the tenant must show that a refusal to give consent to an improvement is unreasonable. But it is not unreasonable for a landlord to make his consent conditional on the payment of a sum of money, and he may also ask the tenant to reinstate the premises to their former condition at the end of the term.

Statutory modifications

The county court has jurisdiction to set aside or modify covenants which prevent a tenant from altering premises in cases where a tenant is compelled to alter premises in order to comply with a statutory requirement: Factories Act 1961 and the Offices, Shops and Railway Premises Act 1963.

IMPROVEMENTS

Introduction

Some leases restrict the tenant's rights to carry out improvements to the property. The covenant may be an absolute or qualified covenant, but a qualified covenant is more usual. A qualified covenant which prohibits a tenant from carrying out improvements without the landlord's consent is subject to the statutory proviso that consent is not to be unreasonably withheld: s.19(2) Landlord and Tenant Act 1927.

An improvement is an addition or alteration which makes the leasehold premises in some way better than before rather than simply making the premises as good as new: *Wates* v. *Rowland* (1952). But it is not necessarily an addition or alteration which increases the value of the leasehold property. It may simply be an alteration which allows the tenant to use the premises more advantageously. It is important to distinguish improvements from non-improving alterations in cases where there is a qualified covenant. This is because tenants with qualified covenants can only rely on the statutory proviso if the contemplated alteration amounts to an improvement. The definition of an improvement favours tenants since the test of deciding whether an alteration is an improvement is decided with reference to the tenant's position and not the landlord's: see the Woolworth and Lambert (1936–8) litigation considered below.

Absolute covenants

An absolute covenant will state that the tenant is not to make any alterations to the premises. For this purpose, 'alterations' include alterations which improve the leasehold premises. No alterations can be made unless the landlord is prepared to give his consent to the improvements. The tenant cannot compel a landlord to give his consent even if the improvement will be of mutual benefit to both landlord and tenant.

Qualified covenants

Landlord's consent

A qualified covenant prohibiting the tenant from carrying out an improvement without the landlord's consent or licence is subject to the two following statutory provisos:

Payment required: Landlords often require a sum of money in return for their consent to an improvement. The statutory proviso stipulates that landlords are not entitled to any sums of money in return for their consent: s.19(3) Landlord and Tenant Act 1927. The proviso is subject to three exceptions: s.19(2)(3) Landlord and Tenant Act 1927. The payment of a reasonable sum of money can be demanded:

(a) if the improvement involves structural alterations; or
(b) if the improvement damages or diminishes the value of neighbouring premises owned by the landlord; or
(c) for legal or other expenses incurred in connection with the consent.

In addition, the landlord is entitled to demand an undertaking from the tenant to reinstate the premises in the condition in which they were before the improvement was carried out.

Unreasonably withholding consent: A landlord must not withhold his consent to an improvement unreasonably: s.19(2) Landlord and Tenant Act 1927. The principles which the courts adopt when deciding whether a landlord has been unreasonable in refusing to give his permission to an improvement by the tenant were considered in the Woolworth and Lambert litigation where a qualified covenant was subject to the proviso in s.19(2).

Woolworth & Co. Ltd leased two adjacent sites, which included a lease of premises from Lambert. Woolworth wished to enlarge these premises by building onto the adjacent site thereby creating a unit straddling both sites. Woolworth asked for Lambert's consent to the improvement. Lambert gave a conditional refusal, and said that they would only give their consent if Woolworth either paid £7000 in damages or reinstated the premises at the end of the term. The proposed improvement would destroy the separate character of the building leased from Lambert.

In the first round of litigation the Court of Appeal held that although the proposed alterations were improvements for the purpose of s.19(2) Landlord and Tenant Act 1927, the tenant had not proved to the court's satisfaction that Lambert had withheld its consent unreasonably: *F.W. Woolworth & Co. Ltd* v. *Lambert* (1936); part of the reason being that the burden of proof is on the tenant to show that the landlord has withheld his consent unreasonably. Woolworth had failed to prove that £7000 was an unreasonable sum to demand in return for the landlord's consent to the proposed improvement.

Woolworth applied again for the Lambert's consent to the improvement whereupon Lambert refused to give their consent. Lambert asked the court for a declaration that the alterations were not an 'improvement' for the purposes of s.19(2). The Court of Appeal held that the proposed alterations were an 'improvement', and further that Lambert had refused its consent unreasonably: *Lambert* v. *F.W. Woolworth & Co. Ltd* (1938). Lambert lost the second round for the simple reason that they failed to give a qualified consent based on the payment of a reasonable sum by way of damages: see Lord Justice Mackinnon's comments.

Remedy of declaration

A tenant has a statutory right to ask the court to make a declaration that the landlord has unreasonably withheld his consent to the making of an improvement to the leasehold premises: s.53(1)(b) Landlord and Tenant Act 1954. The High Court and county court have concurrent jurisdiction.

Secure tenant's improvements

Landlord's consent required

Secure tenants are only permitted to improve a dwelling-house with their landlord's consent: s.97 Housing Act 1985. This is a strict term of secure tenancies and covers all improvements including the erection of a wireless or television aerial: s.97 Housing Act 1985.

Unreasonably withholding consent

The landlord is not to withhold his consent to improvements unreasonably: s.97(3) Housing Act 1985: see pp.176–9 for a judicial consideration of the general principles which the courts consider when applying this test.

When determining whether or not the landlord has withheld his consent to improvements unreasonably the court is directed to consider the extent to which the improvement would be likely to:

(a) make the dwelling-house, or any other premises less safe for the occupiers;
(b) cause the landlord to incur expenditure which it would be unlikely to incur if the improvement were not made; or
(c) reduce the price which the dwelling-house would fetch if sold on the open market or the rent which the landlord would be able to charge on letting the dwelling-house.

But in each case the onus is on the landlord to show that consent was not withheld unreasonably: s.98(1) Housing Act 1985.

Improvement of dwellings

Improvement notices

Part VII Housing Act 1985 empowers local authorities to serve improvement notices on landlords in respect of dwellings which either lack standard amenities or are capable of being repaired to comply with specified standards at a reasonable cost: see ss.209-238 Housing Act 1985.

Area improvement

Part VIII Housing Act 1985 empowers local authorities to designate an area as a 'housing action area' or a 'general improvement area' whereupon the local authority has wide powers to improve properties within the designated area, to grant owners contributions towards improvements and powers to purchase property compulsorily: see ss.239-263 Housing Act 1985.

Chapter 18

Ending the Relationship of Landlord and Tenant–Overview

ENDING THE RELATIONSHIP

Leases are characterised by the fact that they are created for a certain duration and must necessarily end at some point in time. The termination of tenancies was formerly a matter of contract and regulated by common law rules. All tenancies must be terminated by the appropriate common law method in order to end the landlord and tenant relationship. Since many tenancies fall within one of the statutory schemes, the tenant may well have a right to continue in possession even though the contractual term has ended and the tenancy has been determined at common law. A landlord and tenant relationship is only finally brought to an end when the tenant's right to exclusive possession has been extinguished and the landlord has regained possession.

It is important to distinguish between the method or procedure by which a tenancy is terminated, and ending the landlord and tenant relationship. This is because the landlord and tenant relationship does not necessarily end upon the termination of the tenancy. For example, a tenant may have a contractual or statutory right to renew his tenancy when the original term expires, giving rise to a new tenancy but continuing the landlord and tenant relationship. Alternatively, the tenant may be able to take advantage of statutory protection and remain in possession after the tenancy has been determined.

Since the common law regulating the termination of tenancies is overlaid by the statutory schemes, it is essential to give due consideration to the interrelationship between the two when analysing a factual landlord and tenant problem involving issues of possession. The starting point is to work out the common law method of terminating the tenancy in conjunction with the relevant statutory provisions and procedures where appropriate.

TERMINATION AT COMMON LAW

At common law the method of ending the tenancy is dictated by the type of tenancy and any relevant contractual term or agreement. A fixed term

TERM CERTAIN

Effluxion of Time

Lease expires automatically when the term ends

Option to Determine (break clause)

Either party may have the option to terminate a fixed term lease mid-term. The option must be exercised in strict accordance with its terms.

PERIODIC TENANCY

Notice to Quit

Either party may give notice that the tenancy will end after a stated period of time. The notice must be:
(a) served on the correct day
(b) of the appropriate length
(c) in the correct form.

Merger

Tenant acquires the freehold by agreement, and the tenancy merges into the freehold

L (freehold) ↓ T

Surrender

The tenant surrenders the remainder of the lease to the landlord by consent:

L ↑ T (remainder of lease)

Forfeiture

A lease may contain a forfeiture clause (proviso for re-entry) which enables the landlord to evict the tenant e.g.:
(a) for breach of covenant;
(b) upon the tenant's insolvency;
(c) upon the tenant's death.
The correct procedural requirements must be observed.

Fig. 3 Termination at common law.

tenancy will expire automatically at the end of the contractual term whereas a periodic tenancy can carry on indefinitely unless and until one of the parties takes steps to end it and serves a valid 'notice to quit' on the other. A notice to quit served by the landlord gives the tenant notice that he will be required to give up possession of the leasehold premises after a specified period of time. A notice to quit served by the tenant provides the landlord with notice of a tenant's intention to end the landlord and tenant relationship after a specified period of time.

A distinction can be drawn between the intended duration of a fixed term lease and its premature termination. The parties to a fixed term lease may wish to terminate the lease mid-term, e.g. because the leasehold premises no longer meet their requirements or because the lease has become burdensome. Express provision may be made in a lease for this eventuality enabling a tenant to surrender up the remainder of the term, or the landlord may consent to a surrender in any event. Alternatively, the landlord may wish to sell his interest to the tenant, in which case the two estates will merge. One further method by which a fixed term tenancy may be terminated mid-term is by way of forfeiture for breach of covenant.

IMPACT OF STATUTORY SCHEMES

Relationship between the common law and statutory schemes

Although a tenancy may have been determined at common law it does not necessarily follow that the relationship of landlord and tenant has ended. The majority of the statutory schemes contain provisions which affect the ending of landlord and tenant relationships. This is because the statutory schemes are designed to protect tenants, each scheme working in a different way. For example, one feature of a Rent Act protected tenancy is that a tenant is automatically entitled to a statutory tenancy when the protected tenancy has been terminated, thus prolonging the relationship indefinitely. A business tenancy does not give the tenant security of tenure in this way, but a business tenant does have a statutory right to ask his landlord for a new business tenancy when his existing tenancy expires. Thus in both these cases there is the possibility of the continuation of the landlord and tenant relationship after the original tenancy has been terminated.

The statutory schemes are superimposed onto the common law framework, and take effect in completely different ways. Nonetheless, a tenancy must always be determined by the relevant common law method either prior to or concurrent with any prescribed statutory procedure for its termination. In following the complex statutory procedural steps it is easy for landlords to overlook the fact that the tenancy may not have been terminated at common law, e.g. where a landlord has served the prescribed statutory notice to determine a periodic business tenancy but has omitted to serve a notice to quit to terminate it at common law. This omission could prolong possession proceedings as the tenant would be entitled to claim that the tenancy has not been validly terminated.

Surrender

There is nothing to prevent a tenant from agreeing to surrender his tenancy to the landlord.

THE STATUTORY SCHEMES

The broad effect of each scheme is summarised in the text below, but since each scheme operates in a unique way the relevant statutory provisions will be found in later chapters.

Residential sector

Rent Act regulated tenancy

Rent Act tenants have security of tenure which protects them in two different ways as follows, with the result of prolonging the relationship of landlord and tenant beyond the contractual term.

Statutory tenancy

A statutory tenancy is created automatically when a protected tenancy is terminated if the tenant occupies the residence as his home. A statutory tenancy has been graphically described as a 'status of irremoveability' because of the difficulties landlords experience in trying to regain possession. A statutory tenancy can be transferred to up to two generations of the tenant's family by succession provided that there are members of the family who qualify under the scheme's 'inheritance' provisions.

Possession order

A landlord can only obtain possession of the leasehold premises if he obtains a court order for possession. A possession order will only be granted in circumstances where the landlord can satisfy the court that he is entitled to possession on the basis of one of a limited number of statutory grounds of possession: s.98 Rent Act 1977. It is very often the case that a landlord will be unable to obtain a possession order. This is either because none of the grounds applies or because the court has a discretion in the matter which it exercises in favour of the tenant and refuses to grant a possession order.

Common law termination

The relationship between the common law method of terminating a Rent Act regulated tenancy and the statutory scheme can be illustrated by the following example. Tony rents a flat, which is his only home, from Loser on a monthly tenancy which is protected by the Rent Act 1977. Since a monthly periodic tenancy has been created all the normal common law rules relating to the termination of periodic tenancies apply. Thus Loser can only end the tenancy at common law by serving a valid notice to quit. Tony's tenancy attracts all the protection afforded by the Rent Act 1977. If Tony's Rent Act protected tenancy is determined by a valid notice to quit given by Loser, he automatically becomes a statutory tenant. Loser will not be able to regain possession unless he can satisfy a court that he ought to be granted possession on the basis of one of the statutory grounds for possession.

If, however, Tony wishes to give up the tenancy, whether contractual or statutory, he may do so. He has to serve a notice to quit and remains liable for rent during the period of notice unless the landlord agrees to accept earlier surrender.

Long tenancies at a low rent

Long tenancies (exceeding twenty-one years) which fall within the scope of Part I Landlord and Tenant Act 1954 are automatically continued by statute after the end of the contractual term, giving rise to a statutory tenancy which is regulated by the Rent Act 1977: s.1 Landlord and Tenant Act 1954. A long tenancy at a low rent is not terminated until the tenancy has been determined at common law and the statutory procedure for terminating the tenancy has been followed.

If the landlord terminates the tenancy this does not have the effect of ending the landlord and tenant relationship because the ending of the tenancy by the prescribed statutory procedure has the triggering effect of creating a statutory tenancy regulated by the Rent Acts. A landlord can only regain possession of the premises either if the tenant agrees to a surrender of the tenancy or one of the Rent Act grounds for possession applies. Therefore, in effect, a person who has a long tenancy at a low rent will enjoy the same protection as an ordinary Rent Act tenant.

Right to extend or enfranchise: The Leasehold Reform Act 1967 gives some long leaseholders the statutory right to extend their lease by fifty years or to purchase the freehold compulsorily: s.1 Leasehold Reform Act 1967. These provisions have a wide effect, and give tenants a stake in the property. They have two differing effects upon the expiry of the tenancy: the landlord and tenant relationship may be prolonged if the tenant extends his lease; or, alternatively, the tenant may end the landlord and tenant relationship if he chooses to buy out the landlord's interest completely. The new lease or freehold may be transferred, e.g. by sale.

Restricted contract: Landlords will always be able to obtain possession where the contract is a restricted contract although the tenant can ask for a possession order to be postponed for a few months.

Protected shorthold

A protected shorthold tenant has no security of tenure and the tenant must give up possession when the term expires. The tenancy can be ended mid-term by the tenant upon notice. A landlord may be able to end the tenancy mid-term by forfeiture for breach of covenant.

Registered housing associations

This category of residential tenant has no security of tenure, and is specifically exempt from the protection afforded by the Rent Acts.

Assured tenancies

Assured tenancies are treated as if they were business tenancies in spite of their residential nature. They are protected in two ways by Part II Landlord and Tenant Act 1954. First of all, an assured tenancy will continue until it is determined by the prescribed statutory provisions. Secondly, an assured tenant has a statutory right to apply for a new tenancy.

An assured tenancy may be ended mid-term by the tenant by surrender or the appropriate notice. The tenancy can be forfeited by the landlord or by a superior landlord.

Secure tenants

A secure tenant has protection comparable to the protection afforded to Rent Act tenants. A possession order must be obtained from a court in order to terminate a secure tenancy and the tenant must be given notice of any proceedings for possession: s.83 Housing Act 1985. Landlords can only obtain possession if a court is satisfied that one of a limited number of statutory grounds applies: s.84 Housing Act 1985.

Fixed-term secure tenancies may be terminated mid-term by a procedure which is analogous to forfeiture. A landlord must follow the prescribed procedure and apply to the court for a 'termination order': s.82(3) Housing Act 1985. If the court grants a termination order, a periodic tenancy will automatically arise unless the court grants a possession order at the landlord's request.

Business sector

Business tenancies

Part II Landlord and Tenant Act 1954 operates completely differently from the security of tenure provisions found in the statutory schemes relating to the residential sector. There are two main ways in which the statute protects the tenant as follows.

Continuation: A business tenancy will not end when the term expires unless the landlord has observed the strict statutory procedure and time-table for its termination in addition to terminating the tenancy at common law; the business tenancy is continued automatically by statute until so terminated: s.24 Landlord and Tenant Act 1954.

Renewal: A business tenant has a statutory right to apply for a renewal of his tenancy at a commercial market rent. Thus there is a possibility that the parties may continue in a landlord and tenant relationship under a new lease when the original term has expired. The original business tenancy is continued in the interim. A landlord is entitled to ask for a market rent for this period: s.24A Landlord and Tenant Act 1954.

Compensation

A landlord may be obliged to compensate the tenant when the tenancy ends. The compensation may be paid in respect of authorised improvements which the tenant has made: s.1 Landlord and Tenant Act 1927. Alternatively, a landlord may have to pay the tenant compensation for loss of goodwill where the landlord has successfully refused an application for a new tenancy because he requires possession of the premises himself: s.37 Landlord and Tenant Act 1954.

Agricultural sector

Agricultural holdings

Agricultural tenants have a wide measure of security of tenure which restricts the landlord's rights to regain possession of the agricultural holding on the termination of the tenancy or death of the tenant.

Notices to quit

There are a number of statutory restrictions which operate to provide agricultural tenants with a minimum period of notice of twelve months unless the landlord obtains a certificate of bad husbandry from an Agricultural Land Tribunal: Part III Agricultural Holdings Act 1986.

Succession

Members of the tenant's family have statutory rights to succession on the death or retirement of the tenant in the case of certain tenancies of agricultural holdings: Part IV Agricultural Holdings Act 1986.

Compensation for disturbance

Even if the landlord is successful in terminating the tenancy in accordance with the provisions of the Agricultural Holdings Act 1986 he may have to pay the tenant compensation for disturbance: Part V Agricultural Holdings Act 1986.

Agricultural workers

A statutory tenancy is created automatically upon the termination of an agricultural worker's protected occupancy provided that the agricultural worker occupies the dwelling-house as his residence: s.4 Rent (Agriculture) Act 1976. A statutory tenancy gives an agricultural worker security of tenure which is comparable to the security of tenure afforded to Rent Act tenants, save that there is only one right of succession to a statutory tenancy under the provisions of the Rent (Agricultural) Act 1976.

Chapter 19

Termination at Common Law

Once a tenancy is terminated it puts an end to a property interest in land. This has certain consequences for the tenant which cannot always be compensated for in damages. It is for this reason that the common law requires the parties to comply with the relevant procedures, and has leant against termination if these procedures have not been complied with.

The main common law methods of terminating tenancies are set out in the text below. Fixed term tenancies generally end by effluxion of time or by the exercise of an option to determine, and periodic tenancies by way of notice to quit. Both types of tenancy can be terminated at common law by merger or surrender if this is agreed between the parties. Alternatively, some landlords may have grounds for forfeiting a lease and evicting a tenant mid-term; see Chapter 20. Finally, a lease may be disclaimed (disowned) in special narrowly prescribed circumstances.

EFFLUXION OF TIME

A fixed term lease or tenancy will expire automatically at common law when the last day of the term expires through effluxion of time, i.e. by reason of the passage of time. Only fixed term tenancies expire by effluxion of time.

The lease or tenancy agreement will set out the length of term agreed and its commencement date, and the expiry date can be calculated from this if it is not expressly stated. Whilst the relationship of landlord and tenant ends at common law once the term expires, it may of course be continued or prolonged by statute. The common law requires no formalities for the termination of tenancies by effluxion of time: *Cobb* v. *Stokes* (1807).

OPTIONS TO DETERMINE, RENEW AND PURCHASE

Introductory

The parties to a fixed term lease may by express agreement insert an option into the lease which has certain consequences on the question of the lease's termination. Options may take a number of forms. Three of the commonest types of option are options to determine a tenancy, options to renew the lease, and options to purchase the freehold. The first terminates the tenancy whereas the other two options give a tenant the possibility of remaining in the premises either under a new lease or through purchasing the freehold.

The point of incorporating an option into a long lease is to give the parties some flexibility so that either the landlord and tenant relationship can be ended early or the tenant is given the opportunity of enlarging his interest in the premises.

Options to determine, renew and purchase should, strictly speaking, be considered in the context of express covenants. But since for all practical purposes they impinge upon the termination of a tenancy they are considered in this chapter.

Option to determine

A fixed term lease may contain an option conferring a right on either party to terminate a lease mid-term which is referred to as a 'break clause'. The option to determine was traditionally designed to enable the tenant to break the lease mid-term, and is a useful right if the lease has become onerous, e.g. where the tenant is unable to pay rent after a rent review. The option is generally exercisable only by the tenant. But if there is any ambiguity as to who is entitled to exercise the option, it may only be exercised by the tenant: *Dann* v. *Spurrier* (1803).

If the option is validly exercised, the tenancy will end. The lease will set out any conditions which are attached to the option, and these must be complied with strictly. It is common for leases to stipulate that the option can only be exercised if the tenant has fulfilled all his obligations under the lease and served a formal notice within a specified period, e.g. a long lease might be determinable at the end of every fifth or seventh year. Thus if a tenant wishes to terminate a twenty-one year lease in its seventh year pursuant to an option to determine exercisable at the end of the seventh and fourteenth year of the term on written notice given six months prior to the seventh or fourteenth anniversary of the lease, the tenant should give his landlord written notice of this fact not later than six and a half years into the term. If the tenant misses this deadline, he will be unable to break the lease until the fourteenth year unless the landlord agrees to accept a surrender of the remainder of the term.

Option to renew

A fixed term lease may contain an option granting the tenant the right to renew the lease at the end of the term, e.g. for a further seven or fourteen years. The option will set out the terms and conditions for the lease's renewal, which must be complied with. An option to renew will normally be exercised at or near the end of the term. It is appropriate to consider renewal in the context of terminating a tenancy since the tenant has the opportunity of electing to renew the lease upon its termination.

Restrictions

Options which purport to grant the renewal of a lease for a term exceeding sixty years from the termination of the lease are made void by statute: Law of Property Act 1922, Sch XV para 7(2). Options to renew which have the effect of creating perpetually renewable leases should be avoided.

Enforcement

Tenants who wish to renew their lease must comply with the lease's precise conditions for renewal. In practice, leases generally require the tenant to serve a renewal notice on the landlord, at or towards the end of the existing lease, as a prerequisite for exercising an option to renew. Any prescribed time-table must be complied with strictly since the option generally makes time of the essence.

Conditions precedent

The right to renew is often made conditional upon the proper performance of the lease's obligations. These conditions must be complied with before the lease can be renewed, and their compliance is a condition precedent for renewal. In other words, landlords will not be forced to renew leases in favour of tenants who have defaulted in their obligations under the existing lease. This is based on two unstated principles. Firstly, that a landlord should not be forced to renew a landlord and tenant relationship with a bad tenant. Secondly, that a good tenant should be rewarded with the opportunity of renewing his lease.

The imposition of a condition precedent could lead to injustice if it were applied strictly so that any breach, however trivial or understandable, would disentitle a tenant from his right to renew. For example, a tenant may have set off payments of rent against a non-repairing landlord and fail to pay rent for that reason only. This issue was considered by the Court of Appeal in *Bassett* v. *Whiteley* (1982) where Lord Justice Waller said that:

> 'I have no hesitation in saying that, when one has a tenant who has performed throughout the currency of the lease all his obligations but who on one occasion...withholds the rent because he wishes to put some pressure upon his landlord to do some repairs, he has

reasonably performed and observed 'the several stipulations herein contained" '.

This decision demonstrates that some judges are prepared to adopt a flexible construction of covenants to renew and are prepared to take into account the tenant's conduct throughout the term. However, it has to be said that, in the main, judges are more inclined to debar a tenant from renewing a lease where there is a failure to comply with extensive obligations even where the tenant could show good reason for the non-compliance: *Kitney* v. *Greater London Properties Ltd* (1984). A tenant was precluded from exercising an option to renew by virtue of part breaches of a negative covenant in *Bass Holdings Ltd* v. *Morton Music Ltd* (1987).

Terms of renewed lease

General: The new lease will be granted on identical terms to the existing lease which means that no new clauses can be added or variations introduced to the new lease. The new lease will be for the same period and on the same terms as the original lease unless contrary provisions are expressly provided for. An express option to renew is distinct from a statutory right of renewal or continuation, and is based on a common agreement between the parties.

Rent: The option clause often provides for arbitration machinery to determine the new rent levels where the parties fail to reach agreement. It has been held that a clause which provided for renewal of a twenty-one year lease at a rent 'to be agreed between the parties' was to be determined subjectively by an arbitrator, according to what the landlord and tenant would have agreed if they had been negotiating the rent themselves: *Thomas Bates & Sons Ltd* v. *Wyndham's (Lingerie) Ltd* (1981). This test was applied in *Lear* v. *Blizzard* (1983) where it was also held that since an arbitrator had no authority to introduce any variation between the terms of the original lease and the new lease, he had no power to add a premium to take account of anticipated inflation during the currency of the new term. This conclusion was reached notwithstanding the evidence before the court of the practice of either adding a premium to protect the landlord against inflation and a static rent or of including rent review machinery in long leases.

One further problem is the effect that improvements are to have on the new rent. Since the rent is to be assessed on the basis of subjective criteria, an arbitrator should consider the question of past expenditure on improvements: per Lord Justice Buckley in the *Thomas Bates* case. This test was applied in *Lear* v. *Blizzard* where the lease had been assigned after improvements had been carried out by the tenant. It was held that the onus was on the assignee to show that he had paid or contributed towards the improvements, and that they were to be disregarded only to the extent that the assignee satisfied the arbitrator that he had contributed in money or money's worth to their value.

Registration

An option to renew should be registered as an 'estate contract' in the unregistered system of conveyancing: Land Charges Act 1972 s.4(1), and p.23. But it does not require registration in the registered system of conveyancing since it creates an 'overriding interest' which overrides other interests without being required to be registered: *Webb* v. *Pollmount* (1966). Options to renew run with the land and are therefore enforceable by assignees: *Isteed* v. *Stonely* (1580).

Options to purchase

A lease may contain an option to purchase which entitles the tenant to purchase the freehold. In other words, the tenant buys out the landlord's freehold interest in the premises and in doing so, ends the tenancy.

If an option to purchase is validly exercised it will create the relationship of vendor and purchaser. This has the effect of terminating the landlord and tenant relationship (since the lease's terms will be unenforceable) unless the lease contains provisions to the contrary: *Nightingale* v. *Courtney* (1954).

Options to purchase have different qualities from options to renew. An option to purchase is an interest in land which is collateral to the lease and, therefore, independent of the landlord and tenant relationship: *Woodfall* v. *Clifton* (1905). This means that it cannot bind an assignee of the landlord's reversion unless it is duly registered either as an estate contract in the case of unregistered land or by entry on the land register where the land is registered; although the benefit of the option passes to an assignee of the term upon the assignment of the lease: *Griffith* v. *Pelton* (1958).

Exercise of option

The option should be exercised during the currency of the lease. The lease will generally provide that the tenant must give the landlord a specified period of notice in writing as a condition precedent of the exercise of the option, and any such condition precedent must be strictly complied with. The parties will then be placed in the position of vendor and purchaser, and provision will be made for the price to be paid for the reversion in the terms of the option.

Some long residential leaseholders have statutory rights to purchase the freehold compulsorily from their landlords under the provisions of the Leasehold Reform Act 1967 in which case the appropriate statutory procedure should be complied with: see pp.272–3.

NOTICE TO QUIT

Application

Periodic tenancies are terminated by the service of a notice to quit by either party, giving the other notice of an intention to terminate the tenancy. Some fixed term leases require the service of a notice under the express terms of the lease. Finally, a number of statutory provisions regulate some notices to quit.

Effect of

A notice to quit given by one of two joint tenants is sufficient to terminate the tenancy. See *Greenwich London Borough* v. *McGrady* (1982) for a hard case on this point.

A valid notice to quit has the effect of ending the current tenancy when the notice expires. A notice to quit cannot be waived or retracted once it has been served on the other party, except with the consent of both parties. Thus if a tenant serves a notice to quit and then changes his mind and stays on in the leasehold premises after the date the notice to quit expires, and the landlord agrees to this, the position is that the former tenancy has been terminated effectively but that the tenant stays on under a new agreement: *Clark* v. *Grant* (1949).

There has to be some clear evidence, however, before the existence of a new tenancy will be inferred by the acts of the parties after a notice to quit has expired. Thus the acceptance of rent by the landlord is only prima facie evidence, and not conclusive evidence, of the existence of a new tenancy. It must still be shown that the parties intended to create a new tenancy: *Doe d. Cheny* v. *Batten* (1775).

The effect of a notice to quit can be contrasted with a right to forfeit a lease. First of all, a landlord can waive his right to forfeit a lease but cannot waive the service of a valid notice to quit. Secondly, the payment and acceptance of rent after a ground for forfeiture of a lease has arisen constitutes a waiver of the forfeiture whereas a demand for rent by itself after a notice to quit has expired does not. This is because the rules relating to forfeiture are stricter since forfeiture terminates a tenancy prematurely whereas a deemed waiver of a notice to quit would result in the creation of a new proprietary interest.

Validity

In order for a notice to quit to be valid it must comply with the requirements set out below; minor inaccuracies do not invalidate a notice to quit: *Doe d. Cox* v. *Roe* (1802).

Form

A notice to quit must set out a clear intention to terminate the tenancy on a specified date by the party giving notice: *Gardner* v. *Ingram* (1889). But it does not have to be in writing or comply with any formality unless required to do so either by the terms of the lease or by statute: *Ahearn* v. *Bellman, Sedgwick* v. *Ahearn* (1879).

Statutory form: A number of statutes prescribe the form a notice to quit should take.

Business tenancies: Notices relating to business tenancies should be in the prescribed statutory form or substantially to the like effect: Landlord and Tenant (Notices) Regulations 1957 SI 1957 No 1157 made under s.66 Landlord and Tenant Act 1954.

Residential tenancies: Section 5 of the Protection from Eviction Act 1977 renders a notice to quit of residential premises invalid unless it complies with the statutory requirements as to form and content. The notice must be in writing and contain the information prescribed by regulations made by the Secretary of State and set out in the Notices To Quit (Prescribed Information) Regulations 1980 (SI 1980 No 1624): see Appendix.

Agriculural holdings: The Agricultural Holdings Act 1986 ss. 25–33 sets out detailed provisions regulating notices to quit. For example, s. 25 provides for a minimum length of twelve months for notices to quit of agricultural holdings.

Length

General rule: The length of a notice to quit can be agreed between the parties by way of a special stipulation: *Bridges* v. *Potts* (1864). In the absence of a special stipulation, a periodic tenancy will be determined by applying the common law rules. At common law, a notice to quit should correspond to the length of the term unless the periodic tenancy is a yearly periodic tenancy or longer. In other words, a weekly tenancy requires one week's notice and a monthly tenancy one month's notice.

Yearly tenancy: A yearly periodic tenancy or longer requires at least six months' notice expiring at the end of the first or any subsequent year of the tenancy: *Right d. Flower* v. *Darby* (1786). Its expiry date is not linked to the rent days but must coincide with one of the tenancy's anniversary dates.

Residential tenancies: The minimum length for a notice to quit of a residential tenancy is prescribed by s.5 Protection from Eviction Act 1977 as 'not less than four weeks before the date on which it is to take effect'. This gives tenants of residential premises a minimum notice of four clear weeks. If a landlord states a shorter period the notice is invalid and a new notice must be served stating a fresh period of four weeks.

Expiry date

A notice to quit expires on the date on which it is stated to take effect unless the parties have agreed a special stipulation. The expiry date must coincide with the relevant anniversary so that it expires at midnight on the day before the anniversary of the tenancy's commencement date. If the expiry date does not coincide with the relevant anniversary, the notice to quit will be invalid, and a new notice to quit will have to be served stating a new expiry date which dovetails correctly with the tenancy's anniversary date.

Service of notice

The notice to quit must be given to the immediate landlord or tenant by the other party. A landlord cannot, for example, serve a notice on a sub-tenant for he is not the sub-tenant's 'immediate' landlord: *Pleasant* v. *Benson* (1811). Alternatively a duly authorised agent can be appointed to serve the notice to quit acting on behalf of his principal. If the notice to quit is served by an agent, this fact must appear on the notice: *Lemon* v. *Lardeur* (1946).

Service on tenant: A landlord's notice to quit must be served correctly on the tenant although it is not, strictly speaking, necessary to address it to him (although this is a desirable practice): *Doe d. Matthewson* v. *Wrightman* (1801).

Method of service: The notice may be served either personally by the landlord or tenant, by a duly authorised agent, by registered post or recorded delivery, by ordinary post, or by leaving it at the tenant's house unless the lease contains express provisions to the contrary: s.196(4) Law of Property Act 1925 which is reproduced in s.93 Agricultural Holdings Act 1986.

If service by registered post or recorded delivery is being relied upon, a copy of the original documentation should be kept with a note of the date on which the notice was posted together with the address of the post office from which it was posted, in case it has to be relied upon later in possession proceedings. Service will have been effected at the time of postal delivery: *R* v. *Slawstone Inhabitants* (1852). Incidentally there is a presumption that the notice has been delivered where the posting can be proved: s.196(4) Law of Property Act 1925.

It does sometimes happen that the tenant has disappeared, in which case there is no alternative but to serve the notice at the leasehold premises or at the tenant's last known address. The main point to note here is that the notice should be of the correct length and delivered in proper time.

Sub-tenants

It is only the immediate landlord who can serve a notice to quit. This means that a head landlord cannot serve a notice to quit on a sub-tenant because it is the tenant who is the sub-tenant's immediate landlord.

Joint tenancies

The position of joint tenants to a periodic tenancy is that as soon as one joint tenant serves a notice to quit, the tenancy ends: *Doe d. Aslin* v. *Summersett* (1830). This principle was explained in the more modern authority of *Leek & Moorlands Building Society* v. *Clark* (1952) where Lord Justice Somervell stated that 'if a joint enterprise is due to terminate on a particular day, all concerned must agree if it is to be renewed or continued beyond that day.' These authorities were followed in *Greenwich London Borough* v. *McGrady* (1982) where the Court of Appeal held that a wife's notice to terminate a joint tenancy was effective. This incidentally led to the husband losing his secure tenancy since the relevant legislation only gives security where the landlord gives a notice to quit, and does not provide security where the tenant gives notice to quit.

SURRENDER

A surrender occurs where the landlord obtains the lease from the tenant who has surrendered it up. Both fixed term and periodic tenancies can be surrendered although tenants with periodic tenancies would usually serve a notice to quit rather than effect a surrender.

There are numerous reasons for terminating a tenancy by surrender. For example, a tenant may surrender the residue of a fixed term lease in return for the grant of a new lease on different terms; a tenant who is in breach of covenant may agree to surrender up his lease voluntarily rather than try to resist forfeiture proceedings; a surrender may be in the interests of tax planning or estate management.

The main effect of surrender is that it stops rent accruing. If the tenant remains in occupation after a surrender the landlord should not claim rent unless he wishes to affirm the tenancy, but can bring an action for use and occupation: *Shaw* v. *Lomas* (1888). Note also that a tenant cannot be sued for breaches of covenant which occurred after the surrender although he will be liable for breaches of covenant which were committed prior to the surrender: *Brown* v. *Blake* (1912).

To constitute surrender, there must be both a surrender of the lease by the tenant, and acceptance of the surrender by the landlord. In other words, surrender can only occur by joint agreement and not by unilateral action. Otherwise a tenant could attempt to avoid his obligations under the lease by surrendering it before the term expires.

The law recognises two types of surrender: express surrender which is subject to legal formalities, and surrender by operation of law which is an informal surrender.

Express surrender

An express surrender is a surrender which is made by deed or, in some cases, in writing. It is desirable for a tenant to sign a formal deed of surrender for a surrender to be express. This is because the surrender operates as a conveyance of a leasehold interest to the landlord, and the general rule is that conveyances of land are void unless made by deed: s.52 Law of Property Act 1925. However, some short leases not exceeding three years are exempt from the requirement of a deed by s.54(2) Law of Property Act 1925 in which case writing is sufficient to convey the property to the landlord: see pp. 17 and 21.

By operation of law

A surrender by operation of law occurs when the parties act in a way which is wholly inconsistent with the continuation of the tenancy so that it is said to be terminated.

If the surrender is neither effected by deed nor by any form of writing it is not void for the purpose of conveying the leasehold interest to the landlord since there is an express exception to conveyancing formalities in the case of surrenders which occur 'by operation of law': s.52(2)(c) Law of Property Act 1925. This is a common sense exception because there are cases where a tenant terminates his tenancy informally by way of surrender e.g. by giving up possession or by taking up a new lease on terms which are inconsistent with the former lease. In these cases the surrender is said to take place 'by operation of law' rather than by express agreement.

Business tenancies

If a tenant enters into a contract to surrender up a business tenancy and then fails to give up possession, the contract cannot be enforced by the landlord unless a court had sanctioned the agreement made between the parties. This is the effect of s.38(1) Landlord and Tenant Act 1954 which prevents contracting out of Part II of that Act without the court's consent: see *Tarjomani* v. *Panther Securities Ltd* (1984).

Surrender-back clauses

A 'surrender back clause' is a clause in a lease which stipulates that if a tenant wishes to assign the lease he must first offer to surrender it to the landlord before offering to assign it to a third party. If the landlord accepts the surrender there will be no assignment. On the other hand, if the landlord does not accept the surrender, the tenant is then free to assign it in the normal way.

A surrender back clause clearly fetters the rights of the tenant since it makes the offer of surrender back to the landlord a condition precedent of any assignment. Nonetheless they are in common use, and provide landlords with an opportunity of exercising control over the choice of occupant of the leasehold premises.

It has been argued unsuccessfully that surrender-back clauses are invalid in the case of qualified covenants against assignment on the ground that they contravene the spirit of s.19(1) Landlord and Tenant Act 1927 which stipulates that consent to an assignment is not to be unreasonably withheld. But the Court of Appeal held in *Bocardo SA* v. *S & M Hotels and Another* (1979) that s.19(1) did not purport to limit the freedom of contract of the parties to forbid assignments but merely provides that where the landlord's consent is required it should not be unreasonably withheld.

Sub-leases

The termination of a term by surrender does not by itself terminate any sub-tenancies of the term which might exist since surrender does not destroy the rights of sub-tenants. Any existing sub-tenancy will continue unless the sub-tenant also consents to a surrender: *Pleasant* v. *Benson* (1811).

By comparison a forfeiture of the tenancy will destroy the rights of a sub-tenant: see p.221. Landlords who agree to accept a surrender of the tenancy as an alternative to bringing forfeiture proceedings for breach of covenant by the tenant should note that one consequence of accepting a surrender is that the rights of any sub-tenancy will be preserved: *Great Western Railway Company* v. *Smith* (1876).

Finally, the general rule that surrender does not destroy the rights of sub-tenants has no application to statutory tenancies: *Solomon* v. *Orwell* (1954). This is because it only applies to estates in land. A statutory tenant has a right of occupation but no estate in land which can be surrendered. Thus a surrender by a statutory tenant will destroy the rights of any sub-occupiers.

MERGER

Merger is the converse of surrender in that merger occurs when the tenant retains the lease and acquires the reversion, in comparison with surrender where the landlord obtains the residue of the lease. When the landlord and tenant's proprietary interests unite as a result of merger the tenancy is terminated, and the landlord's reversion is said to drop down and 'drown' the tenant's term.

Parties' intention

Merger will only occur if the tenant agrees to accept the reversion. This is the result of the equitable principle that merger would not occur if it was contrary to the tenant's interests. This rule is now set out in s.185 Law of Property Act 1925 which states that there is no merger by operation of law if there would be no deemed merger in equity. Thus a landlord cannot force his reversionary interest on the tenant. Even when the reversion and term are held by the same person, there is no merger if it is intended that the term be kept alive: *Capital and Counties Bank Limited* v. *Rhodes* (1903).

Sub-leases

The head landlord is entitled to the benefits of the covenants in any sub-lease by virtue of the provisions of s.139 Law of Property Act 1925: this also applies to surrender. Merger does not detroy sub-leases, and the effect of a merger on sub-leases is the same as on surrender.

Long leases

Two special forms of merger fall for consideration in the context of long leases since certain long leaseholders are entitled to extend their leases and/or purchase the freehold compulsorily under the provisions of the Leasehold Reform Act 1967: see pp.272–5 for a full treatment of these two forms of merger.

DISCLAIMER

Insolvency

Right to disclaim

If an individual landlord or tenant becomes bankrupt or a company landlord or tenant goes into liquidation, his affairs will be taken over by a trustee in bankruptcy and liquidator respectively. Both trustees in bankruptcy and liquidators have statutory powers to disclaim leases which might otherwise be onerous. The effect of disclaimer is that it terminates the tenancy as between the original landlord and tenant if there are no other parties involved: *Re Finley* (1888). But the position is more complicated if sub-tenancies exist or where there has been an assignment.

The Court of Appeal held in *Eyre and Others* v. *Hall and Another* (1986) that a trustee in bankruptcy was entitled to disclaim a lease which contained stringent restrictions. The lease contained an absolute prohibition against assignment, full repairing covenants and a restriction on use to a dwelling-house.

Disclaimer of gift

Gifts of leasehold property under a will can be disclaimed by the recipient in which case the lease is not terminated but falls into the residue of the estate or passes as if there was an intestacy: *Re Backhouse, Westminster Bank Ltd* v. *Shaftesbury Society* (1931). There may be many reasons for disclaiming a gift of leasehold property, e.g. because of onerous inheritance tax liabilities.

Disclaimer in war

Statutory provisions were introduced during the Second World War to enable leases to be disclaimed on account of war damage which could be implemented in the event of another war: Landlord and Tenant (War Damage) Acts 1939 and 1941.

Chapter 20

Termination by Forfeiture

Forfeiture of the lease is the ultimate penalty paid by certain tenants, e.g. those who are found to be in breach of covenant or who become insolvent. Forfeiture is sometimes referred to as a 'right of re-entry' since the main consequence of forfeiture is that the landlord regains possession of the leasehold premises by ending the lease prematurely and evicting the tenant. A landlord can only terminate the lease by forfeiture for breach of covenant if the lease contains an express provision for forfeiture. The lease will set out the precise circumstances in which the landlord is entitled to forfeit the tenant's lease. But it should be noted that even if these terms are satisfied, the court will not necessarily agree to a forfeiture of the lease since the courts tend to 'lean against forfeiture', particularly in cases where the tenant has made good the breach or where it is trivial in nature.

RIGHT TO FORFEIT

The grounds on which a landlord is entitled to forfeit a lease will be set out in the lease.

Breach of covenant

By far the commonest ground of forfeiture is for breach of covenant, e.g. breach of repairing obligations or breach of a covenant prohibiting assignment. There is an important academic distinction in this context between a breach of 'covenant' and a breach of 'condition'. The distinction is that a lease can be forfeited for a breach of condition regardless of whether the lease does or does not contain a forfeiture clause. By contrast, a landlord can only forfeit a lease for breach of covenant if the lease contains forfeiture provisions.

The vast majority of terms in a lease are indeed covenants. But from time to time a term in the lease will be construed as a condition where there is conditionality, e.g. the lease is to be granted upon condition that the tenant carries out specified repairs to the premises.

Rent arrears

The vast majority of leases contain forfeiture provisions for non-payment of rent. The words 'whether formally demanded or not' generally appear in the provision because forfeiture could not be sought at common law unless the landlord made a formal demand for rent. It is for this reason that leases expressly dispense with the necessity of a formal demand.

Tenant's insolvency

It is common for forfeiture clauses to provide for forfeiture upon the tenant's insolvency. There are two types of insolvency: the tenant may become personally insolvent through bankruptcy, or alternatively, a company tenant may become insolvent and be wound up through a liquidation.

Limitation period

The limitation period for forfeiture proceedings, as in all proceedings relating to land, is twelve years: s.15(1) Limitation Act 1980. This means that the landlord must pursue any right to forfeit the lease within twelve years of the date on which the right to forfeit the lease accrued.

Construction of forfeiture clause

The courts will construe forfeiture clauses literally, applying normal contractual principles: *Doe d. Spencer* v. *Goodwin* (1815). If there is any doubt or ambiguity whatsoever, the clause will be construed in the tenant's favour.

WHO CAN FORFEIT?

The tenant's immediate landlord is entitled to forfeit the lease regardless of whether he is the original landlord or an assignee of the reversion. This is because s.141(1) Law of Property Act 1925 expressly assigns the benefit of a right of re-entry to the reversion enabling assignees to enforce a proviso for re-entry in the lease.

RE-ENTRY

A legal distinction is drawn between re-entry and regaining possession. Landlords who wish to terminate a lease on the grounds of forfeiture can only do so by re-entry under the terms of the forfeiture provision. This does not mean that the landlord has to take physical possession of the leasehold premises (although once forfeiture has been completed he will be entitled to bring possession proceedings if the tenant remains in occupation). In other words, landlords have to do some act which amounts to re-entry in order to forfeit the lease but may not in fact obtain possession until judgment is given for possession. Note that one consequence of this distinction is that if there is an interval between re-entry and possession, the lease is not terminated until judgment for possession is given.

Methods

Forfeiture only occurs when the landlord performs some act which shows his clear intention to forfeit and terminate the lease: *Roberts* v. *Davey* (1833).

Peaceable entry

There is no reason why, in principle, a tenant should not give up possession voluntarily once strong grounds for forfeiture have arisen, e.g. as a result of breaches of covenant. If the landlord re-enters under the forfeiture clause this is proof of his intention to end the tenancy. Where this occurs, the landlord is said to regain possession by 'peaceable entry'. Tenants are generally reluctant to give up possession of leasehold premises without a fight, and landlords will usually have to commence possession proceedings against a tenant in order to gain re-entry of the leasehold premises. Peaceable entry occurs where the landlord re-enters leasehold premises without legal proceedings, and uses no force to do so. Note that landlords are obliged by statute to obtain the court's consent before forfeiting a lease of residential premises.

Residential tenancies

It is unlawful for a landlord to re-enter residential premises without the court's consent. Section 2 of the Protection From Eviction Act 1977 provides that a landlord must always bring legal proceedings in order to forfeit a residential lease. This means that possession of residential premises should be taken through court proceedings and not by peaceable entry.

Failure to comply with this provision may result in the landlord or his agent being prosecuted for unlawful eviction. The main defence open to a landlord or his agent is if they can establish beyond reasonable doubt (to the satisfaction of a jury) that there were reasonable grounds for believing that the occupier had ceased to reside in the premises: *R* v.

Davidson-Acres (1980). To this extent, peaceable entry of residential premises is still possible.

Legal proceedings

The commencement of legal proceedings will provide the clearest evidence of the landlord's intention to end the lease. Landlords should accordingly commence legal proceedings by serving a writ on the tenant requesting the tenant to give up possession in reliance on the lease's forfeiture provisions. This writ should be served on the tenant.

In this case, the taking of possession proceedings is equivalent to the landlord actually re-entering the premises. The landlord will be able to regain possession if the tenant gives up possession voluntarily or if he wins his case for possession in court.

WAIVER

There is nothing to compel a landlord to forfeit a lease; it is simply an option open to him if grounds for forfeiture arise. The law takes this principle one stage further. The right to forfeit a lease can be lost if the landlord has performed some act which is deemed to be an acknowledgement of the continuance of the lease after the right to forfeit occurred. This is known, rather confusingly, as 'waiver' since the landlord's actions are said to waive the right to forfeit the lease. The principle of waiver was developed by the courts who traditionally leaned against forfeiture because it led to the eviction of the tenant before the lease's term ended.

Elements of waiver

In order for waiver to be established it must be shown that the landlord knew of the breach of covenant when he treated the lease as continuing. Waiver will occur either in situations where the landlord has continued the tenancy when he had express knowledge of grounds for forfeiture, or, alternatively, it can be implied from matters which are within a landlord's knowledge.

Knowledge of the breach

The landlord must have knowledge that a breach of covenant has occurred before he can be said to have waived his right to forfeit in respect of the said breach. The question commonly arises as to what extent a landlord is fixed with the knowledge of agents appointed to manage or supervise the leasehold property on his behalf.

This question was settled by the decision of the court in *Metropolitan Properties* v. *Cordery* (1979). The tenant in that case had sub-let his tenancy in breach of covenant against sub-letting. The sub-tenant lived quite openly at the premises and the porters in charge knew of the change in the occupation of the premises. The Court of Appeal had no hesitation in those circumstances in imputing the agent's knowledge to the landlord. Lord Justice Megaw relied heavily on a line of agency cases which establish that when one party is employed by another, he has a duty to communicate information to his employer. In this case there was no difficulty in showing that a reasonable time had elapsed in which the porters could have communicated the change in occupation to the landlords. But it has to be added that a landlord would probably not be imputed with his agent's knowedge in the rare case where there is strong evidence to show that there was insufficient time for information to have been communicated to a landlord before the act of waiver occurred.

Finally, publication in a specialist journal or paper will not amount to notice to all the world. The Court of Appeal have held that the publication of a winding up order against an insolvent company tenant in the *London Gazette* did not impute notice or knowledge to the landlords of the winding up: *Official Custodian for Charities and Others* v. *Parway Estates Developments Ltd* (1984), discussed with considerable authority in the chapter on Leases in *Receivers* by G.Lightman and G.Moss, Sweet & Maxwell, 1986.

Clear act of waiver

There must be some clear and positive act by the landlord acknowledging the continuance of the tenancy. One of the most frequently relied upon acts is the demand and acceptance of rent by the landlord: *Central Estates (Belgravia) Ltd* v. *Woolgar (No 2)* (1973).

It has been held *per incuriam* (not binding) that in determining whether a landlord has waived his right to forfeit the lease where no acceptance or demand for rent is involved, the court is free to look at all the circumstances of the case and to consider whether the act of the landlord relied on is so unequivocal that, when considered objectively, it can only be regarded as having been done consistently with the continued existence of a tenancy at the relevant date: per Lord Justice Slade in *Expert Clothing Service and Sales Ltd* v. *Hillgate House Ltd and Another* (1985).

Examples of waiver

The rules regarding waiver of forfeiture apply to all breaches of covenant alike: *London and County (A and D) Ltd* v. *Wilfred Sportsman Ltd* (1969).

The following examples simply illustrate the application of these principles in a variety of situations.

Rent

There is an authoritative line of cases which establishes that an unqualified demand for rent due, acceptance of rent due or the taking of steps to recover rent due after the grounds for forfeiture have arisen, amounts to waiver. For example, the Court of Appeal held that a demand for rent in knowledge of a breach of covenant effected a waiver in *Central Estates (Belgravia) Ltd* v. *Woolgar* (No. 2) (1972), where Lord Denning MR said that:

> '...if it is sought to say that an existing lease *continues in existence* by waiver of forfeiture, then the intention of the parties does not matter. It is sufficient if there is an unequivocal act done by the landlord which recognises the existence of the lease after having knowledge of the ground of forfeiture'.

In *Segal Securities Ltd* v. *Thoseby* (1963) Mr Justice Sachs held that a demand for rent 'without prejudice' constituted a waiver. Acceptance of rent due after a breach of covenant not to sub-let waived any right to forfeit in *Scala House and District Property Co.* v. *Forbes* (1974). In each of these cases the landlord was held to have affirmed the continuance of the lease by taking a step and making a demand under the lease's provisions that works towards its continuance.

The above line of cases can easily be distinguished from *Church Commissioners for England* v. *Nodjoumi and Others* (1986) where it was held that a right to forfeit a lease on the ground of arrears of rent could not be waived by the service of a forfeiture notice. Counsel's argument that the s.146 notice calling on the tenant to pay arrears of rent amounted to a recognition of the continued existence of the lease was rejected on the basis that the service of a s.146 notice is a necessary prerequisite to forfeiture and cannot, therefore, be said to affirm the opposite.

Repairs

A landlord will waive his right to forfeit a lease for breach of a tenant's repairing covenant if he gives the tenant notice of his intention to enter the premises to carry out the repairs himself and, where appropriate, intention to recover the cost from the tenant: *Doe d. De Rutzen* v. *Lewis* (1836).

Others

In *Marche* v. *Christodoulakis* (1948) Mr Justice Pritchard held that the service of a notice to quit giving the tenant a date in the future to give up possession, constituted an affirmation of the lease.

Effect of waiver

Waiver only relates to past breaches of covenant. This means that if a landlord has waived forfeiture, perhaps inadvertently, the waiver of forfeiture will not extend to future breaches occurring after the waiver: s.148 Law of Property Act 1925. If the tenant commits further breaches of covenant after the landlord's waiver of his right to forfeit for the past breaches, the landlord can bring forfeiture proceedings based on the new breaches of covenant provided, of course, that he has not subsequently waived his right to forfeit in respect of those new breaches too.

In this context, it is important to distinguish 'continuing' breaches of covenant from 'once and for all breaches'. In the case of continuing breaches, grounds for forfeiture will continually reoccur. For example, breaches of a repairing covenant. On the other hand, a once and for all breach cannot reoccur e.g. a sub-letting in breach of covenant. Thus in the former case, if a landlord has waived past breaches of a repairing covenant, this will not preclude him from bringing forfeiture proceedings in respect of further breaches: *Coward* v. *Gregory* (1866). In contrast, if a landlord has waived a breach of covenant against sub-letting, e.g. by accepting rent from the sub-tenant when knowing of the breach, that is a once and for all breach which has been waived for all purposes: see *Scala House and District Property Co Ltd* v. *Forbes* (1973) below. It cannot be argued that the tenant is in continuing breach of covenant by allowing the sub-tenant to remain in possession: *Walrond* v. *Hawkins* (1875).

FORFEITURE PROCEEDINGS

Procedure

A landlord cannot enforce a right of re-entry and regain possession of the leasehold premises without first serving the statutory s.146 notice: s.146 Law of Property Act 1925. The only exception to this rule is where the only breach of covenant is non-payment of rent: s.146(11) Law of Property Act 1925.

Section 146 notice

Contents

The notice must contain the precise details of the breach complained of, and be addressed to the tenant: s.196(2) Law of Property Act

1925. There is no prescribed statutory form for the notice but its contents must conform with the statutory requirements. The statutory requirements regarding content are that the notice must specify the breach complained of, require the tenant to remedy it (if this is possible) and ask for monetary compensation for the breach: s.146(1) Law of Property Act 1925. If the Leasehold Property (Repairs) Act 1938 applies, the notice must also inform the tenant of his right to serve a counter-notice: see Chapter 15.

Particularise breach: A notice could be rendered invalid if it fails to specify the matters complained of with sufficient particularity. It has been held that a notice stating that the tenant was in breach of his repairing obligations was bad, on the grounds that it failed to give details of the want of repair: *Fletcher* v. *Nokes* (1897).

Remediable breaches: If the breach is capable of being remedied i.e. is a remediable breach, the notice must ask the tenant to remedy it. But there is no necessity to set out what the tenant should do to remedy the breach. The test for determining whether a breach of covenant was 'capable of remedy' for the purposes of s.146(1)(b) has been held by the Court of Appeal to depend on whether the harm suffered by the landlords by the relevant breach was capable of being remedied in practical terms: *Expert Clothing Service and Sales Ltd* v. *Hillgate House Ltd and Another* (1985). The breach complained of by the landlords in the *Expert Clothing* case was a breach of covenant to reconstruct the interior of the premises within a specified time. The Court of Appeal held that the landlords suffered no additional harm by giving the tenant an opportunity to remedy the breach by requiring them to remedy the breach in the s.146 notice.

Irremediable breaches: Some breaches of covenant cannot be remedied by the tenant, e.g. a breach of a user covenant, and they amount to once and for all breaches. There is no need for a landlord to ask a tenant to remedy an irremediable breach as this is a contradiction in terms. For example, the Court of Appeal have held that a breach of a covenant prohibiting assignment or sub-letting is a once and for all breach of covenant and is incapable of being remedied: *Scala House and District Property Co Ltd* v. *Forbes* (1973).

RELIEF AGAINST FORFEITURE

General

The courts have a wide jurisdiction for granting relief from forfeiture. The tenant has a statutory right to apply for relief from forfeiture under s.146(2) Law of Property Act 1925 during possession proceedings.

If the tenant applies for relief, the court may either grant the relief sought or refuse it. In reaching a decision the court will take into account the conduct of the parties, and any other circumstances which it thinks fit including the tenant's financial circumstances. The Court of Appeal have affirmed the following sentence in Woodfall: 'The court will consider the conduct of the tenant, the nature and gravity of the breach and its relation to the value of the property to be forfeited': *Cremin* v. *Barjack Properties Ltd* (1985). This wide discretion enables the court to grant relief in even the most unusual circumstances, for example, a breach of a covenant against immoral user: *Central Estates (Belgravia) Ltd* v. *Woolgar* (No 2)(1972).

If the tenant is granted relief from forfeiture, it will be on terms decided by the court so that the tenant may be ordered to bear the costs of the proceedings, to pay compensation to the landlord and any other penalty which the court thinks appropriate in the circumstances.

Interested third parties

Assignees

Relief from forfeiture can be granted where there has been a breach of covenant against assignment or sub-letting after the 1st January 1926, even though this is an irremediable breach: s.146(8) Law of Property Act 1925.

Sub-tenants

The effect of forfeiture proceedings is that they destroy the rights of sub-tenants: *Great Western Railway Co* v. *Smith* (1876). A sub-tenant will invariably wish to apply for relief from forfeiture since the tenancy's forfeiture will automatically terminate any sub-lease unless the sub-tenant is granted relief from forfeiture irrespective of the relief, if any, granted to the tenant. Section 146(4) Law of Property Act 1925 gives sub-tenants a statutory right to apply for relief against forfeiture.

The court has equitable powers to grant relief to sub-tenants over and above its statutory power as contained in s.146(4) which limits the tenant to making an application in the course of possession proceedings. This point was affirmed in a case where Mr Justice Nicholls granted relief to a Building Society when it was too late to grant relief under s.146(4) in the rare case where the Building Society had not been told that the landlord had taken possession of the leasehold premises: *Abbey National Building Society* v. *Maybeech Ltd and Others* (1984). This means that tenants can ask for relief after any forfeiture proceedings have ended or where the landlord has entered peaceably. They would otherwise be unable to seek relief owing to the fact that the scope of s.146(4) is limited to applications in possession proceedings.

If relief is granted by a court, the lease can be vested in the sub-tenant provided that it does not entitle the sub-tenant to a longer term than he had under the original sub-tenancy. The court may, however, take into account the automatic continuation of a business tenancy falling within the scope of Part II Landlord and Tenant Act 1954, and order a new term within the limits imposed by Part II: *Cadogan* v. *Dimovic* (1984).

Mortgagees

Many leases have mortgages secured upon them since tenants often raise a mortgage on a lease from a mortgagee (lender). A mortgagee will wish to know whether he can exercise any rights to relief from forfeiture should the landlord commence forfeiture proceedings against the tenant. If the forfeiture proceedings were successful, the mortgagee would lose the value of his security since the lease would be extinguished upon forfeiture.

A mortgagee has a right to relief from forfeiture, and is placed in an identical position to sub-tenants so that he may obtain a new term as a substituted security: *Chelsea Estates Investment Trust Co Ltd* v. *Marche* (1955).

Non-payment of rent

There are wide powers relieving a tenant from forfeiture if the sole ground for forfeiture is non-payment of rent: see Chapter 12 at p.118 for the relevant provisions.

Tenant's bankruptcy

The statutory period in which the tenant can apply for relief against forfeiture following its bankruptcy is one year: s.146(10) Law of Property Act 1925. The Court of Appeal have held that there is no inherent jurisdiction to grant relief outside this time period: *Official Custodian of Charities and Others* v. *Parway Estates Developments Ltd* (1984).

Breach of repairing covenant

General

A breach of a repairing covenant is a remediable breach which is capable of being remedied since the tenant will be given a reasonable opportunity to put the premises into repair. In fact the s.146 notice specifically requires tenants to remedy the breach. The courts tended to lean against forfeiture for breach of repairing covenant in cases where tenants made good the lack of repair.

Tenants are entitled to apply for relief prior to the landlord's re-entry under the provisions for relief from forfeiture as contained in s.146(2). In *Smith* v. *Metropolitan City Properties Ltd* (1985) the tenant argued that the court had an inherent equitable jurisdiction to grant relief from forfeiture in cases falling outside the scope of s.146(2) and attempted to rely on the *Maybeech* case. But Mr Justice Walton followed the case of *Official Custodian for Charities* v. *Parway* (1984) when he held that s.146 sets out the court's jurisdiction exhaustively. This line of cases creates anomalies in the court's jurisdiction to grant relief which are undesirable, and run counter to the former equitable principles, save that s.146(10) was framed to reflect the former position relating to bankrupts.

Long leases

Long leaseholders fall into a special category since their main repairing liability is to make good any dilapidations at the end of the term. At the same time their repairing liability will be to 'keep' the premises in repair throughout the term. In practice long leaseholders will theoretically be in breach of covenant at any time during the term that the premises are out of repair. But statute has intervened so that landlords must make a special case before bringing proceedings against long leaseholders mid-term for breach of repairing covenant. For this purpose long leases are defined as terms of seven years or more with more than three years to run, excluding agricultural holdings: ss. 1 and 7 Leasehold Property (Repairs) Act 1938. These statutory rules were developed to assist long leaseholders to prevent them from being harrassed mid-term for relatively minor breaches of repairing covenant: see Chapter 15 at p.158 for the relevant statutory provisions.

LAW REFORM

The Law Commission reported on forfeiture in 1985 and stated that:

'The law of forfeiture has become unnecessarily complicated, is no longer coherent and gives rise to injustices.'

(see 'Forfeiture of Tenancies', Law Com No 142 dated the 21st of March 1985 Para 1(1)).

The Law Commission considered forfeiture in the context of the rights of both landlords and tenants to terminate a tenancy when the other has been at fault in breaking its terms. The Law Commission made the radical recommendation that a tenant should in future have a right to terminate a lease when a landlord has broken its terms broadly analogous to the right enjoyed by most landlords today. Accordingly, two separate schemes of 'termination orders' were recommended by the Law Commission. The first related to a new system for termination by landlords in place of the existing system of forfeiture. The second contains a new system for the termination of tenancies by tenants. The report sets out new procedural recommendations together with guide-lines on which courts could base forfeiture decisions. Those with derivative powers, e.g. sub-tenants and mortgagees, were given separate consideration.

Termination by landlords

The Law Commission recommended that the grounds on which landlords could base an application for a termination order, 'termination order events', should be as follows. Firstly, for breach of covenant without the need for any forfeiture clause in the lease. Secondly, for disguised breaches of covenant which cover all events on the happening of which a landlord would be expected to protect himself. Thirdly, insolvency events.

Waiver

The Law Commission recommended a relaxation of the present rules relating to waiver after stating that:

'The law which now governs the circumstances in which a landlord is debarred by waiver from forfeiting a tenancy on a particular ground is unsatisfactory'

(see para 6.1 of their report).

Termination by tenants

The Law Commission recommended that the grounds for a termination order, 'termination order events', should be confined to actual breaches of covenant by a landlord. Courts would have the power to either make an 'absolute order' ending the tenancy or a 'remedial order' which would end the tenancy if the landlord failed to take remedial action within a specified time. Tenants whose tenancy ended because of a termination order obtained by him should have a right to damages from the landlord for the value of the tenancy and consequential losses.

Chapter 21

Rights upon Termination

LANDLORD'S RIGHTS

The landlord's main concern at the end of a lease is to recover vacant possession and to ensure that all outstanding rent is paid, that any dilapidations are made good, and that any damage or deterioration is adequately compensated for.

Possession

The position at common law is that there is an implied contract under which the tenant should give up vacant possession peaceably at the end of the term: *Henderson* v. *Squire* (1869). But it has already been seen that this position has been modified enormously by legislation giving tenants rights to remain in possession beyond the contractual term. Reference should always be made to the appropriate statutory provisions.

Sub-tenants

The common law position is that sub-tenancies fall in with the term. This means that any sub-tenancies created by tenants should be terminated in order to give vacant possession to the landlord. Indeed many sub-tenancies are commonly expressed to end one day before the end of the tenant's own term. In the event that the tenant fails to obtain possession from a sub-tenant, he is liable to the landlord in damages and for any costs which the landlord incurs in regaining possession from the sub-tenant.

But landlords should check to see whether the sub-tenant has a statutory right to remain in possession, for some categories of sub-tenancies are granted statutory rights at the end of the contractual term irrespective of the tenant's rights, e.g. under the provisions of the Rent Act 1977 and Part II of the Landlord and Tenant Act 1954. This can result in the anomalous situation of the landlord regaining possession from the tenant but not from the sub-tenant.

Rent

The remedies for non-payment of rent and related sums are dealt with in Chapter 12.

Holding over

Landlords are entitled to recover double the rent or double the rent's value if the tenant 'holds over' (remains in possession) after the tenancy has ended. But in practice this remedy is seldom used since the majority of tenants have a statutory right to remain in possession after the term has ended.

Dilapidations

The majority of leases, particularly commercial leases, will make provision for dilapidations. Even the most basic residential tenancy agreement is likely to have been made on condition that a deposit is paid to cover possible breakages and damage to the premises. Remedies for disrepair are considered in Chapter 15.

TENANT'S RIGHT TO REMOVE CERTAIN FIXTURES

General principles

It is self-evident that tenants are entitled to remove their own personal belongings and effects from the premises, i.e. chattels. But if a tenant has fixed items to the premises, then he will wish to know whether he is entitled to remove them. In many cases the answer will be clear cut, e.g. a picture hung on a wall can be removed by the tenant.

There are, however, situations in which it is not clear whether the item in question is a chattel or a fixture. In these cases the legal criterion which is applied is the twofold test of degree and purpose of annexation. Once it is established that an item is indeed a fixture, the central question is whether it is a fixture which must be left behind or whether it falls into one of the categories of tenant's fixtures which can be removed. The term 'landlord's fixture' is sometimes used for the purpose of distinguishing tenant's fixtures from other fixtures which cannot be removed and accordingly fall into the landlord's possession at the end of the lease.

The general rule is that fixtures cannot be removed because they have become part of the land itself. The law relating to fixtures results from the operation of the land law doctrine that whatever is fixed to the land becomes part of it: *quicquid plantatur solo, solo cedit*. In other words, personal chattels could be removed but not fixtures which had become part of the land.

The courts upheld the tenant's right to remove three types of fixtures, namely trade fixtures, agricultural fixtures, and domestic and ornamental fixtures by way of a qualification or exception to the principle of *quicquid plantatur solo, solo cedit*. The development of the rules relating to the tenant's right to remove tenant's or trade fixtures was a mitigation of the general rule that they should be left behind as part of the land: per Vice-Chancellor Kindersley in *Gibson* v. *Hammersmith and City Rly Co* (1863).

Landlord and tenant disputes over fixtures centre on the question of whether a fixture is a tenant's fixture which can be removed together with the subsidiary question of the amount of damage, if any, that will be caused by removal. Figure 4 illustrates these general principles:

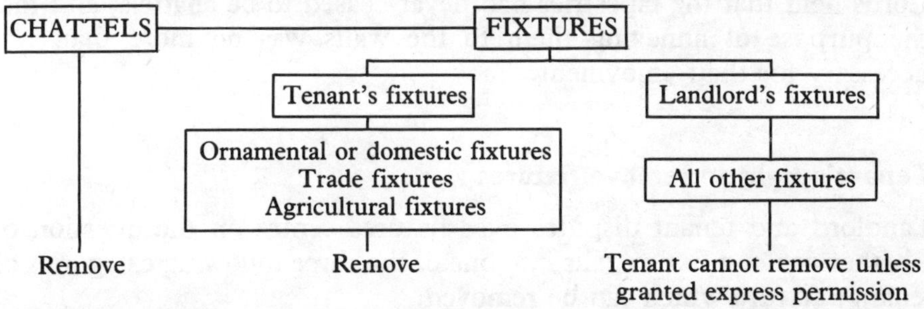

Distinction between chattels and fixtures

It is not always possible to categorise items as chattels or fixtures for the simple reason that their nature changes according to the way in which they are used. For example, Tommy rents a garden flat with its own patio, and keeps a few loose bricks in a garden shed which he from time to time assembles into a barbecue in summer; the bricks will remain as chattels. But if Tommy cements the bricks together to form a permanent patio barbecue there would be an argument for saying that they were sufficiently attached to the land to have become fixtures, thereby making the bricks the property of his landlord. The general law decides borderline cases by applying the twofold test of the degree and purpose of annexation.

Degree of annexation

The starting point is a consideration of the degree to which the item is annexed to the land or premises. An item can only be classified as a fixture if it is annexed to the land or a building on the land in a substantial way, e.g. a fireplace. But if an item merely rests on the land by reason of its weight it does not become a fixture. Thus a free-standing greenhouse has been held to be a chattel which is removeable: *Dibble Ltd* v. *Moore* (1970).

Purpose of annexation

The common law relaxed the degree of annexation test in cases where it could be shown that the purpose of annexation was simply to allow the owner of the item to enjoy it as a chattel. Otherwise the degree of annexation test would have operated harshly and given the landowner a windfall in cases where the owner of the chattel clearly had no intention of conveying a gratuitous benefit to the landowner. In *Leigh* v. *Taylor* (1902), the leading case on this point, the House of Lords had to consider whether tapestries tacked onto wooden frames and then nailed onto the walls of a mansion house were chattels or fixtures. The House of Lords held that the tapestries had never ceased to be chattels, and that the purpose of annexing them to the walls was no more than was necessary for their enjoyment.

Tenant's right to remove fixtures

Landlord and tenant disputes over fixtures centre on the question of whether or not a fixture falls into one of the three following categories of tenant's fixture which can be removed.

Ornamental or domestic fixtures

Items which the tenant fixes to the premises for his own domestic convenience or for purely ornamental purposes can be removed: *Elliott* v. *Bishop* (1854). The injustice of allowing landowners to retain valuable items was recognised in the early cases, as illustrated in *Leigh* v. *Taylor* (above). In *Spyer* v. *Phillipson* (1931) the tenant was held to be entitled to remove valuable antique panelling, mantelpieces and ceilings which he had installed at great expense, provided that he paid for the reinstatement of the premises. But this category extends only to items which are complete in themselves and which can be removed without causing substantial damage to the building.

Ornamental items: The item must be specifically ornamental to qualify as a tenant's fixture and not simply an accessory: *Buckland* v. *Butterfield* (1820). For example, a cornice can be removed if it is ornamental: *Avery* v. *Cheslyn* (1835). But items which were considered ornamental when first introduced may later be viewed as ordinary household accessories, e.g. it has been said that marble chimney pieces were not necessarily ornamental once they had become common: *Bishop* v. *Elliott* (1855).

Domestic items: All manner of items of domestic utility may be removed provided that this does not cause substantial damage: for example, ovens, kitchen ranges, stoves and grates: *Grymes* v. *Boweren* (1830). But note that items which were put in during the construction of the premises, such as windows and doors, form part of the premises and cannot accurately be described as fixtures: modern built in kitchens might conceivably fall into this category.

Trade fixtures

If a tenant fixes items to the premises for the purposes of trade, he may remove those fixtures which have an independent character and can be converted into chattels, but any damage must be made good: *Poole's Case* (1703). For example, a tenant is entitled to remove engines and machinery, boilers, pumps and vats which are set into mortar or stone, or screwed or fastened into the ground.

Agricultural fixtures

An agricultural holdings tenant has a statutory right to remove engines, machinery, fencing or any other fixture regardless of whether it is used for an agricultural purpose or not, and buildings which he has erected on the holding: s.10 Agricultural Holdings Act 1986. The right is qualified in certain respects. For example, the tenant must give the landlord at least one month's written notice of his intention to remove the fixture or building, and must remove it before the last two months of the term: ss.10(1) and 10(3)(b) Agricultural Holdings Act 1986. In addition, the tenant can remove fruit trees and fruit bushes which he has planted before the end of the tenancy if the agricultural holding is a market garden: s.79(4) Agricultural Holdings Act 1986.

Effect of custom

In some cases the tenant's right to remove fixtures is controlled by custom.

Liability to repair damage

If a tenant removes fixtures he is liable at common law to repair any damage caused by the removal, and many leases state this expressly. The Court of Appeal held in *Mancetter Developments Ltd* v. *Garmanson Ltd and Another* (1986) that where a tenant has a right to remove fixtures it was a condition of the exercise of this right that the tenant make good any damage caused by their removal. Lord Justice Dillon interpreted this as a requirement to make good the premises to the extent of leaving them in 'a reasonable condition'. The landlord in *Mancetter Developments* was held to be entitled to compensation from a tenant who had failed to put right damage caused by the removal of extractor fans and pipes.

LANDLORD'S REMEDIES

A landlord can either bring proceedings for compensation in contract if the tenant has broken a covenant in the lease to leave the premises in repair or he can sue in tort for waste (as in *Mancetter Developments*): see pp.145–6 on waste. The measure of damages is the value of the fixtures as chattels: *Clark* v. *Holford* (1848).

If the landlord knows in advance that the tenant is likely to remove landlord's fixtures, the landlord may apply to the court for an injunction preventing their removal: *Sunderland* v. *Newton* (1830).

Licensees

A licensee has no right to remove fixtures from the premises when his licence ends unless it is made an express term of the contract: *Never-Stop Railway (Wembley) Ltd* v. *British Empire Exhibition* (1924).

Time for removal

The tenant is only entitled to remove fixtures to which he is entitled during the lease's term: *Poole's Case* (1703). If the tenant fails to remove fixtures to which he is entitled either during the tenancy or within a reasonable time after it has ended, the fixtures become the landlord's property: *Smith* v. *City Petroleum Co Ltd* (1940).

Chapter 22

Business Tenancies: Objectives of Legislation

LEGISLATIVE PROVISIONS

Business tenancies are subject to the provisions of Part I of the Landlord and Tenant Act 1927 ('the 1927 Act') and Part II of the Landlord and Tenant Act 1954 ('the 1954 Act'). These statutory provisions only become significant towards the end of the term when questions regarding a business tenant's right to renewal or compensation for improvements and goodwill arise. The business tenancy itself is not regulated in any way by statute during the period of the contractual term. This is in stark contrast to the security of tenure legislation applicable to residential tenancies. But since business tenancies are the product of commercial contracts, Parliament has not felt it necessary to erode the parties' freedom to contract on their own terms.

Business tenants are primarily concerned about opportunities to renew their lease at a market rent, compensation for disturbance if they are forced to give up possession at the end of their lease, and compensation for improvements which they have made to the premises. The following example illustrates these problems.

Tea was granted a twenty-one year lease of No. 1 George Street by Lemon, which is due to expire in the next twelve months. The property is on three floors. Tea runs a snack bar from the ground floor, and has recently sub-let the two upper floors to Sugar for office use. Ten years ago, Tea spent £10,000 refurbishing the snack bar, kitchen and staff area on the ground floor. Tea wishes to renew his lease when it expires, but if this is not feasible, he wants to be compensated for the improvements which he has made to the premises. In addition, he would want to be compensated for the loss of goodwill that would result from the subsequent relocation of his snack bar trade to new premises since he will undoubtedly lose many of his regular customers. Sugar is also worried about her position since she has only just managed to establish herself in business and fears the consequences of a forced move to new premises.

LEGISLATION'S OBJECTIVES

The legislative objective underlying the provisions relating to business tenancies is to provide a statutory framework which a tenant can utilise to negotiate a new lease on commercial terms or be provided with compensation for disturbance where this was not possible owing to the landlord's own business or redevelopment plans. In addition, business tenants have a specific statutory right to compensation for authorised improvements when they leave the premises at the end of the term.

Prior to the introduction of legislation, some business tenants had been faced with the unenviable choice of either accepting the landlord's terms for renewal or being forced to relocate their businesses. Parliament felt that it was wrong that some business tenants were being faced with demands for exorbitant rent increases simply in order to retain possession of their trading premises, and found this form of commercial blackmail abhorrent.

The 1927 Act introduced compensation for the loss of goodwill, or the grant of a lease in lieu of, for the first time. These provisions were repealed by the 1954 Act which introduced a comprehensive statutory procedure for the renewal of business leases, and also provided for compensation for disturbance in circumstances where a tenant's application for renewal was refused through no fault of his own. Amendments were later made to the 1954 Act by the Law of Property Act 1969. The 1927 Act also provides for the payment of compensation for improvements, and this part of the 1927 Act is still in force.

The renewal schemes of the 1927 and 1954 Acts worked quite differently. A tenant was entitled to renewal almost by default under the now repealed provisions of the 1927 Act. This is because a tenant had to show that the sum which could be awarded to him by way of compensation for loss of goodwill would not adequately compensate him for the relocation of his business to alternative premises. It was far from easy for business tenants to prove that they fell into this category. In any event, a landlord could often defeat such an application for a new tenancy by relying on any one of a number of statutory provisions, e.g. where he made an offer of alternative accommodation, or where he could establish that the grant of a new lease would not be consistent with good estate management. Both these provisions were excluded in the 1954 Act.

One keenly felt exception to the scope of the 1927 Act was its exclusion of professional businesses. This is because goodwill very often accounts for a major part of the value of a professional's business, leaving him without any remedy or compensation for disturbance. The 1954 Act remedied this defect and includes professions within its definition of business: s.23(2) Landlord and Tenant Act 1954. The 1927 Act was also criticised for including a minimum trading period of five years from the premises. Only tenants who had traded from the premises for five years or more qualified for compensation for loss of goodwill, and accordingly only this category of tenant was qualified to apply for a renewal. The 1954 Act cut back the minimum term for qualifying leases to six months: s.43(3) Landlord and Tenant Act 1954.

The 1954 Act set up a completely new procedure for the renewal of business leases. Business tenants now have a statutory right to apply for a new business lease towards the end of their existing lease if the tenancy falls within the scope of the 1954 Act. The grounds on which a landlord could object to the grant of a new lease were cut down. Provision was made for the automatic continuation of the business lease if negotiations for a new lease were still being conducted after the lease had ended. Meanwhile, a landlord was entitled to apply for an interim market rent. If the parties fail to reach agreement, there is a statutory procedure which a tenant can use in order to apply for a renewal of his business tenancy. The courts have jurisdiction to order a new tenancy, to settle its terms including rent, and to make compensation orders where appropriate.

Chapter 23

The Scope of the 1954 Act

THE RIGHT TO RENEW

The aim of Part II of the Landlord and Tenant Act 1954 ('the 1954 Act') is to give a business tenant an automatic right to renew a business lease at the end of his term at a commercial rent for a term of not more than fourteen years.

Landlords may oppose a renewal application in limited circumstances where either the tenant has broken his obligations or the landlord requires vacant possession of the premises for his own use or in order to demolish or reconstruct them. A tenant will qualify for compensation for disturbance in all cases, except where his application for renewal has been refused because he has broken his obligations under the lease: see Chapter 25.

The procedure for renewal under the 1954 Act is based on strict procedural rules. Each party is required to serve the other with formal notice of their respective intentions within strict time limits.

SCOPE OF THE 1954 ACT

Meaning of business tenancy

The 1954 Act only applies to business tenancies which are occupied by the tenant for the purpose of a business: s.23.

Tenancy

There must be a tenancy: s.23 Landlord and Tenant Act 1954. The tenancy will usually be for a fixed term or may be periodic in nature. The House of Lords have held that tenancies at will do not fall within the Act's scope: *Wheeler* v. *Mercer* (1957). The decision in *Hagee* v. *Erikson* (1975) goes further since it established that even if the tenancy at will was created by an express written instrument it does not come within the ambit of the 1954 Act.

The 1954 Act does not apply to licences and is restricted to tenancies. The courts will consider the intention of the parties in determining whether a licence or tenancy has been created: *Shell-Mex B.P. Ltd* v. *Manchester Garages Ltd* (1971). But if exclusive possession at a rent for a term has been granted the agreement will in all likelihood be a tenancy: see *Street* v. *Mountford* (1985) discussed at pp.63–4.

Business

The expression 'business' is widely defined by the 1954 Act and goes beyond normal commercial trading activities. For this purpose a business includes 'a trade, profession or employment and includes any activity carried on by a body of persons whether corporate or unincorporate': s.23(2) Landlord and Tenant Act 1954. In the case of individuals the expression is limited to 'trade, profession or employment'; it does not include recreational or leisure activities which do not have a direct commercial nature. Thus in *Abernethie* v. *A.M.L.J. Kleinman Ltd* (1970), the Court of Appeal held that running a Sunday school from a former greengrocer's shop was not a business. The Court of Appeal applied similar reasoning in *Lewis* v. *Weldcrest Ltd* (1978) and held that the taking in of lodgers could not be regarded as an occupation within the description of a 'trade, profession or employment' in view of the lack of commercial advantage. Thus in the case of individuals there has to be some element of attempted profit or commercial use in order to bring the tenancy within the scope of the 1954 Act.

Corporate and unincorporated bodies

Section 23(2) provides that 'any activity carried on by a body of persons' is a business. At first, it appears that separate statutory rules apply to corporate and unincorporate bodies, as compared with individuals, so that prima facie any activity undertaken by a corporate or unincorporated body constitutes a business. For example, the expression has been held to include the running of a members' tennis club: *Addiscombe* v. *Crabbe* (1957).

However, the Court of Appeal have held that the words in s.23(2) must correlate to the conception of a trade, profession or employment, in *Hillil Property Investment Co. Ltd* v. *Naraine Pharmacy Ltd* (1979). The tenant owned two adjoining shops which he converted into one large pharmacy. He had used a third shop for storing the waste construction materials, but intended to open a retail shop when the work was completed. The Court of Appeal held that the third shop was not occupied for the purpose of the tenant's business since it was not being used for the purpose of the tenant's pharmacy business or any other business carried on by the tenant, e.g. accountancy operations.

Government departments

Premises occupied by a government department automatically fall within the scope of the 1954 Act regardless of purpose: s.56(4) Landlord and Tenant Act 1954.

Occupation for business purposes

Occupation

The 1954 Act depends upon the occupation of premises by the tenant for the purpose of a business. All business leasehold premises are within its scope regardless of size or value. This is in sharp contrast to the residential tenancy schemes which only operate within certain rateable value limits. The application of the 1954 Act depends upon the tenant's occupation and the purposes of his occupation.

The question of whether a tenant is in occupation for the purpose of a business or not is an evidential question. The word 'occupation' is given its ordinary meaning. The courts take into account the tenant's use and control of the premises when deciding this question. This gives rise to few difficulties in the case of a single tenant since it is relatively easy to detect a sham. But it is harder to decide whether a company tenant is in occupation. Representative occupation is essential, and it is necessary to consider the degree of control exercised over the premises by the company's representative: *Hancock and Willis* v. *G.M.S Syndicate Ltd* (1982). The Court of Appeal considered whether a company tenant who let out twenty furnished service apartments was in occupation of the leasehold premises for the purpose of a business in *Lee-Verhulst (Investments) Ltd* v. *Harwood Trust* (1972). It was held that the entire premises were occupied by the tenant because of the degree of control and extent of services provided by the company's representatives. This case can be contrasted with the Court of Appeal decision in *Chapman* v. *Freeman* (1978) where they held that a cottage used by staff employed by the tenant at his hotel nearby was not occupied for the purpose of a business, but merely for the convenience of the business: see also *Groveside Properties Ltd* v. *Westminster Medical School* (1983). A tenant who is in the business of sub-letting lock-up garages does not occupy the holding: *Trans Britannia Properties Ltd* v. *Darby Properties Ltd* (1986).

Joint tenants

Special problems are posed by joint tenancies where one or some only of the joint tenants occupy the premises for the purpose of a business, e.g. where the tenancy is held by a partnership. It is no longer necessary for all the joint tenants to be in occupation in order to apply for the lease's renewal: s.41A Landlord and Tenant Act 1954 added by s.9 Law of Property Act 1969.

Absences

The position is complicated where the tenant goes out of occupation of the premises but intends to renew his tenancy. A temporary absence occurred in *I. & H. Caplan Ltd* v. *Caplan* (1963) when the tenant ceased trading, leaving the premises empty for seven months when he discontinued his general clothing business but intended to carry on his ladies' garment line. It was held that the thread of continuity of business user had not been broken so the tenant could not be said to have ceased to occupy the premises for the purpose of a business.

Where the tenant is temporarily out of occupation, he is recognised as having constructive occupation. This happened in *Morrison Holdings Ltd* v. *Manders Property* (1976) where circumstances forced the tenant to leave his business premises when they were destroyed by fire. The Court of Appeal held that the tenant could not be said to have gone out of occupation since the absence was not of the tenant's own volition, coupled with the fact that he intended to return when the premises were fit for occupation. Lord Justice Scarman applied the following test in the *Morrison Holdings* case:

> 'a tenant must either show that he is continuing in occupation for the purposes of a business carried on by him, or, if events over which he has no control have led him to absent himself from the premises, if he continues to exert and claim his right to occupancy'.

Breach of covenant

The 1954 Act has no application in cases where the tenant is carrying on a business in breach of a covenant prohibiting business user unless the landlord has consented to the business use: s.23(4) Landlord and Tenant Act 1954; see also *Bell* v. *Alfred Franks and Bartlett Co. Ltd* (1980).

Mixed user

Special rules apply where there is mixed business and residential user. A residential tenancy with significant business use may fall within the scope of the 1954 Act. On the other hand, a business tenancy with minimal business user and significant residential use may not be brought within the Act's scheme, and may indeed be regulated by residential protective legislation, e.g. the Rent Act 1977.

In order for a tenancy with mixed business and residential use to come within the 1954 Act's scope, the business use has to form a significant part of the tenant's occupation and not merely be incidental to his residence. This principle can be illustrated by comparing the two following Court of Appeal decisions.

In *Cheryl Investments* v. *Saldanha* (1978) the landlord objected to a tenant's claim to a Rent Act tenancy by producing evidence to show that the tenant had surreptitiously changed the use of the Knightsbridge flat which he rented by setting up an import business at the premises. The Court of Appeal held that the business use was a significant purpose of the occupation. The same Court of Appeal considered the case of *Royal Life Saving Society* v. *Page* (1978) at the same time. In this instance the tenant had been granted an express licence to use one room in a flat as a medical consulting room but, in fact, did very little professional work there. The Court of Appeal found that the only significant purpose for which the tenant occupied the holding was a residential one, and that the actual use made of the business licence was only incidental to his use of the flat as his home.

Exclusions

The 1954 Act is specifically excluded in the following cases:

(a) agricultural holdings: s.43(1)(a) Landlord and Tenant Act 1954;
(b) mining leases: s.43(1)(b) Landlord and Tenant Act 1954;
(c) licensed premises: s.43(1)(d) Landlord and Tenant Act 1954. The Act does not apply to licensed premises. But it does apply where the consumption of alcohol is an adjunct to a hotel or restaurant business. Accordingly, the Act applies to:
(i) hotels and restaurants and other premises which are genuinely used for receiving visitors and where a substantial part of the business does not concern the sale of intoxicating liquor. The Court of Appeal refused to apply the 1954 Act to a pub where the proportion of non-alcoholic business (which included the provision of overnight accommodation) was only 16 to 18 per cent of the total takings;
(ii) premises genuinely used for judicial, administrative or public purposes to which the holding of a liquor licence is merely ancillary;
(iii) refreshment rooms at railway stations.
(d) tenancies granted to tenants who hold an office, appointment or employment from the landlord which depends upon that appointment. The purpose of the lease must be set out in writing after the 30th September 1954 (Act's commencement date) for the exception to apply: s.43(2) Landlord and Tenant Act 1954;
(e) tenancies for terms of six months or less are excluded by s.43(3), unless:
(i) there is a provision for renewal, or
(ii) the tenant alone or together with any business predecessor has been in occupation for more than twelve months.

Note that all periodic tenancies fall within the scope of the 1954 Act and cannot be excluded, regardless of the length of time that the tenant or his predecessor has been in occupation, even where this is for less than six months: see Woodfall at p. 2376 para 2-0655.

Contracting out

A business tenant's right to renewal was regarded as sacrosanct by the legislators of the 1954 Act. Accordingly the circumstances in which the parties can exclude it are limited. Prospective landlords and tenants cannot contract out of the 1954 Act's renewal provisions except with the consent of a court: s.38(4) Landlord and Tenant Act 1954 and *Cardiothoracic Institute* v. *Shrewdcrest Ltd* (1986). The application for consent must be made by joint agreement prior to the grant of a fixed term tenancy: s.38(4)(a) Landlord and Tenant Act 1954. A court has power to authorise the exclusion of the Act's renewal provisions as set out in ss. 24–28.

The holding

The 1954 Act distinguishes the premises which are leased from the 'holding' in cases where the tenant is only occupying part of the leasehold premises for the purpose of a business. The holding refers only to that part which is occupied for the purpose of a business, and excludes any part of the premises which is not occupied by the tenant or by an employee: s.23(3) Landlord and Tenant Act 1954. The holding does not, therefore, include any part which is either sub-let or not in the occupation of the tenant or his employees.

If only part of the premises are occupied by the tenant or by his employees he is only entitled to renew the tenancy in respect of the holding. The Court of Appeal held that where tenants ran a business of sub-letting part of the premises as flats, the holding excluded the flats sub-let as they were not in the tenant's occupation: *Bagettes Ltd* v. *G.P. Estate Co Ltd* (1956). Thus in the example set out at p.231 in Chapter 22, Tea will only be able to apply to Lemon for a renewal of the ground floor of No. 1 George Street since this is the extent of his holding. But since Part II extends to sub-tenants, Sugar can make a separate application for renewal for the part of the premises which she occupies for the purpose of her own business.

Chapter 24

Renewal Procedure

The procedure for renewal under the provisions of Part II of the 1954 Act depends on the service and counter-service of statutory forms within strict time limits. The tenant has the right to apply to the court for renewal if the landlord refuses his renewal request. Meanwhile the tenancy will be continued by statute beyond the contractual term date pending the disposal of the matter. Likewise, if neither party takes the necessary procedural steps to end the tenancy it will be continued. But in some cases the parties will have reached agreement regarding renewal, rendering much of the 1954 Act's procedural requirements redundant. There are two main alternative procedures depending on whether it is the landlord or the tenant who initiates proceedings. The landlord can initiate proceedings by serving a notice to terminate the tenancy stating whether or not he objects to renewal. Alternatively, the tenant can apply for renewal. As a general rule of thumb, it will be in the tenant's interests to wait for the landlord to initiate proceedings for termination rather than to apply for renewal straight off. The relevant forms are available from law stationers. The notices may either be served personally, by delivery or by registered or recorded delivery: s.66(4) Landlord and Tenant Act 1954 applying s.23 Landlord and Tenant Act 1927.

CALCULATING TIME LIMITS

The time limits prescribed by Part II of the 1954 Act are calculated by months. The word 'month' means calendar month so that the period of *x* months ends upon the corresponding date in the appropriate subsequent month. This is often referred to as the 'corresponding date rule', and was explained by Lord Diplock in the House of Lords decision of *Dodds* v. *Walker* (1981) in the following terms:

> 'the period ends on the corresponding date in the appropriate subsequent month i.e. the day of that month that bears the same number as the day of the earlier month on which the notice was given'.

The House of Lords held that the tenant had made his application out of time in *Dodds* v. *Walker*. He had applied for a new tenancy on the 31st of

January which was held to be more than four months after the giving of the landlord's notice on the 30th September: applied in *Riley Investments* v. *Eurostile Holdings* (1985)–see below.

COMPETENT LANDLORD

If there are a number of landlords owing to the grant of sub-tenancies it is important for the tenant to know who his opposite number is. For this purpose Part II of the 1954 Act defines the 'competent landlord' as the person who either owns the fee simple or who has a tenancy which will not expire within fourteen months and in respect of which no notice to end it has been served: s.44(1) Landlord and Tenant Act 1954. In other words, the competent landlord will either be the owner of the premises or a tenant whose tenancy will not end for at least fourteen months. If the identity of the competent landlord changes in the course of proceedings, the tenant must join the new competent landlord to those proceedings: *Rene Claro (Haute Coiffure) Ltd* v. *Halle Concerts Society* (1969). A tenant can find out who the competent landlord is by serving a notice asking for this information: s.40 (2)-(4) Landlord and Tenant Act 1954.

TERMINATION BY LANDLORD

Section 25 notice

A landlord can terminate a business tenancy which falls within the scope of Part II of the 1954 Act by serving a statutory s.25 notice of termination if the tenant has taken no steps to terminate or renew the tenancy: s.25(1) Landlord and Tenant Act 1954.

The s.25 notice must specify a termination date. The earliest point in time at which the tenancy can be ended is at the end of the contractual term, and the termination date can be no earlier: s.25(3) Landlord and Tenant Act 1954. This will normally be the date on which a fixed term tenancy expires by effluxion of time. But in the case of a periodic tenancy, the landlord does not have to ensure that the termination date coincides with the anniversary of the tenancy although it must not be earlier than the date on which the tenancy could end by a notice to quit: see s.25(3) Landlord and Tenant Act 1954 and *Commercial Properties Ltd* v. *Wood* (1968).

Statutory requirements

A s.25 notice must comply with the statutory requirements otherwise it will be invalid unless the invalidity is waived. Small slips will not invalidate a notice: *Barclays Bank Ltd* v. *Ascot* (1961). Section 25 notices are, however, required to be in the correct statutory form and must comply with the relevant regulations. Thus where a section 25 notice not only omitted the landlord's name and address but gave a misleading implication, it was held to be invalid: *Morrow* v. *Nadeem* (1986). If it transpires, however, that the notice is invalid, a landlord has no choice but to serve a fresh notice of six months but not more than twelve.

(a) The notice must specify the date of termination: s.25(1) Landlord and Tenant Act 1954. This should be calculated with care.
(b) A landlord must give a tenant 'not more than twelve nor less than six months' notice of the tenancy's termination: s.25(2) Landlord and Tenant Act 1954. In other words, the s.25 notice should ideally be served not more than twelve and not less than six months before the date of termination specified, which should coincide with the end of the contractual term.
(c) The notice must contain a clause requiring the tenant to notify the landlord in writing, within two months after the s.25 notice is given, whether or not he is willing to give up possession: s.25(5) Landlord and Tenant Act 1954. If this clause is omitted the notice will be invalid.
(d) The notice must state whether the landlord intends to oppose an application to court for renewal, and if so, state on which of the grounds in s.30 he would do so: see chapter 25. It is important for landlords to plan their campaign for possession early so that the s.30 grounds can be stated with accuracy because they cannot be added to nor amended later: *Hutchinson* v. *Lamberth* (1984). Conversely, if a landlord relies on all or most of the grounds it reduces credibility and can create a poor impression in court.

Statement of intention

The tenant has 'two months after the giving of the notice' by the landlord in which to serve a counter-notice stating whether he is willing to give up possession. If he states that he is willing to give up possession he loses any right of renewal: *De Havilland (Antiques) Ltd* v. *Centrovincial Estates (Mayfair) Ltd* (1971). Failure to serve this statement in the two month period will also result in the tenant losing his right to apply for a new tenancy: *Chiswell* v. *Griffon Land and Estates Ltd* (1975). But if he states that he is unwilling to give up possession in his statement notice, he can apply to the courts for a new tenancy if it is not possible to negotiate a new tenancy directly with his landlord. Correspondence between the parties has been held to amount to an effective counter-notice in special circumstances: *Lewington* v. *Trustees for the Protection of Ancient Buildings* (1983). A counter-notice has the same effect as a tenant's s.26 request for a new tenancy.

Tenant's application to court

A tenant has 'not less than two nor more than four months' in which to apply to the court for a new tenancy after the service of a s.25 notice or s.26 request: s.29 (3) Landlord and Tenant Act 1954. The court will not hear an application which is made outside these time limits. It has been held that the dates are calculated with reference to the 'corresponding date rule': *E Riley Investments* v. *Eurostile Holdings* (1985). In other words the period ends on the corresponding date in the subsequent second, third or fourth month. In the *Riley Investment* case a landlord served a s.25 notice on 23 March and the tenant applied to court for a new tenancy on 23 May. The landlord argued that the application was premature and invalid because they had not been given two months notice after giving the s.25 notice. The Court of Appeal held that the 'not less than two month period' ended on 23 May so that the tenant's application was not invalid.

TENANT'S REQUEST FOR RENEWAL

Section 26 request

A tenant is entitled to serve a s.26 notice requesting a new tenancy which is to commence on a date which is 'not more than twelve nor less than six months' after the request is made: s.26(2) Landlord and Tenant Act 1954. This gives the landlord six to twelve months' notice of the request. But this rule is subject to the proviso that the proposed tenancy's commencement date is not to be earlier than the date on which the current tenancy ends or can be ended: proviso to s.26(2) Landlord and Tenant Act 1954. This means that a tenant cannot apply for a new tenancy any earlier than twelve months before his current tenancy ends.

A tenant cannot request a new tenancy under s.26 if the landlord has already served a s.25 notice: s.26(4) Landlord and Tenant Act 1954. If the tenant is in receipt of a s.25 notice the correct procedure is to counter-notice stating his unwillingness to give up possession, and to apply to the court for a new tenancy if necessary: see above.

Qualifying tenancies

Tenants whose tenancies fall within the scope of Part II of the 1954 Act with terms of more than a year may request a new tenancy. The current tenancy must be for a term certain exceeding one year or for a term of years certain and thereafter from year to year: s.26(1) Landlord and Tenant Act 1954.

Tenant's proposals

The s.26 request must set out the tenant's proposals as to the property which is to be comprised in the new tenancy: s.26(3) Landlord and Tenant Act 1954. The property may be the whole or part of the property in the current tenancy. More specifically, the request must propose the rent to be payable and the tenancy's other terms: s.26(3) Landlord and Tenant Act 1954. These have been held to include a proposal as to the tenancy's duration: *Sidney Bolsom Investment Trust Ltd* v. *E Karmios & Co. (London) Ltd* (1956).

Notice of opposition

A landlord may oppose a s.26 request 'within two months' of it being made stating the statutory s.30 grounds of opposition which he intends to rely on: s.26(6) Landlord and Tenant Act 1954, and see Chapter 25. If he fails to oppose the request within this two month period, the tenant is entitled to a new tenancy. Otherwise, the matter is initially one for negotiation. But if negotiations break down the tenant can apply to the court for a new tenancy 'not less than two nor more than four months' after making the request: see s.29(3) discussed above. Note that any application for a new tenancy which is made outside these time limits will generally be struck out: *Meah* v. *Sector Properties Ltd* (1974). However, the Court of Appeal have extended the time for a tenant's application for a new tenancy in circumstances where there had been an agreement between the parties to suspend the time limits whilst negotiations were going on: *Ali* v. *Knight* (1984).

SUMMARY

The following permutations commonly arise:

(a) the tenant may wish to give up possession in any event at the end of the term: s.27 (fixed term) and s.26(4) (periodic tenancy);

(b) the landlord may wish to terminate the tenancy in which case he should serve a 's.25 notice' not earlier than twelve and not later than six months before the termination date specified in the notice. The notice should contain one or more of the s.30 grounds of opposition. The tenant has two to four months in which to apply for a new tenancy;

(c) the tenant may initiate renewal by making a formal application for a new tenancy not earlier than twelve and not later than six months before the termination date specified by serving a 's.26 notice' setting out his proposals. The landlord has two months in which to respond by serving a counter-notice opposing the grant of a new tenancy and stating which of the grounds in s.30 the opposition is based on;

(d) the parties may have failed to end the tenancy effectively e.g. by serving an invalid notice in which case a new notice should be served complying with the requirements of Part II of the 1954 Act;
(e) in either case the parties may reach a joint agreement to renew the term resulting in a new lease being granted by agreement.

These alternatives are set out in diagrammatic form in Fig. 5.

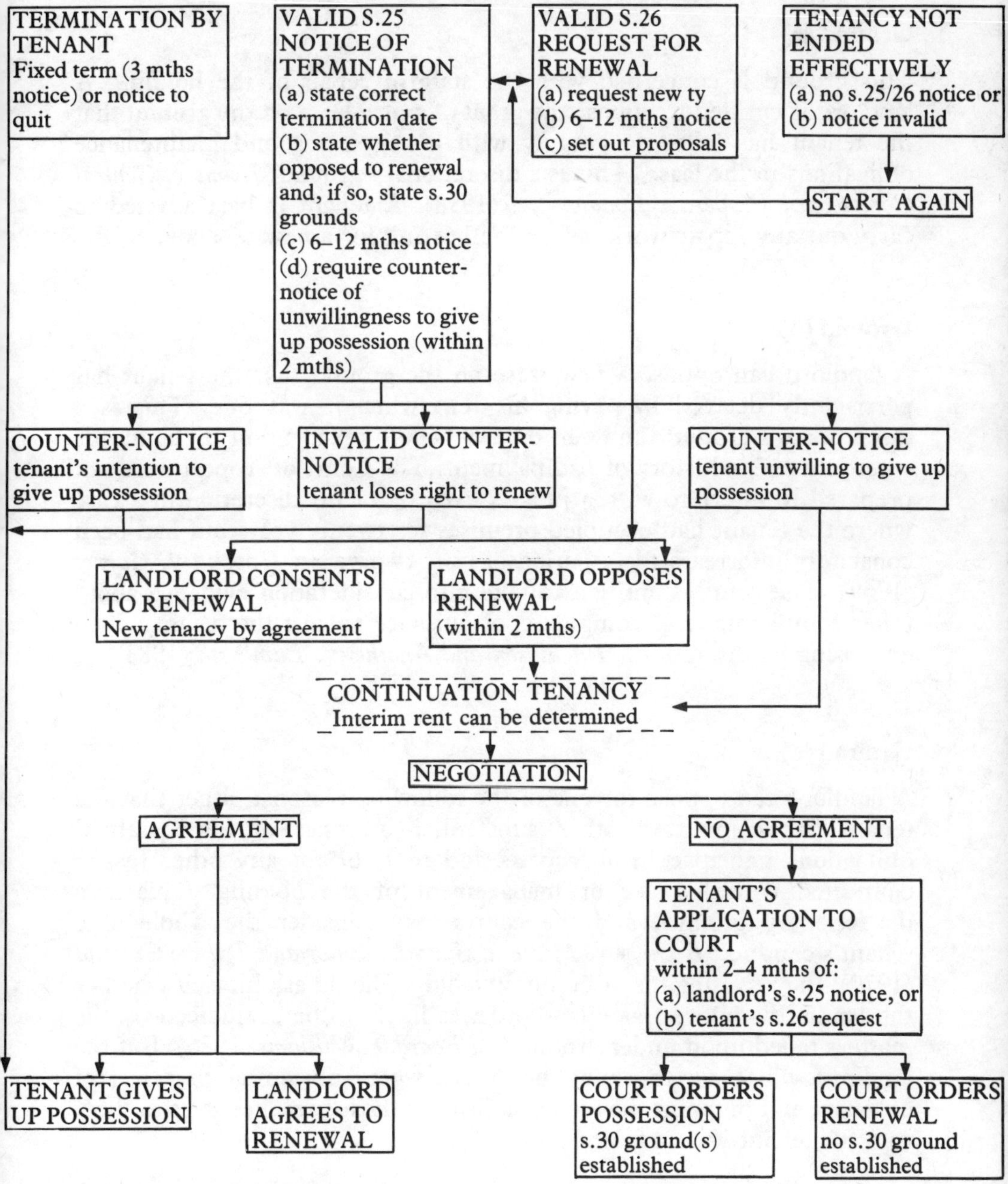

Fig. 5 Procedure for renewal or possession of business tenancies.

GROUNDS OF OPPOSITION

A landlord is entitled to oppose an application for a new tenancy on one or more of the following seven statutory grounds set out in s.30(1)(a)–(g) of the Landlord and Tenant Act 1954. The grounds most commonly relied upon by landlords to oppose renewal are grounds (f) and (g).

Ground (a)

This ground is concerned with the state of repair of the holding. A landlord is entitled to oppose the grant of a new lease on the ground that the tenant has failed to comply with his repairing and maintenance obligations in the lease. This is a discretionary ground: *Lyons* v. *Central Commercial Properties London Ltd* (1958). A tenant is best advised to carry out any repair work before the hearing for a new tenancy.

Ground (b)

A landlord can oppose a new lease on the ground that the tenant has persistently delayed in paying his rent when it was due. This is a discretionary ground, and can only be safely relied upon by landlords where there is a history of bad payment. The Court of Appeal were not prepared to interfere with a judge's exercise of his discretion in a case where the tenant had occupied premises for twenty years but had been constantly in arrears for a period of over two years: *Hopcutt* v. *Carver* (1969). The court is entitled to take into consideration evidence about other complaints, e.g. complaints of nuisance against the tenant, when exercising its discretion: *Hutchinson and Another* v. *Lamberth* (1983).

Ground (c)

A landlord can oppose for one of the following reasons: either that the tenant has committed other substantial breaches of his leasehold obligations i.e. apart from repairs and rent, or for any other reason connected with his use or management of the holding. This is a discretionary ground, and the courts may consider the whole of a tenant's conduct: *Eichner* v. *Midland Bank Executor and Trustee Co. Ltd* (1970). In exercising his discretion the judge should ask himself whether the landlord's interest as a landlord was likely to be prejudiced by the matters relied upon under ground (c): *Beard* v. *Williams* (1986). But the landlord will have to show that there were substantial breaches of covenant and pinpoint the responsibility for those breaches so as to show that the tenant was at fault.

Ground (d)

A landlord can oppose a new tenancy if he is willing to provide or has secured alternative accommodation for the tenant. The offer of alternative accommodation must be made before the notice of opposition is served. The alternative accommodation must satisfy the following criteria, of reasonableness of terms and suitability respectively:

(a) the terms of the alternative accommodation are reasonable. For this purpose, the terms of the current tenancy and any other relevant circumstances are taken into account; and
(b) whether the alternative accommodation is suitable for the tenant's requirements including the requirement to preserve goodwill. For this purpose the class and nature of the tenant's business is taken into account in addition to the situation, extent and facilities of the holding.

Ground (e)

A landlord can oppose a new tenancy on the ground of uneconomic sub-letting. The rationale is that a landlord's reversionary interest should not be depreciated in value. A landlord can only rely on this ground where a property he owns is sub-let and the current tenancy was created by a sub-letting of part of the premises. This is a discretionary ground which is determined in the first instance by reference to two valuations. The rents 'reasonably obtainable' of the parts sub-let are aggregated and compared with the rent which would be 'reasonably obtainable on a letting of the property as a whole': s.30(1)(e) Landlord and Tenant Act 1954. Ground (e) is rarely used because it is difficult to show differentials between market values.

Ground (f)

A landlord can regain possession in cases where he can show that he intends to demolish or reconstruct the holding or a substantial part of it or alternatively where he intends to carry out substantial construction work on the holding or part of it. This ground is determined on the narrow issue of whether it is reasonable to obtain possession of the holding for the purposes of reconstruction or demolition.

If a landlord can enter to carry out the proposed works under the terms of the lease, e.g. under a covenant to carry out alterations and improvements, he may not be able to establish a need for possession of the holding: *Heath* v. *Drown* (1973) and *Price* v. *Esso Petroleum Company Ltd* (1980); compare *Leathwoods Ltd* v. *Total Oil (Great Britain) Ltd* (1984). Moreover, a tenant may be able to resist a landlord's claim for possession on ground (f) if the tenant is willing to give the landlord access to the holding for the purpose of carrying out the work: s.31A Landlord and Tenant Act 1954, added by s.7(1) Law of Property Act 1969. But the Court of Appeal has held that a tenant is not entitled to rely on s.31A if the landlord cannot carry out the proposed work without interfering with the tenant's business use of the holding to a substantial extent: *Redfern* v. *Reeves* (1979); 'Demolition, Reconstruction and the 1954 Act', Legal notes by S.Murdoch (1986) 279 EG 687.

Ground (f) is commonly relied upon by landlords, and may be the only ground on which they can oppose a new tenancy. A bare assertion of intention is not sufficient: *Betty's Cafes Ltd* v. *Phillips Furnishing Stores Ltd* (1959). Thus if there is a succession of fences to be surmounted it cannot be said that a landlord intends reconstruction or demolition. The landlord in *Cunliffe* v. *Goodman* (1950) was found not to have formed this intention since there were a number of fences yet to be surmounted, e.g. obtaining planning permission for her schemes. Lord Asquith stated:

> 'In the case of neither scheme did she form a settled intention to proceed. Neither project moved out of the zone of contemplation–out of the sphere of the tentative, the provisional and the exploratory–into the valley of decision'.

A landlord should, therefore, plan well in advance if he intends to rely on ground (f) so as to ensure that his scheme has passed out of the 'zone of contemplation' into the 'valley of decision'. But it has been held that a letter from a bank manager promising finance for redevelopment is sufficient evidence of finance being available for redevelopment: *Daf Motoring Centre (Gosport) Ltd* v. *Hutfield & Wheeler Ltd* (1982). The courts require proof of a landlord's intention to demolish or reconstruct at the time of the hearing: *Morris Marks* v. *British Waterways Board* (1963).

The work must either amount to demolition or reconstruction. Reconstruction goes beyond refurbishment. The issue is whether a 'substantial part' of the premises is being reconstructed, and that is a question of degree when looking at the entire works proposed: *Atkinson* v. *Bettison* (1955) and *Joel* v. *Swaddle* (1957).

Ground (g)

A landlord is entitled to possession if he can show that he intends to occupy the holding either for the purposes (or partly for the purposes) of a business to be carried on by him there or as his residence. A landlord does not occupy by reletting: *Jones* v. *Jenkins* (1985). The court has no discretion and there are no issues of reasonableness.

Landlord's intention

Once again, the landlord will have to satisfy a court of his intention, in this case to occupy. The House of Lords held that this was an objective test in *Westminster City Council* v. *British Waterways Board* (1984). In that case the tenant Council leased a wharf as a street cleaning depot. The landlords opposed their appplication for a new tenancy on the ground that they intended to change the use to a marina which they would occupy. The tenant Council indicated that it would refuse planning permission for this change of use. The House of Lords held further that the landlords had established a reasonable prospect of success in their notional planning appeal and their case under ground (g), and that the tenant's objection was not a legitimate planning objection since it was designed to preserve their own occupation of the cleaning depot.

Purposes of a business

A landlord must show that he intends to occupy the holding for the purpose of a business carried on therein. In cases where the landlord intends to demolish the holding, the Court of Appeal has held that the holding is the vacant site on which the landlord proposes to erect a building so that it cannot be argued that he is not occupying the holding: *Cam Gears Ltd* v. *Cunningham* (1981); compare *Nursey* v. *P. Currie (Dartford) Ltd* (1959) as distinguished in *J.W.Thornton Ltd* v. *Blacks Leisure Group PLC* (1986).

Business is defined by s.23(2): see pp.232–3. A landlord has a reasonable time in which to enter into occupation from the termination of the lease: *Method Development Ltd* v. *Jones* (1971).

Five year rule

Ground (g) is subject to the rule that the landlord must have owned the interest for five years before he is entitled to oppose a new tenancy on the basis of ground (g) in cases where he purchased his interest subject to the existing tenancy: s.30(2) Landlord and Tenant Act 1954. This is designed to prevent sales of a landlord's interest which is subject to a business tenancy in the last five years of a lease to a third party who intends to demolish or reconstruct. The test is whether in the last five years of the business tenancy (ending on the lease's termination) the landlord either purchased his interest or his interest was created: s.30(2) Landlord and Tenant Act 1954. 'Purchased' means bought for money: *H.L. Bolton (Engineering) Co. Ltd* v. *T.J. Graham & Sons Ltd* (1957).

CONTINUATION AND INTERIM RENT

Continuation

A statutory continuation tenancy is automatically created by s.24 of the Landlord and Tenant Act 1954 if renewal negotiations or proceedings continue beyond the termination date. This is the only form of statutory tenancy relating to business tenancies. The continuation tenancy is designed to fill the vacuum between the termination of the business tenancy and the grant of a new tenancy under the 1954 Act's renewal procedure. There are two main advantages of the device of a continuation tenancy. First, that the business tenant is given some small measure of security of tenure insofar as the continuation tenancy can only be terminated in accordance with the provisions of Part II of the 1954 Act. Second, that the terms of the lease are continued beyond the contractual term, save that there is provision for a procedure to determine an interim rent.

Interim rent

Landlords are now entitled to apply to the courts for the determination of an interim rent which it would be reasonable for the tenant to pay while the tenancy continues: s.24A Landlord and Tenant Act 1954 added by s.3(1) Law of Property Act 1969. This provision enables landlords to obtain a market rent during the continuation tenancy which may be higher than the rent paid under the former business tenancy. It also prevents tenants from abusing the scheme of the 1954 Act by spinning out the continuation tenancy for as long as possible by delaying tactics with a view to paying the contractual rent (which may have fallen behind the market rent) for as long as possible.

There is no reason why a tenant cannot apply for an interim rent. He may choose to do so where, for example, the premises are out of repair owing to the landlord's neglect of his repairing obligations. This happened in *Fawke* v. *Chelsea (Viscount)* (1980) where the Court of Appeal held that lack of repair could be taken into account in assessing the interim rent which the tenant had applied for. Lord Justice Goff stated:

> 'I do not see anything in s.24A which requires the court, in determining what rent is reasonable for the tenant to pay, albeit by reference to a hypothetical letting, to shut its eyes to known facts'.

Where the tenant applies for an interim rent, the rent is payable from the date on which proceedings were commenced which, for this purpose, is the date on which the landlord opposed the application for a new tenancy: *Thomas* v. *Hammond-Lawrence* (1986).

The parties can agree an interim rent without having recourse to the courts: s.24A(3) and s.34(1) Landlord and Tenant Act 1954. But if the court determines the matter the interim rent will be assessed on the basis of what would be a reasonable rent for a tenant to pay as a yearly tenancy: s.24(A)(1) Landlord and Tenant Act 1954: see *Charles Follett Ltd* v. *Cabtell Investment Co. Ltd* (1986) for an application of these principles.

Determination of

Comparables: A court will have regard to comparables when determining an interim rent. If there are no relevant comparables it can be guided by the rents of neighbouring properties. A court will not put the parties to the delay and expense of a new trial unless the figures arrived at are so obviously wrong that some substantial wrong or miscarriage of justice has resulted: *Halberstam* v. *Tandalco Corporation NV and Another* (1985).

The interim rent is calculated with reference to the statutory calculation for rent under any new tenancy which may be granted, although the two calculations are not identical: compare s.24A and s.34 Landlord and Tenant Act 1954.

The three main differences between these two calculations are that, first, an interim rent is payable for the entire premises whilst a new rent will be set for the holding. Second, an interim rent is calculated on the notional assumption that a yearly periodic tenancy has been granted whereas a new rent is calculated with reference to the length of the new term. Third, an interim rent is determined on the basis of the subjective test of what would be reasonable for the tenant to pay during the continuation tenancy whereas a new rent is based on the objective criteria of what the holding might reasonably be expected to be let for to a willing tenant in the open market. In both cases the terms of the lease are taken into account.

In determining the interim rent payable s.24A(3) directs the court to take into account the following factors:

(a) the rent payable under the former business tenancy. There is no binding decision on whether the interim rent can be lower than the contractual rent although there are dicta to indicate that the courts can fix an interim rent at less than the market rent since the courts are directed to consider what would be a reasonable amount for the tenant to pay: per Lord Justice Goff in *Fawke* v. *Viscount Chelsea* (1980), applying Mr Justice Megarry's reasoning in *English Exporters (London) Ltd* v. *Eldonwall Ltd* (1973). This approach is markedly different from the approach of Mr Justice Stamp in *Regis Property Co. Ltd* v. *Lewis & Peat Ltd* (1970) who applied strict valuation criteria with a modification to reflect the hypothetical yearly tenancy;

(b) the application of s.34(1) as if the continuation tenancy were a yearly tenancy. Section 34(1) directs the court as to matters which should be disregarded, e.g. effect of tenant's occupation on rent, goodwill, improvements, and value attributable to a licence in the case of licensed premises: see p.238;

(c) the application of s.34(2) as if the tenancy were a yearly tenancy. Section 34(2) directs the court how to deal with certain improvements.

When payable

An interim rent is payable from the date on which the landlord made his application under s.24A. This date will either be the date proceedings commenced, or the termination date specified in a landlord's s.25 notice or tenant's s.26 notice, whichever is later. For this purpose it has been held that proceedings commence when the application to determine the interim rent is made and not substantive legal proceedings. Landlords should, therefore, apply for an interim rent from the appropriate termination date if they wish to back-date the interim rent as far as possible: *Steam Properties Ltd* v. *Davis* (1972): see p.250.

TERMS OF NEW TENANCY

The parties can either agree the terms of the new tenancy or they may be determined by the court in default of agreement: s.33 Landlord and Tenant Act 1954. But the landlord cannot insist on terms which are more onerous than those in the current tenancy: *Cardshops Ltd* v. *Davies* (1971).

The court has power to grant a new term not exceeding fourteen years on such terms as it thinks reasonable under all the circumstances: ss.33–5 Landlord and Tenant Act 1954. In exercising this power the court is directed by s.35 to consider the terms of the current tenancy and all relevant circumstances. If one of the parties wishes to change the terms of the current tenancy the onus falls on that party to satisfy the court that the proposed term is fair and reasonable in all the circumstances: *O'May* v. *City of London Real Property Co. Ltd* (1983).

Duration

The maximum duration is fourteen years. The court can set very short terms in special circumstances, e.g. where the tenant needs a little time to move out of possession: *CBS United Kingdom Ltd* v. *London Scottish Properties Ltd* (1985). But a new tenancy granted by the court cannot begin prior to three months after the termination of proceedings relating to the tenant's application: s.64(1) Landlord and Tenant Act 1954.

Premises

The court cannot enlarge the holding so that the premises under the new tenancy are greater than the original holding: *G.Orlik (Meat Products)* v. *Hastings & Thanet Building Society* (1975).

Rent

Determination of

Likewise the rent payable under the new tenancy can be agreed between the parties or determined by the court in default of agreement. The court will consider any suitable comparables. If none is available it can take judicial notice of general increases in rent in the area: *National Car Parks* v. *Colebrook Estates Ltd* (1982). The court may insert a rent review clause if the length of the term warrants it: *Re No. 88 High Road, Kilburn* (1959).

The zoning method of valuation has been applied in appropriate circumstances in *James (Gowns) Ltd* v. *Harlow Development Corporation* (1979) where Judge Finlay Q.C. explained the zoning method in the following terms:

> 'This is a process whereby a notional superficial area of the premises is determined with a view to ascertaining the proper rent by applying to that notional superficial area the rent per sq.ft appropriate to that part of the premises which is designated as zone [X]... There are therefore [Y] zones, all differentiated according to...'.

In *Charles Follet Ltd* v. *Cabtell Investment Co. Ltd* (1986) Mr Cullen QC said in giving judgment that the 'expert eye of some steeped in current market conditions applying his judgment, carried more weight than the exercise of making percentage adjustments expressed with precision to rents of different premises, particularly when such adjustments were being made by witnesses with no recent experience of market conditions'.

Disregards

If the court is asked to determine the rent payable, s.34(1) directs the court to disregard the following.

Occupation by tenant: Any effect that the fact that the tenant or his predecessor has been in occupation has on rent: s.34(1)(a) Landlord and Tenant Act 1954.

Goodwill: Any goodwill attached to the holding as a result of the fact that the tenant or his predecessor has carried on business there: s.34(1)(b) Landlord and Tenant Act 1954.

Improvements: Any effect which improvements have on rent in cases where the improvement was carried out by a person who was a tenant provided that the improvement was not a leasehold obligation: s.34(1)(c)(2) Landlord and Tenant Act 1954.

For the improvement to be disregarded it must either have been carried out during the current tenancy or satisfy the twenty-one year condition. This condition will be met if the improvement was completed not more than twenty-one years before the tenant applied for a new tenancy, and the holding or the part affected by the improvement has been let as a business tenancy at all times since the improvement was completed with the then tenant remaining in possession at the end of each tenancy.

Licensed premises: In the case of licensed premises, an addition to the holding's value attributable to the licence if the benefit of the licence belongs to the tenant: s.34(1)(d) Landlord and Tenant Act 1954.

Guarantors

The court has power to require the tenant to provide a guarantor of his obligations under the new tenancy: *Cairnplace Ltd* v. *CBL (Property Investments Co. Ltd)* (1983).

Chapter 25

Compensation for Disturbance and Improvements

COMPENSATION FOR DISTURBANCE

Entitlement

In certain cases a tenant will be entitled to compensation for disturbance under the provisions of s.37 of the Landlord and Tenant Act 1954 when an application for renewal is turned down. Compensation can be awarded where the tenant is precluded from renewing his lease through no fault of his own. Compensation is payable where the landlord's opposition to the grant of a new lease is successfully based on the ground of uneconomic sub-letting, demolition or reconstruction by the landlord, or the landlord's own occupational needs: see s.30 Landlord and Tenant Act 1954, grounds (e) (f) and (g) discussed at pp.246–8.

Contracting out

Landlords and tenants can contract out of the 1954 Act's compensation provisions by excluding or modifying them by agreement in cases where the business occupation has been for less than five years: s.38(2)(3) Landlord and Tenant Act 1954.

Contracting out by agreement is void in the following circumstances: s.38(2) Landlord and Tenant Act 1954. First, where the tenant has occupied the holding for the purpose of a business for five years or more prior to the lease's termination. Second, if there has been a change of occupier during the five years prior to the lease's termination where there is continuity of the business so that the successor carries on the business of the former occupier. This means that if there has been a change of occupier in the five years prior to termination the right to compensation can be excluded unless each occupier succeeded to the business of his predecessor.

Note that even if the lease is for a term of more than five years, landlords occasionally exclude or modify the Act's compensation provisions just in case the tenant should leave within five years or where the tenant or business changes.

Amount of compensation

A tenant is entitled to compensation calculated by multiplying the rateable value of the holding by the appropriate multiplier: s.37(2)(b) Landlord and Tenant Act 1954. If a tenant has occupied the premises for the purpose of a business for fourteen years before the tenancy's termination he is entitled to twice the amount of compensation, calculated by multiplying twice the rateable value by the appropriate multiplier: s.37(2)(a)(3) Landlord and Tenant Act 1954. In *Edicron Ltd* v. *William Whiteley Ltd* (1984) the tenant occupied the first floor of a building continuously for over fourteen years, and the second and third floors for less than fourteen years. The Court of Appeal had to decide whether the tenant qualified for double compensation for all three floors, there being no doubt that they qualified for double compensation in respect of the first floor. It was held that the tenant was entitled to double compensation for the holding they occupied, namely the first, second and third floors by virtue of their occupation of the first floor for over fourteen years. The test is not whether they occupied the entire holding for fourteen years but whether they occupied the 'premises' for fourteen years.

In both cases the appropriate multiplier from the 7th May 1985 is 3: Landlord and Tenant Act 1954 (Appropriate Multiplier) Order 1984 (SI 1984 No 1932). The appropriate multiplier was originally 2, and rose to 21/4 in 1981: see the Landlord and Tenant Act 1954 (Appropriate Multiplier) Regulations 1981 (SI 1981 No 69). The current formula can be represented by the following equations:

(a) ordinary level of compensation

$$3 \times \text{RV (holding)}$$

(b) where 14 years business occupation

$$3 \times 2\ \text{RV} = 6 \times \text{RV (holding)}$$

Rateable value of the holding

Compensation is calculated with reference to the rateable value of the holding. For this purpose the rateable value is determined with reference to the valuation list in force at the date on which the landlord's s.25 or tenant's s.26 notice is given: s.37(5)(a) Landlord and Tenant Act 1954. If no value is shown for the holding but the premises are valued, the rateable value for the holding is calculated by apportioning the value or by aggregating the values shown: s.37(5)(b) Landlord and Tenant Act 1954. Disputes about the correct rateable value for the holding can be referred to the Commissioners of Inland Revenue: s.37(5) Landlord and Tenant Act 1954.

Right to compensation

The tenant's right to compensation for disturbance only arises at the time he leaves the premises. Since the regulations setting the appropriate multiplier change from time to time, the relevant multiplier is the multiplier in force at the date the tenant leaves the premises: *Cardshops Ltd* v. *John Lewis Properties Ltd* (1983). Some landlords have invariably been caught out by rises in the level of compensation payable since 1981.

COMPENSATION FOR MISREPRESENTATION

A tenant is further entitled to be compensated for any misrepresentation or concealment of material facts by the landlord which resulted in the landlord obtaining possession: s.55 Landlord and Tenant Act 1954. In this case the amount of compensation is the measure of damage or loss sustained by the tenant as the result of the possession order or refusal of his application for renewal: s.55 Landlord and Tenant Act 1954.

COMPENSATION FOR IMPROVEMENTS

Part I of the 1927 Act provides for the payment of compensation for improvements. The right to compensation is only applicable to authorised improvements, and does not arise until the end of the lease.

Position under the lease

Business leases generally incorporate a tenant's repairing covenant together with either an absolute covenant prohibiting improvements or a qualified covenant which permits improvements subject to the tenant obtaining the landlord's prior consent. If the lease contains a qualified covenant against improvements the 1927 Act adds the proviso that the landlord's consent is not to be unreasonably withheld: see s.19(2) Landlord and Tenant Act 1927 in Appendix 1. The test for determining whether a landlord has refused his consent unreasonably is subjective to the extent that the courts will look at the position from the tenant's vantage point: *Lambert* v. *Woolworth & Co.* (1938) discussed at p.188.

Thus most business tenants have the opportunity of carrying out improvements lawfully without breaking the terms of their lease and will fall into one of three categories. First, the tenancy may be subject to a qualified covenant, in which case the tenant can rely on the proviso in s.19(2). Second, if the lease is completely silent the tenant can go ahead in any event. Third, even in cases where the lease contains an absolute prohibition on improvements, the landlord may give the tenant express permission to carry out improvements.

The word 'improvement' may not appear in the lease which may use the generic term 'alteration' to include both alterations and improvements: see p.187. Finally, the law draws a distinction between work which constitutes a repair and work which amounts to an improvement each being governed by different covenants in the lease, and only improvements qualify for compensation: see pp.142–3 for the distinction between repair and improvement.

The scope of the 1927 Act

The holding

The 1927 Act applies to 'holdings' which are defined as any premises held under a lease which are used either wholly or partly for carrying on a trade or business: s.17(1) Landlord and Tenant Act 1927. The premises must, therefore, be used for a trade or business.

Exclusions

The following premises are specifically excluded from the scope of the 1927 Act by s.17:

(a) premises let under a mining lease;
(b) agricultural holdings;
(c) holdings let to tenants who are employees of the landlord. The contract must be in writing and set out the purpose for which it is created for the exclusion to operate if the tenancy is created after the 24th March 1927 (commencement date of the 1927 Act);
(d) premises used to carry on a profession unless the premises are used regularly for carrying on a profession, in which case the tenancy qualifies for compensation;
(e) premises used for sub-letting as residential flats.

Comparison with the 1954 Act

The holdings to which Part II of the Landlord and Tenant Act 1954 applies are defined differently and different exclusions apply: see pp.238–9. This means that there can be situations where a tenant may qualify for compensation under the 1927 Act but may not fall within the scope of the 1954 Act. For example, tenants of licensed premises cannot apply for a new tenancy under the provisions of the 1954 Act but may claim compensation for improvements under the 1927 Act: s.43(1)(d) Landlord and Tenant Act 1954.

Authorisation

Section I of the 1927 Act entitles a tenant to compensation for certain authorised improvements carried out by the tenant which benefit the landlord at the termination of the tenancy when he leaves the holding. Improvements can include demolition and rebuilding. The tenant in *National Electric Theatres Ltd* v. *Hudgell* (1939) submitted plans for shops with flats above, the leasehold premises having been used as a cinema. It was held that the proposed works would be an improvement for the purposes of the 1927 Act.

Improvements which fail to qualify

A tenant is not entitled to compensation in the following cases:

(a) where the improvement is made before the 25th March 1928: s.2(1)(a) Landlord and Tenant Act 1927;
(b) improvements which were carried out as a result of an obligation in the lease imposed on the tenant or his predecessor for valuable consideration: s.2(1)(b) Landlord and Tenant Act 1927.
(c) improvements carried out in the last three years of a lease: s.2(1)(c) Landlord and Tenant Act 1927;
(d) if the landlord offers to carry out the proposed improvement himself in return for a reasonable increase in rent within two months after the tenant has made a claim: s.2(1)(d) Landlord and Tenant Act 1927;
(e) if the improvement was begun before the 1st October 1954 as a result of a statutory obligation: s.48(1) Landlord and Tenant Act 1954.

Authorisation procedure

The tenant must obtain prior authorisation from his immediate landlord before carrying out the work. The authorisation procedure is based on a system of written notices.

Notice of intention

The tenant should serve a written notice on the immediate landlord setting out his intention to make the improvement, together with a specification and plan showing both the proposed improvement and the part of the premises which will be affected by it: s.3 (1) Landlord and Tenant Act 1927. A notice of intention to carry out an improvement may be made by implication in a letter asking for a contribution and completed when an architect's final drawings have been served on the landlord: *Deerfield Travel Services Ltd* v. *Wardens and Society of the History of Art of the London Leathersellers of the City of London* (1983).

Notice of objection

The landlord has three months in which to serve a counter-notice objecting to the improvements. But the landlord has no grounds for objecting to it if the improvement has to be carried out as a result of a statutory obligation: s.3(1) Landlord and Tenant Act 1927. A tenant may go ahead with the improvement if no notice of objection is served within three months of the tenant's own notice. If a notice of objection has been served, then he can only go ahead with the certification of a court.

Immediate landlord

Although notice is served on the immediate landlord he may in turn claim compensation from the head landlord when his own term expires: s.8 Landlord and Tenant Act 1927. The landlord or any superior landlord to whom the tenant's notice is passed on is entitled to object to the proposed improvement. This provision applies where there is more than one landlord owing to the grant of sub-lease by the tenant.

Court certification

The tenant can apply for authorisation from the court if the landlord objects to his proposed improvement. A court may certify the improvement if it is satisfied that it will add to the letting value of the premises, is reasonable and suitable to the character of the premises and will not diminish the value of any other property belonging to the landlord: s.3(1) Landlord and Tenant Act 1927. The court will only certify the improvement if it is satisfied that the superior landlords have been notified and have had a chance to be heard.

Confirmation of completion

It is a good idea for tenants to ask their landlords to confirm that the improvement was executed: s.7(6) Landlord and Tenant Act 1927. This avoids lengthy disputes at a later stage when a claim for compensation is made. In cases where the landlord refuses to confirm the completion of the improvement, the tenant may apply to the court for a certificate of completion.

Contracting out

Landlords cannot contract out of the statutory provisions relating to compensation for improvements after the 8th February 1927: s.9 Landlord and Tenant Act 1927.

Compensation claims

The procedure for claiming compensation is also based on the service of statutory notices.

Claims notice

The tenant must serve a written notice on the landlord claiming compensation within strict time limits. The time limits are either calculated with reference to the method of termination or geared to the time limits of the 1954 Act: s.47 Landlord and Tenant Act 1954.

Method of termination

The time limits for claiming compensation vary according to the way in which the tenancy is terminated as follows:

(a) by effluxion of time
The period for claiming compensation in respect of fixed term leases expiring automatically at the end of the term by effluxion of time is not less than three months and not earlier than six months before the tenancy ends.
(b) by forfeiture
The time limits for claims vary according to whether the re-entry is peaceable or by court order. If the tenancy is terminated by peaceable re-entry pursuant to a forfeiture clause compensation should be claimed three months from the date of re-entry. On the other hand, if the forfeiture occurs as a result of a court order the time for claiming compensation is three months from the date on which the order becomes effective or when the order ceases to be the subject of an appeal.
(c) by notice to quit
Where the tenancy is ended by a notice to quit served by either the landlord or tenant, or by a notice under the Landlord and Tenant Act 1954, the time limit is three months from the date on which the notice to quit is given: s.47 Landlord and Tenant Act 1954. This is subject to the following proviso:

> 1954 Act applicable
> If the 1954 Act applies to the tenancy, and the tenant has made a s.26 request for a new tenancy, the tenant has three months from the date on which the landlord gives notice of his opposition to the grant of a new tenancy in which to claim compensation, or three months from the last day on which he could have given notice (if he has failed to do so): proviso to s.47 Landlord and Tenant Act 1954.

Amount of compensation

A statutory formula sets a ceiling for the amount of compensation which a tenant may claim in the absence of any express agreement. The compensation cannot exceed 'the net addition to the value of the holding as a whole' directly resulting from the improvement: s.1(1)(a) Landlord and Tenant Act 1927. This has been judicially construed to mean the benefit to the property less any detriment: *National Electric Theatres* v. *Hudgell* (1939). The purposes for which the premises are to be used after the tenancy's termination can also be taken into account: s.1(2) Landlord and Tenant Act 1927. In other words, if it can be shown that the landlord intended to demolish the premises, or carry out structural alterations or change their user, the effect of any such demolition, alteration, or change of user on the additional value attributable to the improvement will be taken into account.

There is also a statutory ceiling on compensation where the work which constituted the improvement is out of repair. The appropriate formula is the reasonable cost of carrying out the improvement at the termination of the tenancy, less the cost, if any, of putting the works which constitute the improvement into repair except where that cost is covered by the tenant's liability under a repairing covenant or agreement: s.1(1)(b) Landlord and Tenant Act 1927.

Finally, the court determining the amount of compensation is entitled to reduce it to take into account any benefit which the tenant or his predecessor may have received from the landlord in consideration of the improvement: s.2(3) Landlord and Tenant Act 1927. The operation of this reduction has always been very uncertain.

FURTHER READING

Casebook on Rent Review and Lease Renewal by D.Brahams and Mark Pawlowski, Collins, 1986.
Letting Business Premises 5th ed, by T.Aldridge, Oyez, 1985.
Renewal of Business Tenancies by Reynolds and Clark, STEW, 1985.

Chapter 26

Long Residential Tenancies at Low Rents

Long tenancies at low rents fall within the scope of two statutes which co-exist together, namely Part I of the Landlord and Tenant Act 1954 ('the 1954 Act') and the Leasehold Reform Act 1967 ('the 1967 Act'): see pp.231–3 for an introduction to the legislative objectives. Part I of the 1954 Act provides long leaseholders with security of tenure analogous to that enjoyed under the Rent Acts whilst the 1967 Act gives tenants a right to extend their lease or enfranchise. Although these provisions and the Rent Act 1977 are mutually exclusive, a long leaseholder is entitled to Rent Act protection if the long tenancy is ended in accordance with the provisions of Part I of the 1954 Act.

PROTECTION UNDER THE 1954 ACT

The objective of Part I of the 1954 Act is to provide long leaseholders at low rents with security of tenure when their tenancy ends since the low rent payable would otherwise remove long tenancies at low rents from Rent Act protection. Since the aim of the 1954 Act is to grant security of tenure to long leaseholders comparable to that enjoyed by Rent Act protected tenants, many of the statutory provisions adopt the terminology of the Rent Act or adopt some of the Rent Act's provisions directly. Thus, for example, the premises are referred to as the 'dwelling house'.

Meaning of long tenancy at a low rent

In order for a tenant to qualify for security of tenure under Part I of the 1954 Act or the extensive rights under the 1967 Act he must have a long lease, which for this purpose must exceed twenty-one years, at a low rent.

Long tenancy

A long tenancy is defined as a tenancy which was granted for a term certain exceeding twenty-one years from the date of grant: s.2(4) Landlord and Tenant Act 1954; s.146(2) Rent Act 1977; and *Roberts* v.

Church Commissioners for England (1972). If the tenancy can be ended early by the tenant exercising a break clause in the lease it does not qualify as a long tenancy; s.2 Landlord and Tenant Act 1954.

Low rent

A tenancy is at a low rent if either no rent is payable or the rent payable is less than two-thirds of a specified rateable value figure on the 'appropriate day': s.2(5) Landlord and Tenant Act 1954 and s.5 Rent Act 1977. This means that a comparison of the rent payable with the specified rateable value as assessed on the appropriate day will decide the matter conclusively. In determining the amount payable by way of rent, payments for rates, services, repairs, maintenance and insurance are all disregarded: s.2(7) Landlord and Tenant Act 1954.

Rateable value on appropriate day: The property's rateable value is calculated with reference to the rateable value of the leasehold premises as set out in the valuation list on the 'appropriate date'. The entirety of the premises may be rated in the valuation list. Alternatively, the premises may form part of premises which are rated in which case the rateable value will have to be apportioned between the parts. On the other hand, the leasehold premises may straddle more than one property which is rated, in which case the relevant rateable values will have to be aggregated together in order to determine the rateable value for the leasehold premises: see s.25 (1) Rent Act 1977.

The appropriate date is prima facie the 23rd March 1965. If the dwelling did not appear in the valuation list on that date, e.g. because it was built after that date, the appropriate day is the date on which the dwelling was first shown in the valuation list: s.25(3) Rent Act 1977. The rateable values are the same as under the Rent Acts: see Chapter 27. In the case of properties rated on or before the 22nd March 1973 which have a rateable value in excess of £400 in Greater London or £200 elsewhere, the appropriate day is the 22nd March 1973 s.5 Rent Act 1977, s.2(5) Landlord and Tenant Act 1954.

Qualifying tenants

Tenants with long tenancies at low rents will qualify for the protection of Part I of the 1954 Act if the 'qualifying condition' is fulfilled. The qualifying condition is that the tenancy would have been Rent Act protected but for the low rent: s.2 (1) Landlord and Tenant Act 1954. This condition was explained by Lord Denning MR in *Herbert* v. *Byrne* (1964), who stated:

> 'You are to look at the position at the end of the lease, and ask

yourself whether the leaseholder would have been protected if it had not been a tenancy at a low rent, but a short lease at a rack rent. If the leaseholder would have qualified under the old Rent Acts for protection on the expiry of such a short lease, he qualifies now, under the Act of 1954, for protection on the expiry of the long lease'.

Note that if any of the statutory exemptions to the Rent Act are applicable, the tenancy will not be a tenancy which would have been Rent Act protected but for the low rent payable: see ss. 4–16 Rent Act 1977 considered in Chapter 27.

Meaning of landlord

If there is more than one landlord owing to the creation of sub-tenancies, the tenant should ensure that he is dealing with the correct landlord. For the purpose of Part I of the 1954 Act, the 'competent landlord' is either the person who owns the freehold or a leasehold interest which is five years longer than the tenant's: s.21 Landlord and Tenant Act 1954. Note that the meaning of competent landlord is quite differently defined for the purpose of Part II of the 1954 Act: see s.44 (1) Landlord and Tenant Act 1954, where he must either own the freehold or have a lease which will not expire within fourteen months.

Continuation of tenancies

Part I of the 1954 Act (like Part II) uses the vehicle of a statutory continuation tenancy to fill the vacuum between the end of the tenant's contractual term and either the resumption of possession by the landlord or the date on which a statutory tenancy commences: s.3 Landlord and Tenant Act 1954. This means that a long tenancy is automatically continued beyond the contractual term for an indefinite period, unless the tenant gives up possession or an agreement has been reached entitling him to a statutory tenancy when his term ends.

Termination by landlord

Part I of the 1954 Act prescribes a statutory procedure which a landlord must follow in order to terminate the tenancy effectively. A long tenancy cannot be terminated unilaterally by the landlord prior to the end of the term, 'the term date': s.4 (1) Landlord and Tenant Act 1954. Accordingly, any 'termination date' proposed by the landlord must either be the term date or a later date.

In order to terminate a tenancy, a landlord must serve a notice of termination on the tenant at least six months before the termination date specified in the notice, but not more than twelve months from that date: s.4(2) Landlord and Tenant Act 1954. The 1954 Act draws a distinction between landlords who wish to resume possession at the end of the lease, and those who are willing to grant a statutory tenancy. In the former case, the live issue will be whether the landlord can make out one or more of the section 12 grounds for possession. In the latter case, the main issues will be the terms of the statutory tenancy.

The landlord's notice of termination must include the following matters or it will be invalid:

(a) specify the premises which the landlord believes to be or to be likely to be, the premises qualifying for protection; and
(b) either:
 (i) contain proposals for a statutory tenancy in which case the notice is known as a 'landlord's notice proposing a statutory tenancy', or
 (ii) contain notice of the fact that the landlord proposes to apply to the court for possession, stating the statutory grounds on which the landlord relies, if the tenant is not willing to give up possession at the date of termination: s.4(3) Landlord and Tenant Act 1954. In this case the notice is referred to as 'a landlord's notice to resume possession'.
(c) invite the tenant to notify the landlord in writing within two months of the giving of the landlord's notice whether he is willing to give up possession.

Landlord's notice proposing a statutory tenancy

A landlord has the option of setting out concrete proposals as to the terms of the statutory tenancy which he proposes to grant. A landlord's notice should contain the following details:

(a) the premises which will constitute the dwelling-house;
(b) the rent, intervals at which rent is payable, and whether the rent is to be payable in advance or in arrears;
(c) state whether any initial repairs are to be carried out on the dwelling-house, and if so, what. 'Initial repairs' are specified repairs: s.8 (1) Landlord and Tenant Act 1954;
(d) allocate responsibility for any initial repairs as between landlord and tenant. A landlord is entitled to the 'cost reasonably incurred' of any initial repairs which have to be carried out as a result of a tenant's failure to carry out his repairing obligations: s.8 (1) Landlord and Tenant Act 1954;
(e) and any other proposals as to the terms which the landlord may wish to include: ss.4(3)(a), 7(2)(3) Landlord and Tenant Act 1954.

Statutory tenancy's terms

By agreement: The terms of a statutory tenancy can be settled as between landlord and tenant without recourse to the courts: s.7(1) Landlord and Tenant Act 1954. But if the parties fail to reach agreement by a time which is two months prior to the date of termination specified in the landlord's notice proposing a statutory tenancy, the landlord's notice ceases to have effect unless an application has been made to have these matters determined by a court: s.7(2) Landlord and Tenant Act 1954. If a landlord's notice lapses in this way, a continuation tenancy will arise under the provisions of s.3.

The effect of this provision is that it establishes a time scale to which the parties can work, and helps to concentrate the parties' minds on achieving a settlement whilst avoiding the costs of going to court. The onus, in these circumstances, is placed by statute on the landlord to apply to have any disputed terms of the proposed statutory tenancy determined by a court: s.7(5) Landlord and Tenant Act 1954. A landlord must apply not later than two months before the termination date, otherwise his notice will lapse, and he will have to serve a fresh notice with a new date of termination, giving at least six months notice of termination: s.7(2) Landlord and Tenant Act 1954.

Determination by a court: If it falls on a court to determine the terms of the statutory tenancy, Part I of the 1954 Act sets out principles to follow in order, determining terms regarding repairs so as to strike a reasonable balance between landlord and tenant: s.9 Landlord and Tenant Act 1954. For example, if a court has to determine what initial repairs should be carried out by a landlord, if any, the court should not go further than the initial repairs which the landlord proposed carrying out in his notice proposing a statutory tenancy without the landlord's consent: s.9 (1) Landlord and Tenant Act 1954.

Landlord's notice to resume possession

Again, the tenant has two months in which to notify the landlord in writing as to whether he is willing to give up possession: s.4(4) Landlord and Tenant Act 1954. If he is, that will usually be the end of the matter unless he attempts to negotiate some financial settlement in return for giving up possession.

Grounds for possession

A landlord can only resume possession, where a tenant is unwilling to leave at the termination date specified in his notice, if he can establish one or more of the statutory grounds in s.12. These grounds incorporate the Rent Act's discretionary grounds for possession, namely Cases 1–9 in Schedule 15: see Chapter 27 for details. In addition, possession can be obtained where a landlord proposes to demolish or reconstruct the premises for redevelopment purposes: see the case-law in respect of s.30 (1)(f) at pp.246–8, regarding a similar provision in Part II of the 1954 Act, but noting the differences in criteria.

If a landlord is unsuccessful in establishing a statutory ground for possession, he has no alternative but to accept the fact that a statutory tenancy has been brought into existence, unless the tenant changes his mind and decides to give up possession, which is unlikely.

Termination by the tenant

Where a tenant wishes to terminate the long tenancy, he should give the 'immediate landlord' at least one month's written notice of his intention: s.5 (1) Landlord and Tenant Act 1954. Incidentally, a tenant can terminate a tenancy notwithstanding the fact that he initially responded to a landlord's notice to resume possession by electing to retain possession and later changed his mind: s.5(3) Landlord and Tenant Act 1954.

Statutory tenancy

Terms of

The court's duty in determining the terms of the statutory tenancy under the provisions of section 7 (1) is to act fairly between the parties, and one of the matters for consideration is the rights and obligations of the parties under the previous contractual term. But the Court of Appeal have held that it would not be fair to incorporate all the covenants from a previous fixed term lease into a statutory tenancy which might continue for an unlimited period given the right to succession: *Etablissement Kamira* v. *Schiazzano* (1984).

Mention has already been made of the statutory principles which a court should observe in determining the terms as to repairs. In the case of repairs, they should not exceed what is required to bring the dwelling-house into good repair, unless the landlord has specified repairs in a notice proposing a statutory tenancy (in which case, see above): s.9(1) Landlord and Tenant Act 1954. The standard of repair is borrowed from *Proudfoot* v. *Hart* (1890): s.9(2) Landlord and Tenant Act 1954, and see p.139.

A statutory tenancy takes effect as if it were a statutory tenancy under the Rent Acts: s.6 Landlord and Tenant Act 1954. This means that a tenant will have security of tenure, the right to register a fair rent, and the possibility of the tenancy being transferred to members of the tenant's family upon his death. A statutory tenancy gives a tenant a personal right to occupy the dwelling-houses as his residence indefinitely, but he cannot assign the tenancy to another person.

THE 1967 ACT

Objectives

The 1967 Act (as amended by the Housing Act 1974) was aimed at righting the injustice that Parliament felt was caused to tenants occupying premises on long leases. The legislation's aim was to enable tenants to secure rights to 'purchase' their homes despite the contractual arrangements subsisting between the parties. Many felt that long residential leaseholders had a 'moral entitlement' to the property. Accordingly, the right to buy the freehold or at least to extend the lease by fifty years compulsorily was created. The basis of valuation for the purchase of the freehold gives effect to the view taken by the Parliamentary majority that in equity the bricks and mortar belong to the qualifying leaseholder. It is fair to add that many landlords take the view that the 1967 Act does not strike the right balance between the interest of society and the landlord's property rights, and argue that landlords ought, at the very least, to be reimbursed at the property's full market value.

Meaning of long tenancy at a low rent

A long tenancy at a low rent is defined in similar terms in both the 1954 and 1967 Acts. Nonetheless there are significant differences, so that a long tenancy may fall within the scope of one Act but not the other.

Long tenancy

A long tenancy is defined as a tenancy which was granted for a term certain exceeding twenty-one years from the date of grant, regardless of whether the tenant can terminate the tenancy before the end of the term or not: s.3(1) Leasehold Reform Act 1967 and *Eton College* v. *Bard and Another* (1983).

Low rent

A tenancy is let at a low rent when rent is not payable at a yearly rate equal to or more than two-thirds of the rateable value on the appropriate day or, if later, the first day of the term: s.4 Leasehold Reform Act 1967.

In determining the amount payable by way of rent, payments for services, repairs, maintenance and insurance are all disregarded: s.4(1)(b) Leasehold Reform Act 1967.

The 1967 Act adds the proviso that a tenancy shall not be regarded as a tenancy at a low rent if at the commencement of the tenancy the rent payable exceeded two-thirds of the 'letting value' of the property. The House of Lords held in *Johnson* v. *Duke of Westminster and Others* (1986), that a property's letting value includes a premium paid by the tenant for the grant of the tenancy. Bringing the premiums paid into account brought the Westminster tenancies within the scope of the 1967 Act. Lord Griffiths explained the rationale in the following terms:

> 'A premium was manifestly part of the value that the landlord received for letting the premises unless it could be attributed to other benefits such as furniture and so forth and there was no reason why it should be excluded from the letting value of the premises'.

Rateable value on appropriate day

The original appropriate day for calculating the property's rateable value was 23 March 1965, the date taken by the 1954 Act and Rent Act 1977: s.4(1)(a) Leasehold Reform Act 1967. If the dwelling did not appear in the valuation list at that date, the first date on which it appeared. The maximum rateable value figures for the dwelling must not be more than a specified figure on an ascertainable date. The original limits were £400 in Greater London and £200 elsewhere: s.1(1)(a) Leasehold Reform Act 1967. But this has been modified as follows.

If the tenancy was created on or before 18 February 1966 and rated separately before 1 April 1973, the tenancy will be within the scope of the 1967 Act if the rateable value does not exceed £1500 in Greater London and £750 elsewhere: s.1(6) Leasehold Reform Act 1967. The question whether a retrospective reduction of rateable value can be taken into account in determining whether the rateable value exceeds the limit of £1,500 on 1 April 1973 was considered in *Marfarquahar* v. *Phillimore and Another* (1986). The Court of Appeal upheld the judge's decision in favour of the tenant, namely the retrospective reduction of the rateable value to below £1,500. A tenancy which is created after 18 February 1966 but rated after 1 April 1973 is subject to limits of £1000 in Greater London or £500 elsewhere: s.1(5)(b) Leasehold Reform Act 1967. Tenancies created on or before 18 February 1966 but not rated until on or after 1 April 1973 have rateable value limits of £1500 in Greater London and £750 elsewhere.

Finally, if the long lease was granted between the end of August 1939 and the beginning of April 1963, the tenancy is not to be regarded as a tenancy at a low rent if the rent payable under the long tenancy exceeded two-thirds of the letting value of the property at the time that the tenancy commenced: proviso to s.4(1) Leasehold Reform Act 1967.

Occupation

The 1967 Act only confers rights to enfranchise or extend on tenants who occupy the house as their 'residence': s.1(1) Leasehold Reform Act 1967 and *Duke of Westminster* v. *Oddy* (1984), and see Chapter 27 for the relevant case-law defining occupation as a residence.

Meaning of house

A 'house' is defined as including 'any building designed or adapted for living in and reasonably so called': s.2(1) Leasehold Reform Act 1967. But the 1967 Act does not include all premises which are occupied as a residence because this could result in complicated landholdings in cases where the premises are part only of a building. For example, if a tenant were able to enfranchise a bed-sitting room of part of a floor in a large tenanted property it would mean that the other tenants and their landlords could not enforce obligations normally entered into under a lease on a freeholder of a bed-sitting room, given that there is at present no developed system of law whereby positive obligations can be enforced against a freeholder. Accordingly, the 1967 Act draws physical distinctions between different premises, and defines 'houses' with particularity.

If an entire building is let to a tenant as a house, the tenant will be able to enfranchise. Buildings which are divided horizontally are differentiated from buildings which are divided vertically.

Horizontal divisions: If the building is divided horizontally into different units, the separate units cannot be enfranchised since they are excluded from the definition of a 'house': s.2(1)(a) Leasehold Reform Act 1967. For example, horizontal flats in a purpose-built block cannot be enfranchised. But if the entire building which is so sub-divided is leased to a single tenant, he is entitled to enfranchise the building as a whole. These two permutations can be illustrated in a diagrammatic house:

✓
Building as a whole may be a 'house'

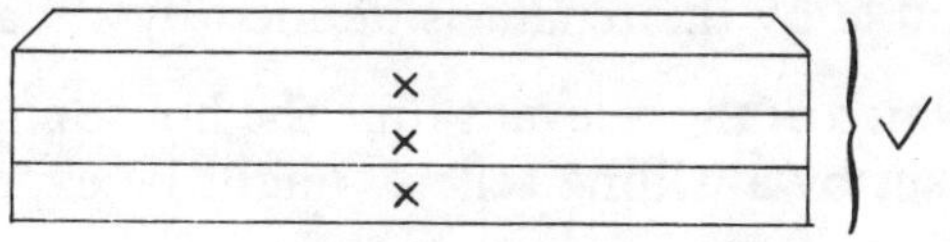

× Horizontal flats/units are not 'houses'

Vertical divisions: Where a building is divided vertically, the units into which it is divided may be a 'house': s.2(1)(b) Leasehold Reform Act

1967, but the building as a whole is not a 'house'. This is illustrated as follows:

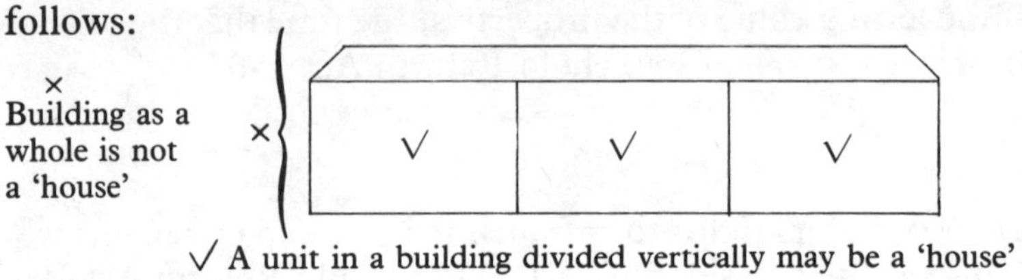

Enfranchisement or extension

General provisions

Where a tenant has a right to enfranchise or to an extended lease, he should give his landlord notice of his desire to exercise his statutory rights: s.5(1) Leasehold Reform Act 1967. If there has been an assignment, the assignee is entitled to exercise the statutory rights: s.5(2) Leasehold Reform Act 1967. Sub-tenants with sub-tenancies lawfully granted out of a long tenancy at a low rent also qualify: s.5(4) Leasehold Reform Act 1967. Finally, members of the tenant's family who are resident in the house can succeed to the tenant's rights when he dies: s.7 Leasehold Reform Act 1967.

Time limits

The normal time limit relating to claims to land of twelve years is applicable. Thus a tenant who made a claim for enfranchisement six years after his claim accrued was held to be entitled to enfranchise and could not be said to have abandoned his claim: *Collin* v. *Duke of Westminster and Others* (1985).

Enfranchisement

Where a tenant has notified a landlord in writing of his desire to enfranchise, and the tenancy falls within the scope of the 1967 Act, the landlord is bound to grant the tenant a fee simple estate: s.8 Leasehold Reform Act 1967.

Price

The price payable by the tenant is defined by s.9 as:

'the amount which at the relevant time the house and premises, if sold in the open market by a willing seller...might be expected to realise...'

The price is calculated after taking into account a number of statutory assumptions which vary according to the house's rateable value.
Rateable value below £1000 or £500: The following assumptions are made by s.9(1) if the house falls below the rateable value limits of £1000 and

£500 for Greater London and elsewhere respectively (see s.9(1A) Leasehold Reform Act 1967 added by the Housing Act 1974, s.118(4) and subsequently amended by s.23 Housing and Planning Act 1986):

(a) that the landlord is selling subject to the existing tenancy on the assumption that this Act conferred no right to acquire the freehold or an extended lease, and where the tenancy has been extended, that the tenancy will end on the original date;
(b) that it is being sold subject to any rent charges payable, but these are not to exceed the annual (low) rent payable under the tenancy at the relevant time;
(c) that it is sold subject to the same rights and burdens as in the sale to the tenant.

Thus the price is calculated on an open market valuation of the freehold on the assumption that there is a deemed extension of the lease for fifty years. The site will have to be valued and a theoretical 's.15' rent calculated. The figure for rent will combine the rent under the lease and the rent payable under a hypothetical fifty year lease, and will, therefore, depend on how long the existing lease has to run. The 'relevant time' is the date of the tenant's notice: s.37(1)(d) Leasehold Reform Act 1967.

Rateable value above £1000 or £500: A number of statutory assumptions are made where the rateable value exceeds £1000 in Greater London and £500 elsewhere by s.9(1A) Leasehold Reform Act 1967 added by the Housing Act 1974 s.118(4), for example:

(a) that there is a deemed continuation of the tenancy under the provisions of Part I of the 1954 Act, but that the tenant has no liabilities to repair, maintain or decorate;
(b) that a deduction is made for any increase in the value of the house resulting from improvements carried out by the tenant at his own expense, or by his predecessors.

Note that there is no assumption that the tenant has been granted a fifty year lease. But if the tenant enfranchises after a lease extension, the price will be valued 'subject to the tenancy': s.9(1A) Leasehold Reform Act 1967. The Court of Appeal considered the question of whether the price for the freehold was to be determined by taking into account the extended lease in three similar cases in *Mosley* v. *Hickman* (1986). The effect would be to reduce the purchase price by at least fifty per cent to take into account the fact that each of the three tenants had already obtained an extended lease. The Court of Appeal held that the words 'subject to the tenancy' in s.9(1A) meant subject to the existing extended tenancy so that the freehold valuation took into account the extended lease. This result means that it may well be in a tenant's interests to take an extended fifty year lease in order to obtain a substantially discounted price for the freehold later.

Other factors: The 1967 Act proceeds on the assumption that the tenant is paying for the site value and not for the bricks and mortar. In all cases the price will be calculated on the basis of a number of material factors. A valuer will take into account the value of the rent payable under the long tenancy; the level of site values; the length of the existing term; and the site's development potential.

Right to buy upheld

The trustees for the Duke of Westminster's estate challenged a tenant's right to buy the freehold under the provisions of the 1967 Act compulsorily without adequate compensation to the landlord. The matter went to the European Court of Human Rights in Strasbourg where the trustees tried to establish that the compulsory purchase of property for no reason other than to confer a private benefit was unreasonable and infringed Article 1 of the Convention on Human Rights. Briefly, Article 1 as paraphrased provides that a person should not be deprived of his ordinary contractual rights by legislation unless such deprivation could be shown to be in the public interest. The European Court rejected this claim, and held in its judgment that:

> '...the compulsory transfer of property from one individual to another might constitute a legitimate means for promoting the public interest. The enhancement of social justice within the community could properly be described as being in the public interest...'.

The court added that:

> 'In deciding whether the legislation complied with the public interest test, the margin of appreciation available to the legislature in implementing social and economic policies should be a wide one, and the legislature's judgment as to what serves the public has to be respected unless it is manifestly without reasonable foundation.

This decision resulted in the forced sale of eighty houses in a prime residential area in London at a loss of £2,529,903 to the trustees: *James* v. *United Kingdom* (1986).

Extension

Where a tenant has notified his landlord in writing of his desire for an extended lease, the landlord is obliged to accede to this: s.14 Leasehold Reform Act 1967. But the tenant will have to pay the reasonable costs incurred by the landlord in investigating his rights to an extended lease, valuing the house and premises, and executing the new lease: s 14(2) Leasehold Reform Act 1967. A tenant only has a right to one new lease of fifty years: s.16 Leasehold Reform Act 1967.

Terms

The new lease is granted on the same terms as the existing tenancy except where they need to be modified to take into account the fact that the rent payable shall be a ground rent for the site only: s.15 Leasehold Reform Act 1967.

Landlord's overriding rights

A landlord has an overriding right to obtain possession of the premises on the grounds that he proposes to reconstruct or demolish the premises for redevelopment purposes: s.17(1) Leasehold Reform Act 1967. The application cannot be made any earlier than twelve months prior to the end of the lease: Leasehold Reform Act 1967.

A tenant is entitled to compensation if the landlord is granted possession. The amount of compensation is calculated on the basis of his interest as a sitting tenant on the assumption that he had an extended lease for fifty years: s.17(2) and Schedule 2 para 5 Leasehold Reform Act 1967. But a dispossessed tenant is not compensated for the loss of the right to enfranchise.

Valuation disputes

A leasehold valuation tribunal (at The Lands Tribunal) has jurisdiction to deal with disputes if the parties cannot agree the price to be payable for enfranchising under s.9, the 's.15 rent' or the amount of compensation payable to a tenant: s.21(1) Leasehold Reform Act 1967.

Chapter 27

Rent Act Protected Tenancies

MEANING OF PROTECTED TENANCY

A protected tenancy is defined by s.1 of the Rent Act 1977 as a 'tenancy under which a dwelling-house (which may be a house or part of a house) is let as a separate dwelling'. Security of tenure is considered in Chapter 28. Rent limits and restrictions on premiums have already been considered separately in Chapters 10 and 11 respectively.

The case-law regarding the definition of a protected tenancy is highly developed, largely owing to litigation by landlords hoping to regain possession by showing that a tenancy is outside the scope of the Rent Act. These attempts on the part of landlords have met with a notable lack of success since the definition of a protected tenancy meets the Parliamentary objective of providing tenants of residential property with security of tenure. Even the recently exploited loop-hole of creating artificial licences has been closed so that very few agreements can constitute a licence nowadays: see Chapter 6. Each word of the definition of a protected tenancy in s.1 has been judicially considered and the following words merit attention:

Tenancy

The Rent Act includes all residential tenancies within certain rateable value limits within its scope. This means that a residential tenancy is prima facie Rent Act protected, unless it is specifically excluded by way of one of the statutory exemptions. Licences are excluded from full Rent Act protection.

Dwelling-house

The premises must be capable of being used as a 'dwelling house'. In other words, the premises must have a structural suitability. This is a question of fact: *Horford Investments* v. *Lambert* (1974). The correct approach is to ask whether the premises were the 'home' of anybody, per Lord Greene MR in *Curl* v. *Angelo* (1948). A caravan with raised wheels which was connected to permanent services has been held to be a dwelling house: *Makins* v. *Elson* (1977).

A dwelling house may be part of a house; that is a flat or one or more rooms in a house. Thus the Court of Appeal held that a three year letting of a hotel room qualified for Rent Act protection in *Luganda* v. *Service Hotels Ltd* (1969).

'As'

The courts take into consideration the purpose of the letting which may be ascertained from the lease, where appropriate, in the first instance. The circumstances surrounding the letting may also provide assistance. But if a blank is drawn then the actual use of the premises is decisive: *British Land Co. Ltd* v. *Herbert Silver (Menswear) Ltd* (1958).

'A separate'

The fact that s.1 is to be read in the singular was underlined in the decision of *Horford Investments Ltd* v. *Lambert* (1974). The facts concerned two adjoining nineteenth century dwelling houses let to the tenant on two 21 year leases. Both houses were divided up into rooms and flats. The Court of Appeal held that neither tenancy was Rent Act protected owing to the plurality of dwellings in each house. The words 'a separate dwelling' do not include several separate dwellings.

Accordingly, the dwelling referred to must be a separate entity which is used exclusively by the tenant. Logically, this would mean that the Rent Act would automatically be precluded where accommodation is shared. However, there are special provisions dealing with shared accommodation so that certain categories of tenants are brought within the full protection of the Rent Acts, notwithstanding the fact that they share accommodation with other tenants: see s.22 Rent Act 1977 at p.304. Tenants who share accommodation with their landlord have very limited protection under a restricted contract: see s.21 Rent Act 1977 at p.304.

'Dwelling'

'Dwelling' is not given a technical meaning. The courts simply consider whether the dwelling contains the essential living rooms. This has been defined in a homely way:

> 'a living room is a room where you cook, eat, sleep and put your feet on the fender'.
> (Per Lord Radcliffe in *Goodrich* v. *Paisner* (1956).)

STATUTORY EXCEPTIONS

Tenancies which meet the statutory definition of a protected tenancy are excluded from Rent Act protection if they fall within any one or more of the statutory exceptions set out in ss.4-16.

Rateable value too high

A tenancy is not a protected tenancy if the dwelling house's rateable value was too high on the 'appropriate day': s.4 Rent Act 1977. The 'appropriate day' is 23 March 1965 (in the case of properties for which a rateable value was shown in the valuation list then in force) or the date on which the dwelling house first appears in the valuation list: s.25(3) Rent Act 1977. This rateable value should be compared with the three classes which are lettered A–C by s.4: see Appendix 1. If the dwelling house falls within any one of the classes A–C, the tenancy is excluded from Rent Act protection. The following chart represents the various permutations:

Chart showing rateable value limits

Appropriate day	Rateable value (RV) limit for London	Rateable value (RV) limit elsewhere
CLASS A		
On or after 1 April 1973	Rent Act excluded if RV exceeds £1500 on appropriate day	Rent Act excluded if RV exceeds £750 on appropriate day
CLASS B		
On or after 22 March 1973	Rent Act excluded if RV exceeds £600 on appropriate day	Rent Act excluded if RV exceeds £300 on appropriate day
	and	*and*
but before 1 April 1973	on 1 April 1973 RV exceeded £1500	on 1 April 1973 RV exceeded £750
CLASS C		
Before 22 March 1973	Rent Act excluded if RV exceeds £400 on appropriate day	Rent Act excluded if RV exceeds £200 on appropriate day
	and	*and*
	on 22 March 1973 RV exceeded £600	on 22 March 1973 RV exceeded £300
	and	*and*
	on 1 April 1973 RV exceeded £1500	on 1 April 1973 RV exceeded £750

It may be necessary to apportion the rateable value where the dwelling -house forms part only of the property as valued. Similarly, where more than one property comprises the tenancy, the rateable values will have to be aggregated accordingly: see s.25(1) Rent Act 1977 at p.264.

Tenancies at a low rent

A tenancy is excluded from the scope of the Rent Act if the rent payable is less than two-thirds of the rateable value of the dwelling-house on the 'appropriate day': s.5 Rent Act 1977. To be excluded, the rent payable must be less than two-thirds of the rateable value on the appropriate day: see p.264.

Qualifying shared ownership leases

A shared ownership lease is a lease granted at a premium by a public body which gives the tenant a right to acquire the freehold, or a lease granted at a premium by a housing association for a term of 99 years or more. These leases are excluded from the Rent Act. This case was added by Schedule 4 para. 1 Housing and Planning Act 1986: see also p.318.

Dwelling-house let with other land

The provisions relating to dwelling-houses which are let with other land are complicated by the fact that they are regulated by two sections which at first reading may appear to be contradictory: ss.6, 26 Rent Act 1977, and *Pender* v. *Reid* (1948). The Rent Act does not exclude dwelling-houses let with land other than the site of the dwelling-house, but does exclude dwelling-houses which are let with agricultural land exceeding two acres in extent.

In order to determine whether a dwelling-house is outside the scope of the Rent Act by reason of the fact that it is let with land other than its site, one has first to ask whether the land is let as an adjunct to the dwelling-house or whether the dwelling-house is let together with some other land. The tenancy will fall within the scope of the Rent Act where the land let is simply an adjunct, e.g. three acres of open land (not agricultural land) situated behind the dwelling-house and let with it, secondly, whether the 'other land' is agricultural land. If it is not agricultural land, the dwelling-house and the other land are prima facie within the Rent Act's scope. But if the 'other land' is indeed agricultural land the Rent Act will only be excluded where the agricultural land exceeds two acres.

The question of whether the dwelling-house is let together with other land is a purely factual one. If the tenant has been granted other land, it need not have been let at the same time by the same lease: *Mann* v. *Merrill* (1945).

Payments for board or attendance

This exclusion is commonly relied upon by landlords who are in a position to provide board or attendance when the tenancy commences. It is important to separate out the provisions relating to board and attendance since valuation criteria apply in the case of attendance but not board.

General provisions

Payments for board or attendance must genuinely be provided for in good faith in order for the exclusion to operate: s.7(1) Rent Act 1977 and *Palser* v. *Grinling* (1948).

Meaning of board: The Rent Act does not define 'board' but its accepted definition is the provision of daily meals. Partial board is sufficient to bring the tenancy outside the scope of the Rent Act. But if the provision of food is minimal then it will not count for this purpose, owing to the operation of the '*de minimis* rule' in law which excludes items which are too insignificant to be taken into account when applying a rule of law. Megarry has suggested that the dividing line appears to fall between the early morning cup of tea which would be *de minimis* and breakfast which would constitute board: see Megarry on the Rent Acts. Pettit suggests that a continental breakfast would constitute board today: Pettit on *Private Sector Tenancies*, 2nd ed., 1981.

Meaning of attendance: 'Attendance' is likewise not defined but has been judicially construed to mean the provision of a personal service to the tenant which will be of benefit to him in his use or enjoyment of the premises: *Palser* v. *Grinling* (1948) per Viscount Simon. The emphasis here is on a personal service to the tenant, e.g. delivery of post and removal of refuse. Attendance does not include the provision of services by a landlord to a number of tenants living communally, e.g. cleaning of common parts.

Attendance must form a substantial part of rent: The amount of rent fairly attributable to attendance must form a substantial part of the whole rent in order for this exclusion to operate: s.7(2) Rent Act 1977. This provision does not apply to board, and poses the following questions: how should the attendance provided be valued, how substantial must the value of the attendance be to avoid the Rent Act, and when should the valuation be made?

The question of how to value the attendance is far from straightforward in the absence of any statutory guidelines. The cost to the landlord may well be less than the theoretical value to the tenant. This is especially true where the landlord provides attendance to a number of tenants in a block. The courts take account of both the cost to the landlord and the value to the tenant in order to arrive at an arithmetic figure, having regard to the entire arrangement before determining whether the attendance forms a substantial part of the whole rent or not. But arithmetic alone does not provide an answer: per Lord Justice Scarman in *Woodward* v. *Docherty* (1974).

The House of Lords case of *Palser* v. *Grinling* (1948) sets out the following valuation guidelines in the context of a block of flats. First, the total cost to the landlord of providing the attendance is ascertained. Second, the proportion of services which can properly be described as attendance is calculated. Third, consideration is given to how far the attendance is for the landlord's benefit and how far to the tenant's. Fourth, the proportion of annual cost attributable to attendance is calculated and apportioned between individual tenants according to the number of rooms in each flat excluding bathrooms. Finally, in special circumstances, a tenant will have a greater or smaller portion attributed to him.

Once the true value attributable to attendance is calculated it is compared with the rent paid in order to ascertain whether it forms a substantial part of the rent or not. At present a substantial part seems to be more than thirteen per cent: see *Williams* v. *Docherty* (slightly less than 14% is substantial) and *Bowness* v. *O'Dwyer* (12% is not substantial) (1948).

The material time for calculating attendance is at the tenancy's commencement: *Palser* v. *Grinling*. This can work to the landlord's detriment in cases where the cost of providing the services did not originally form a substantial part of the rent but has since risen to a substantial amount. On the other hand, if the character of the letting changes in a fundamental way so that it can be brought within s.7, the court may consider this factor: *Seabrook* v. *Mervyn* (1950).

Lettings to students

If an educational institution grants a tenancy to a student who is either pursuing or intends to pursue a course of study the tenancy will be excluded from Rent Act protection if the institution is a 'specified educational institution': s.8 Rent Act 1977. A specified educational institution includes universities, polytechnics and certain further educational establishments: The Protected Tenancies (Exceptions) Regulations 1974 (SI 1974 No. 1336) as amended by the Further Education Regulations 1975 (SI 1975 No. 1054); and the Protected Tenancies (Further Exemptions) Regulations 1976 (SI 1976 No. 905). Students renting accommodation from educational institutions will, at best, have a restricted contract.

Holiday lettings

The exclusion of holiday lettings from Rent Act protection was introduced in 1974 when Parliament extended Rent Act protection to furnished lettings: s.2(1)(b) Rent Act 1974. Prior to the Rent Act 1974, there was an important distinction between furnished and unfurnished accommodation since furnished accommodation could be excluded from the Rent Act then in force. The Rent Act 1974 abolished this distinction but introduced new exclusions of its own, namely holiday lettings and the resident landlord exclusion.

If the tenant is conferred with the right to occupy the dwelling for the purpose of a holiday, the tenancy is excluded from the Rent Act. The exploitation of this exclusion has led to a proliferation of 'holiday' lettings in unlikely locations, e.g. holiday lettings in 'sunny Kilburn'.

'Holiday' is not defined by the Rent Act, but has the dictionary meaning of a 'period of cessation of work or period of recreation': relied upon in *Buchman* v. *May* (1978). The tenancy's terms will be the starting point but the courts also take into account the factual circumstances of the letting to see if they are consonant with its terms. In this case, the onus is on the tenant to show that the purported holiday letting is a sham.

It is not sufficient for the tenancy agreement simply to specify that the purpose of the letting is a holiday in order for the exclusion to operate. There must also be a genuine holiday letting. *R* v. *Rent Officer for the London Borough of Camden ex parte Plant and Others* (1981) provides a warning to landlords. In that case the landlord permitted a holiday letting of a flat to be renewed at the end of the first six month term when he knew that none of the tenants was going to occupy the flat for the purposes of a holiday and that the tenants were in fact students studying to become nurses.

Out of season lettings

Since holiday lettings have a seasonal nature, the Rent Act incorporates special provisions for regaining possession of premises which are let out of season for terms of up to eight months: see Schedule 15, case 13. Rent Act 1977 at p.298. But out-of-season lettings of holiday accommodation do not fall within the exclusion unless of course they are let for out-of-season holidays.

Agricultural holdings

Agricultural holdings are excluded from the Rent Act 1977, but have their own regulatory legislation, namely the Agricultural Holdings Act 1986: s.10 Rent Act 1977.

Resident landlords

One of the most popular Rent Act exclusions for owner-occupiers is the resident landlord exception: s.12 Rent Act 1977. This is particularly true in urban areas where there is always a demand for rented accommodation owing to scarcity, and where owners supplement their income from letting out rooms in their own home. Owner–occupiers who have purchased their property with a mortgage should note that it is customary for bank and building society mortgage agreements to prohibit letting part or all of the premises.

The resident landlord exception was introduced in 1974 when the furnished lettings exception was abolished. It is thought that one reason why Parliament included the resident landlord exception was to avoid social embarrassment arising out of the close proximity of a landlord and tenant living in the same building: per Lord Justice Scarman in *Bardrick* v. *Vernon* (1976). Landlords could previously have asked tenants to leave furnished dwellings in the same building. The same result can be achieved under the resident landlord exception.

Section 12 of the Rent Act imposes three conditions which must be satisfied before the resident landlord exclusion operates:

Condition (a)

The dwelling-house must form part only of a building (which is not a purpose built block of flats). The landlord's dwelling-house must form part of the same building as the tenant's. A landlord who converted a building into flats and then moved into a two storey extension which was structurally tied to the original house was held not to be occupying the same building because there was no internal connecting door between the main house and his extension: *Bardrick* v. *Vernon* (1976).

Purpose-built blocks of flats are specifically excluded from the scope of the resident landlord exception by condition (a). Conversions may qualify as purpose-built blocks of flats according to the facts of a case. It has been suggested that the reason for the exclusion of purpose-built flats from the resident landlord exception is that they are places where people can lead separate lives without embarrassment: per Sir John Arnold in *Barnes* v. *Gorsuch & Another* (1981). For this purpose a 'purpose-built block of flats' is a building containing two or more flats, and a 'flat' is a dwelling-house which is separated horizontally from another: Schedule 2 para 4 Rent Act 1977.

Condition (b)

The landlord must have occupied another dwelling-house as his residence at the time the tenancy was granted. The criteria for the landlord's residence requirement are identical to the criteria which a tenant must satisfy in order to qualify as a statutory tenant: Schedule 2 para 5 Rent Act 1977: see s.2(1) at p.286.

Condition (c)

The landlord must have occupied another dwelling in part of the building or flat, as the case may be, at all times since the tenancy was granted. The Court of Appeal have held that residence by one of several joint landlords satisfies this condition: *Cooper and Others* v. *Tait and Another* (1984).

Periods of disregard

Two periods can be disregarded for the purpose of calculating whether the landlord has been in continuous occupation for the purpose of condition (c): Schedule 2 para 1 Rent Act 1977.

Twenty-eight day period: This period of disregard is designed to cover a sale of the property by a resident landlord to another resident landlord: Schedule 2 para 1(a) Rent Act 1977. Up to twenty-eight days of non-residence may be disregarded so that a prospective landlord need not go into possession immediately upon the old landlord leaving the premises. The prospective landlord can extend the twenty-eight day period to six months if the prospective landlord notifies the tenant in writing of his intention to take up occupation.

If a prospective landlord avails himself of the statutory period of disregard, no statutory tenancy can be created during the transitional period between sale and taking up possession.

Two year period: The two year period of disregard operates in two situations. Firstly, in cases where a resident landlord vests his interest in trustees: Schedule 2 para 1(c) Rent Act 1977. It can be relied upon by a landlord who goes out of residence for a period of up to two years and meanwhile vests his interest in trustees (to be held on trust for himself). It has been suggested that the effect of this provision is that landlords can take advantage of the s.12 exemption without taking up residence, namely by vesting their interest in different trustees every two years.

Secondly, the two year period of disregard applies to cases where a deceased landlord's interest vests in his personal representatives. The personal representatives may recover possession from a tenant during the transitional period between the resident landlord's death and sale. This enables them to sell with vacant possession: Sched 2 para 2A Rent Act 1977, added by s.65 Housing Act 1980 by way of a codification of the rule in *Landau* v. *Sloane* (1980) which applies to interests which vested in the personal representatives of a resident landlord who died before 28 November 1980 (Act's commencement date).

Exception to section 12: There is one situation where the requirements of s.12 are satisfied, but where a protected tenancy still arises: where the tenancy is granted to a protected or statutory tenant. This prevents landlords from using s.12 to deprive a tenant of his protection: s.12(2) Rent Act 1977.

Landlord's interest belongs to a local authority

Tenancies granted by housing co-operatives are also excluded from the scope of the Rent Act 1977: s.16 Rent Act 1977. The Housing Associations Act 1985 does not provide tenants with security of tenure.

A housing co-operative is a society, company or body of trustees with which a housing co-operative agreement was made: s.27B Housing Act 1985 added by Schedule 5 para. 15 Housing and Planning Act 1986.

Landlord's interest belongs to a housing association

Tenancies granted by housing associations are excluded from the scope of the Rent Act 1977: s.15 Rent Act 1977. The Housing Associations Act 1985 does not provide tenants with security of tenure.

Landlord's interest belongs to a housing co-operative

Tenancies granted by housing co-operatives are also excluded from the scope of the Rent Act 1977: s.16 Rent Act 1977. The Housing Associations Act does not provide tenants with security of tenure.

A housing co-operative is a society, company or body of trustees with which a housing co-operative agreement was made: s.27B Housing Act 1985 added by Schedule 5 para. 15 Housing and Planning Act 1986.

Assured tenancies

A new statutory exclusion was added when assured tenancies were introduced by ss.79-117 of the Housing Act 1980: s.16A Rent Act 1977. An assured tenancy is treated as though it is a business tenancy, and Part II of the Landlord and Tenant Act 1954 applies: see Chapters 22 to 25.

Business tenancies

The Rent Act 1977 and Part II of the Landlord and Tenant Act 1954 are mutually exclusive: s.24(3) Landlord and Tenant Act 1954, and see pp.237–8 for problems regarding mixed business and residential user.

Chapter 28

Security of Tenure for Rent Act Regulated Tenants

OVERVIEW OF SECURITY OF TENURE

The Rent Act 1977 provides security of tenure in two ways. First, by automatically continuing a protected tenancy on the termination of the contractual term by the creation of a statutory tenancy: s.2(1)(a) Rent Act 1977. Second, by restricting the grounds on which a landlord can regain possession: s.98 Rent Act 1977.

STATUTORY TENANCY

A statutory tenancy will only arise at the end of a protected tenant's contractual term if the following two conditions are fulfilled.

Prior protected tenancy

First, the contractual tenancy must be a protected tenancy which has been terminated: s.2(1)(a) Rent Act 1977. A statutory tenancy only arises at the end of the contractual term. This can occur in one of two ways. Either by the termination of the tenancy by one of the common law methods of termination, e.g. notice to quit, whereupon the tenant is referred to as a 'statutory tenant by virtue of his previous protected tenancy': s.2(4) Rent Act 1977. Alternatively, by succession upon the death of the tenant, whereupon the tenant is referred to as a 'statutory tenant by succession': s.2(5) Rent Act 1977. One of two joint tenants in occupation may claim a statutory tenancy: *Lloyd* v. *Sadler* (1978). Finally, the protected tenancy must vest in the tenant immediately before its termination. In *Smalley* v. *Quarrier* (1975) the tenant in possession under a protected tenancy was disqualified from becoming a statutory tenant because he had been adjudicated bankrupt. The tenant was held not to be a tenant immediately before the tenancy terminated because it had already tenancy vested in the trustee in bankruptcy.

Occupation as a residence

Second, the tenant must occupy the dwelling-house as his residence in order to qualify as a statutory tenant. This is a factual question. For example, in *Skinner* v. *Geary* (1931) the tenant lived in another house and the dweling-house was not occupied by the tenant for ten years. The Court of Appeal held that no protection existed where the tenant was not in actual occupation. There are a number of special cases as follows:

Companies

A company tenant cannot on the termination of its contractual tenancy acquire a statutory tenancy either for itself or for a resident occupier: see *Firstcross Ltd* v. *East West Ltd and Another* (1980) for a summary of the cases. A company cannot be said to 'reside' in premises, and cannot enjoy the rights of a statutory tenant which are purely personal: *Reidy* v. *Walker* (1933).

Sub-letting

If the entire premises have been sub-let the tenant is not in occupation, and, accordingly, does not qualify for a statutory tenancy. But if a tenant only sub-lets part of the premises he is entitled to a statutory tenancy of the entire premises: *Baker* v. *Turner* (1950).

Two cases which illustrate the difficulties in applying these principles are *Crowhurst* v. *Maidment* (1952) and *Berkeley* v. *Papadoyannis* (1954). The tenant in *Crowhurst* v. *Maidment* (1952) sub-let the first and second floors but remained in possession of the ground floor; an order for possession of the first and second floors was granted. The case was distinguished by the Court of Appeal in *Berkeley and Another* v. *Papadoyannis* (1954) on similar facts. The tenant had sub-let parts of the house but had from time to time occupied different rooms in the house, and it was held that he was entitled to protection of the entire house.

Matrimonial home

The court has wide powers to transfer a tenancy to a non-tenant spouse under the provisons of s.7 of the Matrimonial Homes Act 1967 as amended. Thus if a home is occupied by a non-tenant spouse, e.g. by the deserted wife of a tenant husband, the non-tenant's occupation is protected by a protected or statutory tenancy upon the termination of a marriage: see Chapter 26 on the 'Family Home' in *Housing Law* by Arden and Partington, Sweet & Maxwell, 1983.

Temporary absence

A temporary absence does not of itself deprive a tenant of Rent Act protection, e.g. a tenant sea captain who is away for months at a time but leaves his wife and children in occupation: often cited example given by Lord Justice Scrutton in *Skinner* v. *Geary* (1931).

Even a prolonged absence will not bring the tenancy outside the Rent Act's protection in an appropriate case. The Court of Appeal held that a tenant's absence of eighteen months was a temporary absence in circumstances where the tenant left the dwelling-house to nurse his parents up to the time of their death and then spent time working on their house which he inherited before putting it on the market: *Richards and Others* v. *Green* (1983). The same result was applied in *Tickner* v. *Hearn* (1961) where there was a lengthy absence through mental illness. But in *Brown* v. *Brash and Ambrose* (1948) protection was lost where imprisonment was the cause of absence. In *Tickner* v. *Hearn* the tenant's daughter remained in occupation whereas in *Brown* v. *Brash* there was no visible sign of an intention to return after the tenant's common law wife and children left the premises.

Non-occupying tenants will invariably lose their protection if they leave no visible evidence of their intention to return, since a non-occupying tenant prima facie forfeits his right to a statutory tenancy: per Lord Justice Asquith in *Brown* v. *Brash and Ambrose*. To retain protection, the non-occupying tenant must show both an intention to return (*animus possidendi*) and visible evidence of this intention (*corpus possessionis*):

Animus possidendi: A tenant must show his intention to return to the dwelling-house as his home. Thus in *Tickner* v. *Hearn* the tenant was held to have established an intention to return even though she had been in a mental hospital for six years and was unlikely to be fit enough to return. A vague wish or hope will not be sufficient evidence of intention to return: *Cove* v. *Flick* (1954).

Corpus possidendi: The courts place reliance on any visible evidence of an intention to return. This evidence may take the form of furniture and personal effects or the occupation of one or more members of the tenant's family. For example, in *Tickner* v. *Hearn*, reliance was placed on the continued occupation of the daughter maintaining the tenant's physical possession when taken with the tenant's furniture: per Lord Justice Willmer.

Two-homes man: There is no reason why a person should not have two dwelling-houses and occupy them both as his home. The question for consideration is whether he can have a statutory tenancy based on 'occupation as a residence' if he lets one of the homes. Although the two-homes cases all turn on their own precise facts, the House of Lords have extrapolated the following propositions in *Hampstead Way Investments Ltd* v. *Lewis-Weare and Another* (1985).

First, a person can have two homes so that if either of them was let to him his tenancy would be Rent Act protected: applying *Langford Property Co. Ltd* v. *Tureman* (1949). Second, where a person was a tenant of two different parts of the same house under separate lettings, and split his living activities between the two parts, neither tenancy would normally be protected; unless there was, in substance, a single letting: applying *Wimbush* v. *Cibulia* (1949). Third, where a person owned one dwelling-house which he occupied as his home for most of the time and was a tenant of another dwelling-house which he occupied rarely or for limited purposes, it was a question of fact and degree whether he occupied the latter dwelling-house as his second home: applying the *Langford* case (above).

In the *Hampstead Way Investments* case, the House of Lords held that a statutory tenant of a flat who moved with his family into a house nearby but who continued to sleep at the flat five nights a week after working in a night club, was not occupying the flat as his residence.

In *Kavanagh* v. *Lyroudias* (1985), a difficult border-line case, the tenant occupied two dwelling-houses using one for sleeping purposes and the adjoining house for normal living purposes and meals. The landlord was granted possession of the adjoining house. The Court of Appeal held that the test to be applied was whether the use of the premises concerned extended to all those activities which were essential to enable them to exhibit the characteristics of a complete home: considered by the House of Lords in the *Hampstead Way Investments* case but distinguished on its facts.

Terms and conditions

General position

A tenant is entitled to the benefit of all the terms and conditions of the original tenancy insofar as they are consistent with the provisions of the Rent Act: s.3(1) Rent Act 1977. It has been held that a landlord is entitled to an agreed sum for redecoration at the end of the tenancy: *Boyer* v. *Warbey* (1953). A statutory tenancy is not assignable and is merely a personal right of occupation.

Access

A statutory tenant is obliged to give the landlord access for the purpose of carrying out repairs: s.3(2) Rent Act 1977.

Assignment prohibited

A statutory tenancy is a personal privilege and cannot be assigned: *Keeves* v. *Dean* (1924). The special case of the transfer of a matrimonial home tenancy to a non-tenant spouse has been considered: see p.287.

Statutory tenancy by succession

A statutory tenancy can be transferred by succession upon the death of a tenant. This provision enables members of a deceased tenant's family to inherit the tenancy upon his death. For this purpose, the deceased tenant is referred to as 'the original tenant', and may have held either a protected or statutory tenancy. The transfer is referred to as a 'transmission'.

Transmission operates in favour of two classes, namely the surviving spouse and other members of the tenant's family.

Surviving spouse

The surviving spouse, if any, of the original tenant will succeed to the tenancy if that spouse resides in the dwelling-house immediately before the tenant's death 'if and so long as he or she occupies the dwelling-house as his or her residence': Schedule 1 para 2 Rent Act 1977 as amended by s.76 Housing Act 1980. Where the tenant died prior to 28 November 1980 only a widow but not a widower could succeed.

Family members

A member of the original tenant's family who resided with him at the time of and for a period of six months immediately before his death may succeed to the tenancy 'if and so long as he occupies the dwelling-house as his residence': Schedule 1 para 3 Rent Act 1977. This provision only applies in cases where there is no qualifying surviving spouse.

The word 'family' is not used in a technical sense. The courts apply the common-sense test of what the ordinary man would say if asked whether the individual was a member of the tenant's family or not, the 'family nexus test': *Brock* v. *Wollams* (1949). Adopted and illegitimate children, in-laws and grandparents all qualify as family. The line was drawn at platonic relationships between men and women in *Carega Properties SA* v. *Sharratt* (1979) where the House of Lords held that a platonic friend who had lived with the tenant (who was fifty years his senior) for eighteen years, was not a member of the tenant's family although he called the tenant 'Aunt Nora'.

Special principles apply to unmarried couples. If the relationship is permanent and results in children there is little doubt of the family nexus being established today: *Dyson Holdings Ltd* v. *Fox* (1975). But this was not always the case: *Gammins* v. *Ekins* (1950). Furthermore, if the relationship is short-lived or is complicated by the fact that one of the parties is lawfully married to another, the courts have shown a reluctance to uphold the family nexus: see *Watson* v. *Lucas* (1980) and *Helby* v. *Rafferty* (1979). This means that the court has to sift through evidence of the parties' personal circumstances to determine this issue in the case of unmarried couples which, in this author's view, is unedifying, particularly as the hearing will follow the death of a partner.

If there is more than one member of the family who can qualify as the tenant's successor, the courts will have to determine this issue if there is a dispute. In *Williams* v. *Williams* (1970) a father and son failed to agree to the statutory succession of the tenancy whereupon the Court of Appeal upheld a test based on relative merits including 'relative hardship'. The widower was granted the tenancy on grounds of age and income, even though there was evidence to suggest that he had treated the deceased badly and had lived a separate life whilst the son supported his mother and paid the bills: widowers now qualify to succession as of right: see p.290.

Residence requirement

Transmission of a statutory tenancy will only occur if and so long as the claimant occupies the dwelling-house as his residence: Schedule 1 paras 2 and 3 Rent Act 1977. Members of the tenant's family must reside with the tenant for at least six months prior to his death in order to qualify.

Residence has its ordinary meaning: per Evershed MR in *Edmunds* v. *Jones* (1975). The courts are sometimes prepared to extend the meaning of residence in cases where a member of the tenant's family could not, technically, be described as 'residing with' the tenant for six months where the tenant has spent the last months of his life in hospital: per Lord Justice Russell in *Foreman* v. *Beagley* (1969).

Two transmissions

Two transmissions of the statutory tenancy are possible provided that there is a qualifying claimant: Schedule 1 paras 5-7 Rent Act 1977. In the natural course of family life, Parliament envisaged a first transmission to the surviving spouse with a second transmission to a member of the tenant's family. No further transmissions are possible after the death of the second successor.

Termination of statutory tenancies

By landlords

A landlord can only recover possession either by consent or if one of the statutory grounds for possession can be enforced in cases where the tenant occupies the dwelling-house as his residence. However, circumstances may change with the passage of time so that it is conceivable that a tenancy can be brought out of the Rent Act's scope, e.g. the tenant may cease to occupy the dwelling as his residence: see pp. 99-102 *Private Sector Tenancies*, 2nd ed., by P.H. Pettit (1981, Butterworths), for an analysis of possible changes which may bring a statutory tenancy outside the scope of the Rent Act.

By tenants

The tenant must give the landlord notice of his intention to give up possession. This must be at least four weeks in duration: s.5 Protection from Eviction Act 1977. If there is no express contractual period of notice, the tenant must give at least three months' notice: s.3(3) Rent Act 1977. One consequence of these rules is that a landlord can claim at least four weeks rent after being told of the tenant's intention to leave.

OBTAINING POSSESSION

Overview

A landlord can only obtain possession of a dwelling-house which is let on a protected tenancy or subject to a statutory tenancy if the tenancy has been ended correctly at common law, and, one or more of the statutory grounds for possession apply, unless the landlord is willing to provide suitable alternative accommodation: s.98(1) Rent Act 1977.

The first point to check is whether the tenancy has been terminated correctly at common law, e.g. by service of a valid notice to quit. Next the particular circumstances of the case will have to be examined in order to ascertain whether one or more of the statutory grounds for possession apply. These grounds are divided into discretionary grounds where the court has a discretion as to whether or not to grant possession, and mandatory grounds where the court must order possession: Schedule 15 Rent Act 1977. These grounds are known as Cases 1 to 6 and 8 to 10 (discretionary) and Cases 11 to 20 (mandatory): Case 7 was repealed by s.152(3) Housing Act 1980. Obviously, a landlord who can make out a case for one of the mandatory cases is in a stronger position than a landlord who has to rely on the court's exercise of its discretion in respect of a discretionary case.

In any event, the landlord may be able to recover possession by offering alternative accommodation, say by granting a twenty year lease of suitable premises. This may be the only commercially viable alternative where the dwelling-house could fetch a large sum if refurbished and sold with vacant possession.

Finally, many landlords reach agreement for the surrender of the tenancy in return for a fixed sum. The fixed sum is commonly calculated as a multiplier of the dwelling-house's rateable value. This has advantages for both parties because the landlord then recovers vacant possession, and the tenant has funds which can be used as a deposit for his own house purchase if so desired.

Overriding discretion of reasonableness

If the landlord chooses to recover possession by one of the discretionary grounds or by offering suitable alternative accommodation the courts have an overriding discretion, and will only grant a possession order if it considers it reasonable to do so: s.98(1) Rent Act 1977. There is no overriding discretion in relation to the mandatory cases.

The court will consider all the relevant circumstances as at the date of the hearing when applying their overriding discretion: per Lord Greene MR in *Cumming* v. *Danson* (1942). Matters which have been taken into account include the following circumstances. The professional needs of the tenant: *MacDonnell* v. *Daly* (1969). Additional income obtained by a low income tenant who took in paying guests where alternative accommodation was offered: *Warren* v. *Austen* (1947). Environmental factors are important: *Redspring Ltd* v. *Francis* (1973). Any failure by the tenant to fulfil his obligations will be considered but may not be conclusive. The Court of Appeal have upheld a judge's refusal to grant possession against a tenant who was breaking a covenant by keeping a dog: *Bell London and Provincial Properties* v. *Reuben* (1946).

Discretionary grounds for possession: Schedule 15

Case 1

A landlord may recover possession if either any rent due has not been paid or where an obligation under the lease has been broken or not performed.

Non-payment of rent: A landlord should first send the tenant a 'letter before action' demanding payment with the threat of legal proceedings if the arrears are not paid by a certain date. But no possession proceedings can be commenced if the rent is then paid because the material date is the commencement of legal proceedings: *Bird* v. *Hildage* (1948). If proceedings are commenced the court will look at the entire history of rent payments when exercising its discretion.

Breach of tenant's other obligation: A landlord may bring possession proceedings in respect of any breach or non-performance of an obligation. The obligation may either be express or implied, but must be an obligation of the tenancy and not a collateral obligation. Restrictive covenants have been construed widely for this purpose. For example, the activities of a tenant who was the chairman of a Turkish Cypriot organisation in London were held to be in breach of a covenant prohibiting business use in *Florent* v. *Horez* (1983).

Case 2

Case 2 comprises two different but related grounds for possession.

Nuisance or annoyance: First, possession proceedings may be brought where the tenant or any person residing with him has been guilty of conduct which is a nuisance or annoyance to adjoining occupiers. For this purpose, 'nuisance' has been construed in its technical sense of committing a nuisance in tort. 'Annoyance', on the other hand, has been interpreted in a wider sense to include anything which disturbs neighbouring occupiers. For example, a tenant's undue familiarity with the landlord's sixteen year old daughter was held to constitute an annoyance to the landlord who lived in the flat above the tenant: *Whitbread* v. *Ward* (1952).

Conviction for using dwelling-house for immoral or illegal purposes: Second, possession may be obtained where the tenant has been convicted of using the dwelling-house for immoral or illegal purposes. In order for possession to be maintained on the grounds of a conviction, the landlord has to establish that the dwelling-house had some connection with the crime for which the tenant was convicted, e.g. it was used to store stolen property: *S. Schneider & Sons Ltd* v. *Abrahams* (1925). Minor isolated illegal acts may not be sufficient to bring the tenant within Case 2.

Case 3

The tenant's neglect of the premises may entitle the landlord to possession under Case 3 if the condition of the dwelling-house has deteriorated as a result. Case 3 also applies to neglect by sub-tenants and lodgers.

Case 4

Similarly, a deterioration in the condition of furniture provided for the tenant's use can be made the basis of possession proceedings. Case 4 applies to deterioration owing to ill-treatment by the tenant or a lodger or sub-tenant.

Case 5

If the tenant serves a notice to quit and then changes his mind and decides to remain in the dwelling-house, the landlord may be able to recover possession if he can show that he would be seriously prejudiced if he did not obtain possession because of a sale or letting which he has agreed. Case 5 is designed to protect landlords who might otherwise be liable to a third party for breach of a sale or letting contract.

Case 6

A landlord may be entitled to possession if a regulated tenant (protected or statutory) has sub-let his tenancy or a protected tenant has assigned his tenancy without the consent of his landlord; a statutory tenant cannot assign his personal right to a tenancy. A landlord's consent should always be procured to an assignment regardless of the terms of the lease: see *Pazgate Ltd* v. *McGrath and Others* (1984).

Case 8

Case 8 is relied upon by landlords who can satisfy a court that possession of the dwelling-house is reasonably required from a tenant employee for another employee for occupation as a residence. Two conditions have to be satisfied with regard to the existing tenant employee and prospective tenant employee respectively.

First, the landlord will have to prove that the employee (the prospective tenant), is engaged in full-time employment by himself or by one of his tenants, and that the contract of employment was made conditional on the provision of housing.

Second, the landlord will have to show that the present tenant was employed by himself or by a former landlord, that the dwelling-house was let to him in consequence of that employment, and that he has ceased to be in that employment.

Case 9

A landlord may recover possession where the dwelling-house is reasonably required for occupation as a residence by himself, or by one of his children who is over eighteen, a parent or a parent-in-law. Each element of Case 9 must be satisfied.

If the landlord requires it for himself this has a wide meaning and covers his household, e.g. his wife and any children who are minors; the other categories of relatives are construed literally. In the case of joint landlords, the dwelling-house must be required for occupation by both or all the landlords: *McIntyre* v. *Hardcastle* (1948). A landlord will not succeed under Case 9 if he simply requires vacant possession for resale rather than for the purpose of occupation as a residence.

The landlord will have to show that one of the specified categories of relative has a genuine need for the dwelling-house in order to satisfy a court that it is 'reasonably required' for their occupation: *Kennealy* v. *Dunne* (1977). A landlord's present housing needs are only one factor, and the courts have demonstrated their willingness to take into account a probable future change of circumstances. A possession order was suspended for a maximum period of twelve months from the date of the hearing and was to be issued on the death of the landlord's mother in *Kidder* v. *Birch and Another* (1983) so that the landlord could remain with her elderly mother until she died but plan for her future accommodation at the same time.

The court will consider whether the tenant or claimant tenant will suffer the greater hardship in the circumstances when deciding whether to grant a possession order on the general issue of reasonableness. A possession order on Case 9 was refused in *Fernandes* v. *Parvardin and Another* (1982) where the judge had held that greater hardship would be caused by granting it than by refusing it since no suitable alternative accommodation was available to the tenants: possession was recovered under Case 11.

Possession will not be ordered in a case where the landlord became the landlord by purchase. This provision is designed to prevent landlords selling on their interest to another landlord who can make out a Case 9 ground for possession.

Case 10

Landlords may recover possession under Case 10 if a regulated tenant has sub-let the premises for more than the amount of rent which is recoverable for the part sub-let. Case 10 also has a similar application to restricted contracts.

Mandatory grounds for possession: Schedule 15

Notices

A landlord should provide a tenant with written notice of the fact that possession may be recovered under a specified mandatory case for possession when the tenancy is granted, although the courts do have a discretion to dispense with this requirement if it is just and equitable to make a possession order.

Case 11

Owner-occupiers who let their property, e.g. while they are abroad, can rely on Case 11, as amended by the Rent (Amendment) Act 1985, in order to regain possession. A number of conditions have to be satisfied. First, the owner-occupier must have occupied the dwelling-house as his residence before the tenancy was granted. Temporary occupation will suffice: *Naish* v. *Curzon and Another* (1984). Second, the tenant should be given written notice of the fact that possession might be recovered under Case 11 (a Case 11 notice) before the tenancy commences, although this provision can be dispensed with by the courts. But the requirement of a Case 11 notice will not be dispensed with where the tenant has been given the misleading impression that he was being granted an ordinary tenancy: *Bradshaw and Another* v. *Baldwin-Wiseman* (1985). Third, to recover possession the owner-occupier has to satisfy one of conditions (a) and (c) to (f) in Part V of Schedule 15 of the Rent Act 1977, namely:

(a) that the dwelling-house is required as a residence for the owner or any member of his family who resided with him when he last occupied the dwelling-house;
(c) in cases where the owner has died, that a member of his family residing with him at his death requires the dwelling-house as a residence;
(d) in cases where the owner has died, that the dwelling-house is required by a successor in title as his residence;
(e) in cases where the dwelling-house was mortgaged before the tenancy was granted, that the mortgagee requires vacant possession for the purposes of a forced sale in circumstances where the owner has defaulted in his mortgage repayments;
(f) that the dwelling-house is no longer suitable to the owner's needs having regard to his place of work.

The 1985 amendment was introduced to deal with the situation of an occupier who had renewed a tenancy of a dwelling-house without first returning into occupation before the further letting. Previously, the law had required the tenant to return into occupation between lettings, and this had proved impracticable for occupiers who had been posted abroad and did not or could not return into occupation before granting a further letting. The amendment has been held to have retrospective effect: *Hewitt* v. *Lewis* (1985).

Case 12

A landlord who plans to retire to the dwelling-house can recover possession from a tenant under Case 12 when he retires from regular employment. The owner should have given the tenant written notice of this intention when the tenancy was granted, although this provision can be dispensed with by the courts. Thus a second retirement home can be purchased and let out prior to retirement without the normal risks attendant to creating a regulated tenancy. But in order to recover possession the court must be satisfied that one of the conditions (b) to (e) in Part V of the Rent Act 1977 is satisfied. Conditions (c) to (e) have already been considered in the context of Case 11. Condition (b) is most commonly relied upon, and simply states that the owner has retired from regular employment and requires the dwelling-house as his residence.

Case 13

If a landlord grants out-of-season lettings of holiday accommodation, he can recover possession provided that the letting is for a term certain not exceeding eight months, and, the landlord gave the tenant written notice of his intention to recover possession under Case 13 when the tenancy was granted.

Case 14

Specified educational institutions who grant tenancies to students can recover possession under Case 14. The tenancy must be for a term certain not exceeding twelve months, and the landlord must have given the student a written 'Case 14 notice' informing him that possession might be recovered under this case.

Case 15

Possession can be recovered under Case 15 of dwelling-houses let to ministers of religion provided that the tenant was given a 'Case 15 notice' in writing informing him of this fact when the tenancy was granted.

Case 16

Possession can be recovered from agricultural workers under Case 16.

Case 17

Case 17 is a narrowly defined case which only applies to dwelling-houses which the landlord requires for the occupation of a person which he employs in agriculture in the course of an amalgamation.

Case 18

Case 18 applies to agricultural tenants.

Case 19

Landlords who grant protected shortholds can recover possession under Case 19 at the end of the term: introduced by s.55 Housing Act 1980, see Chapter 30.

Case 20

Service-men who let out their dwelling-house may recover possession under Case 20: introduced by s.67 Housing Act 1980.

Suitable alternative accommodation

If the landlord wishes to recover possession of the dwelling-house by granting the tenant alternative accommodation, that accommodation must be both available to the tenant, and suitable within the meaning of Part IV of Schedule 15 to the Rent Act 1977. The accommodation must either be available at the date of the hearing for possession or, at the latest, the date on which the possession order is to take effect: *Topping* v. *Hughes* (1925).

Availability

The burden is on the landlord to show that suitable alternative accommodation is available. He can do this by producing a Housing Authority certificate which certifies that the local authority will provide suitable alternative accommodation for the tenant by a date specified in the certificate. These are rare, but when granted constitute conclusive evidence that suitable accommodation will be available for the tenant so that there is no further issue as to suitability.

The second, and most common way in which a landlord can establish that alternative accommodation is available, is to prove that he can personally provide the tenant with alternative accommodation which is suitable.

Suitability

Where the landlord has personally made arrangements for the provision of alternative accommodation, he must satisfy the court that the accommodation will provide the tenant with security of tenure, and meet certain statutory requirements as to suitability.

Security of tenure

A court can only deem accommodation to be suitable if it confers security of tenure. A landlord will have to satisfy a court that the premises will either be let on a Rent Act protected tenancy or give the tenant security of tenure which is reasonably equivalent to that enjoyed by a protected tenant.

Tenant's needs

A landlord will have to satisfy a court that the accommodation is reasonably suitable to the needs of the tenant and his family in that it meets the two following 'relevant conditions':

(a) proximity to place of work
This is always a question of fact and degree. In *Yewbright Properties Ltd* v. *Stone* (1980) the Court of Appeal upheld the judge's finding that a flat in East Dulwich was not proximate to the tenant's place of work in and around the SW6 area.

(b) and is either:
(i) comparable to local authority accommodation provided to a similar tenant with regard to its rental and extent of accommodation; *or*
(ii) is reasonably suitable to the means of the tenant, and to the needs of the tenant and his family as regards extent and character.

The Court of Appeal held in *Hill and Others* v. *Rochard and Another* (1983) that in determining whether the alternative accommodation offered is suitable to the tenant's needs as regards extent and character, a court can only take into account the tenant's housing needs. This was an unusual case: see 'Suitable alternative accommodation and the environment' an article by H. Wilkinson in 266 EG 1166 for a commentary.

The tenants in *Hill* v. *Rochard* (1983) had refused the offer of a modern detached four bedroomed house situated on a pleasant estate on the outskirts of a country village. They considered that this house would not match their life-style since they had been leasing a large country house with an adjoining field for which they paid £2,100 per annum. Lord Justice Dunn, in an unusual policy statement said in *Hill* v. *Rochard* (1983) that:

> 'Even on a liberal construction of the statutory provisions I do not think that the Rent Acts were intended to protect incidental advantages of that kind. The Rent Acts are concerned with the provision of housing and accommodation'.

A landlord may fail to obtain possession in a case where the extent of accommodation is comparable or better on the grounds that its character is unsuitable. When determining this matter, the courts take into consideration the needs of an individual tenant. Environmental matters may be taken into account. In *Redspring* v. *Francis* (1973) the court held that a flat which was situated in a busy road, next to a fried fish shop, close to a public house, and with no access to a garden was not reasonably suitable to the tenant's needs in view of the fact that her flat was in a quiet residential road and that she had the use of a back garden even though the alternative flat was larger.

But a line is drawn somewhere. In *Siddiqui* v. *Rashid* (1980) the Court of Appeal held that the word 'character' does not include such matters as proximity to the tenant's friends and leisure activities. In this case the tenant occupied a room in London and attended a London mosque although his work was in Luton. The landlords offered the tenant alternative accommodation which had proximity to his work in Luton. But the tenant refused the offer on the grounds that a move would take him away from his friends in London. The Court of Appeal held that 'character' only related to the property itself and not to peripheral matters such as proximity to a mosque and cultural centre.

Finally, if furniture was provided for the tenant's use under his tenancy, the landlord will have to satisfy a court that either similar furniture will be provided or furniture which is reasonably suitable to his needs.

FURTHER READING

Rent Acts (Amended and Annotated), 2nd ed, Sweet & Maxwell, 1981.
Rent Acts–Selected Case Law Guide, loose-leaf publication up-dated with Supplements by the Institute of Rent Officers Educational Trust.
The Rent Acts: Volumes 1–3 by R. Megarry, Sweet & Maxwell (in preparation).

Chapter 29

Lessees Under Restricted Contracts

MEANING

Certain lessees who are excluded from full Rent Act protection have a very limited degree of security of tenure under a restricted contract together with a right to register a reasonable rent: see p.99 in Chapter 10. A restricted contract arises in the three following situations:

Where rent includes payment for furniture or services

If a contract for the occupation of a dwelling-house includes payment for the use of furniture or services it will amount to a restricted contract provided that it falls within certain rateable value limits: s.19 Rent Act 1977. The contract may be either a licence or a tenancy: *R* v. *Battersea, Wandsworth, Mitcham and Wimbledon Rent Tribunal, ex parte Parikh* (1975). But the occupier must have exclusive occupation of the part which he is entitled to use: see p.63 for the distinction between exclusive possession and exclusive occupation.

Rateable value limits

The dwelling must not have a rateable value of more than £1,500 in London or £750 elsewhere if the appropriate day is on or after 1 April 1973: see p.278 for the meaning of 'appropriate day'. If the appropriate day is before 1 April 1973, the rateable value should not exceed £400 in London and £200 elsewhere on that date, and, should not exceed the aforementioned limits of £1,500 and £750 on 1 April 1973: s.19(3),(4) Rent Act 1977.

Occupation as a residence

The dwelling must be occupied as a residence. This is a question of fact. Generally speaking, occupation of a hotel room will not amount to occupation as a residence unless the reality is that the purported hotel provides the occupiers with a residence, e.g. bed-sitting accommodation: see *Luganda* v. *Service Hotels Ltd* (1969). Company lettings cannot be restricted contracts because a company cannot occupy a dwelling as a residence.

Payment for use of furniture or services

The amount of payment for the use of furniture or services need not be high in relation to the total rent: compare the test in s.7(2) Rent Act 1977 at p.280. But the amount of payment which reflects this use may be so small that it is left out of account by the application of the '*de minimis* rule': see p.280.

Furniture

Whether an item is to be regarded as 'furniture' is a question of fact applying current standards of what is considered to be furniture: *Gray* v. *Fidler* (1943). Furniture includes gas and electrical fires and appliances in addition to tables, beds and chairs. Fixtures cannot be regarded as furniture as they are part of the fabric of the dwelling.

Services

Services are statutorily defined to include attendance, the provision of heating or lighting, the supply of hot water, and any other facility: s.19(8) Rent Act 1977. Contracts which include payments for board, however, cannot be a restricted contract if the value of the board to the tenant forms a substantial part of the whole rent: s.19(5)(c) Rent Act 1977 and compare s.7(1) Rent Act 1977 at p.280.

Exceptions

There are a number of contracts which are specifically excluded from becoming restricted contracts. These include contracts which create regulated tenancies, contracts granted by local authority and Crown landlords, holiday lettings, rent free contracts, and protected occupancies within the meaning of the Rent (Agriculture) Act 1976: s.19(5) Rent Act 1977.

Resident landlord

The second situation in which a restricted contract arises is in the case of a tenancy which would have been Rent Act protected but for the fact that there is a resident landlord, even though the rent may not include payments for the use of furniture or services: s.20 Rent Act 1977, and see pp. 282–4 on resident landlord exception.

Sharing with landlord

The third situation in which a restricted contract arises is in the case of a tenant who shares some accommodation with his landlord. If a tenant has exclusive occupation of some accommodation ('the separate accommodation') and shares some other accommodation with the landlord ('the shared accommodation'), the letting will be a restricted contract and cannot amount to a Rent Act protected tenancy: s.21 Rent Act 1977. For example, where the tenant shares bathroom and kitchen facilities with the landlord but has his own bedroom. This is really another way of saying that the tenant has a resident landlord, save that it applies to licences too: s.21(1a) Rent Act 1977.

Compare sharing with others

By contrast if a tenant has exclusive occupation of some accommodation ('the separate accommodation') and shares some other accommodation ('the shared accommodation') with persons other than the landlord, the letting may amount to a protected tenancy if it falls within the Rent Act definition of a protected tenancy: s.22 Rent Act 1977. For example, if a number of persons occupy a house and enjoy common bathroom and kitchen facilities. In this situation the occupier may be entitled to a protected tenancy of his own separate accommodation, provided that he has 'a separate dwelling' within the definition of a protected tenancy: see s.1 Rent Act 1977 at pp.276–7. In other words, his separate accommodation must contain the essential living rooms.

REASONABLE RENT

A person with a restricted contract is entitled to apply to the rent tribunal in order to register a reasonable rent: s.77 Rent Act 1977. This has little practical value to most tenants who are in a vulnerable category owing to their limited security of tenure.

SECURITY OF TENURE

Persons occupying a dwelling under a restricted contract have limited security of tenure. They can apply for the postponement of an order for possession for a maximum period of up to three months if the contract was made after 28 November 1980: s.102A Rent Act 1977 added by s.69(3) Housing Act 1980. The maximum period for the suspension of a possession order is six months (renewable) for contracts made before this date: s.103(1) Rent Act 1977.

FURTHER READING

Private Sector Tenancies by P.H. Pettit, chapters 5,8, and 11, 2nd ed., Butterworths, 1981.

Chapter 30

Protected Shorthold and Assured Tenancies

INTRODUCTORY

The Housing Act 1980 introduced shorthold protected tenancies and assured tenancies with the aim of encouraging more people to rent out residential property privately.

PROTECTED SHORTHOLD TENANCIES

Definition

A protected shorthold tenancy is defined by s.52(1) Housing Act 1980 as 'a protected tenancy' which is 'granted for a term certain of not less than one year nor more than five years' and meets the statutory conditions.

Protected tenancy

'Protected' is not defined by the Housing Act 1980. Presumably it imports into the meaning the fact that a shorthold tenant originally had protection so far as rent was concerned: see p.307 below. Licences do not qualify as protected shortholds; there must be a tenancy.

Fixed term

The tenancy must be for a fixed term of between one and five years in duration. A periodic tenancy cannot be a protected shorthold.

Conditions

All tenancies must satisfy the two following conditions:

condition (a)
The landlord must not be able to terminate the tenancy prematurely before the end of the term, except in pursuance of a right to forfeit for non-payment of rent or breach of any other covenant: s.52(1)(a) Landlord and Tenant Act 1954.

condition (b)
Before the tenancy is granted, the landlord must give the tenant a valid notice (complying with regulations made by the Secretary of State) stating that the tenancy is to be a protected shorthold tenancy: s.52(1)(b) Landlord and Tenant Act 1954. The Protected Shorthold Tenancies (Notice To Tenant) Regulations 1981 (SI 1981 No. 1579) set out the statutory form of notice.

At the time of writing tenancies in London must satisfy condition (c). But the Draft Protected Shorthold Tenancies (Rent Registration) Order 1987, when implemented, will revoke conditions for all registration areas.

condition (c)
There must either be:
(i) a registered rent for the dwelling-house at the time the tenancy is granted;
(ii) or a rent which does not exceed the amount specified in a certificate of fair rent, and, an application for the registration of a rent must be made not later than twenty-eight days after the beginning of the term.

This condition originally applied to all protected shortholds throughout the country: s.52(1)(c) Landlord and Tenant Act 1954 and see also p.99 in Chapter 10. But it was soon recognised that the protected shorthold would be a flop unless landlords were given some further inducement to grant them. Accordingly, landlords outside London were given the opportunity to grant protected shortholds at a market rent, and condition (c) was retained in London only: Protected Shorthold Tenancies (Rent Registration) Order 1981 (SI 1981 No. 1578). One consequence of this is that protected shortholds outside London are not really protected in any real sense. The tenancy is simply a contractual arrangement for a fixed term at a market rent. The only unusual features are that there is an absolute prohibition upon assignment, and that the tenant has an option to terminate the tenancy upon short notice: see below.

In London, protected shorthold tenancies can only be granted if the tenancy is let at a registered fair rent. For this purpose the Rent Act procedure for registering rents applies: see pp.96–9 in Chapter 10. A landlord is only given one month to register a fair rent after the tenancy's commencement, if no rent has been registered, and then only in cases where he has obtained a certificate of rent from the rent officer.

If there is no existing registered rent a landlord may apply to the rent officer for a certificate of fair rent under the provisions of s.69 of the Rent Act 1977. The certificate will stipulate the amount which, in the rent officer's opinion, is a fair rent. This is the maximum amount which can be charged until a fair rent is subsequently registered. The fair rent will not necessarily be the same as the amount stated in the certificate.

Subletting or assignment

Subletting: A tenant is not prohibited from sub-letting. But if a tenant sub-lets the whole or part of the dwelling-house for a 'continuous period' from the grant of the protected shorthold, a landlord may be able to recover possession from a sub-tenant in the event of the tenancy being forfeited against the tenant: see the rather complicated provisions of s.54(1)(3) Housing Act 1980.

Assignment: A tenant is prohibited from assigning his protected shorthold: s.54(2) Housing Act 1980. This prohibition also applies to sub-lettings during the 'continuous period'. The court, however, is empowered to effect an assignment from a tenant spouse to a non-tenant spouse in the event of a divorce or judicial separation under the provisions of s.24 of the Matrimionial Causes Act 1973.

Termination

By landlords: A landlord cannot terminate a protected shorthold before the term expires except in reliance on a forfeiture clause for breach of covenant: see condition (a) above.

By tenants: A tenant, on the other hand, may terminate the tenancy prematurely by giving notice in writing: s.53 Housing Act 1980. The minimum period of notice must be one month in cases where the term is two years or less, and three months in all other cases: s.53(2) Housing Act 1980. This limits the length of time for which a landlord can claim rent after being notified of termination to either one month or three months.

ASSURED TENANCIES

An assured tenancy is a tenancy granted by a landlord who is an approved body and either constructs the dwelling-house or has carried out work on a dwelling-house involving expenditure of a prescribed amount: see page 48 for the figures. Part II of the Landlord and Tenant Act 1954 will apply, and not the Rent Act 1977.

Definition

Tenancy

There must be a 'tenancy under which a dwelling-house is let as a separate dwelling', which would, when created, have been a Rent Act protected tenancy or a housing association tenancy but for the fact that it satisfies the conditions of an assured tenancy: s.56(1) Housing Act 1980 as amended by s.12 Housing and Planning Act 1986. The definition of an assured tenancy borrows the terminology of the statutory definition of a Rent Act protected tenancy, e.g. licences are excluded: see p.276. In other words, the tenancy must satisfy the requirements of a Rent Act protected tenancy or a housing association tenancy: see p.49 on housing association tenancies. There are no statutory rent limits: see pp.99–100 in Chapter 10. Neither is there any security of tenure, simply a procedure for renewal which restricts a landlord's right to possession.

Conditions

The tenancy must comply with the following conditions:

Landlord condition: The landlord must be a body approved by the Secretary of State: s.56(1),(3),(4) Housing Act 1980. The number of bodies who have applied to become 'approved bodies' is very small indeed.

If there is a variation in the approved bodies by the Secretary of State, and the approval of a landlord is removed, it will not have effect on current tenancies and the renewal of tenancies granted before approval was removed: s.57(1). However, the landlord will no longer satisfy the 'landlord condition' with regard to future lettings.

If the landlord ceases to be an approved body (for reasons other than a variation in the bodies approved by the Secretary of State), a period of three months is disregarded if the tenancy would otherwise become either a Rent Act protected tenancy or a housing association tenancy: s.57(2) Housing Act 1980. In effect, this gives a landlord who loses approval (because he fails to meet the statutory conditions), three months in which to assign his interest to an approved body, or he otherwise runs the risk of the tenancy becoming Rent Act protected.

Conditions for newly erected buildings: Two conditions must be satisfied:

(a) the dwelling-house must be or form part of a building which was erected on land on which construction work first began on or after 8th August: s.56(1) Housing Act 1980 as amended by s.12 Housing and Planning Act 1986; and
(b) the premises must not previously have been occupied by any person

as his residence except as an assured tenancy: s.56 Housing Act 1980, as amended by s.12 Housing and Planning Act 1986.

Conditions for buildings to which work has been carried out: Three conditions must be satisfied:

(a) the qualifying works have been carried out within the period of two years before the grant; and
(b) the dwelling-house is fit for human habitation at the date of grant; and
(c) since the qualifying works were carried out no part of the dwelling-house has been occupied by any person as his residence except under an assured tenancy.

Application of Part II of the Landlord and Tenant Act 1954

Part II applies subject to modifications so that assured tenants can apply for renewal of their tenancies at the end of their term as if they were business tenants: s.58 Housing Act 1980; see Chapters 22 to 25 on business tenancies.

CONCLUDING REMARKS

There can be little doubt that a greater diversification of residential tenancies is desirable to meet demand for accommodation. There is some evidence to suggest that landlords have now taken advantage of the new protected shorthold tenancy but not of assured tenancies. Undoubtedly, one of the reasons why the construction industry has not favoured assured tenancies is because of the fear that a Labour government might take the tenancies out of the scope of the Landlord and Tenant Act 1954 and into Rent Act protection. The extension of the scope of assured tenancies to include existing buildings will ensure a greater number of such tenancies.

The protected shorthold is gradually becoming accepted at the bottom end of the residential market. It is not yet known whether the protected shortholds which are being granted really represent new property being made available for residential occupation. It seems that some landlords have persuaded occupiers to take up protected shortholds who formally had been granted contracts designed to avoid the Rent Acts, e.g. sham licence agreements, now outlawed by the House of Lords decision in *Street* v. *Mountford* (1985), and purported holiday lettings. There is also evidence that some occupiers who in reality had a Rent Act protected tenancy unbeknown to themselves have agreed to accept a protected shorthold. In some cases tenants have been beguiled by the word 'protected' and preferred a written protected tenancy agreement to an informal oral tenancy.

Chapter 31

Secure Tenancies

INTRODUCTORY

Secure tenancies were first introduced by the Housing Act 1980 in order to provide council tenants with security of tenure comparable to that enjoyed by Rent Act tenants. These provisions were drawn largely on the Rent Act 1977. They were subsequently consolidated into Part IV of the Housing Act 1985 and further amended by the Housing and Planning Act 1986.

DEFINITION

Tenancy

A secure tenancy is defined as a 'tenancy under which a dwelling-house is let as a separate dwelling' using the well known words of the definition of a Rent Act protected tenancy: s.79 Housing Act 1985. But there are a number of material differences between the definition of a secure tenancy and the definition of a Rent Act protected tenancy. First, secure tenancies specifically include licences: s.79(3) Housing Act 1985. Secondly, there is a 'landlord condition' and a 'tenant condition'.

Landlord and tenant conditions

The landlord must be a local housing authority, new town corporation, urban development corporation, the Development Board for Rural Wales, the Housing Corporation, a housing trust which is a charity, a registered housing association or an unregistered housing association which is a co-operative housing association: s.80 Housing Act 1985.

The tenant must occupy the dwelling-house as his only or principal home: s.81 Housing Act 1985. If the tenancy is a joint tenancy, then at least one of the tenants must occupy the dwelling as his only or principal home. There is no comparable tenant condition for protected tenants who may assign or sub-let their tenancy provided that this is not prohibited by the tenancy agreement, although statutory tenants must occupy the dwelling-house as a residence.

Exclusions

The statutory exclusions are set out in Schedule 1 of the Housing Act 1985. The following tenancies are not secure tenancies: long tenancies, tenancies granted to certain of the landlord's employees, e.g. rent-free accommodation provided to policemen; tenancies granted to firemen; tenancies of land required for development; accommodation for homeless persons; temporary accommodation for persons taking up employment; short-term arrangements; temporary accommodation made available to a tenant while work is carried out at his principal home; agricultural holdings; licensed premises; student lettings; business tenancies within the scope of Part II of the Landlord and Tenant Act 1954; and almshouses: Schedule 1 of the Housing Act 1985.

SECURITY OF TENURE

Termination

General

A landlord can only regain possession of a secure tenancy by a court order on one of a limited number of statutory grounds for the tenancy's termination: s.82(1) Housing Act 1985.

By forfeiture

A landlord's right to obtain possession of a fixed term tenancy by forfeiture pursuant to a forfeiture provision in the lease is strictly curtailed. A tenant is entitled to a periodic tenancy as of right if the courts would have granted forfeiture: s.82(3) Housing Act 1985.

Termination of first fixed term

If the first secure tenancy ('the first tenancy') is a fixed term tenancy, a periodic tenancy will arise automatically when it ends, unless a further secure tenancy is granted. The position is represented by the following diagram.

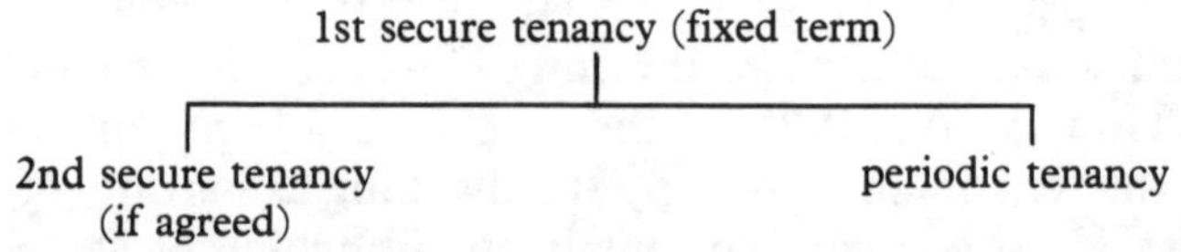

The type of periodic tenancy, e.g weekly or monthly, will be worked out with reference to the periods for which rent was payable under the secure tenancy: s.86 Housing Act 1985.

Termination proceedings

The procedure for terminating a secure tenancy commences with a termination notice, in the prescribed statutory form, served by the landlord specifying the ground of possession which the landlord intends to rely on and particularising the ground.

Grounds for possession

A court is only entitled to grant the landlord possession on one or more of the statutory Grounds 1 to 16 set out in Schedule 2 Parts 1-3 of the Housing Act 1985. There are no mandatory grounds for possession, as in the Rent Act 1977. A landlord must either show that it is reasonable for a court to grant possession or that suitable alternative accommodation is available, or both.

Meaning of suitable alternative accommodation: The court may order possession on the basis of Grounds 9 to 16 if suitable alternative accommodation is available. Suitable alternative accommodation is defined by Schedule 2 Part IV of the Housing Act 1985 with regard to the needs of the tenant and his family. The court must consider the following factors:

(a) the accommodation granted in practice to tenants with similar needs;
(b) the distance of the accommodation from the place of work or education of the tenant or any member of his family;
(c) the distance of the accommodation from the home of any member of the tenant's family, if proximity is essential to the well-being of that family member or to the tenant. For example, this is an appropriate consideration, important if elderly or sick relatives are being cared for;
(d) the tenant's accommodation needs and means;
(e) the terms on which the accommodation is available, and the terms of the secure tenancy;
(f) whether furniture is provided, if it was previously provided.

Grounds for possession–if considered reasonable

A court has a discretion as to whether to grant possession on one or more of Grounds 1 to 8, but cannot make a possession order unless it considers it reasonable to do so: s.84(2)(a) Housing Act 1985. The court may adjourn any possession proceedings on Grounds 1 to 8 for such period as it thinks fit: s.85(1) Housing Act 1985. But it may impose conditions as to the payment of rent arrears (if any), and rent unless this would cause the tenant exceptional hardship or be otherwise unreasonable: s.85(3) Housing Act 1985.

Ground 1: Where the rent due has not been paid or where the tenant has broken or failed to perform one of the tenancy's obligations: ground 1 is in identical terms to Schedule 15, Case 1 of the Rent Act 1977; see p.293.

Ground 2: Where the tenant or a person residing with him has been guilty of conduct which is a nuisance or annoyance to neighbours or has been convicted of using the dwelling-house for illegal or immoral purposes: ground 2 is in identical terms to Schedule 15, Case 2 of the Rent Act 1977; see p.294. Landlords are often under pressure to seek possession on ground 2 from neighbouring tenants complaining about a tenant's conduct, particularly in high rise blocks of council flats and high density council estates.

Ground 3: Where the tenant or a person residing with him has allowed the condition of the dwelling-house to deteriorate through acts of waste or neglect or default: ground 3 is in identical terms to Schedule 15, Case 3 of the Rent Act 1977; see p.294.

Ground 4: Where the tenant or a person residing with him has allowed the condition of furniture provided by the landlord to deteriorate owing to ill-treatment: ground 4 is in identical terms to Schedule 15, Case 4 of the Rent Act 1977; see p.295.

Ground 5: Where the tenant induced the landlord to grant the tenancy by a false statement. The landlord will have to show that the false statement was made knowingly or recklessly.

Ground 6: Where the tenancy was assigned to the tenant or to the tenant's predecessor for a premium as part of an assignment by way of exchange. Tenants are entitled to exchange tenancies under the provisions of s.92. If the tenant or his predecessor paid a premium for an assignment by way of exchange they risk losing the tenancy altogether. Ground 6 is designed to penalise tenants who trade their tenancies for a lump sum.

Ground 7: Where the dwelling-house forms part of premises used primarily for non-residential purposes, a landlord may seek possession on the ground that the tenant is guilty of such conduct that it would not be right for him to continue in occupation, having regard to the purpose for which the building is used.

Ground 8: Where the accommodation has been made available to the tenant temporarily whilst works were being carried out on his previous home.

Grounds for possession–suitable alternative accommodation is available

A court cannot make an order for possession on Grounds 9 to 11 unless it is satisfied that suitable alternative accommodation will be available for the tenant when the order takes effect: s.84(2)(b) Housing Act 1985.

Ground 9: Where the dwelling-house is overcrowded so as to make the occupier guilty of an offence.

Ground 10: Where the landlord intends (within a reasonable time of obtaining possession) either to demolish or reconstruct the building or to carry out work on it, and cannot reasonably do so without obtaining possession. *Ground 10A:* Where the landlord intends to redevelop as part of a redevelopment scheme (ground added by s.9 Housing and Planning Act 1986).

Ground 11: Where the landlord is a charity, possession may be recovered if the tenant's continued occupation of the dwelling-house would conflict with the objects of the charity.

Grounds for possession–reasonable and suitable alternative accommodation available

A court cannot make an order for possession on Grounds 12 to 16 unless it both considers it reasonable to make the order, and is satisfied that suitable alternative accommodation will be available for the tenant when the order takes effect: s.84(2)(c) Housing Act 1985. The court may adjourn any possession proceedings on Grounds 12 to 16 for such period as it thinks fit: s.85(1) Housing Act 1985. But it may impose conditions as to the payment of rent arrears (if any), and rent unless this would cause the tenant exceptional hardship or be otherwise unreasonable: s.85(3) Housing Act 1985.

Ground 12: Where the landlord requires the dwelling-house for an employee and it forms part of a building which is mainly used for non-residential purposes or is situated in a cemetery.

Ground 13: Where the dwelling-house has been adapted for physically disabled persons, and is needed for a disabled person, and, there is no longer such a person residing there.

Ground 14: Where the landlord is a housing association or trust which only lets dwelling-houses for occupation to persons whose circumstances (apart from financial circumstances) make it especially difficult to obtain housing. The landlord must show that there is either no longer such a person residing in the dwelling-house or that the person has received an offer of a secure tenancy elsewhere, and, that the dwelling-house is required for occupation of such a person.

Ground 15: Where the dwelling-house forms part of a group of dwellings which is let for persons with special needs, and there is no longer anyone residing in the dwelling-house with a special need. The landlord must show that there is a social service or special facility in close proximity, and further, that the dwelling-house is required for a person who has those special needs.

Ground 16: Where the tenant is occupying accommodation which is more extensive than is reasonably required by the tenant.

Possession order

If a court does make a possession order against a tenant, it has power to stay or suspend or postpone its execution for as long as it thinks fit: s.85(2) Housing Act 1985. But it may impose conditions as to the payment of rent arrears (if any), and rent unless this would cause the tenant exceptional hardship or be otherwise unreasonable: s.85(3) Housing Act 1985.

Possession of matrimonial homes

If a tenant's spouse or former spouse has rights of occupation under the Matrimonial Homes Act 1983, that spouse has rights identical to the tenant in respect of an adjournment, stay, suspension or postponement of possession proceedings: s.85(5) Housing Act 1985.

SUCCESSION

Where the tenant dies, there is the possibility of the tenancy being transferred to the tenant's spouse or another member of the tenant's family: s.87 Housing Act 1985. The only persons qualified to succeed the tenant are a spouse or family member who 'occupies the dwelling-house as his only or principle home at the time of the tenant's death'. Only one right of succession is permitted. This means that if a tenant's spouse succeeds to the tenancy on the tenant's death, any children living in the dwelling- house as their principle home have no rights of succession since the spouse is the preferred successor: ss. 87, 89(2)(a) Housing Act 1985.

ASSIGNMENT AND SUB-LETTING

Assignment

The general rule is that the assignment of secure tenancies is prohibited. Public sector landlords provide housing for those with certain needs:

s.91 Housing Act 1985. It is a personal privilege which is non-assignable. The main exception, apart from the special case of matrimonial homes, is an assignment by way of exchange. Council home exchanges are permitted by s.92 of the Housing Act 1985 with the written consent of the landlord.

Sub-letting and lodgers

Tenants are permitted to take in lodgers: s.93(1)(a) Housing Act 1985. But they are not permitted to sub-let without the landlord's written consent: s.93(1)(b) Housing Act 1985. Such consent is not to be unreasonably withheld: s.94 Housing Act 1985.

REPAIRS AND IMPROVEMENTS

Repairs

A statutory scheme has recently been established under which a tenant is entitled to carry out landlord's repairs and can recover the cost from his landlord: see the 'Right to Repair Scheme' at pp.169–70.

Improvements

A tenant is not permitted to carry out improvements without the written consent of his landlord: s.97(1) Housing Act 1985. For this purpose, 'improvement' has the wide meaning of any alteration or addition, and includes putting up a television aerial and decorating the exterior: s.97(2) Housing Act 1985. A landlord cannot increase rent on account of improvements made by the tenant: s.101(10) Housing Act 1985.

Reimbursement

A tenant is entitled to be reimbursed for any authorised improvements which he has made at the end of the term, provided that they add to the notional market price or to the rent which the landlord may be able to charge: s.100 Housing Act 1985. But a tenant is not entitled to receive more than the cost of the improvement after deducting any grants which were provided: s.100(2) Housing Act 1985.

VARIATION OF TERMS

The terms of the tenancy (apart from the payment of rent and related sums) can be varied by agreement or pursuant to a 'notice of variation' served on the tenant inviting comments: ss. 102-3 Housing Act 1985.

The tenant's only real sanction in the event of a rent variation is to serve a notice to quit and leave if he opposes the variation unsuccessfully: s.103(9) Housing Act 1985.

INFORMATION AND CONSULTATION

Landlords have a statutory duty to furnish tenants with information about its secure tenancies explaining in simple language its terms and the provisions of Parts IV and V of the Housing Act 1985: s.104 Housing Act 1985. Furthermore, landlords have a statutory obligation to maintain arrangements whereby tenants are consulted on matters of housing management: s.105 Housing Act 1985.

THE RIGHT TO BUY

The Housing Act 1980 introduced the right to buy: see now Part V Housing Act 1985 as amended by the Housing and Planning Act 1986. Broadly speaking, a tenant has a right to buy his dwelling-house from the landlord on favourable terms coupled with a right to a mortgage provided he is not bankrupt: s.118, Housing Act 1985. The right to buy is preserved on disposal to a private sector landlord: s.171A Housing Act 1985 added by s.8 Housing and Planning Act 1986.

The purchase price is calculated using the notional open market price which the dwelling-house would fetch if sold by a a willing vendor, as the base figure: s.127 Housing Act 1985. But the tenant is not required to pay an open market price since he is entitled to a discount according to the length of time he has occupied the dwelling-house as a public sector tenant: s.129 and Schedule 4 Housing Act 1985 as amended by s.2 Housing and Planning Act 1986. The discount, in the case of a house, is for a minimum of 32 per cent, plus one per cent for each complete year by which the qualifying period exceeds two years up to a maximum of 60 per cent of the purchase price at present. In the case of a flat the minimum discount is 44 per cent plus two per cent for each complete year by which the qualifying period exceeds two years up to a maximum of 70 per cent: s.129(2A) Housing Act 1985 as amended by s.2 Housing and Planning Act 1986. A tenant who is entitled to a right to buy but not entitled to a full mortgage has a right to a 'shared ownership lease' at a premium: s.143(1) Housing Act 1985.

FURTHER READING

Encyclopaedia of Housing Law and Practice by A. Arden, Sweet & Maxwell, updated work.

Chapter 32

The Future

RESIDENTIAL PREMISES

Security of tenure

Security of tenure and rent control in residential tenancies have been a political football since the Second World War. Those on the left fervently believe that the operation of a free market would result in landlords using their much stronger position at common law to oppress and exploit tenants. Those on the right however believe with equal passion that only the liberalisation of statutory controls leading eventually to a free market can restore the private rented sector to its former glory. The left point out that liberalisation would inevitably lead to those landlords who were able to seeking possession doing so in order to sell and make a quick profit. The right insist that there is a huge number of empty homes which nobody risks letting with all the consequences of security of tenure. They go on to say that the stagnation produced by an economy in which there is only a very small private rented sector reduces mobility and employment opportunities.

Whatever the merits or demerits of the two opposing arguments may be certain facts stand out fairly clearly. It must be recognised as a political impossibility for any administration to repeal the twin pillars of interventionism—security of tenure and rent control—at least within the foreseeable future. There would be too many who would lose too much. Abolition of security of tenure and rent control for tenancies granted from a future date might be feasible. Nevertheless the howls of protest and promises of repeal of such legislation after the next election would still deter prospective landlords from venturing their properties on the market.

Decline in rented sector

Apart from the renting of very expensive properties in Central London to foreigners and corporations, there is a continuing decline in the private rented market. This sector has declined from providing over 60% of homes in 1947 to less than 10% in 1985. Today over 60% of homes are owner occupied as compared with 26% in 1947. A further 25% are rented from local authorities, rising from 13 per cent in 1947: see Table 3 at p. 30 of *The Politics of Legislation, The Rent Act 1957* by M.J.Barnett for a break-down of figures up until 1964; the Department of Environment is the source of the figures available in 1986. This decline must surely be terminal and irreversible. The number of private rented tenancies is reducing at the rate of 100,000 homes a year. The following table shows figures for the number of privately rented homes in Great Britain:

PRIVATELY RENTED HOMES
including housing associations

	Total (000s)	Percentage
1974	3,205	16.3
1975	3,083	15.5
1976	2,984	14.8
1977	2,897	14.2
1978	2,818	13.7
1979	2,738	13.1
1980	2,667	12.7
1981	2,595	12.3
1982	2,532	11.9
1983	2,472	11.5
1984	2,416	11.1

Figures are for Great Britain
Source: Department of the Environment

As property prices continue to increase well beyond the rate of inflation it is inevitable that all those who can will take on large mortgages in the confident hope that the increase in property values will lead to a tidy gain free of tax. The annual capital gain made on residential property in most parts of Britain has on average greatly exceeded the interest payable upon borrowing the price of the property at the rates charged on mortgages since 1970. Income tax relief on the first £30,000 makes the net gain for the property owner even more impressive. Unless and until the property market crashes it can only be folly for anyone who could afford to not to buy. Hence the private rented sector caters largely for those who for one reason or another cannot leap aboard the owner occupier gravy train.

Whatever alterations are made to landlord and tenant law the fundamental economics underlying the change away from private renting will not alter in the foreseeable future. The argument between left and right on protection for residential tenants will therefore become still less significant than it already is in terms of the number of homes affected. The private rented sector will continue to provide shelter largely for rich foreigners, company directors, students, and those unable to obtain either a mortgage or a council home until property prices rise to a level where those without capital will not be able to buy at all.

Reforming the law

Although the rented sector is declining in size, the number of disputes and the complexity of the Rent Acts will ensure the survival of plenty of work for lawyers in that field. The Rent Acts are a sad reflection upon their many authors, governments of both complexions, parliamentary committees and draftsmen. The fact that this area of law has been such a political football has resulted in absurdly over-complicated legislation and cases. It is a bitter irony that in the three areas of law which most directly impinge upon those who cannot afford lawyers, namely landlord and tenant, consumer credit and employment, parliament in its wisdom has seen fit to enact the most cumbersome and indigestible legislation studded with technical concepts and the worst sort of legalese.

There are, however, many ways in which the law relating to the private rented sector could be improved. Apart from the impossible dream of scrapping the Rent Acts and starting again with a fresh sheet of paper, Occam's razor, and a respect for intelligibility, there are many minor amendments which could prove highly beneficial.

Rent Bill

The present Conservative Government has made a number of public pronouncements about its intention to reform the Rent Acts by introducing legislation to end private rent controls. But it put off its controversial Rent Bill which was not included in the 1985 legislative time-table as anticipated. One of the hopes of the protagonists for the abolition of rent control was that the scrapping of controls could help to bring up to half a million private empty homes into occupation. Given the fact that a property can have its value reduced to two-thirds or even a half merely by creating an oral weekly tenancy falling within the scope of the Rent Acts, the commercial landlord of residential property is likely to fade away into insignificance. The Small Landlords Association represents the interests of those who regard the abolition of rent control as the last chance for the private residential sector which has shrunk so severely.

Service charges

In numerical terms, one of the most disputed issues between landlords and tenants is the level of service charges. This applies not only in the residential sector but equally to the commercial sector. The tenant is frequently in a very weak position because of his inability to control the standard of service and the cost passed on to him.

The business tenant does not even have the protection offered by section 19 of the Landlord and Tenant Act 1985: see Chapter 11 at pp.109–10 for the test of reasonableness in respect of residential tenancies. At least the business tenant may have the financial resources to take advice about his position and litigate to protect himself.

The private residential tenant is in a much more difficult position unless an active and well funded tenant's association is willing to do battle. Unless the private tenant is fortunate enough to qualify for legal aid, litigation about service charges conducted at his own expense is liable to prove an enormous waste of money. The determination of issues in service charge litigation often requires many well paid expert witnesses and ranges across a catalogue of complaints–and hence is expensive. The costs incurred and the risk of losing mean that such litigation is not for any private individual except for the man who litigates on principle.

The problem of service charges could to some extent have been averted if the Law Society had put pressure on solicitors to draft appropriate protection into modern leases. Whilst the greatest attention to detail is given in leases to matters which might be in issue once in a blue moon, service charge covenants usually contain no protection whatsoever for the tenant against the corrupt, incompetent or extravagant landlord. Therefore Parliament must step into the breach once again.

The fundamental difficulty is that the person in control of the nature, quality and cost of services, i.e. the landlord, is not the person who benefits from, suffers under or pays for the same. The only solution to the problem is for a statutory scheme under which control is given to the tenants. By far the most successful arrangement for a building or development with multiple tenancies from the point of view of an honest landlord and the majority of the tenants, is a tripartite set-up. The landlord transfers the management of the building to a company which is owned and controlled by the tenants. Each tenant covenants with the company to pay service charges. The covenant contains suitable protection against undue increases and overcharging. The company, whose officers may either be paid professionals or tenants, gets on with the job of running the building. All tenants exercise control over it through a shareholding.

Whilst such a scheme does solve many problems it still leaves some. There will inevitably be disputes between tenants as to the nature and standard of services desired. The only way of dealing with that difficulty is for more attention to be given to protection in the drafting of the tenant's covenant to pay service charges. However under this scheme the parsimonious tenant is bound to find that a majority of his neighbours is as oppressive as a landlord.

There are many large property developers selling on long leases who set up such a scheme themselves. In that way they can rid themselves of all the wrangles which always arise. However this is only a comparatively recent phenomenon and so the only practical way of introducing such a scheme to protect tenants generally is through legislation. The only comprehensive legislation is in relation to public sector service charges payable after the exercise of the right to buy where special considerations apply to safeguard tenants who are likely to have low incomes: s.125 Housing Act 1985 as amended by s.4 Housing and Planning Act 1986.

The simplest and most effective way of achieving the desired effect would be to give companies owned and controlled by the majority of the tenants of one building a right to buy the freehold from the landlord. Clearly the right to buy would need to be circumscribed carefully. However, it would not be too difficult to set out a number of criteria so that in the main tenants' companies could buy out landlords of blocks of flats on long leases. Such legislation however is unlikely to extend to the business sector and so at the least business tenants should have some protection by provisions similar to section 19 of the Landlord and Tenant Act 1985.

The Nugee Committee, chaired by Mr Edward Nugee Q.C. and set up in 1984, recommended reforms to tackle the problems of management in blocks of residential flats in a report published in November 1985, which would affect about half a million tenants, mainly occupying flats in mansion blocks in London and the South-East. The Committee recommended that residents should have the collective right of first refusal to purchase the block where the landlord wished to dispose of his interest.

The Government responded by proposing a Bill which would give tenants important new rights of tenure and management, announcing its proposals on the 8th April 1986. In essence, the Government accepts the recommendations of the Nugee Committee, but goes further in two respects. First, the Government proposed that the residents of blocks wholly or substantially occupied by long leaseholders should have the right to purchase the landlord's interest at market price if they satisfied a court that the landlord has persistently failed in his duties. Second, the Government recommended that more should be done to involve residents in the selection of managing agents by giving recognised residents' associations a right to require the landlord to consult them about the appointment of agents and to consult them thereafter, whilst endorsing the Nugee Committee's views.

The Government endorsed the recommendation of the Nugee Committee for the development of the procedure for appointing a receiver and manager if a landlord or his agent neglected the property or failed to carry out the necessary work: this novel relief was granted by Mr Justice Goulding in *Hart and Others* v. *Emelkirk Ltd* (1982), discussed at p. 165. In addition, proposals to vary leases which contained important defects and to tighten the control over monies paid into service charge accounts and reserves were approved.

Resolving disputes

The Royal Institution of Chartered Surveyors recommended the establishment of a code of practice and the introduction of an inexpensive means of resolving disputes rather than changing the present system, in a memorandum published in January 1986 in response to the Nugee Report. It rejected the argument that difficulties between landlords and tenants over maintenance and service charges in blocks of flats could be solved by the Government's proposal to grant the occupier the right to buy the freehold. The RICS takes the view that the root cause of the problems with blocks of flats is a lack of managerial expertise, and emphasises the fact that efficient management and good maintenance cost money. Many tenants are unwilling to recognise this, and invariably fail to budget properly, particularly at the lower end of the residential market.

BUSINESS TENANCIES

Whilst the legislation controlling the private residential sector owes much of its complexity to the tussles between left and right the legislation affecting business tenancies is a model of good sense. The Landlord and Tenant Act 1954 Part II is and has been politically uncontroversial. It is an Act which seeks to strike a balance between the interest of the landlord in obtaining a market rent and being free to re-enter under certain circumstances, and the interest of the tenant in not losing the goodwill of his business when his lease expires. The fact that no major amendments have been made or argued about testifies for the fairness and commercial wisdom of the Act. One can therefore make relatively safe predictions about its future and assume that it is likely to remain for the foreseeable future in substantially the same form as it is now.

The success of this legislation certainly does add some support to those who argue that, whilst security of tenure and rent control result in a frozen and stagnant market, security of tenure itself is acceptable for residential tenants. Ignoring for the moment the major differences between the nature of the security offered to Rent Act and to business tenants, the crucial distinction between the two is in the level of rent.

While the business tenant must pay the market rent calculated on renewal on the available comparables, the Rent Act tenant need only pay the market rent ignoring any scarcity factor. That formula requires an exercise of supreme illogicality in order to be applied and results in a level of rent which bears no resemblance to what is available on the market.

Would the abolition of rent control and the preservation of security of tenure for Rent Act tenants provide a satisfactory compromise? It would not, for a number of reasons. The absence of a normal market and the fact that this absence is liable to continue for the foreseeable future for the reasons set out above mean that the removal of rent control would result in sky-high rents. Landlords would for the most part take the opportunity of raising the rent in the hope of possession and sale to an owner occupier. The market would be utterly distorted and so any procedure whereby rents had to be fixed at the market rent would be of no help to the tenant. Once a market is destroyed through the forces of interventionism it takes a long time to return to its former state.

Furthermore, whilst most business tenancies are created for a term of several years, Rent Act tenancies on the whole are not. A system whereby on expiry of a lease of say, five years, the procedure of notices, counter-notices, negotiation over new terms and agreement or litigation is gone through makes commercial sense. In the case of a monthly tenancy it would not. Above and beyond all of these factors it must be borne in mind that the largest category of those in the private rented sector are those who are too poor to get a mortgage. Increased rents through the absence of rent control would mean that the taxpayer, through the housing benefits which would be necessary to prevent homelessness, would end up providing a windfall to landlords.

PUBLIC SECTOR

The public sector tenancy has entered the political arena in the 1980s. Under Margaret Thatcher council homes have been sold by the thousand and those who would or could not buy have been given some statutory protection. Until the Housing Act 1980 it was assumed that local authorities were such benign institutions that there was no need to protect their tenants. Prior to such protection council tenants were legally in an extremely weak position. As a matter of fact they were well protected given the existence of reasonably fair policies by most local authorities and the tenants' ability to take the matter up with local councillors. However, it is surely an unsatisfactory state of affairs for people to have no remedy at law against arbitrary decisions about their housing made by a local authority.

The major problem areas which arise, however, are the failure of local authorities to keep their buildings in good repair and to prevent environmental pollution by noise, graffiti, rubbish etc. The law does provide remedies in these areas but they are not often exploited as fully as they might be. Those tenants not poor enough to be supported by legal aid may well find such remedies too expensive. However there undoubtedly is a great deal of uncomplaining acceptance of appalling conditions by tenants, which is explicable both by a kind of stoicism and by ignorance of remedies. Perhaps the major future trend in the field of public sector tenancies will be that word will get around the council estates that if the local authority is signally failing to honour its legal obligations there are remedies available, and council tenants will be more willing to safeguard their rights through the courts.

LEASEHOLD OBLIGATIONS

Implied covenants

The Law Commission published a report in 1975 recommending the codification of the implied obligations of landlord and tenant: 'Obligations of Landlords and Tenants', the Law Commission No. 67, 11 June 1975. The Report's objective was to produce a restatement of the general law regulating the parties' relationship as set out in a draft Landlord and Tenant (Implied Covenants) Bill. No new remedies for breach of covenant were suggested. It is this author's view that it is highly desirable that this Bill should pass into legislation in order to create a modern code of leasehold obligations applicable to all fixed term tenancies, and to do away with a body of complicated anachronistic law once and for all.

The Law Commission classified implied covenants as either 'overriding covents' which would apply in any event, or 'variable covenants' which could be modified or excluded by the parties. Overriding covenants would include covenants for possession and quiet enjoyment (which were to be strengthened), derogation from grant and rent. The Committee recommended the strengthening of the tenant's obligations by the introduction of overriding covenants designed to protect the premises, e.g. to prevent encroachment, to inform landlords of adverse proceedings, and not to permit a nuisance (wider than tenant-like duty).

A large body of the Law Commission's recommendations were focussed on repairing obligations where it was perceived that the law was inadequate, with a large number of disputes arising out of inadequately expressed agreements and obscure law. All the recommended repairing covenants were classified as variable covenants, apart from re-enacting what is now s.11 of the Landlord and Tenant Act 1985: see pp.147–53. The proposed implied repairing obligations were correlated to the length of the lease's term. The following categorisation was recommended:

(a) residential lettings for less than seven years where it was thought inappropriate to make a tenant responsible for repairs;
(b) furnished residential lettings of up to twenty years;
(c) all other lettings up to twenty years;
(d) all lettings whether residential or not for over twenty years.

Other variable covenants include a right of re-entry and outgoings.

Express covenants

The Law Commission's more recent recommendations relating to the reform of the law of forfeiture and user covenants have already been considered: see pp.223–4.

Appendix 1

Statutes–Select Sections

COMMON LAW PROCEDURE ACT 1852

Tenant paying all rent, with costs, proceedings to cease

212. If the tenant or his assignee do or shall, at any time before the trial in such ejectment, pay or tender to the lessor or landlord, his executors or administrators, or his or their attorney in that cause, or pay into the court where the same is depending, all the rent and arrears, together with the costs, then and in such case all further proceedings on the said ejectment shall cease and be discontinued; and if such lessee, his executors, administrators, or assigns, shall, upon such proceedings as aforesaid, be relieved in equity, he and they shall have, hold, and enjoy that demised lands, according to the lease thereof made, without any new lease.

LAW OF PROPERTY ACT 1925

Contracts, Conveyances and other Instruments

Contracts for sale, etc., of land to be in writing

40. (1) No action may be brought upon any contract for the sale or other disposition of land or any interest in land, unless the agreement upon which such action is brought, or some memorandum or note thereof, is in writing, and signed by the party to be charged or by some other person thereunto by him lawfully authorised.

(2) This section applies to contracts whether made before or after the commencement of this Act and does not affect the law relating to part performance, or sales by the court.

Conveyances to be by deed

52. (1) All conveyances of land or of any interest therein are void for the purpose of conveying or creating a legal estate unless made by deed.

(2) This section does not apply to:

(a) assents by a personal representative;

(b) disclaimers made in accordance with s.54 of the Bankruptcy Act 1914 or not required to be evidenced in writing;

(c) surrenders by operation of law, including surrenders which may, by law, be effected without writing;

(d) leases or tenancies or other assurances not required by law to be made in writing;

(e) receipts not required by law to be under seal;
(f) vesting orders of the court or other competent authority;
(g) conveyances taking effect by operation of law.

Creation of interests in land by parol

54. (1) All interests in land created by parol and not put in writing and signed by the persons so creating the same, or by their agents thereunto lawfully authorised in writing, have, notwithstanding any consideration having been given for the same, the force and effect of interests at will only.

(2) Nothing in the foregoing provisions of this Part of this Act shall affect the creation by parol of leases taking effect in possession for a term not exceeding three years (whether or not the lessee is given power to extend the term) at the best rent which can be reasonably obtained without taking a fine.

Rent and benefit of lessee's covenants to run with the reversion

141. (1) Rent reserved by a lease, and the benefit of every covenant or provision therein contained, having reference to the subject-matter thereof, and on the lessee's part to be observed or performed, and every condition of re-entry and other condition therein contained, shall be annexed and incident to and shall go with reversionary estate in the land, or in any part thereof, immediately expectant on the term granted by the lease, notwithstanding severance of that reversionary estate, and without prejudice to any liability affecting a covenantor or his estate.

(2) Any such rent, covenant or provision shall be capable of being recovered, received, enforced, and taken advantage of, by the person from time to time entitled, subject to the term, to the income of the whole or any part, as the case may require, of the land leased.

(3) Where that person becomes entitled by conveyance or otherwise, such rent, covenant or provision may be recovered, received, enforced or taken advantage of by him notwithstanding that he becomes so entitled after the condition of re-entry or forfeiture has become enforceable, but this subsection does not render enforceable any condition of re-entry or other condition waived or released before such person becomes entitled as aforesaid.

(4) This section applies to leases made before or after the commencement of this Act, but does not affect the operation of:

(*a*) any severance of the reversionary estate; or
(*b*) any acquisition by conveyance or otherwise of the right to receive or enforce any rent covenant or provision;

effected before the commencement of this Act.

Obligation of lessor's covenants to run with reversion

142. (1) The obligation under a condition or of a covenant entered into by a lessor with reference to the subject-matter of the lease shall, if and as far as the lessor has power to bind the reversionary estate immediately expectant on the term granted by the lease, be annexed and incident to and shall go with that reversionary estate, or the several parts thereof, notwithstanding severance of that reversionary estate, and may be taken advantage of and enforced by the person in whom the term is from time to time vested by conveyance, devolution in law, or otherwise; and, if and as far as the lessor has power to bind the person from time to time entitled to that reversionary estate, the obligation aforesaid may be taken advantage of and entered against any person so entitled.

(2) This section applies to leases made before or after the commencement of this Act, whether the severance of the reversionary estate was effected before or after such commencement:

Provided that, where the lease was made before the first day of January eighteen hundred and eighty-two, nothing in this section shall affect the operation of any severance of the reversionary estate effected before such commencement.

This section takes effect without prejudice to any liability affecting a covenantor or his estate.

Restrictions on and relief against forfeiture of leases and underleases

146. (1) A right of re-entry or forfeiture under any proviso or stipulation in a lease for a breach of any covenant or condition in the lease shall not be enforceable, by action or otherwise, unless and until the lessor serves on the lessee a notice:

(*a*) specifying the particular breach complained of; and

(*b*) if the breach is capable of remedy, requiring the lessee to remedy the breach; and

(*c*) in any case, requiring the lessee to make compensation in money for the breach;

and the lessee fails, within a reasonable time thereafter, to remedy the breach, if it is capable of remedy, and to make reasonable compensation in money, to the satisfaction of the lessor, for the breach.

(2) Where a lessor is proceeding, by action or otherwise, to enforce such a right of re-entry or forfeiture, the lessee may, in the lessor's action, if any, or in any action brought by himself, apply to the court for relief; and the court may grant or refuse relief, as the court, having regard to the proceedings and conduct of the parties under the foregoing provisions of this section, and to all the other circumstances, thinks fit; and in case of relief may grant it on such terms, if any, as to costs, expenses, damages, compensation, penalty, or otherwise, including the granting of an injunction to restrain any like breach in the future, as the court, in the circumstances of each case, thinks fit.

(3) A lessor shall be entitled to recover as a debt due to him from a lessee, and in addition to damages (if any), all reasonable costs and expenses properly incurred by the lessor in the employment of a solicitor and surveyor or valuer, or otherwise, in reference to any breach giving rise to a right of re-entry or forfeiture which, at the request of the lessee, is waived by the lessor, or from which the lessee is relieved, under the provisions of this Act.

(4) Where a lessor is proceeding by action or otherwise to enforce a right of re-entry or forfeiture under any covenant, proviso, or stipulation in a lease, or for non-payment of rent, the court may, on application by any person claiming as under-lessee any estate or interest in the property comprised in the lease or any part thereof, either in the lessor's action (if any) or in any action brought by such person for that purpose, make an order vesting, for the whole term of the lease or any less term, the property comprised in the lease or any part thereof in any person entitled as under-lessee to any estate or interest in such property upon such conditions as to execution of any deed or other document, payment of rent, costs, expenses, damages, compensation, giving security, or otherwise, as the court in the circumstances of each case may think fit, but in no case shall any such under-lessee be entitled to require a lease to be granted to him for any longer term than he had under his original sub-lease.

(5) For the purposes of this section:

(*a*) 'Lease' includes an original or derivative under-lease; also an agreement for a lease where the lessee has become entitled to have his lease granted; also a grant at a fee farm rent, or securing a rent by condition;

(*b*) 'Lessee' includes an original or derivative under-lessee, and the persons deriving title under a lessee; also a grantee under any such grant as aforesaid and the persons deriving title under him;

(*c*) 'Lessor' includes an original or derivative under-lessor, and the persons deriving title under a lessor; also a person making such grant as aforesaid and the persons deriving title under him;

(*d*) 'Under-lease' includes an agreement for an underlease where the underlessee has become entitled to have his underlease granted;

(*e*) 'Underlessee' includes any person deriving title under an underlessee.

(6) This section applies although the proviso or stipulation under which the right of re-entry or forfeiture accrues is inserted in the lease in pursuance of the directions of any Act of Parliament.

(7) For the purposes of this section a lease limited to continue as long only as the lessee abstains from committing a breach of covenant shall be and take effect as a lease to continue for any longer term for which it could subsist, but determinable by a proviso for re-entry on such a breach.

(8) This section does not extend:

(i) To a covenant or condition against assigning, underletting, parting with the possession, or disposing of the land leased where the breach occurred before the commencement of this Act; or

(ii) In the case of a mining lease, to a covenant or condition for allowing the lessor to have access to or inspect books, accounts, records, weighing machines or other things, or to enter or inspect the mine or the workings thereof.

(9) This section does not apply to a condition for forfeiture on the bankruptcy of the lessee or on taking in execution of the lessee's interest if contained in a lease of:

(*a*) Agricultural or pastoral land;

(*b*) Mines or minerals;

(*c*) A house used or intended to be used as a public-house or beershop;

(*d*) A house let as a dwelling-house, with the use of any furniture, books, works of art, or other chattels not being in the nature of fixtures;

(*e*) Any property with respect to which the personal qualifications of the tenant are of importance for the preservation of the value or character of the property, or on the ground of neighbourhood to the lessor, or to any person holding under him.

(10) Where a condition of forfeiture on the bankruptcy of the lessee or on taking in execution of the lessee's interest is contained in any lease, other than a lease of any of the classes mentioned in the last subsection, then:

(*a*) if the lessee's interest is sold within one year from the bankruptcy or taking in execution, this section applies to the forfeiture condition aforesaid;

(*b*) if the lessee's interest is not sold before the expiration of that year, this section only applies to the forfeiture condition aforesaid during the first year from the date of the bankruptcy or taking in execution.

(11) This section does not, save as otherwise mentioned, affect the law relating to re-entry or forfeiture or relief in case of non-payment of rent.

(12) This section has effect notwithstanding any stipulation to the contrary.

General definitions

205. (1) (xxvii) 'Term of years absolute' means a term of years (taking effect either in possession or in reversion whether or not at a rent) with or without impeachment for waste, subject or not to another legal estate, and either certain or liable to determination by notice, re-entry, operation of law, or by a provision for cesser on redemption, or in any other event (other than the dropping of a life, or the determination of a determinable life interest); but does not include any term of years determinable with life or lives or with the cesser of a determinable life interest, nor, if created after the commencement of this Act, a term of years which is not expressed to take effect in possession within twenty-one years after the creation thereof where required by this Act to take effect within that period; and in this definition the expression 'term of years' includes a term for less than a year, or for a year or years and a fraction of a year or from year to year.

LANDLORD AND TENANT ACT 1927

Part I
Compensation for Improvements and Goodwill on the Termination of Tenancies of Business Premises

Tenant's right to compensation for improvements

1. (1) Subject to the provisions of this Part of this Act, a tenant of a holding to which this Part of this Act applies shall, if a claim for the purpose is made in the prescribed manner [and within the time limited by section 47 of the Landlord and Tenant Act 1954] be entitled, at the termination of the tenancy, on quitting his holding, to be paid by his landlord compensation in respect of any improvement (including the erection of any building) on his holding made by him or his predecessors in title, not being a trade or other fixture which the tenant is by law entitled to remove, which at the termination of the tenancy adds to the letting value of the holding:

Provided that the sum to be paid as compensation for any improvement shall not exceed

(*a*) the net addition to the value of the holding as a whole which may be determined to be the direct result of the improvement; or

(*b*) the reasonable cost of carrying out the improvement of the termination of the tenancy, subject to a deduction of an amount equal to the cost (if any) of putting the works constituting the improvement into a reasonable state of repair, except so far as such cost is covered by the liability of the tenant under any covenant or agreement as to the repair of the premises.

(2) In determining the amount of such net addition as aforesaid, regard shall be had to the purposes for which it is intended that the premises shall be used

after the termination of the tenancy, and if it is shown that it is intended to demolish or to make structural alterations in the premises or any part thereof or to use the premises for a different purpose, regard shall be had to the effect of such demolition, alteration or change of user on the additional value attributable to the improvement, and to the length of time likely to elapse between the termination of the tenancy and the demolition, alteration or change of user.

(3) In the absence of agreement between the parties, all questions as to the right to compensation under this section, or as to the amount thereof, shall be determined by the tribunal hereinafter mentioned, and if the tribunal determines that, on account of the intention to demolish or alter or to change the user of the premises, no compensation or a reduced amount of compensation shall be paid, the tribunal may authorise a further application for compensation to be made by the tenant if effect is not given to the intention within such time as may be fixed by the tribunal.

Limitation on tenant's right to compensation in certain cases

2. (1) A tenant shall not be entitled to compensation under this Part of this Act:

(*a*) in respect of any improvement made before the commencement of this Act; or

(*b*) in respect of any improvement made in pursuance of a statutory obligation, or of any improvement which the tenant or his predecessors in title were under an obligation to make in pursuance of a contract entered into, whether before or after the passing of this Act, for valuable consideration, including a building lease; or

(*c*) in respect of any improvement made less than three years before the termination of the tenancy; or

(*d*) if within two months after the making of the claim under s. 1(1) of this Act the landlord serves on the tenant notice that he is willing and able to grant to the tenant, or obtain the grant to him of, a renewal of the tenancy at such rent and for such term as, failing agreement, the tribunal may consider reasonable; and, where such a notice is so served and the tenant does not within one month from the service of the notice send to the landlord an acceptance in writing of the offer, the tenant shall be deemed to have declined the offer.

(2) Where an offer of the renewal of a tenancy by the landlord under this section is accepted by the tenant, the rent fixed by the tribunal shall be the rent which in the opinion of the tribunal a willing lessee other than the tenant would agree to give and a willing lessor would agree to accept for the premises, having regard to the terms of the lease, but irrespective of the value attributable to the improvement in respect of which compensation would have been payable.

(3) The tribunal in determining the compensation for an improvement shall in reduction of the tenant's claim take into consideration any benefits which the tenant or his predecessors in title may have received from the landlord or his predecessors in title in consideration expressly or impliedly of the improvement.

PART II

GENERAL AMENDMENTS OF THE LAW OF LANDLORD AND TENANT

Provisions as to covenants to repair

18. (1) Damages for a breach of a covenant or agreement to keep or put premises in repair during the currency of a lease, or to leave or put premises in repair at the termination of a lease, whether such covenant or agreement is expressed or implied, and whether general or specific, shall in no case exceed the amount (if any) by which the value of the reversion (whether immediate or not) in the premises is diminished owing to the breach of such covenant or agreement as aforesaid; and in particular no damage shall be recovered for a breach of any such covenant or agreement to leave or put premises in repair at the termination of a lease, if it is shown that the premises, in whatever state of repair they might be, would at or shortly after the termination of the tenancy have been or be pulled down, or such structural alterations made therein as would render valueless the repairs covered by the covenant or agreement.

(2) A right of re-entry or forfeiture for a breach of any such covenant or agreement as aforesaid shall not be enforceable, by action or otherwise, unless the lessor proves that the fact that such a notice as is required by section 146 of the Law of Property Act 1925, had been served on the lessee was known either

(*a*) to the lessee; or

(*b*) to an under-lessee holding under an under-lease which reserved a nominal reversion only to the lessee; or

(*c*) to the person who last paid the rent due under the lease either on his own behalf or as agent for the lessee or under-lessee;

and that a time reasonably sufficient to enable the repairs to be executed had elapsed since the time when the fact of the service of the notice came to the knowledge of any such person.

Where a notice has been sent by registered post addressed to a person at his last known place of abode in the United Kingdom, then, for the purposes of this subsection, that person shall be deemed, unless the contrary is proved, to have had knowledge of the fact that the notice had been served as from the time at which the letter would have been delivered in the ordinary course of post.

This subsection shall be construed as one with section 146 of the Law of Property Act 1925.

(3) This section applies whether the lease was created before or after the commencement of this Act.

Provisions as to covenants not to assign, etc., without licence or consent

19. (1) In all leases whether made before or after the commencement of this Act containing a covenant condition or agreement against assigning, under-letting, charging or parting with the possession of demised premises or any part thereof without licence or consent, such covenant condition or agreement shall, notwithstanding any express provision to the contrary, be deemed to be subject

(*a*) to a proviso to the effect that such licence or consent is not to be unreasonably withheld, but this proviso does not preclude the right of the landlord to require payment of a reasonable sum in respect of any legal or other expenses incurred in connection with such licence or consent; and

(*b*) (if the lease is for more than forty years, and is made in consideration wholly or partially of the erection, or the substantial improvement, addition or alteration of buildings, and the lessor is not a Government department or local or public authority, or a statutory or public utility company) to a proviso to the effect that in the case of any assignment, under-letting, charging or parting with the possession (whether by the holders of the lease or any under-tenant whether immediate or not) effected more than seven years before the end of the term no consent or licence shall be required, if notice in writing of the transaction is given to the lessor within six months after the transaction is effected.

(2) In all leases whether made before or after the commencement of this Act containing a covenant condition or agreement against the making of improvements without licence or consent, such covenant condition or agreement shall be deemed, notwithstanding any express provision to the contrary, to be subject to a proviso that such licence or consent is not to be unreasonably withheld; but this proviso does not preclude the right to require as a condition of such licence or consent the payment of a reasonable sum in respect of any damage to or diminution in the value of the premises or any neighbouring premises belonging to the landlord, and of any legal or other expenses properly incurred in connection with such licence or consent nor, in the case of an improvement which does not add to the letting value of the holding, does it preclude the right to require as a condition of such licence or consent, where such a requirement would be reasonable, an undertaking on the part of the tenant to reinstate the premises in the condition in which they were before the improvement was executed.

(3) In all leases whether made before or after the commencement of this Act containing a covenant condition or agreement the alteration of the user of the demised premises, without licence or consent, such covenant condition or agreement shall, if the alteration does not involve any structural alteration of the premises, be deemed, notwithstanding any express provision to the contrary, to be subject to a proviso that no fine or sum of money in the nature of a fine, whether by way of increase of rent or otherwise, shall be payable for or in respect of such licence or consent; but this proviso does not preclude the right of the landlord to require payment of a reasonable sum in respect of any damage to or diminution in the value of the premises or any neighbouring premises belonging to him and of any legal or other expenses incurred in connection with such licence or consent.

Where a dispute as to the reasonableness of any such sum has been determined by a court of competent jurisdiction, the landlord shall be found to grant the licence or consent on payment of the sum so determined to be reasonable.

(4) This section shall not apply to leases of agricultural holdings within the meaning of the Agricultural Holdings Act 1923, and paragraph (*b*) of subsection (1), subsection (2) and subsection (3) of this section shall not apply to mining leases.

LEASEHOLD PROPERTY (REPAIRS) ACT 1938

Restriction on enforcement of repairing covenants in long leases of small houses

1. (1) Where a lessor serves on a lessee under sub-section (1) of section one hundred and forty-six of the Law of Property Act 1925, a notice that relates to a breach of a covenant or agreement to keep or put in repair during the currency of the lease [all or any of the property comprised in the lease], and at the date of the service of the notice [three] years or more of the term of the lease remain unexpired, the lessee may within twenty-eight days from that date serve on the lessor a counter-notice to the effect that he claims the benefit of this Act.

(2) A right to damages for a breach of such a covenant as aforesaid shall not be enforceable by action commenced at any time at which [three] years or more of the term of the lease remain unexpired unless the lessor has served on the lessee not less than one month before the commencement of the action such a notice as is specified in subsection (1) of section one hundred and forty-six of the Law of Property Act 1925, and where a notice is served under this subsection, the lessee may, within twenty-eight days from the date of the service thereof, serve on the lessor a counter-notice to the effect that he claims the benefit of this Act.

(3) Where a counter-notice is served by a lessee under this section, then, notwithstanding anything in any enactment or rule of law, no proceedings, by action or otherwise, shall be taken by the lessor for the enforcement of any right of re-entry or forfeiture under any proviso or stipulation in the lease for breach of the covenant or agreement in question, or for damages for breach thereof, otherwise than with the leave of the court.

(4) A notice served under subsection (1) of section one hundred and forty-six of the Law of Property Act 1925, in the circumstances specified in subsection (1) of this section, and a notice served under subsection (2) of this section shall not be valid unless it contains a statement, in characters not less conspicuous than those used in any other part of the notice, to the effect that the lessee is entitled under this Act to serve on the lessor a counter-notice claiming the benefit of this Act, and a statement in the like characters specifying the time within which, and the manner in which, under this Act a counter-notice may be served and specifying the name and address for service of the lessor.

(5) Leave for the purposes of this section shall not be given unless the lessor proves:

(*a*) that the immediate remedying of the breach in question is requisite for preventing substantial diminution in the value of his reversion, or that the value thereof has been substantially diminished by the breach;

(*b*) that the immediate remedying of the breach is required for giving effect in relation to the [premises] to the purposes of any enactment, or of any byelaw or other provision having effect under an enactment, [or for giving effect to any order of a court or requirement of any authority under any enactment or any such byelaw or other provision as aforesaid];

(*c*) in a case in which the lessee is not in occupation of the whole of the [premises as respects which the covenant or agreement is proposed to be enforced], that the immediate remedying of the breach is required in the interests of the occupier of [those premises] or of part thereof;

(*d*) that the breach can be immediately remedied at an expense that is relatively small in comparison with the much greater expense that would probably be occasioned by postponement of the necessary work; or

(*e*) special circumstances which in the opinion of the court, render it just and equitable that leave should be given.

(6) The court may, in granting or in refusing leave for the purposes of this section impose such terms and conditions on the lessor or on the lessee as it may think fit.

LANDLORD AND TENANT ACT 1954

PART I
SECURITY OF TENURE FOR RESIDENTIAL TENANTS

Security of tenure for tenants under ground leases, etc.

Protection of residential tenants on termination of long tenancies at low rents

1. On the termination in accordance with the provisions of this Part of this Act of a tenancy to which this section applies the tenant shall be entitled to the protection of the [Rent Act] subject to and in accordance with those provisions.

PART II
SECURITY OF TENURE FOR BUSINESS, PROFESSIONAL AND OTHER TENANTS

Tenancies to which Part II applies

23. (1) Subject to the provisions of this Act, this Part of this Act applies to any tenancy where the property comprised in the tenancy is or includes premises which are occupied by the tenant and are so occupied for the purposes of a business carried on by him or for those and other purposes.

(2) In this Part of this Act the expression 'business' includes a trade, profession or employment and includes any activity carried on by a body of persons, whether corporate or unincorporate.

(3) In the following provisions of this Part of this Act the expression 'the holding', in relation to a tenancy to which this Part of this Act applies, means the property comprised in the tenancy, there being excluded any part thereof which is occupied neither by the tenant nor by a person employed by the tenant and so employed for the purposes of a business by reason of which the tenancy is one to which this Part of this Act applies.

Rent while tenancy continues by virtue of s.24

24A. (1) The landlord of a tenancy to which this Part of this Act applies may,

(*a*) if he has given notice under s.25 of this Act to terminate the tenancy; or

(*b*) if the tenant has made a request for a new tenancy in accordance with s.26 of this Act;

apply to the court to determine a rent which it would be reasonable for the tenant to pay while the tenancy continues by virtue of s.24 of this Act, and the court may determine a rent accordingly.

(2) A rent determined in proceedings under this section shall be deemed to be the rent payable under the tenancy from the date on which the proceedings were commenced or the date specified in the landlord's notice or the tenant's request, whichever is the later.

(3) In determining a rent under this section the court shall have regard to the rent payable under the terms of the tenancy, but otherwise subsections (1) and (2) of s.34 of this Act shall apply to the determination as they would apply to the determination of a rent under that section if a new tenancy from year to year of the whole of the property comprised in the tenancy were granted to the tenant by order of the court.

Opposition by landlord to application for a new tenancy

30. (1) The grounds on which a landlord may oppose an application under subsection (1) of s.24 of this Act are such of the following grounds as may be stated in the landlord's notice under s.25 of this Act or, as the case may be, under subsection (6) of s.26 thereof, that is to say:

(*a*) where under the current tenancy the tenant has any obligations as respects the repair and maintenance of the holding, that the tenant ought not to be granted a new tenancy in view of the state of repair of the holding, being a state resulting from the tenant's failure to comply with the said obligations;

(*b*) that the tenant ought not to be granted a new tenancy in view of his persistent delay in paying rent which has become due;

(*c*) that the tenant ought not to be granted a new tenancy in view of other substantial breaches by him of his obligations under the current tenancy, or for any other reason connected with the tenant's use or management of the holding;

(*d*) that the landlord has offered and is willing to provide or secure the provision of alternative accommodation for the tenant, that the terms on which the alternative accommodation is available are reasonable having regard to the terms of the current tenancy and to all other relevant circumstances, and that the accommodation and the time at which it will be available are suitable for the tenant's requirements (including the requirement to preserve goodwill) having regard to the nature and class of his business and to the situation and extent of, and facilities afforded by, the holding;

(*e*) where the current tenancy was created by the sub-letting of part only of the property comprised in a superior tenancy and the landlord is the owner of an interest in reversion expectant on the termination of that superior tenancy, that the aggregate of the rents reasonably obtainable on separate lettings of the holding and the remainder of that property would be substantially less than the rent reasonably obtainable on a letting of that property as a whole, that on the termination of the current tenancy the landlord requires possession of the holding for the purpose of letting or otherwise disposing of the said property as a whole, and that in view thereof the tenant ought not to be granted a new tenancy;

(*f*) that on the termination of the current tenancy the landlord intends to demolish or reconstruct the premises comprised in the holding or a substantial part of those premises or to carry out substantial work of construction on the holding or part thereof and that he could not reasonably do so without obtaining possession of the holding;

(*g*) subject as hereinafter provided, that on the termination of the current tenancy the landlord intends to occupy the holding for the purposes, or partly for the purposes, of a business to be carried on by him therein, or as his residence.

(2) The landlord shall not be entitled to oppose an application on the ground specified in paragraph (*g*) of the last foregoing subsection if the interest of the landlord, or an interest which has merged in that interest and but for the merger would be the interest of the landlord, was purchased or created after the beginning of the period of five years which ends with the termination of the current tenancy, and at all times since the purchase or creation thereof the holding has been comprised in a tenancy or successive tenancies of the description specified in subsection (1) of s.23 of this Act.

(3) Where the landlord has a controlling interest in a company any business to be carried on by the company shall be treated for the purposes of subsection (1)(*g*) of this section as a business to be carried on by him.

For the purposes of this subsection, a person has a controlling interest in a company if and only if either

(*a*) he is a member of it and able, without the consent of any other person, to appoint or remove the holders of at least a majority of the directorship; or

(*b*) he holds more than one-half of its equity share capital, there being disregarded any shares held by him in a fiduciary capacity or as nominee for another person;

and in this subsection 'company' and 'share' have the meanings assigned to them by s.455(1) of the Companies Act 1948 and 'equity share capital' the meaning assigned to it by s.154(5) of that Act.

Rent under new tenancy

34. (1) The rent payable under a tenancy granted by order of the court under this Part of this Act shall be such as may be agreed between the landlord and the tenant or as, in default of such agreement, may be determined by the court to be that at which, having regard to the terms of the tenancy (other than those relating to rent), the holding might reasonably be expected to be let in the open market by a willing lessor, there being disregarded:

(*a*) any effect on rent of the fact that the tenant has or his predecessors in title have been in occupation of the holding,

(*b*) any goodwill attached to the holding by reason of the carrying on thereat of the business of the tenant (whether by him or by a predecessor of his in that business),

[(*c*) any effect on rent of an improvement to which this paragraph applies],

(*d*) in the case of a holding comprising licensed premises, any addition to its value attributable to the licence, if it appears to the court that having regard to the terms of the current tenancy and any other relevant circumstances the benefit of the licence belongs to the tenant.

(2) Paragraph (*c*) of the foregoing subsection applies to any improvement carried out by a person who at the time it was carried out was the tenant, but only if it was carried out otherwise than in pursuance of an obligation to his immediate landlord, and either it was carried out during the current tenancy or the following conditions are satisfied, that is to say:

(*a*) that is was completed not more than twenty-one years before the application for the new tenancy was made; and

(*b*) that the holding or any part of it affected by the improvement has at all times since the completion of the improvement been comprised in tenancies of the description specified in s.23(1) of this Act; and

(*c*) that at the termination of each of those tenancies the tenant did not quit.

(3) Where the rent is determined by the court the court may, if it thinks fit, further determine that the terms of the tenancy shall include such provision for varying the rent as may be specified in the determination.

Compensation where order for new tenancy precluded on certain grounds

37. (1) Where on the making of an application under section 24 of this Act the court is precluded (whether by subsection (1) or subsection (2) of section 31 of this Act) from making an order for the grant of a new tenancy by reason of any of the grounds specified in paragraphs (*e*), (*f*) and (*g*) of subsection (1) of section 30 of this Act and not of any grounds specified in any other paragraph of that subsection [or where no other ground is specified in the landlord's notice under section 25 of this Act or, as the case may be, under section 26(6) thereof, than those specified in the said paragraphs (*e*), (*f*) and (*g*) and either no application under the said section 24 is made or such an application is withdrawn], then, subject to the provisions of this Act, the tenant shall be entitled on quitting the holding to recover from the landlord by way of compensation an amount determined in accordance with the following provisions of this section.

(2) The said amount shall be as follows, that is to say:

(*a*) where the conditions specified in the next following subsection are satisfied it shall be [the product of the appropriate multiplier and] twice the rateable value of the holding,

(*b*) in any other case it shall be [the product of the appropriate multiplier and] the rateable value of the holding.

(3) The said conditions are

(*a*) that, during the whole of the fourteen years immediately preceding the termination of the current tenancy, premises being or comprised in the holding have been occupied for the purposes of a business carried on by the occupier or for those and other purposes;

(*b*) that, if during those fourteen years there was a change in the occupier of the premises, the person who was the occupier immediately after the change was the successor to the business carried on by the person who was the occupier immediately before the change.

(4) Where the court is precluded from making an order for the grant of a new tenancy under this Part of this Act in the circumstances mentioned in subsection (1) of this section, the court shall on the application of the tenant certify that fact.

(5) For the purposes of subsection (2) of this section the rateable value of the holding shall be determined as follows:

(*a*) where in the valuation list in force at the date on which the landlord's notice under section 25 or, as the case may be, subsection (6) of section 26 of this Act is given a value is then shown as the annual value (as hereinafter defined) of the holding, the rateable value of the holding shall be taken to be that value;

(*b*) where no such value is so shown with respect to the holding but such a value or such values is or are so shown with respect to premises comprised in or comprising the holding or part of it, the rateable value of the holding shall be taken to be such value as is found by a proper apportionment or aggregation of the value or values so shown;

(*c*) where the rateable value of the holding cannot be ascertained in accordance with the foregoing paragraphs of this subsection, it shall be taken to be the value which, apart from any exemption from assessment to rates, would on a proper assessment be the value to be entered in the said valuation list as the annual value of the holding;

and any dispute arising, whether in proceedings before the court or otherwise, as to the determination for those purposes of the rateable value of the holding shall be referred to the Commissioners of Inland Revenue for decision by a valuation officer.

An appeal shall lie to the Lands Tribunal from any decision of a valuation officer under this subsection, but subject thereto any such decision shall be final.

(6) The Commissioners of Inland Revenue may by statutory instrument make rules prescribing the procedure in connection with references under this section.

(7) In this section

the reference to the termination of the current tenancy is a reference to the date of termination specified in the landlord's notice under section twenty-five of this Act or, as the case may be, the date specified in the tenant's request for a new tenancy as the date from which the new tenancy is to begin;

the expression "annual value" means rateable value except that where the rateable value differs from the new annual value the said expression means net annual value;

the expression "valuation officer" means any officer of the Commissioners of Inland Revenue for the time being authorised by a certificate of the Commissioners to act in relation to a valuation list.

[(8) In subsection (2) of this section "the appropriate multiplier" means such multiplier as the Secretary of State may by order made by statutory instrument prescribe.

(9) A statutory instrument containing an order under subsection (8) of this section shall be subject to annulment in pursuance of a resolution of either House of Parliament.]

LEASEHOLD REFORM ACT 1967

PART I
ENFRANCHISEMENT AND EXTENSION OF LONG LEASEHOLDS

Tenants entitled to enfranchisement or extension

1. (1) This Part of this Act shall have effect to confer on a tenant of a leasehold house, occupying the house as his residence, a right to acquire on fair terms the freehold or an extended lease of the house and premises where:

(*a*) his tenancy is a long tenancy at a low rent and [subject to subsections (5) and (6) below] the rateable value of the house and premises on the appropriate day is not (or was not) more than £200 or, if it is in Greater London, than £400; and

(*b*) at the relevant time (that is to say, at the time when he gives notice in accordance with this Act of his desire to have the freehold or to have an extended lease, as the case may be) he has been tenant of the house under a long tenancy at a low rent, and occupying it as his residence, for the last [three years] or for periods amounting to [three years] in the last ten years;

and to confer the like right in the other cases for which provision is made in this Part of this Act.

(2) In this Part of this Act references, in relation to any tenancy, to the tenant occupying a house as his residence shall be considered as applying where, but

only where, the tenant is, in right of the tenancy, occupying it as his only or main residence (whether or not he uses it also for other purposes); but

(*a*) references to a person occupying a house shall apply where he occupies it in part only; and

(*b*) in determining in what right the tenant occupies, there shall be disregarded any mortgage term and any interest arising in favour of any person by his attorning tenant to a mortgagee or chargee.

(3) This Part of this Act shall not confer on the tenant of a house any right by reference to his occupation of it as his residence (but shall apply as if he were not so occupying it) at any time when:

(*a*) it is let to and occupied by him with other land or premises to which it is ancillary; or

(*b*) it is comprised in an agricultural holding within the meaning of the Agricultural Holdings Act 1948.

(4) In subsection (1)(*a*) above, 'the appropriate day', in relation to any house and premises, means the 23rd March 1965 or such later day as by virtue of [s.25(3) of the Rent Act 1977] would be the appropriate day for purposes of that Act in relation to a dwelling house consisting of that house.

(4A) Schedule 8 to the Housing Act 1974 shall have effect to enable a tenant to have the rateable value of the house and premises reduced for purposes of this section in consequence of tenant's improvements.

(5) If, in relation to any house and premises, the appropriate day for the purposes of subsection (1)(*a*) above falls on or after 1st April 1973 that subsection shall have effect in relation to the house and premises:

(*a*) in a case where the tenancy was created on or before 18th February 1966, as if for the sums of £200 and £400 specified in that subsection there were substituted respectively the sums of £750 and £1500; and

(*b*) in a case where the tenancy was created after 18th February 1966, as if for those sums of £200 and £400 there were substituted respectively the sums of £500 and £1000.

(6) If, in relation to any house and premises

(*a*) the appropriate day for the purposes of subsection (1)(*a*) above falls before 1st April 1973, and

(*b*) the rateable value of the house and premises on the appropriate day was more than £200 or, if it was then in Greater London, £400, and

(*c*) the tenancy was created on or before 18th February 1966,

subsection (1)(*a*) above shall have effect in relation to the house and premises as if for the reference to the appropriate day there were substituted a reference to 1st April 1973 and as if for the sums of £200 and £400 specified in that subsection there were substituted respectively the sums of £750 and £1500.

Meaning of 'house' and 'house and premises', and adjustment of boundary

2. (1) For purposes of this Part of this Act, 'house' includes any building designed or adapted for living in and reasonably so called, notwithstanding that the building is not structurally detached, or was or is not solely designed or adapted for living in, or is divided horizontally into flats or maisonettes; and

(*a*) where a building is divided horizontally, the flats or other units into which it is so divided are not separate 'houses', though the building as a whole may be; and

(*b*) where a building is divided vertically the building as a whole is not a 'house', though any of the units into which it is divided may be.

RENT (AGRICULTURE) ACT 1976

Protected occupiers in their own right

2. (1) Where a person has, in relation to a dwelling house, a relevant licence or tenancy and the dwelling-house is in qualifying ownership, or has been in qualifying ownership at any time during the subsistence of the licence or tenancy (whether it was at the time a relevant licence or tenancy or not), he shall be a protected occupier of the dwelling-house if:

(*a*) he is a qualifying worker, or

(*b*) he has been a qualifying worker at any time during the subsistence of the licence or tenancy (whether it was at the time a relevant licence or tenancy or not).

(2) Where a person has, in relation to a dwelling-house, a relevant licence or tenancy and the dwelling-house is in qualifying ownership, or has been in qualifying ownership at any time during the subsistence of the licence or tenancy (whether it was at the time a relevant licence or tenancy or not), he shall be a protected occupier of the dwelling-house if and so long as he is incapable of whole-time work in agriculture, or work in agriculture as a permit worker, in consequence of a qualifying injury or disease.

(3) A person who has in relation to a dwelling-house a relevant licence or tenancy shall be a protected occupier of the dwelling-house if:

(*a*) immediately before the licence or tenancy was granted, he was a protected occupier or statutory tenant of the dwelling-house in his own right, or

(*b*) the licence or tenancy was granted in consideration of his giving up possession of another dwelling-house of which he was such an occupier or such a tenant.

(4) In this Act

'protected occupier in his own right' means a person who is a protected occupier by virtue of subsection (1), (2) or (3) above;

'statutory tenant in his own right' means a person who is a statutory tenant by virtue of s.4(1) below and who, immediately before he became such a tenant, was a protected occupier in his own right.

RENT ACT 1977

PART I
PRELIMINARY
PROTECTED AND STATUTORY TENANCIES

Protected tenants and tenancies

1. Subject to this Part of this Act, a tenancy under which a dwelling-house (which may be a house or part of a house) is let as a separate dwelling is a protected tenancy for the purposes of this Act.

Any reference in this Act to a protected tenant shall be construed accordingly.

Statutory tenants and tenancies

2. (1) Subject to this Part of this Act:

(*a*) after the termination of a protected tenancy of a dwelling-house the person who, immediately before that termination, was the protected tenant of the dwelling-house shall, if and so long as he occupies the dwelling-house as his residence, be the statutory tenant of it.

Exceptions

Dwelling-houses above certain rateable values

4. (1) A tenancy is not a protected tenancy if the dwelling-house falls within one of the Classes set out in subsection (2) below.

(2) Where alternative rateable values are mentioned in this subsection, the higher applies if the dwelling-house is in Greater London and the lower applies if it is elsewhere.

Class A

The appropriate day in relation to the dwelling-house falls or fell on or after 1st April 1973 and the dwelling-house on the appropriate day has or had a rateable value exceeding £1500 or £750.

Class B

The appropriate day in relation to the dwelling-house fell on or after 22nd March 1973, but before 1st April 1973, and the dwelling-house

(*a*) on the appropriate day had a rateable value exceeding £600 or £300, and

(*b*) on 1st April 1973 had a rateable value exceeding £1500 or £750.

Class C

The appropriate day in relation to the dwelling-house fell before 22nd March 1973 and the dwelling-house

(*a*) on the appropriate day had a rateable value exceeding £400 or £200, and

(*b*) on 22nd March 1973 had a rateable value exceeding £600 or £300, and

(*c*) on 1st April 1973 had a rateable value exceeding £1500 or £750.

(3) If any question arises in any proceedings whether a dwelling-house falls within a Class in subsection (2) above, by virtue of its rateable value at any time, it shall be deemed not to fall within that Class unless the contrary is shown.

Tenancies at low rents

5. (1) A tenancy is not a protected tenancy if under the tenancy either no rent is payable or, ... the rent payable is less than two-thirds of the rateable value which is or was the rateable value of the dwelling-house on the appropriate day.

(2) Where

(*a*) the appropriate day in relation to a dwelling-house fell before 22nd March 1973, and

(*b*) the dwelling-house had on the appropriate day a rateable value exceeding, if it is in Greater London, £400 or, if it is elsewhere, £200, subsection (1) above shall apply in relation to the dwelling-house as if the reference to the appropriate day were a reference to 22nd March 1973.

(3) In this Act a tenancy falling within subsection (1) above, is referred to as a 'tenancy at a low rent'.

(4) In determining whether a long tenancy is a tenancy at a low rent, there shall be disregarded such part (if any) of the sums payable by the tenant as is expressed (in whatever terms) to be payable in respect of rates, services, repairs, maintenance, or insurance, unless it could not have been regarded by the parties as a part so payable.

(5) In subsection (4) above 'long tenancy' means a tenancy granted for a term certain exceeding 21 years, other than a tenancy which is, or may become, terminable before the end of that term by notice given to the tenant.

5A. (1) A tenancy is not a protected tenancy if it is a qualifying shared ownership lease, that is:

(*a*) a lease granted in pursuance of the right to be granted a shared ownership lease under Part V of the Housing Act 1985, or

(*b*) a lease granted by a housing association and which complies with the conditions set out in subsection (2) below.

(2) The conditions referred to in subsection (1)(*b*) above are that the lease:

(*a*) was granted for a term of 99 years or more and is not (and cannot become) terminable except in pursuance of a provision for re-entry or forfeiture;

(*b*) was granted at a premium, calculated by reference to the value of the dwelling-house or the cost of providing it, of not less than 25 per cent, or such other percentage as may be prescribed, of the figure by reference to which it was calculated;

(*c*) provides for the tenant to acquire additional shares in the dwelling-house on terms specified in the lease and complying with such requirements as may be prescribed;

(*d*) does not restrict the tenant's powers to assign, mortgage or charge his interest in the dwelling-house;

(*e*) if it enables the landlord to require payment for outstanding shares in the dwelling-house, does so only in such circumstances as may be prescribed;

(*f*) provides, in the case of a house, for the tenant to acquire the landlord's interest on terms specified in the lease and complying with such requirements as may be prescribed; and

(*g*) states the landlord's opinion that by virtue of this section the lease is excluded from the operation of this Act.

(3) The Secretary of State may by regulations prescribe anything requiring to be prescribed for the purposes of subsection (2) above.

(4) The regulations may:

(*a*) make different provision for different cases or descriptions of case, including different provision for different areas, and

(*b*) contain such incidental, supplementary or transitional provisions as the Secretary of State considers appropriate,

and shall be made by statutory instrument which shall be subject to annulment in pusuance of a resolution of either House of Parliament.

(5) In any proceedings the court may, if of opinion that it is just and equitable to do so, treat a lease as a qualifying shared ownership lease notwithstanding that the condition specified in subsection (2)(*g*) above is not satisfied.

(6) In this section:

"house" has the same meaning as in Part I of the Leasehold Reform Act 1967;

"housing association" has the same meaning as in the Housing Associations Act 1985; and

"lease" includes an agreement for a lease, and references to the grant of a lease shall be construed accordingly.

Dwelling-houses let with other land

6. Subject to s.26 of this Act, a tenancy is not a protected tenancy if the dwelling-house which is subject to the tenancy is let together with land other than the site of the dwelling-house.

Payments for board or attendance

7. (1) A tenancy is not a protected tenancy if under the tenancy the dwelling-house is bona fide let at a rent which includes payments in respect of board or attendance.

(2) For the purposes of subsection (1) above, a dwelling-house shall not be taken to be bona fide let at a rent which includes payments in respect of attendance unless the amount of rent which is fairly attributable to attendance, having regard to the value of the attendance to the tenant, forms a substantial part of the whole rent.

Lettings to students

8. (1) A tenancy is not a protected tenancy if it is granted to a person who is pursuing, or intends to pursue, a course of study provided by a specified educational institution and is so granted by that institution or by another specified institution or body of persons.

(2) In subsection (1) above 'specified' means specified, or of a class specified, for the purposes of this section by regulations made by the Secretary of State by statutory instrument.

(3) A statutory instrument containing any such regulations shall be subject to annulment in pursuance of a resolution of either House of Parliament.

Holiday lettings

9. A tenancy is not a protected tenancy if the purpose of the tenancy is to confer on the tenant the right to occupy the dwelling-house for a holiday.

Agricultural holdings

10. A tenancy is not a protected tenancy if the dwelling-house is comprised in an agricultural holding (within the meaning of the Agricultural Holdings Act 1948) and is occupied by the person responsible for the control (whether as tenant or as servant or agent of the tenant) of the farming of the holding.

Licensed premises

11. A tenancy of a dwelling-house which consists of or comprises premises licensed for the sale of intoxicating liquors for consumption on the premises shall not be a protected tenancy, nor shall such a dwelling-house be the subject of a statutory tenancy.

Resident landlords

12. (1) Subject to subsection (2) below, a tenancy of a dwelling-house granted on or after 14th August 1974 shall not be a protected tenancy at any time if:

[(*a*) the dwelling-house forms part only of a building and, except in a case where the dwelling-house also forms part of a flat, the building is not a purpose-built block of flats; and

(*b*) the tenancy was granted by a person who, at the time when he granted it, occupied as his residence another dwelling-house which

(i) in the case mentioned in paragraph (*a*) above, also forms part of the flat; or

(ii) in any other case, also forms part of the building; and

(*c*) subject to paragraph 1 of Schedule 2 to this Act, at all times since the tenancy was granted the interest of the landlord under the tenancy has belonged to a person who, at the time he owned that interest, occupied as his residence another dwelling-house which

(i) in the case mentioned in paragraph (*a*) above, also formed part of the flat; or

(ii) in any other case, also formed part of the building

[(2) This section does not apply to a tenancy of a dwelling-house which forms part of a building if the tenancy is granted to a person who, immediately before it was granted, was a protected or statutory tenant of that dwelling-house or of any other dwelling-house in that building.]

(3)...

(4) Schedule 2 to this Act shall have effect for the purpose of supplementing this section.

Miscellaneous

Rateable value and meaning of 'appropriate day'

25. (1) Except where this Act otherwise provides, the rateable value on any day of a dwelling-house shall be ascertained for the purposes of this Act as follows:

(*a*) if the dwelling-house is a hereditament for which a rateable value is then shown in the valuation list, it shall be that rateable value;

(*b*) if the dwelling-house forms part only of such a hereditament or consists of or forms part of more than one such hereditament, its rateable value shall be taken to be such value as is found by a proper apportionment or aggregation of the rateable value or values so shown.

(2) Any questions arising under this section as to the proper apportionment or aggregation of any value or values shall be determined by the county court, and the decision of the county court shall be final.

(3) In this Act 'the appropriate day'

(*a*) in relation to any dwelling-house which, on 23rd March 1965, was or formed part of a hereditament for which a rateable value was shown in the valuation list then in force, or consisted or formed part of more than one such hereditament, means that date, and

(*b*) in relation to any other dwelling-house, means the date on which such a value is or was first shown in the valuation list.

(4) Where, after the date which is the appropriate day in relation to any dwelling-house, the valuation list is altered so as to vary the rateable value of the

hereditament of which the dwelling-house consists or forms part and the alteration has effect from a date not later than the appropriate day, the rateable value of the dwelling-house on the appropriate day shall be ascertained as if the value shown in the valuation list on the appropriate day had been the value shown in the list as altered.

(5) This section applies in relation to any other land as it applies in relation to a dwelling-house.

Land and premises let with dwelling house

26. (1) For the purposes of this Act, any land or premises let together with a dwelling-house shall, unless it consists of agricultural land exceeding 2 acres in extent, be treated as part of the dwelling-house.

Determination of fair rent

70. (1) In determining, for the purposes of this Part of this Act, what rent is or would be a fair rent under a regulated tenancy of a dwelling-house, regard shall be had to all the circumstances (other than personal circumstances) and in particular to:

(*a*) the age, character, locality and state of repair of the dwelling-house,

(*b*) if any furniture is provided for use under the tenancy, the quantity, quality and condition of the furniture; and

(*c*) any premium, or sum in the nature of a premium, which has been or may be lawfully required or received on the grant, renewal, continuance or assignment of the tenancy.

(2) For the purposes of the determination it shall be assumed that the number of persons seeking to become tenants of similar dwelling-houses in the locality on the terms (other than those relating to rent) of the regulated tenancy is not substantially greater than the number of such dwelling-houses in the locality which are available for letting on such terms.

(3) There shall be disregarded:

(*a*) any disrepair or other defect attributable to a failure by the tenant under the regulated tenancy or any predecessor in title of his to comply with any terms thereof;

(*b*) any improvement carried out, otherwise than in pursuance of the terms of the tenancy, by the tenant under the regulated tenancy or any predecessor in title of his;

(*c*),(*d*) ...

(*e*) if any furniture is provided for use under the regulated tenancy, any improvement to the furniture by the tenant under the regulated tenancy or any predecessor in title of his or, as the case may be, any deterioration in the condition of the furniture due to any ill-treatment by the tenant, any person residing or lodging with him, or any subtenant of his.

(4) In this section 'improvement' includes the replacement of any fixture or fitting.

(4A) In this section "premium" has the same meaning as in Part IX of this Act, and "sum in the nature of a premium" means:

(*a*) any such loan as is mentioned in section 119 or 120 of this Act,

...

Part VII
Security of Tenure

Limitations on recovery of possession of dwelling-houses let on protected tenancies or subject to statutory tenancies

Grounds for possession of certain dwelling-houses

98. (1) Subject to this Part of this Act, a court shall not make an order for possession of a dwelling-house which is for the time being let on a protected tenancy or subject to a statutory tenancy unless the court considers it reasonable to make such an order and either:

(*a*) the court is satisfied that suitable alternative accommodation is available for the tenant or will be available for him when the order in question takes effect, or

(*b*) the circumstances are as specified in any of the Cases in Part 1 of Schedule 15 of this Act.

(2) If, apart from subsection (1) above, the landlord would be entitled to recover possession of a dwelling-house which is for the time being let on or subject to a regulated tenancy, the court shall make an order for possession if the circumstances of the case are as specified in any of the Cases in Part II of Schedule 15.

SCHEDULE 15

Section 98

Grounds for Possession of Dwelling-Houses Let on or Subject to Protected or Statutory Tenancies

Part I Cases In Which Court May Order Possession

Case 1

Where any rent lawfully due from the tenant has not been paid, or any obligation of the protected or statutory tenancy which arises under this Act, or

(*a*) in the case of a protected tenancy, and other obligation of the tenancy, in so far as is consistent with the provisions of Part VII of this Act, or

(*b*) in the case of a statutory tenancy, any other obligation of the previous protected tenancy which is applicable to the statutory tenancy.

has been broken or not performed.

Case 2

Where the tenant or any person residing or lodging with him or any sub-tenant of his has been guilty of conduct which is a nuisance or annoyance to adjoining occupiers, or has been convicted of using the dwelling-house or allowing the dwelling-house to be used for immoral or illegal purposes.

Case 3

Where the condition of the dwelling-house has, in the opinion of the court, deteriorated owing to acts of waste by, or the neglect or default of, the tenant or any person residing or lodging with him or any sub-tenant of his and, in the case of any act of waste by, or the neglect or default of, a person lodging with the tenant or a sub-tenant of his, where the court is satisfied that the tenant has not, before the making of the order in question, taken such steps as he ought reasonably to have taken for the removal of the lodger or sub-tenant, as the case may be.

Case 4

Where the condition of any furniture provided for use under the tenancy has, in the opinion of the court, deteriorated owing to ill-treatment by the tenant or any person residing or lodging with him or any sub-tenant of his and, in the case of any ill-treatment by a person lodging with the tenant or a sub-tenant of his, where the court is satisfied that the tenant has not, before the making of the order in question, taken such steps as he ought reasonably to have taken for the removal of the lodger or sub-tenant, as the case may be.

Case 5

Where the tenant has given notice to quit and, in consequence of that notice, the landlord has contracted to sell or let the dwelling-house or has taken any other steps as the result of which he would, in the opinion of the court, be seriously prejudiced if he could not obtain possession.

Case 6

Where, without the consent of the landlord, the tenant has, at any time after

(*a*) ...
(*b*) 22nd March 1973, in the case of a tenancy which became a regulated tenancy by virtue of s.14 of the Counter-Inflation Act 1973
[(*bb*) the commencement of s.73 of the Housing Act 1980, in the case of a tenancy which became a regulated tenancy by virtue of that section.]
(*c*) 14th August 1974, in the case of a regulated furnished tenancy; or
(*d*) 8th December 1965, in the case of any other tenancy,

assigned or sublet the whole of the dwelling-house or sublet part of the dwelling-house, the remainder being already sublet.

Case 8

Where the dwelling-house is reasonably required by the landlord for occupation as a residence for some person engaged in his whole-time employment, or in the whole-time employment of some tenant from him or with whom, conditional on housing being provided, a contract for such employment has been entered into, and the tenant was in the employment of the landlord or a former landlord, and the dwelling-house was let to him in consequence of that employment and he has ceased to be in that employment.

Case 9

Where the dwelling-house is reasonably required by the landlord for occupation as a residence for:

(*a*) himself, or
(*b*) any son or daughter of his over 18 years of age, or
(*c*) his father or mother, or
(*d*) if the dwelling-house is let on or subject to a regulated tenancy, the father or mother of his wife or husband.

and the landlord did not become landlord by purchasing the dwelling-house or any interest therein after

(i) 7th November 1956, in the case of a [tenancy which was then a controlled tenancy];

(ii) 8th March 1973, in the case of a tenancy which became a regulated tenancy by virtue of s.14 of the Counter-Inflation Act 1973;

(iii) 24th May 1974, in the case of a regulated furnished tenancy; or

(iv) 23rd March 1965, in the case of any other tenancy.

Case 10

Where the court is satisfied that the rent charged by the tenant

(*a*) for any sublet part of the dwelling-house which is a dwelling-house let on a protected tenancy or subject to a statutory tenancy is or was in excess of the maximum rent for the time being recoverable for that part, having regard to ... Part III of this Act, or

(*b*) for any sublet part of the dwelling-house which is subject to a restricted contract is or was in excess of the maximum (if any) which it is lawful for the lessor, within the meaning of Part V of this Act, to require or receive having regard to the provisions of that Part.

Part II Cases In Which Court Must Order Possession Where Dwelling-House Subject to Regulated Tenancy

Case 11

Where a person who occupied the dwelling-house as his residence (in this Case referred to as 'the owner-occupier') let it on a regulated tenancy and

(*a*) not later than the relevant date the landlord gave notice in writing to the tenant that possession might be recovered under this Case, and

(*b*) the dwelling-house has not, since

(i) 22nd March 1973, in the case of a tenancy which became a regulated tenancy by virtue of s.14 of the Counter-Inflation Act 1973;

(ii) 14th August 1974, in the case of a regulated furnished tenancy; or

(iii) 8th December 1965, in the case of any other tenancy,

been let by the owner-occupier on a protected tenancy with respect to which the condition mentioned in paragraph (*a*) above was not satisfied, and

(*c*) the court is of the opinion that of the conditions set out in Part V of this Schedule one of those in paragraphs (*a*) and (*c*) to (*f*) is satisfied.

If the court is of the opinion that, notwithstanding that the condition in paragraph (*a*) or (*b*) above is not complied with, it is just and equitable to make an order for possession of the dwelling-house, the court may dispense with the requirements of either or both of those paragraphs, as the case may require.

The giving of a notice before 14th August 1974 under s.79 of the Rent Act 1968 shall be treated, in the case of a regulated furnished tenancy, as compliance with paragraph (*a*) of this Case.

Case 12

Where the landlord (in this Case referred to as 'the owner') intends to occupy the dwelling-house as his residence at such time as he might retire from regular employment and has let it on a regulated tenancy before he has so retired and

(*a*) not later than the relevant date the landlord gave notice in writing to the tenant that possession might be recovered under this Case, and (*b*) the dwelling-house has not, since 14th August 1974, been let by the owner on a protected tenancy with respect to which the condition mentioned in paragraph (*a*) above was not satisfied; and

(*c*) the court is of the opinion that of the conditions set out in Part V of this Schedule one of those in paragraphs (*b*) to (*e*) is satisfied.

If the court is of the opinion that, notwithstanding that the condition in paragraph (*a*) or (*b*) above is not complied with, it is just and equitable to make an order for possession of the dwelling-house, the court may dispense with the requirements of either or both of those paragraphs, as the case may require.

Case 13

Where a dwelling-house is let under a tenancy for a term of years certain not exceeding 8 months and

(*a*) not later than the relevant date the landlord gave notice in writing to the tenant that possession might be recovered under this Case; and

(*b*) the dwelling-house was, at some time within the period of 12 months ending on the relevant date, occupied under a right to occupy it for a holiday.

For the purposes of this Case a tenancy shall be treated as being for a term of years certain notwithstanding that it is liable to determination by re-entry or on the happening of any event other than the giving of notice by the landlord to determine the term.

Case 14

Where the dwelling-house is let under a tenancy for a term of years certain not exceeding 12 months and

(*a*) not later than the relevant date the landlord gave notice in writing to the tenant that possession might be recovered under this Case; and

(*b*) at some time within the period of 12 months ending on the relevant date, the dwelling-house was subject to such a tenancy as is referred to in s.8(1) of this Act.

For the purposes of this Case a tenancy shall be treated as being for a term of years certain notwithstanding that it is liable to determination by re-entry or on the happening of any event other than the giving of notice by the landlord to determine the term.

Case 15

Where the dwelling-house is held for the purpose of being available for occupation by a minister of religion as a residence from which to perform the duties of his office and

(*a*) not later than the relevant date the tenant was given notice in writing that possession might be recovered under this Case, and

(*b*) the court is satisfied that the dwelling-house is required for occupation by a minister of religion as such a residence.

Case 16

Where the dwelling-house was at any time occupied by a person under the terms of his employment as a person employed in agriculture, and

(*a*) the tenant neither is nor at any time was so employed by the landlord and is not the widow of a person who was so employed, and

(*b*) not later than the relevant date, the tenant was given notice in writing that possession might be recovered under this Case, and (*c*) the court is satisfied that the dwelling-house is required for occupation by a person employed, or to be employed, by the landlord in agriculture.

For the purposes of this Case 'employed', 'employment' and 'agriculture' have the same meanings as in the Agricultural Wages Act 1948.

Case 17

Where proposals for amalgamation, approved for the purposes of a scheme under s.26 of the Agriculture Act 1967, have been carried out and, at the time when the proposals were submitted, the dwelling-house was occupied by a person responsible (whether as owner, tenant, or servant or agent of another) for the control of the farming of any part of the land comprised in the amalgamation and

(*a*) after the carrying out of the proposals, the dwelling-house was let on a regulated tenancy otherwise than to, or to the widow of, either a person ceasing to be so responsible as part of the amalgamation or a person who is, or at any time was, employed by the landlord in agriculture, and

(*b*) not later than the relevant date the tenant was given notice in writing that possession might be recovered under this Case, and

(*c*) the court is satisfied that the dwelling-house is required for occupation by a person employed, or to be employed, by the landlord in agriculture, and

(*d*) the proceedings for possession are commenced by the landlord at any time during the period of 5 years beginning with the date on which the proposals for the amalgamation were approved or, if occupation of the dwelling-house after the amalgamation continued in, or was first taken by, a person ceasing to be responsible as mentioned in paragraph (*a*) above or his widow, during a period expiring 3 years after the date on which the dwelling-house next became unoccupied.

For the purposes of this Case 'employed' and 'agriculture' have the same meanings as in the Agricultural Wages Act 1948 and 'amalgamation' has the same meaning as in Part II of the Agriculture Act 1967.

Case 18

Where

(*a*) the last occupier of the dwelling-house before the relevant date was a person, or the widow of a person, who was at some time during his occupation responsible (whether as owner, tenant, or servant or agent of another) for the control of the farming of land which formed, together with the dwelling-house, an agricultural unit within the meaning of the Agriculture Act 1947, and

(*b*) the tenant is neither

(i) a person, or the widow of a person, who is or has at any time been responsible for the control of the farming of any part of the said land, nor

(ii) a person, or the widow of a person, who is or at any time was employed by the landlord in agriculture, and

(*c*) the creation of the tenancy was not preceded by the carrying out in connection with any of the said land of an amalgamation approved for the purposes of a scheme under s.26 of the Agriculture Act 1967, and

(*d*) not later than the relevant date the tenant was given notice in writing that possession might be recovered under this Case, and (*e*) the court is satisfied that the dwelling-house is required for occupation either by a person responsible or to be responsible (whether as owner, tenant, or servant or agent of another) for the control of the farming of any part of the said land or by a person employed or to be employed by the landlord in agriculture, and

(*f*) in a case where the relevant date was before 9th August 1972, the proceedings for possession are commenced by the landlord before the expiry of 5 years from the date on which the occupier referred to in paragraph (*a*) above went out of occupation.

For the purposes of this Case 'employed' and 'agriculture' have the same meanings as in the Agricultural Wages Act 1948 and 'amalgamation' has the same meaning as in Part II of the Agriculture Act 1967.

Case 19

Where thc dwelling-house was let under a protected shorthold tenancy (or is treated under s.55 of the Housing Act 1980 as having been so let) and

(*a*) there either has been no grant of a further tenancy of the dwelling-house since the end of the protected shorthold tenancy or, if there was such a grant, it was to a person who immediately before the grant was in possession of the dwelling-house as a protected or statutory tenant; and

(*b*) the proceedings for possession were commenced after appropriate notice by the landlord to the tenant and not later than 3 months after the expiry of the notice.

A notice is appropriate for this Case if

(i) it is in writing and states that proceedings for possession under this Case may be brought after its expiry; and

(ii) it expires not earlier than 3 months after it is served nor, if, when it is served, the tenancy is a periodic tenancy, before that periodic tenancy could be brought to an end by a notice to quit served by the landlord on the same day;

(iii) it is served

(*a*) in the period of 3 months immediately preceding the date on which the protected shorthold tenancy comes to an end; or

(*b*) if that date has passed, in the period of 3 months immediately preceding any anniversary of that date; and

(iv) in a case where a previous notice has been served by the landlord on the tenant in respect of the dwelling-house, and that notice was an appropriate notice, it is served not earlier than 3 months after the expiry of the previous notice.

Case 20

Where the dwelling-house was let by a person (in this Case referred to as 'the owner') at any time after the commencement of s.67 of the Housing Act 1980 and

(*a*) at the time when the owner acquired the dwelling-house he was a member of the regular armed forces of the Crown;

(*b*) at the relevant date the owner was a member of the regular armed forces of the Crown;

(*c*) not later than the relevant date the owner gave notice in writing to the tenant that possession might be recovered under this Case;

(*d*) the dwelling-house has not, since the commencement of s.67 of the Act of 1980, been let by the owner on a protected tenancy with respect to which the condition mentioned in paragraph (*c*) above was not satisfied; and

(*e*) the court is of the opinion that

(i) the dwelling-house is required as a residence for the owner; or

(ii) of the conditions set out in Part V of this Schedule one of those in paragraphs (*c*) to (*f*) is satisfied.

If the court is of the opinion that, notwithstanding that the condition in paragraph (*c*) or (*d*) above is not complied with, it is just and equitable to make an order for possession of the dwelling-house, the court may dispense with the requirements of either or both of these paragraphs, as the case may require.

For the purposes of this Case 'regular armed forces of the Crown' has the same meaning as in s.1 of the House of Commons Disqualification Act 1975.

Part IV Suitable Alternative Accommodation

5.(1) For the purposes of paragraph 4 above, the relevant conditions are that the accommodation is reasonably suitable to the needs of the tenant and his family as regards proximity to place of work, and either:

(*a*) similar as regards rental and extent to the accommodation afforded by dwelling-houses provided in the neighbourhood by any housing authority for the persons whose needs as regards extent are, in the opinion of the court, similar to those of the tenant and of his family; or

(*b*) reasonably suitable to the means of the tenant and to the needs of the tenant and his family as regards extent and character; and

that if any furniture was provided for use under the protected or statutory tenancy in question, furniture is provided for use in the accommodation which is either similar to that so provided or is reasonably suitable to the needs of the tenant and his family.

(2) For the purposes of sub-paragraph (1)(*a*) above, a certificate of a housing authority stating:

(*a*) the extent of the accommodation afforded by dwelling-houses provided by the authority to meet the needs of tenants with families of such number as may be specified in the certificate, and

(*b*) the amount of the rent charged by the authority for dwelling-houses affording accommodation of that extent,

shall be conclusive evidence of the facts so stated.

PROTECTION FROM EVICTION ACT 1977

PART I

UNLAWFUL EVICTION AND HARASSMENT

Unlawful eviction and harassment of occupier

1. (1)...

(2) If any person unlawfully deprives the residential occupier of any premises of his occupation of the premises or any part thereof, or attempts to do so, he shall be guilty of an offence unless he proves that he believed, and had

reasonable cause to believe, that the residential occupier had ceased to reside in the premises.

Part II
Notice to Quit

Validity of notices to quit

5. (1) No notice by a landlord or a tenant to quit any premises let (whether before or after the commencement of this Act) as a dwelling shall be valid unless
(*a*) it is in writing and contains such information as may be prescribed, and
(*b*) it is given not less than 4 weeks before the date on which it is to take effect.

(2) In this section 'prescribed' means prescribed by regulations made by the Secretary of State by statutory instrument, and a statutory instrument containing any such regulations shall be subject to annulment in pursuance of a resolution of either House of Parliament.

(3) Regulations under this section may make different provision in relation to different descriptions of lettings and different circumstances.

HOUSING ACT 1980

Protected shorthold tenancies

52. (1) A protected shorthold tenancy is a protected tenancy granted after the commencement of this section which is granted for a term certain of not less than one year nor more than five years and satisfies the following conditions, that is to say,
(*a*) it cannot be brought to an end by the landlord before the expiry of the term, except in pursuance of a provision for re-entry or forfeiture for non-payment of rent or breach of any other obligation of the tenancy; and
(*b*) before the grant the landlord has given the tenant a valid notice stating that the tenancy is to be a protected shorthold tenancy; and
(*c*) either a rent for the dwelling-house is registered at the time the tenancy is granted or:
(i) a certificate of fair rent has, before the grant, been issued under s.69 of the 1977 Act in respect of the dwelling-house and the rent payable under the tenancy, for any period before a rent is registered for the dwelling-house, does not exceed the rent specified in the certificate; and
(ii) an application for the registration of a rent for the dwelling-house is made not later than 28 days after the beginning of the term and is not withdrawn.

(2) A tenancy of a dwelling-house is not a protected shorthold tenancy if it is granted to a person who, immediately before it was granted, was a protected or statutory tenant of that dwelling-house.

Assured tenancies

56. (1) A tenancy under which a dwelling-house is let as a separate dwelling is an assured tenancy and not a housing association tenancy (within the meaning of s.86 of the 1977 Act) or a protected tenancy if:

(*a*) the conditions described in section 56A or 56B are satisfied,

(*b*) the interest of the landlord has, since the creation of the tenancy, belonged to an approved body, and

(*c*) the tenancy would, when created, have been a protected tenancy or, as the case may be, a housing association tenancy but for this section.

(2) In this Part of this Act 'assured tenant' means the tenant under an assured tenancy ....

(4) In this Part of this Act 'approved body' means a body, or one of a description of bodies, for the time being specified for the purposes of this Part of this Act in an order made by the Secretary of State.

56A. The first set of conditions referred to in section 56(1)(*a*) above is that:

(*a*) the dwelling-house is, or forms part of, a building which was erected (and on which construction work first began) on or after 8th August 1980, and

(*b*) before the tenant first occupied the dwelling-house under the tenancy, no part of it had been occupied by any person as his residence except under an assured tenancy.

56B. (1) The second set of conditions referred to in section 56(1)(*a*) above is that:

(*a*) qualifying works have been carried out (whether before or after the commencement of this section),

(*b*) the dwelling-house is (or was) fit for human habitation at the relevant date, and

(*c*) since the qualifying works were carried out no part of the dwelling-house has been occupied by any person as his residence except under an assured tenancy,

and, in the case of the first relevant tenancy, that the person (or persons) to whom the tenancy is granted is not (or do not include) a person who was a secure occupier of the dwelling-house before the works were carried out.

LANDLORD AND TENANT ACT 1985

Implied terms as to fitness for human habitation

8. (1) In a contract to which this section applies for the letting of a house for human habitation there is implied, notwithstanding any stipulation to the contrary:

(*a*) a condition that the house is fit for human habitation at the commencement of the tenancy, and

(*b*) an undertaking that the house will be kept by the landlord fit for human habitation during the tenancy.

(2) The landlord, or a person authorised by him in writing, may at reasonable times of the day, on giving 24 hours' notice in writing to the tenant or occupier, enter premises to which this section applies for the purpose of viewing their state and condition.

(3) This section applies to a contract if:

(*a*) the rent does not exceed the figure applicable in accordance with subsection (4), and

(*b*) the letting is not on such terms as to the tenant's responsibility as are mentioned in subsection (5).

(4) The rent limit for the application of this section is shown by the following table, by reference to the date of making of the contract and the situation of the premises:

Table

Date of making of contract	*Rent limit*
Before 31st July 1923	In London: £40 Elsewhere: £26 or £16 (see Note 1)
On or after 31st July 1923 and before 6th July 1957	In London: £40 Elsewhere: £26
On or after 6th July 1957	In London: £80 Elsewhere: £52

Notes

1. The applicable figure for contracts made before 31st July 1923 is £26 in the case of premises situated in a borough or urban district which at the date of the contract had according to the last published census a population of 50,000 or more. In the case of a house situated elsewhere, the figure is £16.

2. The references to 'London' are, in relation to contracts made before 1st April 1965, to the administrative county of London and, in relation to contracts made on or after that date, to Greater London exclusive of the outer London boroughs.

(5) This section does not apply where a house is let for a term of three years or more (the lease not being determinable at the option of either party before the expiration of three years) upon terms that the tenant puts the premises into a condition reasonably fit for human habitation.

(6) In this section 'house' includes

(*a*) a part of a house, and

(*b*) any yard, garden, outhouses and appurtenances belonging to the house or usually enjoyed with it.

Repairing Obligations

Repairing obligations in short leases

11. (1) In a lease to which this section applies (as to which, see s.13 and 14) there is implied a covenant by the lessor

(*a*) to keep in repair the structure and exterior of the dwelling-house (including drains, gutters and external pipes),

(*b*) to keep in repair and proper working order the installations in the dwelling-house for the supply of water, gas and electricity and for sanitation (including basins, sinks, baths and sanitary conveniences, but not other fixtures, fittings and appliances for making use of the supply of water, gas or electricity), and

(*c*) to keep in repair and proper working order the installations in the dwelling-house for space heating and heating water.

(2) The covenant implied by subsection (1) ('the lessor's repairing covenant') shall not be construed as requiring the lessor

(*a*) to carry out works or repairs for which the lessee is liable by virtue of his duty to use the premises in a tenant-like manner, or would be so liable but for an express covenant on his part

(*b*) to rebuild or reinstate the premises in the case of destruction or damage by fire, or by tempest, flood or other inevitable accident, or

(*c*) to keep in repair or maintain anything which the lessee is entitled to remove from the dwelling-house.

(3) In determining the standard of repair required by the lessor's repairing covenant, regard shall be had to the age, character and prospective life of the dwelling-house and the locality in which it is situated.

(4) A covenant by the lessee for the repair of the premises is of no effect so far as it relates to the matters mentioned in subsection (1)(*a*) to (*c*), except so far as it imposes on the lessee any of the requirements mentioned in subsection (2)(*a*) or (*c*).

(5) The reference in subsection (4) to a covenant by the lessee for the repair of the premises includes a covenant

(*a*) to put in repair or deliver up in repair,

(*b*) to paint, point or render,

(*c*) to pay money in lieu of repairs by the lessee, or

(*d*) to pay money on account of repairs by the lessor.

(6) In a lease in which the lessor's repairing covenant is implied there is also implied a covenant by the lessee that the lessor, or any person authorised by him in writing, may at reasonable times of the day and on giving 24 hours' notice in writing to the occupier, enter the premises comprised in the lease for the purpose of viewing their condition and state of repair.

Restriction on contracting out of s.11

12. (1) A covenant or agreement, whether contained in a lease to which s.11 applies or in an agreement collateral to such a lease, is void in so far as it purports

(*a*) to exclude or limit the obligations of the lessor or the immunities of the lessee under that section, or

(*b*) to authorise any forfeiture or impose on the lessee any penalty, disability or obligation in the event of his enforcing or relying upon those obligations or immunities,

unless the inclusion of the provision was authorised by the county court.

(2) The county court may, by order made with the consent of the parties, authorise the inclusion in a lease, or in an agreement collateral to a lease, of provisions excluding or modifying in relation to the lease, the provisions of s.11 with respect to the repairing obligations of the parties if it appears to the court that it is reasonable to do so, having regard to all the circumstances of the case, including the other terms and conditions of the lease.

Leases to which s.11 applies: general rule

13. (1) Section 11 (repairing obligations) applies to a lease of a dwelling-house granted on or after 24th October 1961 for a term of less than seven years.

(2) In determining whether a lease is one to which s.11 applies

(*a*) any part of the term which falls before the grant shall be left out of account and the lease shall be treated as a lease for a term commencing with the grant, (*b*) a lease which is determinable at the option of the lessor before the expiration of seven years from the commencement of the term shall be treated as a lease for a term of less than seven years, and

(*c*) a lease (other than a lease to which paragraph (*b*) applies) shall not be treated as a lease for a term of less than seven years if it confers on the lessee an option for renewal for a term which, together with the original term, amounts to seven years or more.

(3) This section has effect subject to

s.14 (leases to which s.11 applies: exceptions), and

s.32(2) (provisions not applying to tenancies within Part II of the Landlord and Tenant Act 1954).

Service charges

Meaning of 'service charge' and 'relevant costs'

18. (1) In the following provisions of this Act 'service charge' means an amount payable by a tenant of a flat as part of or in addition to the rent

(*a*) which is payable, directly or indirectly, for services, repairs, maintenance or insurance or the landlord's costs of management, and

(*b*) the whole or part of which varies or may vary according to the relevant costs.

(2) The relevant costs are the costs or estimated costs incurred or to be incurred by or on behalf of the landlord, or a superior landlord, in connection with the matters for which the service charge is payable.

(3) For this purpose:

(*a*) 'costs' include overheads, and

(*b*) costs are relevant costs in relation to a service charge whether they are incurred, or to be incurred, in the period for which the service charge is payable or in an earlier or later period.

Limitation service charges: reasonableness

19. (1) Relevant costs shall be taken into account in determining the amount of a service charge payable for a period

(*a*) only to the extent that they are reasonably incurred, and

(*b*) where they are incurred on the provision of services or the carrying out of works, only if the services or works are of a reasonable standard;

and the amount payable shall be limited accordingly.

(2) Where a service charge is payable before the relevant costs are incurred, no greater amount than is reasonable is so payable, and after the relevant costs have been incurred any necessary adjustment shall be made by repayment, reduction or subsequent charges or otherwise.

(3) An agreement by the tenant of a flat (other than an arbitration agreement within the meaning of s.32 of the Arbitration Act 1950) is void in so far as it purports to provide for a determination in a particular manner, or on particular evidence, of any question

(*a*) whether costs incurred for services, repairs, maintenance, insurance or management were reasonably incurred,

(*b*) whether services or works for which costs were incurred are of a reasonable standard, or

(*c*) whether an amount payable before costs are incurred is reasonable.

(4) A county court may make a declaration
(*a*) that any such costs were or were not reasonably incurred,
(*b*) that any such services or works are or are not of a reasonable standard, or
(*c*) that any such amount is or is not reasonable,
notwithstanding that no other relief is sought in the proceedings.

Meaning of 'lease' and 'tenancy' and related expressions

36. (1) In this Act 'lease' and 'tenancy' have the same meaning.
(2) Both expressions include:
(*a*) a sub-lease or sub-tenancy, and
(*b*) an agreement for a lease or tenancy (or sub-lease or sub-tenancy).
(3) The expressions 'lessor' and 'lessee' and 'landlord' and 'tenant', and references to letting, to the grant of a lease or to covenants or terms, shall be construed accordingly.

HOUSING ACT 1985

Limitation of service charges payable after disposal of house by public authority

47. (1) Relevant costs shall be taken into account in determining the amount of a service charge payable for a period
(*a*) only to the extent that they are reasonably incurred, and
(*b*) where they are incurred on the provision of services or the carrying out of works, only if the services or works are of a reasonable standard;
and the amount payable shall be limited accordingly.
(2) Where the service charge is payable before the relevant costs are incurred, no greater amount than is reasonable is so payable and after the relevant costs have been incurred any necessary adjustment shall be made by repayment, reduction of subsequent charges or otherwise.
(3) An agreement by the payer (other than an arbitration agreement within the meaning of s.32 of the Arbitration Act 1950) is void in so far as it purports to provide for a determination in a particular manner or on particular evidence of any question
(*a*) whether an amount payable before costs for services, repairs, maintenance, insurance or management are incurred is reasonable,
(*b*) whether such costs were reasonably incurred, or
(*c*) whether services or works for which costs were incurred are of a reasonable standard.
(4) Where relevant costs are incurred or to be incurred on the carrying out of works in respect of which a grant has been or is to be paid under Part XV (grants for works of improvement, repair or conversion), the amount of the grant shall be deducted from the costs and the amount of the service charge payable shall be reduced accordingly.

PART IV
SECURE TENANCIES AND RIGHTS OF SECURE TENANTS

Security of tenure

79. (1) A tenancy under which a dwelling-house is let as a separate dwelling is a secure tenancy at any time when the conditions described in s.80 and 81 as the landlord condition and the tenant condition are satisfied.

(3) The provisions of this Part apply in relation to a licence to occupy a dwelling-house (whether or not granted for a consideration) as they apply in relation to a tenancy.

(4) Subsection (3) does not apply to a licence granted as a temporary expedient to a person who entered the dwelling-house or any other land as a trespasser (whether or not, before the grant of that licence, another licence to occupy that or another dwelling-house had been granted to him).

The landlord condition

80. (1) The landlord condition is that the interest of the landlord belongs to one of the following authorities or bodies:

a local authority,
a new town corporation,
an urban development corporation,
the Development Board for Rural Wales,
the Housing Corporation,
a housing trust which is a charity, or
a housing association or housing co-operative to which this section applies.

(2) This section applies to

(*a*) a registered housing association other than a co-operative housing association, and

(*b*) an unregistered housing association which is a co-operative housing association.

(3) If a co-operative housing association ceases to be registered, it shall, within the period of 21 days beginning with the date on which it ceases to be registered, notify each of its tenants who thereby becomes a secure tenant, in writing, that he has become a secure tenant.

(4) This section applies to a housing co-operative within the meaning of section 27B (agreements under certain superseded provisions) where the dwelling-house is comprised in a housing co-operative agreement within the meaning of that section.

The tenant condition

81. The tenant condition is that the tenant is an individual and occupies the dwelling-house as his only or principal home; or, where the tenancy is a joint tenancy, that each of the joint tenants is an individual and at least one of them occupies the dwelling-house as his only or principal home.

PART VI
REPAIR NOTICES

Repair Notices

In respect of unfit house

189. (1) Where the local housing authority are satisfied that a house is unfit for human habitation, they shall serve a repair notice on the person having control of the house, unless they are satisfied that the house is not capable of being rendered so fit at reasonable expense.

(2) A repair notice under this section shall:

(*a*) require the person on whom it is served to execute the works specified in the notice within such reasonable time, not being less than 21 days, as is specified in the notice, and

(*b*) state that in the opinion of the authority the works specified in the notice will render the house fit for human habitation.

In respect of house in state of disrepair but not unfit

190. (1) Where the local housing authority

(*a*) are satisfied that a house is in such a state of disrepair that, although not unfit for human habitation, substantial repairs are necessary to bring it up to a reasonable standard, having regard to its age, character and locality, or

(*b*) are satisfied on a representation made by an occupying tenant that a house is in such a state of disrepair that, although not unfit for human habitation, its condition is such as to interfere materially with the personal comfort of the occupying tenant,

they may serve a repair notice on the person having control of the house.

(2) A repair notice under this section shall require the person on whom it is served, within such reasonable time, not being less than 21 days, as is specified in the notice, to execute the works specified in the notice, not being works of internal decorative repair.

Enforcement

Power of local housing authority to execute works

193. (1) If a repair notice is not complied with the local housing authority may themselves do the work required to be done by the notice.

Part VII
Improvement Notices

General conditions for service of improvement notice

209. The general conditions for service of an improvement notice in respect of a dwelling are that the dwelling

(*a*) is without one or more of the standard amenities (whether or not it is also in a state of disrepair),

(*b*) is capable at reasonable expense of improvement to the full standard or, failing that, to the reduced standard, and

(*c*) was provided (by erection or by the conversion of a building already in existence) before 3rd October 1961.

Service of provisional notice: dwellings in general improvement area or housing action area

210. (1) The local housing authority may serve a provisional notice on the person having control of a dwelling in

(*a*) a general improvement area, or

(*b*) a housing action area,

if it appears to the authority that the general conditions for service of an improvement notice are met, but subject to subsection (2) if the dwelling is owner-occupied.

(2) The authority may only serve a provisional notice in respect of a dwelling which is owner-occupied if it appears to them that the circumstances are such that it is not reasonably practicable for another dwelling

(*a*) which is in the same building as, or is adjacent to, the owner-occupied dwelling, and

(*b*) which is not owner-occupied or in respect of which an application for an improvement grant has been approved,

to be improved to the full standard or, as the case may be, to the reduced standard without effecting the improvement to one of those standards of the owner-occupied dwelling.

Acceptance of undertaking to do works

211. (1) In any case where an improvement notice has not yet been served in respect of a dwelling falling within s.210 (certain dwellings in general improvement areas or housing action areas), the local housing authority may accept an undertaking from

(*a*) the person having control of the dwelling, or

(*b*) any other person having an estate or interest in the dwelling,

to improve the dwelling to the full standard or, if in the opinion of the authority it is not practicable at reasonable expense for the dwelling to be improved to the full standard, to the reduced standard.

Power of local housing authority to execute works

220. (1) If the works to be carried out in compliance with an improvement notice have not been carried out in whole or in part within the period for compliance, the local housing authority may themselves carry out so much of the works as has not been completed.

PART IX
SLUM CLEARANCE

Demolition or closing of unfit premises beyond repair at reasonable cost

Power to accept undertaking as to reconstruction or use of unfit house

264. (1) Where the local housing authority are satisfied that a house is unfit for human habitation and not capable of being rendered so fit at reasonable expense, they shall serve on

(*a*) the person having control of the house,

(*b*) any other person who is an owner of the house, and

(*c*) every mortgagee of the house whom it is reasonably practicable to ascertain,

notice of a time (at least 21 days after the service of the notice) and place at which the condition of the house and any offer which he may wish to submit with respect to the carrying out of works, or the future user of the premises, will be considered by the authority.

Demolition or closing order to be made where no undertaking accepted or undertaking broken

265. (1) If no undertaking under s.264 is accepted by the local housing authority or if, where they have accepted such an undertaking

(*a*) any work to which the undertaking relates is not carried out within the specified period, or

(*b*) the house is at any time used in contravention of the terms of the undertaking,

the authority shall forthwith make a demolition or closing order in respect of the premises to which the notice under that section relates.

(2) The authority shall make a demolition order unless

(*a*) they consider it inexpedient to make a demolition order having regard to the effect of the demolition on another building, or

(*b*) s.304(1) applies (listed buildings and buildings protected by notice pending listing),

in which case they shall make a closing order.

(3) The provisions of this section have effect subject to s.300 (power to purchase for temporary housing use houses liable to be demolished or closed).

PART X
OVERCROWDING

Definition of overcrowding

324. A dwelling is overcrowded for the purposes of this Part when the number of persons sleeping in the dwelling is such as to contravene

(*a*) the standard specified in s.325 (the room standard), or

(*b*) the standard specified in s.326 (the space standard).

The room standard

325. (1) The room standard is contravened when the number of persons sleeping in a dwelling and the number of rooms available as sleeping accommodation is such that two persons of opposite sexes who are not living together as husband and wife must sleep in the same room.

(2) For this purpose

(*a*) children under the age of ten shall be left out of account, and

(*b*) a room is available as sleeping accommodation if it is of a type normally used in the locality either as a bedroom or as a living room.

The space standard

326. (1) The space standard is contravened when the number of persons sleeping in a dwelling is in excess of the permitted number, having regard to the number and floor area of the rooms of the dwelling available as sleeping accommodation.

(2)...

(3) The permitted number of persons in relation to a dwelling is whichever is the less of:

(*a*) the number of specified in Table 1 in relation to the number of rooms in the dwelling available as sleeping accommodation, and (*b*) the aggregate for all such rooms in the dwelling of the numbers specified in column 2 of Table 2 in relation to each room of the floor area specified in column 1.

No account shall be taken for the purposes of either Table of a room having a floor area of less than 50 square feet.

Table 1

Number of rooms	*Number of persons*
1	2
2	3
3	5
4	7½
5 or more	2 for each room

Table 2

Floor area of room	*Number of persons*
110 sq ft or more	2
90 sq ft or more but less than 110 sq ft	1½
70 sq ft or more but less than 90 sq ft	1
50 sq ft or more but less than 70 sq ft	½

(4) The Secretary of State may by regulations prescribe the manner in which the floor area of a room is to be ascertained for the purposes of this section; and the regulations may provide for the exclusion from computation, or the bringing into computation at a reduced figure, of floor space in a part of the room which is of less than a specified height not exceeding eight feet.

HOUSING ASSOCIATIONS ACT 1985

PART I
REGULATION OF HOUSING ASSOCIATIONS

Introductory

Meaning of 'housing association' and related expressions

1. (1) In this Act 'housing association' means a society body of trustees or company

(*a*) which is established for the purpose of, or amongst whose objects or powers are included those of, providing, constructing, improving or managing, or facilitating or encouraging the construction or improvement of, housing accommodation, and

(*b*) which does not trade for profit or whose constitution or rules prohibit the issue of capital with interest or dividend exceeding such rate as may be prescribed by the Treasury, whether with or without differentiation as between share and loan capital.

(2) In this Act 'fully mutual', in relation to a housing association, means that the rules of the association

(*a*) restrict membership to persons who are tenants or prospective tenants of the association, and

(*b*) preclude the granting or assignment of tenancies to persons other than members;

and 'co-operative housing association' means a fully mutual housing association which is a society registered under the Industrial and Provident Societies Act 1965 (in this Part referred to as 'the 1965 Act').

(3) In this Act 'self-built' means a housing association whose object is to provide, for sale to, or occupation by, its members, dwellings built or improved principally with the use of its members' own labour.

AGRICULTURAL HOLDINGS ACT 1986

PART I
Introductory

Principal definitions

1. (1) In this Act 'agricultural holding' means the aggregate of the land (whether agricultural land or not) comprised in a contract of tenancy which is a contract for an agricultural tenancy, not being a contract under which the land is let to the tenant during his continuance in any office, appointment or employment held under the landlord.

(2) For the purposes of this section, a contract of tenancy relating to any land is a contract for an agricultural tenancy if, having regard to

(*a*) the terms of the tenancy,

(*b*) the actual or contemplated use of the land at the time of the conclusion of the contract and subsequently, and

(*c*) any other relevant circumstances,

the whole of the land comprised in the contract, subject to such exceptions only as do not substantially affect the character of the tenancy, is let for use as agricultural land.

(3) A change in user of the land concerned subsequent to the conclusion of a contract of tenancy which involves any breach of the terms of the tenancy shall be disregarded for the purpose of determining whether a contract which was not originally a contract for an agricultural tenancy has subsequently become one unless it is effected with the landlord's permission, consent or acquiescence.

(4) In this Act 'agricultural land' means:

(*a*) land used for agriculture which is so used for the purposes of a trade or business, and

(*b*) any other land which, by virtue of a designation under s.109(1) of the Agriculture Act 1947, is agricultural land within the meaning of that Act.

(5) In this Act 'contract of tenancy' means a letting of land, or agreement for

letting land, for a term of years or from year to year; and for the purposes of this definition a letting of land, or an agreement for letting land, which, by virtue of subsection (6) of s.149 of the Law of Property Act 1925, takes effect as such a letting of land or agreement for letting land as is mentioned in that subsection shall be deemed to be a letting of land or, as the case may be, an agreement for letting land, for a term of years.

Restriction on letting agricultural land for less than from year to year

2. (1) An agreement to which this section applies shall take effect, with the necessary modifications, as if it were an agreement for the letting of land for a tenancy from year to year unless the agreement was approved by the Minister before it was entered into.

Tenancies for two years or more to continue from year to year unless terminated by notice

3. (1) Subject to s.5 below, a tenancy of an agricultural holding for a term of two years or more shall, instead of terminating on the term date, continue (as from that date) as a tenancy from year to year, but otherwise on the terms of the original tenancy so far as applicable, unless

(*a*) not less than one year nor more than two years before the term date a written notice has been given by either party to the other of his intention to terminate the tenancy, or

(*b*) s.4 below applies.

Arbitration of rent

12. (1) Subject to the provisions of Schedule 2 to this Act, the landlord or tenant of an agricultural holding may by notice in writing served on the other demand that the rent to be payable in respect of the holding as from the next termination date shall be referred to arbitration under this Act.

(2) On a reference under this section the arbitrator shall determine what rent should be properly payable in respect of the holding at the date of the reference and accordingly shall, with effect from the next termination date following the date of the demand for arbitration, increase or reduce the rent previously payable or direct that it shall continue unchanged.

(3) A demand for arbitration under this section shall cease to be effective for the purposes of this section on the next termination date following the date of the demand unless before the said termination date

(*a*) an arbitrator has been appointed by agreement between the parties, or

(*b*) an application has been made to the President of the Royal Institution of Chartered Surveyors for the appointment of an arbitrator by him.

(4) References in this section (and in Schedule 2 to this Act) in relation to a demand for arbitration with respect to the rent of any holding, to the next termination date following the date of the demand are references to the next day following the date of the demand on which the tenancy of the holding could have been determined by notice to quit given at the date of the demand.

(5) Schedule 2 to this Act shall have effect for supplementing this section.

PART III
NOTICES TO QUIT

Notices to quit whole or part of agricultural holding

Length of notice to quit

25. (1) A notice to quit an agricultural holding or part of an agricultural holding shall (notwithstanding any provision to the contrary in the contract of tenancy of the holding) be invalid if it purports to terminate the tenancy before the expiry of twelve months from the end of the then current year of tenancy.

Appendix 2

Statutory Instruments

THE LANDLORD AND TENANT ACT 1954 (Appropriate Multiplier) ORDER 1984

The Secretary of State for the Environment, as respects England, and the Secretary of State for Wales, as respects Wales, in exercise of the powers conferred on them by section 37(8) of the Landlord and Tenant Act 1954, and of all other powers enabling them in that behalf, hereby make the following Order:

1. This Order may be cited as the Landlord and Tenant Act 1954 (Appropriate Multiplier) Order 1984 and shall come into operation on 7th May 1985.

2. The appropriate multiplier for the purposes of paragraphs (*a*) and (*b*) of section 37(2) of the Landlord and Tenant Act 1954 shall be 3.

3. The previous instrument made in the exercise of the above-mentioned powers and known as the Landlord and Tenant Act 1954 (Appropriate Multiplier) Regulations 1981 is hereby revoked.

Explanatory Note
(This Note is not part of the Order)

This Order increases, from 2¼ to 3, the appropriate multiplier to be used in calculating the amount of compensation to which a tenant may be entitled, under Part II of the Landlord and Tenant Act 1954, where an order for a new tenancy is precluded on certain grounds. The amount of compensation is arrived at by multiplying either the rateable value of the holding or twice the rateable value of the building, as the case may be, by the figure prescribed. The previous multiplier was prescribed by SI 1981/69, which is revoked by the Order.

NOTICES TO QUIT (PRESCRIBED INFORMATION) REGULATIONS 1980
(SI 1980 NO 1624)

1. These regulations may be cited as the Notices to Quit (Prescribed Information) Regulations 1980 and shall come into operation on 28th November 1980.

2. Where a notice to quit is given by a landlord on or after the coming into operation of these regulations to determine a tenancy of any premises let as a dwelling the information prescribed for the purposes of section 5 of the Protection from Eviction Act 1977 (which deals with the minimum length of, and other matters relating to, a notice to quit any premises let as a dwelling) shall be that in the Schedule to these regulations.

SCHEDULE
PRESCRIBED INFORMATION

1. If the tenant does not leave the dwelling, the landlord must get an order for possession from the court before the tenant can lawfully be evicted. The landlord cannot apply for such an order before the notice to quit has run out.

2. A tenant who does not know if he has any right to remain in possession after a notice to quit runs out or is otherwise unsure of his rights, can obtain advice from a solicitor. Help with all or part of the cost of legal advice and assistance may be available under the Legal Aid Scheme. He should also be able to obtain information from a Citizens' Advice Bureau, a Housing Aid Centre, a Rent Officer or a Rent Tribunal Office.

Appendix 3

Law Society/RICS Model Forms of Rent Review Clause (1985 Edition)

MODEL FORM—VARIATION A

Determination in default of agreement by Arbitration with alternative provisions for (*a*) upwards only review, and (*b*) upwards or downwards review

... yielding and paying to the landlord yearly rents ascertained in accordance with the next four clauses hereof without any deduction by equal quarterly payments in advance on the usual quarter days the first payment (being an apportioned sum) to be made on the date hereof

Clause 1

Definitions

In this lease 'review date' means the............................day of....................in the year 19... and in every.............year thereafter and 'review period' means the period starting with any review date up to the next review date or starting with the last review date up to the end of the term hereof

Clause 2

The yearly rent shall be:
(A) until the first review date the rent of £.....and

Provisions for revision of rent in upwards only review

(B) during each successive review period a rent equal to the rent previously payable hereunder or such revised rent as may be ascertained as herein provided whichever be the greater

OR

For revision of rent in upwards or downwards review

(B)(i) during each successive review period such revised rent as may be ascertained as herein provided and
(B)(ii) in the event of a revised rent not being ascertained as herein provided the rent payable for the relevant review period shall be the rent payable immediately prior to the commencement of such period

Clause 3

Ascertainment of amount by arbitrator

Such revised rent for any review period may be agreed at any time between the landlord and the tenant or (in the absence of agreement) determined not earlier than the relevant review date by an arbitrator such arbitrator to be nominated in the absence of agreement by or on behalf of the President for the time being of

the Royal Institute of Chartered Surveyors on the application of the landlord or
(See Note 1) the tenant made not earlier than six months before the relevant review date *but not later than the end of the relevant review period* and so that in the case of such arbitration the revised rent to be awarded by the arbitrator shall be such as he shall decide is the yearly rent at which the demised premises might reasonably be expected to be let at the relevant review date

(A) On the following assumptions at that date:

(i) That the demised premises:

(See Note 2) (*a*) are available to let on the open market without a fine or premium with vacant possession by a willing landlord to a willing tenant for a term of [10] years or the residue then unexpired of the term of this lease (whichever be the longer)

(*b*) are to be let as a whole subject to the terms of this lease (other than the amount of the rent hereby reserved but including the provisions for review of that rent)

(*c*) are fit and available for immediate occupation

(*d*) may be used for any of the purposes permitted by this lease as varied or extended by any licence granted pursuant thereto

(See Note 3) (ii) That the covenants herein contained on the part of *the landlord and* the tenant have been fully performed and observed

(iii) That no work has been carried out to the demised premises which has diminished the rental value and that in case the demised premises have been destroyed or damaged they have been fully restored

(iv) That no reduction is to be made to take account of any rental concession which on a new letting with vacant possession might be granted to the incoming tenant for a period within which its fitting out works would take place

(B) But disregarding:

(i) any effect on rent of the fact that the tenant its sub-tenants or their respective predecessors in title have been in occupation of the demised premises

(ii) any goodwill attached to the demised premises by reason of the carrying on thereat of the business of the tenant its sub-tenants or their predecessors in title in their respective businesses and

(See Note 4) (iii) any increase in rental value of the demised premises attributable to the existence at the relevant review date of any improvement to the demised premises or any part thereof carried out with consent where required otherwise than in pursuance of an obligation to the landlord or its predecessors in title except obligations requiring compliance with statutes or directions of local authorities or other bodies exercising powers under statute or Royal Charter either (*a*) by the tenant its sub-tenants or their respective predecessors in title during the said term or during any period of occupation prior thereto arising out
(See Note 5) of an agreement to grant such term or (*b*) *by any tenant or sub-tenant of the demised premises before the commencement of the term hereby granted so long as the landlord or its predecessors in title have not since the improvement was carried out had vacant possession of the relevant part of the demised premises*

Clause 4

It is hereby further provided in relation to the ascertainment and payment of revised rent as follows:

Further provisions as to Arbitration

(A) The arbitration shall be conducted in accordance with the Arbitration Acts 1950 and 1979 or any statutory modification or re-enactment thereof for the time being in force with the further provision that if the arbitrator nominated pursuant to Clause 3 hereof shall die or decline to act the President for the time being of the Royal Institute of Chartered Surveyors or the person acting on his behalf may on the application of either the landlord or the tenant by writing discharge the arbitrator and appoint another in his place

As to memoranda of ascertainment

(B) When the amount of any rent to be ascertained as hereinbefore provided shall have been so ascertained memoranda thereof shall thereupon be signed by or on behalf of the landlord and the tenant and annexed to this lease and the counterpart thereof and the landlord and the tenant shall bear their own costs in respect thereof

As to interim payments and final adjustments upwards only review

(See Note 6)

(C)(i) if the revised rent payable on and from any review date has not been agreed by that review date rent shall continue to be payable at the rate previously payable and forthwith upon the revised rent being ascertained the tenant shall pay to the landlord any shortfall between the rent and the revised rent payable up to and on the preceding quarter day together with interest on any shortfall at the seven day deposit rate of...........BANK such interest to be calculated on a day to day basis from the relevant review date on which it would have been payable if the revised rent had then been ascertained to the date of actual payment of any shortfall and the interest so payable shall be recoverable in the same manner as rent in arrear or as the case may be as a debt

OR

upwards or downwards review

(See Note 6)

(C)(i) if the revised rent payable on and from any review date has not been agreed by that review date rent shall continue to be payable at the rate previously payable and forthwith upon the revised rent being ascertained the tenant shall pay to the landlord any shortfall between the rent and the revised rent or as the case may be the landlord shall pay to the tenant any excess of the rent paid over the revised rent payable up to and on the preceding quarter day together with interest on any shortfall or as the case may be any excess at the seven day deposit rate of.........BANK such interest to be calculated on a day to day basis from the relevant date on which it would have been payable if the revised rent had then been ascertained to the date of actual payment of any shortfall or any excess and the interest so payable shall be recoverable in the same manner as rent in arrear or as the case may be as a debt

(ii) for the purposes of this proviso the revised rent shall be deemed to have been ascertained on the date when the same has been agreed between the landlord and the tenant or as the case may be the date of the award of the arbitrator

(D) If either the landlord or the tenant shall fail to pay any costs awarded against it in an arbitration under the provisions hereof within twenty-one days of the same being demanded by the arbitrator the other shall be entitled to pay the same and the amount so paid shall be repaid by the party chargeable on demand

MODEL FORM—VARIATION B

Determination in default of agreement by independent valuer acting as an expert with alternative provisions for (*a*) upwards only review and (*b*) upwards or downwards review.

... yielding and paying to the landlord yearly rents ascertained in accordance with the next four clauses hereof without any deduction by equal quarterly payments in advance on the usual quarter days the first payment (being an apportioned sum) to be made on the date hereof

Clause 1

Definitions

In this lease 'review date' means the ...day of...in the year 19... and in every .... year thereafter and 'review period' means the period starting with any review date up to the next review date or starting with the last review date up to the end of the term hereof

Clause 2

The yearly rent shall be: (A) until the first review date the rent of £... and

Provisions for revision of rent in upwards only review

(B) during each successive review period a rent equal to the rent previously payable hereunder or such revised rent as may be ascertained as herein provided whichever be the greater

OR

For revision of rent in upwards or downwards review

(B) (i) during each successive review period such revised rent as may be ascertained as herein provided and

(B)(ii) in the event of a revised rent not being ascertained as herein provided the rent payable for the relevant review period shall be the rent payable immediately prior to the commencement of such period

Clause 3

Ascertainment of amount by independent valuer

(See Note 1)

Such revised rent for any review period may be agreed at any time between the landlord and the tenant or (in the absence of agreement) determined not earlier than the relevant review date by an independent valuer (acting as an expert and not as an arbitrator) such valuer to be nominated in the absence of agreement by or on behalf of the President for the time being of the Royal Institution of Chartered Surveyors on the application of the landlord or the tenant made not earlier than six months before the relevant review date *but not later than the end of the relevant review period* and so that in the case of such valuation the revised rent to be determined by the valuer shall be such as he shall decide is the yearly rent at which the demised premises might reasonably be expected to be let at the relevant review date

(A) On the following assumptions at that date:

(i) That the demised premises:

(*a*) are available to let on the open market without a fine or premium with vacant possession by a willing landlord to a willing tenant for a term of [10] years or the residue then unexpired of the term of this lease (whichever be the longer) (See Note 2)

(*b*) are to be let as a whole subject to the terms of this lease (other than the amount of the rent hereby reserved but including the provisions for review of that rent)

(*c*) are fit and available for immediate occupation

(*d*) may be used for any of the purposes permitted by this lease as varied or extended by any licence granted pursuant thereto

(ii) That the covenants herein contained on the part of *the landlord and* the tenant have been fully performed and observed (See Note 3)

(iii) That no work has been carried out to the demised premises which has diminished the rental value and that in case the demised premises have been destroyed or damaged they have been fully restored

(iv) That no reduction is to be made to take account of any rental concession which on a new letting with vacant possession might be granted to the incoming tenant for a period within which its fitting out works would take place.

(B) But disregarding:

(i) any effect on rent of the fact that the tenant its sub-tenants or their respective predecessors in title have been in occupation of the demised premises

(ii) any goodwill attached to the demised premises by reason of the carrying on thereat of the business of the tenant its sub-tenants or their predecessors in title in their respective businesses and

(iii) any increase in rental value of the demised premises attributable to the existence at the relevant review date of any improvement to the demised premises or any part thereof carried out with consent where required otherwise than in pursuance of an obligation to the landlord or its predecessors in title except obligations requiring compliance with statutes or directions of Local Authorities or other bodies exercising powers under statute or Royal Charter either (*a*) by the tenant its sub-tenants or their respective predecessors in title during the said term or during any period of occupation prior thereto arising out of an agreement to grant such term (See Note 4)

or (b) by any tenant or sub-tenant of the demised premises before the commencement of the term hereby granted so long as the landlord or its predecessors in title have not since the improvement was carried out had vacant possession of the relevant part of the demised premises (See Note 5)

Clause 4

It is hereby further provided in relation to the ascertainment and payment of revised rent as follows:

As to independent valuation

(A)(i) the fees and expenses of the valuer including the cost of his nomination shall be borne equally by the landlord and the tenant who shall otherwise bear their own costs and

(ii) the valuer shall afford the landlord and the tenant an opportunity to make representation to him and

(iii) if the valuer nominated pursuant to Clause 3 hereof shall die delay or become unwilling, unfit or incapable of acting or if for any other reason the President for the time being of the Royal Institution of Chartered Surveyors or the person acting on his behalf shall in his absolute discretion think fit he may on the application of either the landlord or the tenant by writing discharge the valuer and appoint another in his place

As to memoranda of ascertainment

(B) When the amount of any rent to be ascertained as hereinbefore provided shall have been so ascertained memoranda thereof shall thereupon be signed by or on behalf of the landlord and the tenant and annexed to this lease and the counterpart thereof and the landlord and the tenant shall bear their own costs in respect thereof

Provisions as to interim payments final adjustments upwards only review

(See Note 6)

(C) (i) If the revised rent payable on and from any review date has not been agreed by that review date rent shall continue to be payable at the rate previously payable and forthwith upon the revised rent being ascertained the tenant shall pay to the landlord any shortfall between the rent and the revised rent payable up to and on the preceding quarter day together with interest on any shortfall at the seven day deposit rate of........ BANK such interest to be calculated on a day-to-day basis from the relevant review date on which it would have been payable if the revised rent had then been ascertained to the date of actual payment of any shortfall and the interest so payable shall be recoverable in the same manner as rent in arrear

OR

upwards or downwards review

(See Note 6)

(C)(i) if the revised rent payable on and from any review date has not been agreed by that review date rent shall continue to be payable at the rate previously payable and forthwith upon the revised rent being ascertained the tenant shall pay to the landlord any shortfall between the rent and the revised rent or as the case may be the landlord shall pay to the tenant any excess of the rent paid over the revised rent payable up to and on the preceding quarter day together with interest on any shortfall or as the case may be any excess at the seven day deposit rate of.......BANK such interest to be calculated on a day-to-day basis from the relevant review date on which it would have been payable if the revised rent had then been ascertained to the date of actual payment of any shortfall or any excess and the interest so payable shall be recoverable in the same manner as rent in arrear or as the case may be as a debt

(ii) for the purposes of this proviso the revised rent shall be deemed to have been ascertained on the date when the same has been agreed between the landlord and the tenant or as the case may be the date of the determination by the valuer

(D) If either the landlord or the tenant shall fail to pay the moiety of the fees and expenses of the valuer under the provisions hereof within twenty-one days of the same being demanded by the valuer, the other shall be entitled to pay the same and the amount so paid shall be repaid by the party chargeable on demand

MODEL FORM—VARIATION C

Determination in default of agreement to be either by arbitration or by independent valuer acting as expert (at the landlord's option) with alternative

provisions for (*a*) upwards only review and (*b*) upwards or downwards review
...yielding and paying to the landlord yearly rents ascertained in accordance with the next four clauses hereof without any deduction by equal quarterly payments in advance on the usual quarter days the first payment (being an apportioned sum) to be made on the date hereof

Clause 1

In this lease 'review date' means the ....day of..... in the year 19...and in every......year thereafter and 'review period' means the period starting with any review date up to the next review date or starting with the last review date up to the end of the term hereof

Clause 2

The yearly rent shall be:
(A) until the first review date the rent of £... and

(B) during each successive review period a rent equal to the rent previously payable hereunder or such revised rent as may be ascertained as herein provided whichever be the greater **Provisions for revision of rent in upwards only review**

OR

(B)(i) during each successive review period such revised rent as may be ascertained as herein provided and **For revision of rent in upwards or downwards review**

(B)(ii) in the event of a revised rent not being ascertained as herein provided the rent payable for the relevant review period shall be the rent payable immediately prior to the commencement of such period

Clause 3

Such revised rent for any review period may be agreed at any time between the landlord and the tenant or (in the absence of agreement) determined not earlier than the relevant review date at the option of the landlord either by an arbitrator or by an independent valuer (acting as an expert and not as an arbitrator) such arbitrator or valuer to be nominated in the absence of agreement by or on behalf of the President for the time being of the Royal Institution of Chartered Surveyors on the application of the landlord (in exercise of the said option) made not earlier than six months before the relevant review date *but not later than the end of the relevant review period* and so that in the case of such arbitration or valuation the revised rent to be awarded or determined by the arbitrator or valuer shall be such as he shall decide is the yearly rent at which the demised premises might reasonably be expected to be let at the relevant review date **Ascertainment of amount by arbitrator or by independent valuer at the landlord's option (See Note 7)** **(See Note 1)**

(A) On the following assumptions at that date:

(i) That the demised premises:

(*a*) are available to let on the open market without a fine or premium with vacant possession by a willing landlord to a willing tenant for a term of [10] years or the residue then unexpired of the term of this lease (whichever be the longer) **(See Note 2)** (*b*) are to be let as a whole subject to the terms of this lease (other than the amount of the rent hereby reserved but including the provisions for review of that rent)

(*c*) are fit and available for immediate occupation

(*d*) may be used for any of the purposes permitted by this lease as varied or extended by any licence granted pursuant thereto

(See Note 3) (ii) That the covenants herein contained on the part of *the landlord and* the tenant have been fully performed and observed

(iii) That no work has been carried out to the demised premises which has diminished the rental value and that in case the demised premises have been destroyed or damaged they have been fully restored

(iv) That no reduction is to be made to take account of any rental concession which on a new letting with vacant possession might be granted to the incoming tenant for a period within which its fitting out works would take place

(B) But disregarding:

(i) any effect on rent of the fact that the tenant its sub-tenants or their respective predecessors in title have been in occupation of the demised premises

(ii) any goodwill attached to the demised premises by reason of the carrying on thereat of the business of the tenant its sub-tenants or their predecessors in title in their respective businesses and

(See Note 4) (iii) any increase in rental value of the demised premises attributable to the existence at the relevant review date of any improvement to the demised premises or any part thereof carried out with consent where required otherwise than in pursuance of an obligation to the landlord or its predecessors in title except obligations requiring compliance with statutes or directions of Local Authorities or other bodies exercising powers under statute or Royal Charter either (*a*) by the tenant its sub-tenants or their respective predecessors in title during the said term or during any period of occupation prior thereto arising out of an agreement to grant such term or (*b*) *by any tenant or sub-tenant of the demised premises before the commencement of the term hereby granted so long as the landlord or its predecessors in title have not since the improvement was carried out had vacant possession of the relevant part of the demised premises* (See Note 5)

Clause 4

It is hereby further provided in relation to the ascertainment and payment of revised rent as follows:

Further provisions as to arbitration

(A) (In the case of arbitration) the arbitration shall be conducted in accordance with the Arbitration Acts 1950 and 1979 or any statutory modification or re-enactment thereof for the time being in force with the further provision that if the arbitrator nominated pursuant to Clause 3 hereof shall die or decline to act the President for the time being of the Royal Institution of Chartered Surveyors or the person acting on his behalf may on the application of either the landlord or the tenant by writing discharge the arbitrator and appoint another in his place

(B) (In the case of determination by a valuer) (i) the fees and expenses of the valuer including the cost of his nomination shall be borne equally by the landlord and the tenant who shall otherwise each bear their own costs and

As to independent valuation

(ii) the valuer shall afford the landlord and the tenant an opportunity to make representation to him and

(iii) if the valuer nominated pursuant to Clause 3 hereof shall die delay or become unwilling, unfit or incapable of acting or if for any reason the President for the time being of the Royal Institution of Chartered Surveyors or the person acting on his behalf shall in his absolute discretion think fit he may on the application of either the landlord or the tenant by writing discharge the valuer and appoint another in his place

(C) When the amount of any rent to be ascertained as hereinbefore provided shall have been so ascertained memoranda thereof shall thereupon be signed by or on behalf of the landlord and the tenant and annexed to this lease and the counterpart thereof and the landlord and the tenant shall bear their own costs in respect thereof

As to memoranda of ascertainment

(D)(i) If the revised rent payable on and from any review date has not been agreed by that review date rent shall continue to be payable at the rate previously payable and forthwith upon the revised rent being ascertained, the tenant shall pay to the landlord any shortfall between the rent and the revised rent payable up to and on the preceding quarter day together with interest on any shortfall at the seven day deposit rate of.....BANK such interest to be calculated on a day-to-day basis from the relevant review date on which it would have been payable if the revised rent had then been ascertained to the date of actual payment of any shortfall and the interest so payable shall be recoverable in the same manner as rent in arrear

As to interim payments and final adjustments upwards only review

OR

(D)(i) If the revised rent payable on and from any review date has not been agreed by that review date rent shall continue to be payable at the rate previously payable and forthwith upon the revised rent being ascertained the tenant shall pay to the landlord any shortfall between the rent and the revised rent or as the case may be the landlord shall pay to the tenant any excess of the rent paid over the revised rent payable up to and on the preceding quarter day together with interest on any shortfall or as the case may be any excess at the seven day deposit rate of..........BANK such interest to be calculated on a day-to-day basis from the relevant review date on which it would have been payable if the revised rent had then been ascertained to the date of actual payment of any shortfall or any excess and the interest so payable shall be recoverable in the same manner as rent in arrear or as the case may be as a debt

upwards or downwards review

(See Note 6)

(ii) for the purposes of this proviso the revised rent shall be deemed to have been ascertained on the date when the same has been agreed between the landlord and the tenant or as the case may be the date of the award of the arbitrator or of the determination by the valuer.

(E) If either the landlord or the tenant shall fail to pay any costs awarded against it in the case of an arbitration or the moiety of the fees and expenses of the valuer under the provisions hereof within twenty-one days of the same being demanded by the arbitrator or the valuer (as the case may be) the other shall be entitled to pay the same and the amount so paid shall be repaid by the party chargeable on demand.

As to notice by the tenant to trigger landlord's application

(See Note 7)

(See Note 8)

(F) *Whenever a revised rent in respect of any review period has not been agreed between the landlord and the tenant before the relevant review date and where no agreement has been reached as to the appointment of an arbitrator or valuer nor has the landlord made any application to the President for the time being of the Royal Institution of Chartered Surveyors as hereinbefore provided the tenant may serve on the landlord notice in writing referring to this provision and containing a proposal as to the amount of such revised rent (which shall not be less than the rent payable immediately before the commencement of the relevant review period) and the amount so proposed shall be deemed to have been agreed by the landlord and the tenant as the revised rent for the relevant review period and sub-clause (D) (i) hereof shall apply accordingly unless the landlord shall make such application as aforesaid within three months after service of such notice by the tenant. Time shall be of the essence in respect of this provision.*

Table of Cases

Table of Statutes and Statutory Instruments

Note: *Sections of statutes included verbatim in Appendix 2 are indicated by an italic page reference.*

Index